M. Schader · A. Korthaus
Editors

The Unified Modeling Language

Technical Aspects and Applications

With 108 Figures
and 15 Tables

Physica-Verlag
A Springer-Verlag Company

Prof. Dr. Martin Schader
Dipl.-Wirtsch. Inf. Axel Korthaus
Lehrstuhl für Wirtschaftsinformatik III
Universität Mannheim
Schloß
D-68131 Mannheim
Germany

ISBN 978-3-7908-1105-6

Cataloging-in-Publication Data applied for
Die Deutsche Bibliothek - CIP-Einheitsaufnahme
The unified modeling language: technical aspects and applications ; with 15 tables / M. Schader ; A. Korthaus (ed.). - Heidelberg : Physica-Verl., 1998

ISBN 978-3-7908-1105-6 ISBN 978-3-642-48673-9 (eBook)
DOI 10.1007/978-3-642-48673-9

Cover Design: Erich Kirchner, Heidelberg

SPIN 10662121 88/2202-5 4 3 2 1 0 – Printed on acid-free paper

Preface

Most of the articles in this volume are revised versions of papers presented during the 1st GROOM-Workshop on the Unified Modeling Language (UML). GROOM (*Grundlagen objektorientierter Modellierung*) is a working group of the *Gesellschaft für Informatik* (GI), the German Society of Computer Science. The workshop took place at the University of Mannheim (Germany) in October 1997; the local organizers were Martin Schader and Axel Korthaus, Department of Information Systems.

The scientific program of the workshop included 21 talks, presented in German language on Friday, Oct. 10th, and Saturday, Oct. 11th, 1997. Researchers and practitioners interested in object-oriented software development, analysis and design of software systems, standardization efforts in the field of object technology, and particularly in the main topic of the workshop: *"Applications, State of the Art, and Evaluation of the Unified Modeling Language"* had the opportunity to discuss recent developments and to establish cooperation in these fields.

The workshop owed much to its sponsors and supporters

- University of Mannheim
- Faculty of Business Administration, University of Mannheim
- Sun Microsystems GmbH
- Apcon Professional Concepts GmbH.

Their generous support is gratefully acknowledged.

In the present proceedings volume, papers are presented in three chapters as follows.

- UML vs. Other Approaches
- Business Process Modeling and Applications
- Technical Aspects and Concepts

In the first place, we would like to thank the authors for their contributions which made the workshop and this volume a forum for exchanging new ideas. Also, we are very grateful to all colleagues who chaired sessions during the workshop. Especially, we are obliged to Christoph Tapper who helped in many ways. Finally, thanks are extended to Physica-Verlag, Heidelberg, for the excellent cooperation in publishing this volume.

Mannheim, December 1997

Martin Schader
Axel Korthaus

Contents

Part 3: Business Process Modeling and Applications

Part 1

UML vs. Other Approaches

Exchange of UML-Models with EIA/CDIF

R. G. Flatscher

Abteilung für Wirtschaftsinformatik,
Wirtschaftsuniversität Wien, A-1090 Vienna, Austria

Abstract: Exchanging UML model data among tools of different vendors will be done with the technological means developed for the EIA/CDIF interim standards. This paper gives an overview about the development and present state of EIA/CDIF, the meta-metamodel underlying all of CDIF's metamodels, the proposed mapping of the UML meta-metamodel to the CDIF meta-metamodel as well as the officially submitted proposal for a CDIF UML-metamodel.

1 Introduction

Rational's proposal to OMG's (Object Management Group) RFP (Request for Proposal) for OAD (Object Analysis and Design) contains a proposal to address the problem related to exchanging UML (Unified Modeling Language) model data among tools of different vendors. It is proposed that EIA's (Electronic Industries Association) CDIF (CASE Data Interchange Format) interim standards are employed for this purpose.

In order to be able to allow for such a vendor independent exchange format for UML model data, Rational proposed a CDIF-compliant metamodel which is supposed to allow for transferring all UML semantics in a systematic and standardized way.[1]

Where UML 1.1 has been officially adopted as an OMG standard on November 14th, 1997, work is still ongoing in the area of exchanging UML models.

2 EIA'S CASE Data Interchange Format

In 1987 the "CASE Data Interchange Format" (CDIF) committee was founded within the American Electronic Industries Association (EIA) to create a set of standards allowing the interchange of model data among the CASE tools of (different) vendors.

The CDIF committee approached its goal by systematically devising a meta-metamodel first and thereafter defining metamodels according to the expressivenes layed out in its meta-metamodel. It took until 1994 before the framework got stabilized in such a manner that CDIF metamodels representing the semantics of the different modeling methodologies could be finalized and presented as CDIF interim standards.

[1] Cf. UML Interchange Format (1997) and UML M3 (1997) as presented to OMG as part of the initial UML proposal in January 1997.

CDIF Name	*abbrev.*	*status*
Foundation	FND	standard
Common	CMM	standard
Data Modeling	DMOD	standard
Data Flow Modeling	DFM	standard
Presentation Location and Connectivity	PLAC	standard
Data Definition	DDEF	final draft
State Event Modeling	STEV	final draft
Business Process Modeling	BPM	draft
Computer Aided Control Systems Design	CACSD	draft
Expression	EXPR	draft
Object-Oriented Analysis and Design	OOAD	draft
Physical (Object) Relational Database	PORD	draft
Project Management Planning and Scheduling	PMPS	draft

Table 1: The CDIF Metamodels.

An overview of the CDIF architecture can be found on CDIF's website (cf. CDIF W3 (1997)), in Ernst (1997a) or in Flatscher (1996). The standardized CDIF metamodels as of the end of 1997 are given in Table 1.

EIA/CDIF has been co-operating and working with a number of standardization bodies like OMG, ECMA TC33:PCTE, ISO IRDS, ANSI X3L8 (data representation), ANSI X3H4 (open systems repository), IEEE P1175 (task force on professional computing tools). This work has been carried out with informal[2] as well as formal co-operation.

The most important work is doubtlessly the co-operation with ISO/IEC JTC1/-SC7/WG11, which uses the EIA/CDIF interim standards to produce an internationalized ISO version ("ISO/CDIF") of it.

2.1 The CDIF Meta-Metamodel

From 1987 to 1991 the CDIF framework for exchanging CASE data independently of tool vendors had been developed, yielding the "Meta-Metamodel I" set of standards for ensuring the interchangeability of CASE data for tools adhering to these interim standards. Basically, the meta-metamodel defined an extended entity-relationship modeling (EERM) language which allowed for specializing Meta-Entity-Types.

While work started on defining metamodels for exchanging model data for different modeling methodologies[3] it became clear that the meta-metamodel had

[2]Usually informal co-operations exist in the form of CDIF members working on other standard bodies, thereby transferring their CDIF knowledge and interim standards with the knowledge of the EIA/CDIF committee.

[3]A set of concepts building a "CDIF Metamodel" for a certain modeling methodology like for state-/event-models is called a "Subject Area" in terms of CDIF. Although CDIF tries to

to be extended in order to add a viewing mechanism and the ability for Meta-Relationships to be specialized themselves.

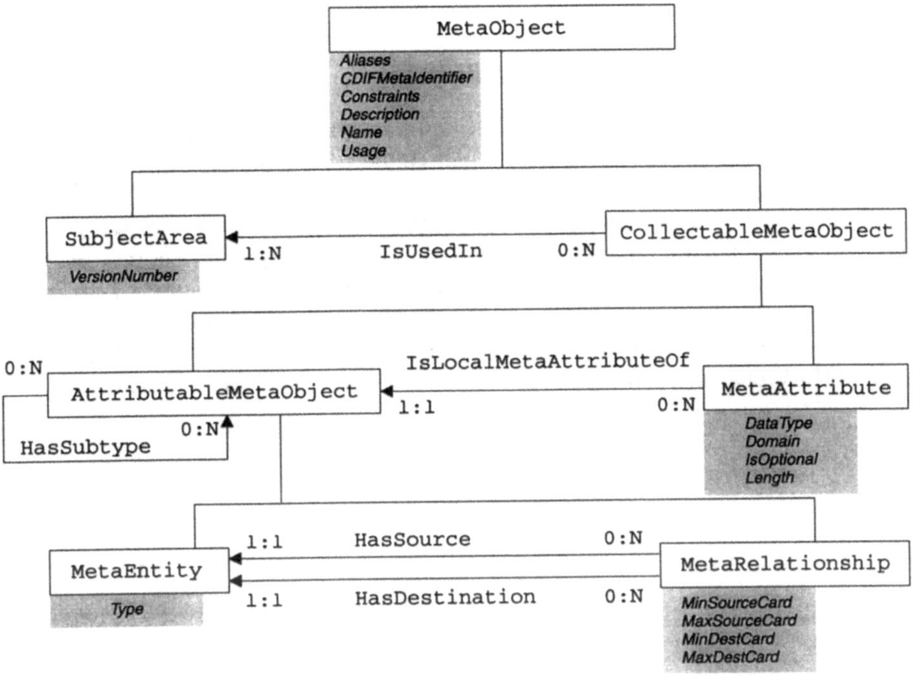

Figure 1: The CDIF Meta-Metamodel.

In 1994 another interim standard for the framework ("Meta-Metamodel II") was finalized which is depicted in Figure 1[4] and described in CDIF FRAMEWORK (1994). As can be seen "MetaEntity" and "MetaRelationship" are specializations of the entity-type "AttributableMetaObject" which allows for assigning "MetaAttribute"s. Due to the recursive relationship type "HasSubtype" on "AttributableMetaObject" specialization is enabled. The viewing mechanism is implemented with the entity types "SubjectArea" and "CollectableMetaObject" and the relationship type "IsUsedIn".

The idea is that the set of all CDIF metamodels constitute the so-called "CDIF Integrated Metamodel" of which any Subject Area employs a subset. This way it became easier to insulate the different CDIF working groups from each other

---

incorporate the most important variations of a subject area it may be possible that specializations exist which are not covered by a CDIF metamodel. For such situations a general extending mechanism has been defined, allowing the tool vendors to extend a CDIF metamodel for the purpose of a data exchange.

[4]Rectangles depict entity types, arrowed lines relationship types and lines without arrows indicate the specialization hierarchy. Instantiable entity types are shown with rectangles with a grey background, abstract ones with a white background. If entity types have attributes defined, they are listed on a grey background right next to the appropriate rectangle.

while defining new metamodels. On the other hand it still has been possible to take advantage of existing definitions by simply incorporating them via an appropriate instantiation of the "IsUsedIn" relationship type of the CDIF Meta-metamodel II.

2.2 The Founding CDIF Metamodel

As mentioned earlier CDIF metamodels represent the CDIF standardized concepts of different modeling methodologies like state/event, data definition, data flow, data modeling and the like. Metamodels conveying the semantics of a particular modeling methodology are called "Semantic Metamodels" by EIA/CDIF.

There is one special CDIF metamodel which does not carry a modeling methodological meaning and exists for the sole purpose of initiating the CDIF metamodeling: "The Foundation Subject Area". This truly fundamental subject area defines the root of any CDIF-compliant metamodel definition and hence is the root of the CDIF UML-metamodel too.

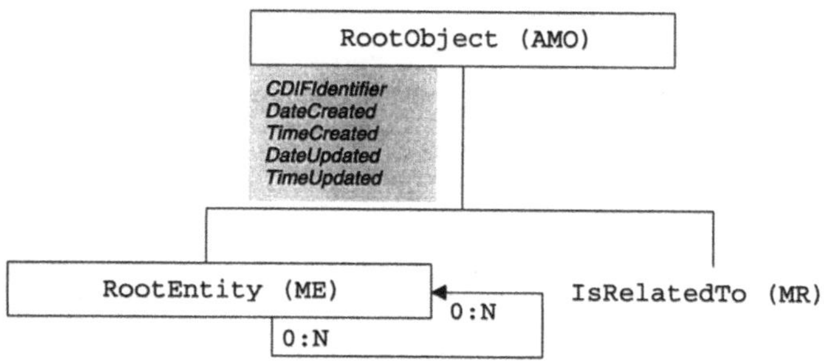

Figure 2: The Founding CDIF Metamodel "Foundation".

Figure 2 depicts this very simple metamodel and as can be seen contains the concepts "RootObject" (an instance of "AttributableMetaObject" and represented with a rectangle), "RootEntity" (an instance of "MetaEntity" and represented as a rectangle) and "IsRelatedTo"[5] (an instance of "MetaRelationship" and represented as a directed line). Any meta-entity in a metamodel descends ultimately from "RootEntity", any meta-relationship from "IsRelatedTo" respectively. The definitions for this Subject Area can be found in CDIF FOUNDATION (1994).

2.3 CDIF Transfer

In CDIF SYNTAX.1 (1994) and CDIF ENCODING.1 (1994) the CDIF rules are set out which allow for a vendor independent exchange of model data by

[5]Note that the fully qualified name of a relationship type is built by using the name of the meta-entity at the source end of the line, the name of the meta-relationship and the name of the target meta-entity at the end of the line indicated by the arrowhead. The constituting names are concatenated by a dot, hence the fully qualified name of the meta-relationship "IsRelatedTo" is "RootEntity.IsRelatedTo.RootEntity".

employing a batch transfer. Every such exchange needs to employ a metamodel descending from the "Foundation Subject Area".

For the purpose of a specific transfer a standardized CDIF subject area may be extended or even a totally proprietary metamodel may be devised as long as it ultimately subclasses the founding meta-entity "RootEntity" and meta-relationship "IsRelatedTo". An exporter is obliged to export all of its information and an importer must be able to import all model data of a CDIF transfer, even concepts the importing tool does not understand ("maximum information transfer rule"). Only after a successful import may the importer discard those concepts it does not understand.

In the beginning of 1996 work started on defining a totally different means of making model data available for exchanging purposes which is documented in Kirkendall (1996, 1997) and entitled "MIDDLEWARE.1". This proposal became a CDIF interim standard in summer 1997 and allows for interrogating (federated) metamodel and model data via OMG's CORBA technology by defining all interfaces with OMG's "Interface Definition Language" (IDL, cf. Flatscher (1997) for an overview).

2.4 UML with EIA/CDIF

Exchanging UML model data with the means of EIA/CDIF first demands a CDIF metamodel which encompasses all data definitions necessary to transport the semantics of all of UML's modeling concepts. This specific CDIF metamodel for UML is defined in the UML Interchange Format (1997).

3 Concepts for Exchanging UML-Models with EIA/CDIF

In order for UML users to understand the differences between the UML and CDIF on a methodological level, the meta-metamodels of both, UML and CDIF need to be compared. The meta-metamodels confine the expressibility of metamodels, hence their paramount importance. Once the concepts used for building metamodels are understood it becomes necessary to understand the concepts represented with metamodels themselves. It can be noted that both, the UML meta-metamodel[6] as well as the CDIF meta-metamodel can be depicted and interpreted as variations of extended entity-relationship models.

It has become customary to abbreviate the term "meta-metamodel" as *M3*, "metamodel" as *M2* and "model" as *M1*, so these abbreviations are applied in the following text also.[7]

---

[6]The UML meta-metamodel objects have no operations defined for them, although the meta-objects MetaOperation and MetaParameter can be used for the UML metamodel.

[7]Using these abbreviations one could restate that UML-CDIF-M2 is defined for exchanging M1-data.

3.1 Aligning UML-M3 with CDIF-M3

As was noted above EIA/CDIF started out by first defining a meta-metamodel which served as the conceptualization of the relevant meta-objects for building metamodels. Rational on the other hand seems to have devised the UML language as a large metamodel by incorporating all kind of different modeling-techniques and documenting/defining notations and semantics for them. The first publically available document of the UML meta-metamodel was part of the initial UML submission to OMG in UML M2 (1997) and aligning it with CDIF and MOF in UML M3 (1997).[8]

Table 2[9] displays the UML M3 concepts and their mappings to the CDIF M3 objects. Where such a mapping was not possible "N/A" has been used instead. It becomes clear that the CDIF M3 at present does not provide the ability for defining members, roles, operations and parameters explicitly, hence these UML concepts cannot be directly expressed in metamodels complying to CDIF.

UML-M3	*CDIF-M3*
MetaObject	MetaObject
MetaModel	SubjectArea
MetaType	AttributableMetaObject
MetaClass	MetaEntity
MetaDataType	Meta-Meta-Attribute "DataType" on MetaAttribute
MetaAssociation	MetaRelationship
MetaRole	N/A
MetaMember	N/A
MetaAttribute	MetaAttribute
MetaOperation	N/A
MetaParameter	N/A
MetaConstraint	Meta-Meta-Attribute "Constraints" on MetaObject

Table 2: Comparing UML M3 Objects with EIA/CDIF's.

The mapping of datatypes defined for UML to CDIF is depicted in Table 3.[10] CDIF has more datatypes defined for its M3 than UML and it is possible to map all of UML's datatypes to CDIF. This mapping is straightforward except for UML's MetaDataType which can be represented with the meta-meta-attribute of CDIF's M3 object MetaAttribute.

[8]It may be safe to assume that a meta-metamodel for UML was devised beforehand by Rational for the purpose of conceptualizing the data-model needed for systematically storing all gathered information with Rational's "Rose" tool.

[9]Cf. UML M3 (1997), p. 3.

[10]Cf. UML M3 (1997), p. 4.

UML-M3	CDIF-M3
MetaDataType	Meta-Meta-Attribute "DataType" on MetaAttribute
MetaBoolean	CDIF-Datatype "Boolean"
MetaEnumeration	CDIF-Datatype "Enumerated"
MetaExpression	CDIF-Datatype "Text"
MetaMultiplicity	CDIF-Datatype "String"
MetaName	CDIF-Datatype "Identifier"
MetaNumber	CDIF-Datatype "Float", CDIF-Datatype "Integer"
MetaPoint	CDIF-Datatype "Point"
MetaString	CDIF-Datatype "String"
MetaTime	CDIF-Datatype "Time", CDIF-Datatype "Date"
MetaUninterpeted	CDIF-Datatype "Text"

Table 3: Aligning UML M3 Data Types with EIA/CDIF.

3.2 The UML CDIF-Metamodel

The UML CDIF-M2 is defined in UML Interchange Format (1997). The format of the definitions does not follow the style of CDIF interim standards, but nevertheless attempts to define the UML concepts which are all shown in Table 4 as briefly as possible. All UML-CDIF-M2 definitions ultimately descend from CDIF FOUNDATION (1994).

UML-Classes Defined for a CDIF Transfer		
Action	ActionExpression	ActionState
ActiveClass	ActivityDiagram	Association
AssociationRole	Attribute	Behavior
BehaviorInstance	BooleanExpression	CallEvent
Class	ClassDiagram	Collaboration
CollaborationDiagram	Component	ComponentDiagram
CompositeState	CompositeState	Constraint
Dependency	DeploymentDiagram	Diagram
Element	Event	FormalParameter
GeneralizableElement	Generalization	Instance
Interaction	Link	LinkRole
Member	Message	Method
Model	ModelElement	Name
Node	Note	ObjectDiagram
Operation	Package	Parameter
PrimitiveType	Pseudostate	Relationship
Responsibility	SequenceDiagram	Signal
SignalEvent	State	StateDiagram
StateMachine	StateVertex	Stereotype

Table 4 continued on next page ...

System	TaggedValue	TimeEvent
Transition	Type	TypeExpression
UseCase	UseCaseDiagram	Value
ViewElement		

Table 4: UML Concepts Defined in the UML CDIF Metamodel.

All UML aggregations and associations are expressed as CDIF MetaRelationships. *Multiplicity* is expressed with the minimum/maximum notation of *CDIF Cardinalities* and stored with the appropriate meta-attributes of MetaRelationship instances.
The definitions of the UML CDIF M2 incorporates in addition a set of default values for UML CDIF meta-attributes. This way only those meta-attributes in a CDIF transfer need to be stated, which differ from these defaults.[11]

3.3 Aligning UML-M2 with CDIF-M2

The UML CDIF M2 incorporates *all* modeling concepts found in UML. Therefore only *one* metamodel was defined by the submittors of UML encompassing class diagramming to state-/transition-modeling. As can be seen from Table 1 EIA/CDIF on the other hand has consistently partitioned its metamodels and has devised separate metamodels for different modeling techniques respectively methodologies it deemed important. Therefore it may be also interesting and important for EIA/CDIF to analyze the UML CDIF M2 and align its concepts with its interim standard M2.

UML-M2	*CDIF-M2*
Action	Action [STEV]
ActionsSequence	ActionDefinition [STEV]
ActionState	Action? [STEV]
Association	Relationship [DMOD]
AssociationClass	Relationship that contains Attributes [DMOD]
AssociationEnd	Role? [DMOD]
Attribute	Attribute [DMOD, STEV]
Boolean	BooleanDataType [DDEF]
Classifier	DefinitionObject [DFM, DMOD, ...]
CompositeState	State referencing "StateDefinition" containing other States [STEV]

Table 5 continued on next page ...

[11]From this it follows that in effect *all* meta-attributes for an UML CDIF transfer are *mandatory*. In the case that such meta-attributes are omitted the default values are used in place.

Constraint	TextualConstraint? [CMMN]
DataType	DataType [DDEF]
Element	RootEntity [FND]
Enumeration	EnumerationDataType [DDEF]
Event	Event [STEV]
Feature	ComponentObject [DFM, DMOD, ...]
GeneralizableElement	InheritableDataModelObject [DMOD]
Generalization	SubtypeSet [DMOD]
Geometry	Point [PLAC]
Guard	Condition [STEV]
Integer	IntegerDataType [DDEF]
Model	Model
ModelElement	SemanticInformationObject [CMMN]
Presentation	PresentationObject.Represents. Semantic-ObjectReference [PLAC]
PrimitiveType	ElementalType [BasicDataType [DDEF]]
State	State [STEV]
StateMachine	StateEventModel
String	StringDataType [DDEF] [StringType]
Time	TimeDataType [DDEF] [TimeType]
Transition	Transition [STEV]
Uninterpreted	Text [CDIF-Datatype]
ViewElement	PresentationInformationObject [CMMN, PLAC]

Table 5: Mapping of UML M2 Concepts to EIA/CDIF's M2 Concepts.

Table 5[12] depicts the findings of Ernst (1997b). Information in square brackets was added by the author and contains hints to the CDIF M2 subject areas of which concepts are referred to. Where in doubt a question mark was appended to the CDIF MetaObject name or a reference to an existing CDIF subject area was omitted. The mapping of the abbreviations to the CDIF subject areas which get referred to in most square brackets can be found in Figure 1.

Should it become possible to partition the final UML CDIF metamodel such that the partitions may be covered by individual CDIF subject areas, UML model data could be transferred to or imported from non-UML tools. This way it would become possible to interchange model data with legacy and specialized tools for which the entire UML CDIF M2 would be inadequate, in addition models created and maintained with legacy tools could be transferred into UML-aware tools.

[12] Cf. Ernst (1997b), p. 6–7.

3.4 Summary and Lookout

This paper introduced the reader first to EIA/CDIF, its meta-metamodel and foundation metamodel which serves as the core for the UML CDIF metamodel introduced with the initial submission of UML to OMG in January 1997. Unlike EIA/CDIF which attempted to partition the set of concepts and definitions into *"subject areas"* concentrating on a specific modeling technique or methodology, the UML CDIF metamodel incorporates *all* of UML's modeling techniques into *one* large metamodel.

The immediate consequence is that all tool providers, commercial as academic alike, need to know all concepts of UML in detail in order to successfully exchange e.g. just State-/Transition model data. Furthermore it becomes almost impossible to successfully transfer model data between tools which are not UML aware[13] and ones which are. Therefore it would be beneficiary to research the possibility of retrofitting the UML CDIF metamodel definitions into the existing EIA/CDIF subject area definitions, at least into the integrated EIA/CDIF metamodel. It may be the case that existing EIA/CDIF definitions need to be extended so it becomes possible to cover UML semantics which are not part of EIA/CDIF at the moment. Preliminary work has started with EIA/CDIF to extend the EIA/CDIF meta-metamodel in a backwardly compatible manner in order to incorporate concepts like *role*, *operation* or *parameter* explicitly into the meta-metamodel.

Another initiative started early 1997 to unify the exchange of model data for a number of different standard bodies which have been already formally or informally worked with EIA/CDIF. This work revolves around the UML CDIF M2 proposal and took the form of an open co-operation of interested parties to carry the EIA/CDIF work further and to finally arrive at an official standard for exchanging UML and MOF data in the process. In this context it is expected that OMG will issue a request for proposal for 1998 to solicit submissions for a *"File-based Model Interchange Facility"* (FMIF) which builds on EIA/CDIF and serves as a standard exchanging mechanism with a planned final OMG vote at the beginning of 1999.

References

CDIF ENCODING.1 (1994): CDIF Transfer Format Encoding—ENCODING.1. CDIF Interim Standard, EIA.

CDIF FOUNDATION (1994): CDIF Integrated Meta-model, Foundation Subject Area. Interim Standard, EIA.

CDIF FRAMEWORK (1994): CDIF Framework for Modeling and Extensibility. Interim Standard, EIA.

CDIF SYNTAX.1 (1994): CDIF Transfer Format Syntax—SYNTAX.1. CDIF Interim Standard, EIA.

[13]There may be plentiful of reasons for such a setting, starting with legacy tools and encompassing highly specialized tools dealing just with a specific modeling methodology only

CDIF W3 (1997): CDIF Internet World Wide Web Site, URL (as of: 1997-11-22): http://www.cdif.org

ERNST, J. (1997a): Introduction to CDIF. Working document, EIA/CDIF Technical Committee, EIA. URL (as of: 1997-11-22): http://www.cdif.org/intro.html

ERNST, J. (1997b): Using the CDIF Transfer Format to exchange UML-models, version 2. Working document, EIA/CDIF Technical Committee, EIA.
URL (as of: 1997-11-22): http://www.cdif.org/liaisons/CDIF-JE-N34-V2.pdf

FLATSCHER, R.G. (1996): An Overview of EIA's CASE Data Interchange Format (CDIF). In: *Rundbrief des GI-Fachausschusses 5.2 Informationssystem Architekturen, 1.*

FLATSCHER, R.G. (1997): Federating Meta-model and Model Data with EIA/CDIF's CORBA Compliant MIDDLEWARE.1 In: *Rundbrief des GI-Fachausschusses 5.2 Informationssystem Architekturen, 1.*

UML Interchange Format (1997): UML-Compliant Interchange Format. Object Management Group, 492 Old Connecticut Path, Framingham, MA 01701, U.S.A. URL (as of: 1997-11-22): http://ftp.omg.org/pub/docs/ad/97-01-13.pdf

UML M2 (1997): Appendix M2: UML Meta-Metamodel. Object Management Group, 492 Old Connecticut Path, Framingham, MA 01701, U.S.A. URL (as of: 1997-11-22): ftp://ftp.omg.org/pub/docs/ad/97-01-06.pdf

UML M3 (1997): Appendix M3: UML Meta-Metamodel Alignment with MOF and CDIF. Object Management Group, 492 Old Connecticut Path, Framingham, MA 01701, U.S.A. URL (as of: 1997-11-22): ftp://ftp.omg.org/pub/docs/ad/97-01-06.pdf

Object-Oriented Modeling Languages: State of the Art and Open Research Questions

U. Frank

Institut für Wirtschaftsinformatik,
Universität Koblenz-Landau, D-56075 Koblenz, Rheinau 1, Germany

"Language is my instrument, but at the same time my problem."

Maturana

Abstract: Object-oriented modeling is used in a growing number of commercial software development projects. But the plethora of approaches and corresponding CASE tools still prevents corporate users from migrating to object-oriented software development methods. Against this background the recent efforts of the Object Management Group (OMG) to standardize object-oriented modeling languages seem to promise substantial benefits: Not only will a standard allow to transfer a model from one CASE tool to another, it will also protect investment in training. However, at the same time it is questionable whether the state of the art in object-oriented modeling is mature enough to allow for standardization. In order to answer this question, we will briefly describe the proposals submitted to the OMG in January 1997. We will then show that there are still essential problems in designing modeling languages which have not been addressed yet.

1 Introduction

During the last decade, object-oriented software development has been adopted in the academic world with remarkable enthusiasm. This is different with corporate software development: Although there is a tremendous marketing push caused by vendors, consultants, and speoialist journals, many companies are hesitating to introduce object-oriented methods[1]. This is for comprehensible reasons: At present time, there are still serio ıs inhibitors of object-oriented software development to overcome. There is laok of *mature technology*. While there are object-oriented programming languages that come with reliable compilers—sometimes embedded in rather convenient environments, today's object-oriented database management systems are usually not suited to replace relational database management systems within corporate information systems. Furthermore, there is *lack of competence*. In order to exploit the benefits offered by the object-oriented paradigm, and to avoid its pitfalls, it is necessary for the developers to gain a deep understanding of the essential concepts. It is certainly not too daring to assume that most software developers do not have these skills today. From a managerial point of view it is risky to provide for the training that is required to develop

[1]To our knowledge there is no representative study on an international scale. A recently conducted empirical study (Schnur 1997) indicates that less than 10% of the german insurance companies use object-oriented software development methods.

these skills: Not only that training is expensive, and its success is hard to predict; furthermore, there is still *lack of standards*. This is the case for object-oriented programming languages and database management systems, as well as for specialized development methods. For this reason protection of investments, both in professional training and in technology (CASE, compilers, etc.), is usually not satisfactory.

Although many companies are still hesitating to introduce object-oriented methods and technologies, there is no doubt that the future (that is at least the next ten years) of corporate software development will be more and more object-oriented—simply because there is no alternative paradigm of similar relevance. In other words: The already big market for object-oriented concepts, training, and technologies can still be expected to grow at a fast pace. However, in order to encourage corporate investments, it is not sufficient to develop mature technologies. In addition, it is crucial to provide reliable standards that foster interoperability and reusability, and protect investments at the same time. Only recently it became apparent that the various dialects of object-oriented modeling will eventually be replaced by an industry standard modeling language: The "Object Management Group" (OMG) issued a request for proposals for object analysis and design (OMG (1996)). The submissions were due at January, 17th, 1997. The review process can be expected not to be completed before the end of 1997. The OMG's request for proposal was one cause for writing this article which will focus on the following questions:

- What are the particular benefits to be expected from standardized modeling languages?
- What is the OMG's intention?
- What are the characteristics of the official proposals to the OMG?
- Is the current state of the art mature enough to allow for standardization?

2 Background of Current Standardization Efforts

While it is no option to standardize a modeling method or even a modeling methodology (see Frank (1997)), the standardization of object-oriented modeling languages promises substantial benefits for the development and utilization of software. Standardized modeling languages will allow for better protection of investments in technologies that depend on those languages—like modeling tools and ODBMS. This is the case for investments into training, too. Standardized modeling language will also improve the chance for exchanging models and interoperability in general, or—in other words—for system integration. Furthermore, standardized modeling languages will foster reusability of existing models, for instance of generic or reference models developed for certain problem areas or domains. Standardized modeling languages are also a prerequisite for the emergence of a market for standardized (implemented) classes for corporate information systems, often referred to as "business objects". It is not possible to establish a market for business classes/objects that have been specified/implemented independent from each other: Usually objects, which are to be used in a certain domain, will interact with other objects/classes. Furthermore, it is important to represent business objects in an illustrative way. For these reasons, the vision of providing standardized business objects in the long run requires application level object models together with a corresponding implementation—either as a class library or as a framework (see Lewis et al. (1995)). Standardizing application level object models implies the existence of a standardized modeling language.

Against this background it is not surprising that there is a growing demand for the standardization of object-oriented modeling languages in the industry. The OMG has addressed this issue in 1992 already by launching the "Object Analysis and Design Special Interest Group" (Kain et al. (1992)). But this group did not succeed to meet its central objective: "To formalise the definitions of the concepts used for analysis and design" (Kain et al. (1992)). Apparently for this failure, the OMG issued a request for proposals for object analysis and design in 1996 (OMG (1996)). The aim of the initiative is to standardize "the interfaces and semantics needed to support the creation and manipulation of a core set of OA&D models that define the structure, meaning, and behavior of object applications" (OMG (1996)). In particular, the standard should support the creation of "static models", "dynamic models", "usage models", and "architectural models". It seems that the OMG is primarily interested in CASE tool interoperability. Nevertheless, the OMG's statements about the purpose of the "OA&D facility" leave a number of questions:

What is the precise objective of the intended standard?

The explicit reference to tool interoperability indicates that the standard is to describe metamodels for those models managed by CASE tools. However, the OMG stresses the conceptual level as well: "An object analysis and design model (hereafter called simply model) is defined as an object that represents the semantics of an analysis or design of a system. A model is used to define and specify the semantics of interest in a particular aspect of the domain." (OMG (1996)) Furthermore, the OMG requires notations which enable "a core set of OA&D diagrams, each of which describes a model, to be communicated between people without semantic loss." (OMG (1996)). Note that tool interoperability and modeling languages as an instrument for system development require different specifications. While a model that is managed by a tool should be suited to incorporate the semantics defined in the corresponding modeling languages, it will also include additional information, like for versioning, user management, etc. Defining a language for communication between people on the other hand requires to take into account human perception and conceptualization.

What is the scope of the (meta) models to be specified?

While the request for proposals provides examples for a number of models that might be part of the standard ("class models", "instance models", "state-transition models", "use-case models", etc.), it does not tell the level of semantics they should incorporate. In other words: What are the stages of the software life-cycle to be covered—in part, or completely—by the modeling languages to be defined? There is evidence that the OMG does not plan a rigid standard anyway:

> "The OA&D facility should not constrain the processes and techniques that OA&D methods use to extract the information needed to determine the semantic content of OA&D models, to ensure the integrity and validity of the content of those models, or to evolve or optimize those models. Nor should the facility constrain OA&D methods from introducing models in addition to the core set." (OMG (1996))

How does the intended standard relate to other standards?

There is no doubt that the standard should be compliant to existing OMG specifications—such as the Interface Definition Language (IDL). However, there are at least two standardization efforts outside the OMG which are concerned with subjects that are obviously related to analysis and design.

Firstly, there is the CASE Date Interchange Format (CDIF), defined by the CDIF division within the Electronic Industries Association (EIA). CDIF is dedicated to support the exchange of models managed by CASE tools. CDIF does not specify the metamodel a tool has to use itself. Instead, it is restricted to the external representations that a tool has to support with its interfaces. With the ISO "Information Resource Dictionary System" (IRDS, ISO (1990)) and the "Portable Common Tool Environment" (PCTE, Wakeman (1993)), an initiative launched by tool vendors, two major standardization efforts are committed to using the CDIF metamodel (CDIF (1996)).

Secondly, there are the activities of the Workflow Management Coalition (WfMC). Similar to the OMG the WfMC is an industry consortium. It aims at a set of standards that are to allow for "open" workflow management systems. In order to achieve this goal the WfMC intends to define a set of interfaces for the components to be integrated (such as office application, DBMS, and so called workflow engines) as well as a "Workflow Process Definition Language" (WPDL, WfMC (1996)). The idea behind this approach is similar to entity relationship modeling and SQL respectively: A workflow type can be modeled using an appropriate modeling language provided by a corresponding tool. The modeling language will then translate into the WPDL which can be interpreted by any workflow engine that has been certified by the WfMC. There is a clear relationship to the mission of the OMG's "Object Analysis&Design Facility": In order to model a workflow, you need to describe the information required and produced within that workflow—for instance by referring to an object model. While both, the EIA (CDIF (1996)) and the WfMC (Anderson (1996)) refer to the OMG, to our knowledge, the OMG itself does not explain its relationship to those approaches, nor does it even mention them.

3 Object-Oriented Modeling Languages: Is there a State of the Art?

Standardizing technologies or concepts requires a mature level of corresponding research activities. With object-oriented modeling, it is impossible to identify a unique scientific community that is dedicated to this subject. This is for a number of reasons. Firstly, object-oriented concepts have various roots, including programming languages, database design, and artificial intelligence. Secondly, there are contributions from authors with either a commercial or a more academic background. Therefore, the selection we made, is a compromise: We will primarily focus on what you could call the "dominating" state of the art. For this purpose, we will have a look at the languages submitted to the OMG early this year. By the time of writing this, some of the proposals have apparently been withdrawn. Nevertheless, we will consider them briefly, since they give an impression of the current state of the art.

3.1 The Proposals to the OMG

Until the deadline at January 17th the following six proposals had been submitted to the OMG:

Company/Consortium	References	Extent (pages)
Taskon; Reich Technologies; Humans and Technology	Taskon (1997)	101
IBM; ObjecTime Limited	IBM (1997)	196
Softeam	Softeam (1997)	37
Platinum Technology	Platinum (1997)	318
Ptech	Cerrato and Ibrahim (1997)	58
Rational Software; Microsoft; Hewlett - Packard; Oracle; Texas Instruments; MCI Systemhouse; Unisys; ICON Computing; IntelliCorp.	Rational (1997a) Rational (1997b) Rational (1997c) Rational (1997d)	> 550

Table 1: Proposals submitted to the OMG

Taskon; Reich Technologies; Humans and Technology

This submission does not claim to describe a complete set of object-oriented modeling languages. Instead, its authors intend to provide an "extension of the UML, and the OML object models" (Taskon (1997)). It originates from a number of previous approaches (like Reenskaug (1995), Wirfs-Brock et al. (1990)). Its main emphasis is on three additional basic concepts: *role model*, *role*, and *port*. Roles emphasize another level of abstraction than classes. A role represents a particular real world object's role within a certain activity. A role model describes the interactions of roles within an activity. Those interactions are invocations of operations in other roles/objects. Apparently role models are to be used mainly during analysis, in order to record systematically the features of classes within a corresponding object model (Taskon (1997)). A port is described as "an abstraction on a variable, permitting the object represented by the adjoining role to execute operations in the object represented by OtherRole." (Taskon (1997)) This concept is not sufficiently explained. We assume that it is similar to—although not equivalent—to delegation, where an object may transparently access operations of its role object (Frank and Halter (1997)). The metamodel itself is defined using the IDL standardized by the OMG. Although this has been encouraged by the OMG, there is no doubt that IDL is not suited to serve as a modeling or specification language, since it lacks relevant concepts (for instance: it is not possible to express cardinalities or more specific constraints).

There is one other suggestion within this proposal that we would like to mention: "system inheritance" is to provide for specializing from "the overall system structure and behavior properties" (Taskon (1997)). As the authors state, such a concept would certainly be helpful for designing reusable frameworks. That, however, would require a precise definition of this type of inheritance—especially how to modify and enhance an inherited system. We could not find such a definition within the proposal. Although Reich claims to be a tool vendor, it seems that this consortium is focusing on the applications of modeling languages rather than on metamodels which would promote tool interoperability. The authors have rather elaborated ideas about the particular models to be used within a software development project. They suggest not less than nine partial views (like "area of concern view", "stimulus-response view", "role list view", "interface view", etc.) together with corresponding modeling notations. The models are described in an informal way (Taskon (1997)).

IBM; ObjecTime Limited

This proposal, submitted by IBM and ObjecTime, covers what may be called the "full range" of common object-oriented modeling: static properties, behavior, and dynamics. Nevertheless, the authors apparently do not intend to define a complete set of languages for object-oriented modeling. While they completely abstract from modeling notations, they put strong emphasis on language semantics and pragmatics. It is characteristic for this outstanding submission that it starts with analyzing the requirements related to modeling languages in general. The authors make the assumption that models may serve a wide range of purposes, which can hardly be determined in advance. To illustrate this point, they distinguish between "general purpose modeling languages", "domain specific modeling languages", and even "application specific modeling languages". Furthermore, they state that modeling languages should take into account concepts which are appropriate for a particular purpose (and particular people) rather than reconstructing programming languages. On the other hand they argue that modeling applied to software development at some point requires formal definitions of the modeling languages. From these assumptions they conclude that there is "need for extensibility", "for language and method independence", and "for formality and interoperability" (IBM (1997)).

The consortium presents a "Core Meta-Model (CMM)" which is the foundation for the models that can be built within this approach. The CMM contains generic concepts which allow to express static, dynamic, and interaction semantics. It is characteristic for the level of abstraction suggested by this proposal that the CMM does not explicitly contain core concepts of object-oriented modeling such as classes or objects. Instead, the CMM provides abstractions which may be specialized further. One of the core abstractions is called "specification". Specification is an abstraction of concepts like type and class: "Specifications representing pure interfaces will have all Features unimplemented, those representing concrete classes will have all Features implemented, and further possibilities exist in between." (IBM (1997)) Compared to other submissions, there is a stronger emphasis on formalization. For this purpose the authors introduce and define a formal language called "Object Constraint Language" (OCL) that is used to specify the CMM. It also helps with the specification of additional modeling languages, since the OCL in general is used to specify invariants within model schemes. Additionally, each "model scheme may define a Grammar for each type of Expression" (IBM (1997))—like invariants or conditions. The proposal includes a few examples of how to specify a model scheme. Smalltalk "design models", for instance, can be introduced by a scheme which includes—among other things—invariants to constrain generalization to single inheritance, or to express that every element within a class has exactly one name. The ability to introduce specialized languages which are defined by concepts in more general languages is a promising approach—last but not least to support the idea of standardized business object models. Notice, however, that extensibility—like the definition of new modeling languages with existing meta concepts—is not sufficient to allow for a straightforward interchange of models expressed in such a new language: Standardized meta concepts do not imply that the special concepts of a particular modeling language will be standardized, too. For instance: If you define a language scheme for a business modeling language, you may want to introduce a concept like "Organizational Unit". It is probably very hard to define such a concept in a way that everybody is willing to accept. Nevertheless a standardized metalanguage allows to determine precisely how a specialized concept was defined—even if you do not agree with it.

Although the authors point to the fact that modeling languages should suit a particular purpose, providing particular modeling languages is not their main concern. Instead, they refer to approaches such as the UML or the OML (IBM (1997)) which they consider as possible applications of their specification. From our point of view, this is a very ambitious, yet substantial approach. To briefly summarize our impression: We think that the strength of this approach marks a possible weakness at the same time. Taking into account the realistic assumptions on requirements for modeling languages, it is certainly a good idea to provide for a high degree of extensibility: Thereby developers (and users) of specific modeling languages will not be restricted to concepts which do not fit their needs. However, by allowing for almost arbitrary specific modeling languages, standardization does not happen on the level of those languages.

Softeam

This submission is based on the "Class Relation method" which was introduced in 1989, and revised later (Desfray (1994)). Softeam's proposal is certainly not as complete as for instance the previous one. In fact, it seems that the authors primarily intend to introduce a few concepts as alternatives to corresponding concepts of the UML. In particular, they suggest an "object flow model" that is to provide a representation of operations behavior. Most remarkable, from our point of view, is the introduction of a special state diagram that is based on the "Hygraph" principle suggested by Harel. It is motivated by the fact that the state charts often used in object-oriented modeling neither allow for a well defined integration with object models, nor do they allow to express generalization/specialization hierarchies. The suggested state diagrams can be decomposed into two different categories (Softeam (1997)). "Control state diagrams" focus on the usage of a class, describing what is to be expected from an instance of this class from an external point of view. The authors state—referring to Desfray (1994)—that control state diagrams can be completely translated into pre- and postconditions. "Trigger state diagrams" represent a particular implementation of a control state diagram. In other words: They describe the actual dynamics a class has to implement in order to satisfy the requirements specified in a corresponding control state diagram. Figure 7 gives an overview of the control state diagram metamodel. The specialized state charts suggested by Softeam promise both a better integration with other partial models, and to take advantage of generalization/specialization. Notice, however, that the corresponding concepts are not defined in the proposal itself—which comprises only about 30 pages. Instead, it is referred to Desfray (1994).

Platinum Technology

Platinum used to be a provider of tools for the development and maintenance of relational DBMS. With the acquisition of Protosoft, the developer of an object-oriented modeling tool called "Paradigm Plus", Platinum became one of the major vendors in this market. "Paradigm Plus" is claimed to support various popular modeling approaches, such as OMT (Rumbaugh et al. (1991), OOSE (Jacobson et al. (1992)), and Booch (1994)). Against this background it is not surprising that Platinum's submission puts strong emphasis on tool interoperability. The proposal includes seven modeling languages, each of which is assigned to a so called "subject area". Each subject area represents a certain view on a system—such as object models, dynamic models, architecture models, etc. The subject areas are defined by seven corresponding metamodels which are tightly coupled.

The concepts shared by all seven metamodels are assigned to an additional subject area called "Foundation and Common Subject Areas", which in turn is defined in a corresponding metamodel.

Notice that the COMMA ("Common object-oriented Methodology Metamodel Architecture") metamodel, proposed by the OPEN consortium (Firesmith et al. (1996)), "had a major influence" (Platinum (1997)) on those metamodels. Furthermore, the metamodels are defined within a common "meta meta model". It is based on the CDIF meta metamodel (EIA (1993), in other words: it uses the concepts defined in this reference model). Therefore the metamodels can be exchanged between all tools which are capable of using the CDIF interchange standard formats.

The meta metamodel provides a few core concepts which are "totally immutable" (Platinum (1997)). "Extensibility" of subject areas can be accomplished by modifying the corresponding metamodels. Notice, however, that extensibility is restricted to the expressive power of the concepts defined in the meta-metamodel. Since those concepts are essentially restricted to data structures, it seems that there is no way to specify constraints that go beyond the description provided by such structures—as it is possible in the metamodel suggested by IBM and ObjecTeam.

The submission includes an extensive description of the meta-metamodel as well as of the metamodels (about 2/3 of the whole document). By referring to an existing standard for exchanging information between CASE tools (CDIF), it is probably of special value for tool providers. However, from our point of view the proposal neglects to consider the requirements of conceptual modeling: A modeling language is not only thought to define models for the purpose of exchanging them between programs. Instead, it is also a tool to support an intellectual endeavor. In other words: It includes pragmatic aspects as well. It seems that these aspects are not Platinum's primary concern—on the contrary: In the past Platinum has gained its reputation as a tool vendor by supporting many modeling languages. In order to hold on to this tradition, the proposal is restricted to metamodels which can be used to define a set of particular modeling languages. To emphasize this point of view, Platinum does not provide a specific notation. Instead, it is argued that the proposed specifications "are fully compatible with the current state of the art in object modeling notations"—a statement that is illustrated by small examples. They refer to other approaches which put more emphasis on notation (Platinum (1997)). Although the "current state of the art" is hard to identify, such a statement is rather daring: Notations only make sense with associated concepts. We doubt that the meta-metamodel allows to express the semantics of any concept that may be useful within object-oriented modeling. For instance: How would you express the specific semantics of delegation (see Frank and Halter (1997)).

Ptech

The authors of this proposal first make a few assumptions on the purpose of modeling languages. They emphasize both, the need to offer a medium to foster effective communication between humans with different professional backgrounds, and the need for tool interoperability (Cerrato and Ibrahim (1997)). They provide metamodels for five types of models: "structural models", "architectural models", "behavioral models", "distributed processing models", and "usage models". It is remarkable that the authors seem to be very much inspired by relational theory. In order to define the concepts they suggest for object-oriented modeling, they often refer to notions such as "set", "domain", "range", or "relation"—for instance: "The associations that implement the relation are named customer and order." (Cerrato and Ibrahim (1997)).

To some degree this proposal benefits from the precision of relational theory. It lacks, however, a specific object-oriented point of view—in other words: The authors seem not to have overcome the separation of function and data. For instance, they speak of "... an operation that can be performed on instances of a class." (Cerrato and Ibrahim (1997)) Although the authors state that their metamodels "guarantee that all Ptech models are logically consistent." (Cerrato and Ibrahim (1997)), the documentation of the metamodels does not seem to be complete. While the metamodels are said to be extensible (Cerrato and Ibrahim (1997)), it is not demonstrated how an extension can be accomplished. Furthermore, there is no language included that would allow to specify additional constraints. From our point of view, the most remarkable aspect of this proposal is the background of the Ptech method: It has been used for "understanding, analyzing, capturing, validating, and documenting business processes and systems." (Cerrato and Ibrahim (1997)) It is surprising that the authors did not add specific requirements for object-oriented modeling languages to be applied in the area of process modeling.

Rational et al.

This submission is backed by a rather impressive consortium including Rational Software, Microsoft, Hewlett-Packard, Oracle, Texas Instruments, and Unisys. The proposed "Unified Modeling Language" (UML) has mainly been developed by Rational Software and has its roots in three well known object-oriented modeling approaches (Booch (1994), Jacobson et al. (1992), Rumbaugh et al. (1991)). The material proposed by the consortium is relatively extensive: It includes 13 documents which cover more than 550 pages. Furthermore, the background of the UML is explained in various textbooks (Booch (1994), Jacobson et al. (1994), Jacobson et al. (1992), Rumbaugh et al. (1991), Derr (1995), White (1994)), and in numerous articles. But it is certainly not the sheer volume, why the UML is regarded as a reference already—often without discussing its qualities. Even within the competing proposals to the OMG the UML seems to have gained an outstanding position. This may be due to the fact that it is associated with three protagonists of the object-oriented modeling arena. Furthermore, it seems that most of the other consortia have accepted the relevance of this proposal, since they describe how their metalanguages, or metamodels respectively, would allow to specify parts of the UML (for instance IBM (1997), Cerrato and Ibrahim (1997))—or they restrict their efforts to providing extensions to the UML (like Softeam (1997)).

Compared to the previous approaches, the UML is based on, the language description submitted to the OMG is much more comprehensive (fig. 12 gives an impression). Although some concepts of the original approaches, such as data flow diagrams, which are part of OMT, are not supported any more, the UML almost appears like a superset of the languages it originates from. It supports nine types of diagrams. Static aspects can be rendered on various levels of abstraction. In addition to *class* or *object diagrams*, *component diagrams* serve to map existing software components and their interrelationships. *Deployment diagrams* can be used to render dependencies between runtime systems across various platforms. Collaboration diagrams allow to express message flows between objects. *Sequence diagrams*, *state diagrams*, and *activity diagrams* serve to render various dynamic aspects. Furthermore, the UML provides *use case diagrams* as suggested in Jacobson et al. (1992). While the variety that comes with those diagrams improves the chances to find a diagram type which is appropriate for a particular view, it can be a burden at the same time, since some of the diagrams (like sequence diagrams, state diagrams, and activity diagrams) are overlapping in a subtle way. For a detailed evaluation of the UML see Frank and Prasse (1997). The 1.1 version of the language, released in July 1997, has adopted the OCL from the IBM/ObjecTime proposal. In addition to the UML and natural language, the OCL is used to specify the abstract syntax and semantics of the UML (Rational (1997d)).

Without any doubt, the UML marks a clear progress compared to its direct predecessors. Nevertheless, it is not completely convincing in the end. It seems questionable whether the extent and variety of concepts provided with the UML will not confuse the prospective users. It is by no means easy to learn and use.

3.2 Resume

Our brief analysis was mainly motivated by the following question: Do the proposals give the impression of a converging and mature field? Considering the different backgrounds and goals of the various contributors, it is certainly not appropriate to speak of a coherent state of the art. Furthermore, we do not think that the submissions are a representative selection of object-oriented modeling languages in general: There are numerous other approaches that contribute to the state of the art as well—from various perspectives (for instance Meyer (1997), Coad (1995), Goldberg and Rubin (1995)). One of them deserves particular attention: The OPEN Modeling Language (OML) which has evolved from a joint research effort called OPEN ("Object - oriented Process, Environment, and Notation"). Different from the companies that submitted their proposals to the OMG, OPEN is an initiative launched solely within an academic context. OPEN has been developed further from a number of previous approaches, like Colbert (1989), Desfray (1994), Firesmith (1992), Graham (1991), Henderson-Sellers and Edwards (1994), Henderson-Sellers (1992). As it is indicated by its name, the members of the initiative clearly want the OPEN specifications to become a standard (Firesmith et al. (1996)). Nevertheless, they did not submit the already existing specifications, because they were not able to fulfill some requirements defined by the OMG: A submitting organization has to be a "contributing member" of the OMG. Additionally, it has to provide a statement about its willingness to make the proposed “technology ... commercially available within 12 months of adoption” (OMG (1996))— whatever that means for modeling languages.

Independent from the question how well the OML compares against other approaches (for a comparison of the UML and the OML see Frank and Prasse (1997)), the regulations imposed by the OMG have rather disturbing consequences: They exclude many potential contributors, especially those with academic intentions, no matter how valuable their proposals might be. Such a procedure does not only jeopardize the quality of the standard to be established. In addition, it may also hinder the acceptance of the standard by those who were not able to express their ideas.

4 Open Research Questions

Assuming that modeling languages are of pivotal importance for the way people perceive and conceptualize real world domains, and how they design software, the design of a general modeling language is a challenging task. This is for various reasons. Firstly, there is *variety*— both in domains and in software systems. For instance, there are certainly essential differences between traffic control systems, vending machines, or marketing information systems. This is the case for the corresponding terminologies as well as for abstractions used to represent system features. Additionally, there is an immense variety of people who use a modeling language—both as readers and writers. Since it can be expected that this variety is accompanied by a wide range of individual perceptions, conceptualizations, and preferences, it is almost impossible to design a language that fits the needs of all potential users. Secondly, there are *trade-offs*. A modeling language should be easy to use. Its notation should be intuitive, which implies that it corresponds to the conceptualizations its users prefer. At the same time it should support the design and implementation of software. At some point, that requires to introduce formal concepts which are suited to be mapped to implementation languages. Furthermore, there is the well known trade-off between quality, cost, and time. While it is difficult to tell how a modeling language relates to this trade-off, we cannot assume that quality, cost, and time are independent of the modeling languages used within a project. Thirdly, there is *arbitrariness*. Like any artificial language, a modeling language should be designed to fit its purpose. However, it cannot be deduced logically from this purpose. This thought alone implies that arbitrary decisions can hardly be avoided. Furthermore, dealing with trade-offs will usually require compromises that will, to a certain degree, reflect individual preferences rather than objective reasons.

Comparing the current state of the art of object-oriented modeling against those challenges reveals a remarkable lack of knowledge. Regarding a modeling language as an instrument for software development would suggest to start with a thorough requirements analysis which would include a number of questions, for instance:

- What are the purposes the language is to be used for?
- Who are the prospective users of the modeling language?
- What are the concepts a language should provide in order to fit their cognitive styles?
- How does an intuitive notation look like?

There is no doubt that answering these questions requires some sort of empirical research. The authors of object-oriented modeling methods or languages sometimes emphasize the experience they have gathered with applying their approach in practice (for instance Firesmith et al. (1996), or Cerrato and Ibrahim (1997)). Vendors and consultants have certainly received some kind of feedback from their customers. However, it is remarkable that up to now there has been no sophisticated study of how people perceive and deal with concepts and notations of object-oriented modeling languages (at least we do not know of any) There have been a few studies on the use of entity relationship (ER) modeling (Hitchman (1995), Goldstein and Storey (1990)). They indicate that ER models are not intuitive at all for many people. Our experience, as well as the similarity between object models and ER models suggest that this is also the case for object— oriented modeling. Approaches like the UML or the OML, which offer a wide range of different modeling languages, can be expected to be even less intuitive for many prospective users. Furthermore, some concepts featured by those languages, such as use cases, are difficult to understand. For this reason, applying them can easily result in bad design (for a detailed analysis of pitfalls see Berard (1997)). In other words: Without substantial knowledge about the way how people perceive and apply modeling concepts, it is hard to tell whether those concepts contribute to software quality—or to "disaster" (Berard (1997)).

Beside the lack of research on user perceptions and preferences, there is a wide range of domains and purposes that suggest the use of modeling languages. To give a few examples: business process (re-) design, workflow management, organizational design, enterprise modeling, design of document management systems, design of integrated circuits, design in the field of computer telephony integration (CTI). During the last years a lot of special purpose modeling approaches have emerged in those fields (for instance: Frank (1997), Frank (1994), ISO (1990), Ould (1995), Schwabe and Ross (1995), Taylor (1995)). While they usually require specialized concepts, many of them are closely interrelated with object-oriented modeling. For instance: Modeling a business process usually requires to refer to information specified within an object model. In order to foster integration, it is helpful to regard documents as objects which require special concepts. None of the modeling languages discussed above includes special concepts to cover one of those domains. Furthermore, one has to take into account that some of those fields are still in a virgin state, although they are of increasing relevance—like business process modeling or enterprise modeling. Against the background of standardization, it is important to notice that additional requirements for modeling languages can be expected from various evolving areas.

While reusability has been a research topic for long, there are two recent approaches that have gained remarkable attention: design patterns (Gamma et al. (1995)) and frameworks (Lewis et al. (1995)). They promise to deliver reusable artifacts which are rather flexible and/or convenient to use. Nevertheless, there is only little experience about how to integrate them in the process of software development. This is especially the case for design patterns since they are—by definition—less formal in nature than frameworks. It seems characteristic that, despite these problems, some of the approaches discussed in 4.1, and 4.2 already feature concepts to describe design patterns (for instance: Rational (1997a), Firesmith et al. (1996))—however, without specifying them in an adequate way (for instance: Rational (1997a) defines a design pattern as "a template collaboration").

In order to specify/standardize modeling languages you need metamodels or metalanguages. Among other things, they should allow for convenient and safe extensions of the corresponding object level languages. At the same time, a metalanguage perspective, as emphasized in IBM (1997) or Platinum (1997), allows to abstract widely from some problems occurring on the level of a particular modeling language—like user perceptions or preferences. For this reason, it may appear that an approach like the one suggested by IBM (1997) provides a satisfactory solution at least for the metalanguage level. However, this is not the case. Within computer science there is a wide range of alternatives. Beside general, well known approaches like predicate calculus, or algebraic specification, there are many special approaches that define representations for metalanguages to be used for CASE tools or Meta CASE tools respectively (for instance: Ebert et al. 1996, Kelly and Smolander (1996)). While there are requirements for metalanguages, like completeness, simplicity, and correctness (see Süttenbach and Ebert (1997)), it is still difficult to compare them in an objective sense: Similar to modeling languages to be used on an object level, metalanguages are artificial. Therefore they are necessarily arbitrary to some degree. This is an important aspect for another reason as well: Even with metalanguages you cannot completely neglect cognitive styles of prospective users: An extensible metalanguage/metamodel is also used by people who have their own ideas about language concepts and notation— although the group of people who work on a meta level is much smaller than the group of those who use a modeling language on an object level.

The current state of the art is not only lacking knowledge which would be required for the specification of modeling languages. In addition, it is not evident which scientific discipline is responsible for filling those gaps. The design of artificial languages as well as the analysis of their use is an essential topic of linguistics. The interaction between language and cognition is subject of cognitive psychology. The specification of languages to be used for software development is part of computer science. Finally, the definition of concepts suited to describe and analyze certain real world domains, like business firms, is subject of disciplines like management science or organization studies. Considering both, the complexity of the open research questions and the fact that there is no single discipline to cover those questions in a satisfactory way, indicates that it will take considerable time before we are able to speak of a mature state of the art in modeling languages.

5 Concluding Remarks

Our overview of the current state of the art has shown that object-oriented modeling is a still an evolving field with relevant problems and challenges still to be overcome. In addition, the field of object-oriented modeling lacks a common focus: There is work on metamodels with more or less formal rigor, while other approaches focus on the application of modeling languages. There is also variety in the backgrounds of people working on various aspects of object-oriented modeling; to name a few: programming languages, database design, artificial intelligence—with motives ranging from purely academic to chiefly commercial.

From an academic point of view, software development in general, conceptual modeling in particular has not reached a level of maturity that would recommend to freeze a certain paradigm by standardizing corresponding modeling languages. Although there has been considerable progress during the last years, we still agree with the authors of an open letter to the OMG (Mellor et al. (1993)) who, in 1993, advised emphatically against a standardization of object-oriented modeling methods (which includes the standardization of modeling languages)[2]:

> "Standardization of this rapidly developing technology will be out of date almost immediately. Not only is standardization futile, but, to the extent that it succeeds, positively dangerous. Standardization will discourage the innovation required to advance and mature the methods."

However, things look different from an economic point of view: There is no doubt that standards are of crucial importance for establishing integrated information systems. Furthermore, they foster reusability, help to protect investments, and decrease transaction cost. Hence, in the end it comes down to the trade-off between the benefits of standardized representations and the pitfalls of investing into premature concepts. This decision is beyond the capabilities of IS research. It finally happens in market-like settings: If enough players see a chance for an equilibrium between the incentives and the cost of standardization, a standard may be established.

References

ANDERSON, M.J. (1996): Draft Workflow Standard—Interoperability. Abstract Specification WFMC-TC-1012, 3-June.

BERARD, E.V. (1997): Be Careful With "Use Cases". URL: http://www.toa.com/pub/html/use_case.html

BOOCH, G. (1994): Object-oriented Design with Applications. 2nd ed., RedwoodCity, Ca.: Benjamin Cummings.

CDIF (1996): Harmonization of CDIF with other Standards Bodies, 96-07-26. URL: http://www.cdif.org/intro.html

[2]In the meantime some of them, like Booch, or Wirfs-Brock, have apparently changed their mind, since they paricipated in the preparation of proposals to the OMG

CERRATO, J. and IBRAHIM, H. (1997): The Ptech Method for Object-Oriented Development Version 1.0. URL: http://www.omg.org/library/schedule/AD_RFP1.html

COAD, P. (1995): Object Models: Strategies, Patterns, and Applications. Englewood Cliffs, NJ: Prentice Hall.

COLBERT, E. (1989): The Object-Oriented Software Development Method: A Practical Approach to Object-Oriented Development. In: *Proceedings of TRI-Ada '89—Ada Technology in Context: Application, Development, and Deployment.* New York: ACM Press 1989, pp. 400–415.

DERR, K.W. (1995): Applying OMT: A practical step-by-step guide to using the object modeling technique. New York: SIGS Books.

DESFRAY, P. (1994): Object Engineering—The Fourth Dimension. Reading, Mass.: Addison-Wesley.

EBERT, J., WINTER, A., DAHM, P., FRANZKE, A., and SÜTTENBACH, R. (1996): Graph Based Modeling and Implementation with EER/GRAL. Thalheim, B. (Ed.): *Proceedings of the 15th International Conference on Conceptual Modeling.* Berlin et al.: Springer, pp. 163–178.

CDIF (1993): Framework for Modeling and Extensibility, EIA/IS-107, Electronic Industries Association, November.

FIRESMITH, D. (1992): Object-oriented requirements analysis and logical design. Chichester.

FIRESMITH, D., HENDERSON-SELLERS, B., GRAHAM, I., and PAGE-JONES, M. (1996): OPEN Modeling Language (OML). Reference Manual. Version 1.0. 8 December 1996. URL: http://www.csse.swin.edu.au/OPEN/comn.html

FRANK, U. (1994): Multiperspektivische Unternehmensmodellierung. Theoretischer Hintergrund und Entwurf einer objektorientierten Entwicklungsumgebung. München.

FRANK, U. (1997): Enhancing Object-Oriented Modeling with Concepts to Integrate Electronic Documents. In: *Proceedings of the 30th HICSS, Vol. VI, ed. by R. H. Sprague, Los Alamitos, Ca.: IEEE Computer Society Press, pp. 127–136.*

FRANK, U. and HALTER, S. (1997): Enhancing Object-Oriented Software Development with Delegation. Arbeitsberichte des Instituts für Wirtschaftsinformatk, Nr. 2, Koblenz.

FRANK, U. and PRASSE, M. (1997): Ein Bezugsrahmen zur Beurteilung objektorientierter Modellierungssprachen—veranschaulicht am Beispiel von OML und UML. Arbeitsberichte des Instituts für Wirtschaftsinformatk, Nr. 6, Koblenz.

GAMMA, E., HELM, R., JOHNSON, R., and VLISSIDES, J. (1995): Design Patterns. Elements of Reusable Object-Oriented Software. Reading/Mass. et al.: Addison-Wesley.

GOLDBERG, A. and RUBIN, K.S. (1992): Object Behaviour Analysis. In: *Communications of the ACM. Vol. 35, No. 9, pp. 48–62.*

GOLDBERG, A. and RUBIN, K.S. (1995): Succeeding with objects, decision frameworks for project management, Reprint. with corr., Reading, Mass.: Addison-Wesley.

GOLDSTEIN, R.C. and STOREY, V.C. (1990): Some Findings on the Intuitiveness of Entity Relationship Constructs. In: Lochovsky, F.H. (Ed.): *Entity Relationship Approach to Database Design and Query.* Amsterdam: Elsevier.

GRAHAM, I. (1991): Object-Oriented Methods. Wokingham et al.: Addison-Wesley.

HENDERSON-SELLERS, B. (1992): A Book of Object-Oriented Knowledge: Object-Oriented Analysis, Design and Implementation. A new Approach to Software Engineering. Englewood Cliffs, NJ: Prentice Hall.

HENDERSON-SELLERS, B. and EDWARDS, J.M. (1994): Book Two of Object-Oriented Knowledge: The Working Object. Object-Oriented SoftwareEngineering: Methods and Management. Sidney et al.: Prentice Hall.

HITCHMAN, S. (1995): Practitioner Perceptions on the Use of some Semantic Concepts in the Entity Relationship Model In: *European Journal of Information Systems, Vol. 4, pp. 31–40.*

IBM; OBJECTIME LIMITED (1997): OMG OA&D RFP Response Version 1.0. URL: http://www.omg.org/library/schedule/AD_RFP1.html

ISO/IEC1990 IRDS Framework. ISO/IEC-Standard 10027. 1990.

ISAKOWITZ, T., STOHR, E.A., and BALASUBRAMANIAN, P.: RMM (1995): A Methodology for Structured Hypermedia Design. In: *Communications of the ACM, Vol. 38, No. 8, pp. 34–44.*

JACOBSON, I., CHRISTERSON, M., JONSSON, P., and OVERGAARD, G. (1992): Object-Oriented Engineering. A Use Case Driven Approach. Reading, Mass.: Addison-Wesley.

JACOBSON, I., ERICSSON, M., and JACOBSON, A. (1994): The Object Advantage. Business Process Reengineering with Object Technology. Wokingham et al.: Addison-Wesley.

KAIN, J.B., CHRISTOPHERSON, M. et al. (1992): Object Analysis and Design. OMG Document 92-10-01.PDF, draft 7.0. URL: http://www.omg.org/library/public-doclist.html

KELLY, S. and SMOLANDER, K. (1996): Evolution and issues in metaCASE. In: *Information and Software Technology. Vol. 38* (Special Issue: Method engineering and meta-modeling), No. 4, pp. 261–266.

LEWIS, T., ROSENSTEIN, L. et al. (eds.) (1995): Object Oriented Application Frameworks. Greenwich, CT: Manning.

MELLOR, S.J., SHLAER, S., BOOCH, G., RUMBAUGH, J., SALMONS, J., BABITSKY, T., ADAMS, S., and WIRFS-BROCK, R.J. (1993): Premature methods standardization considered harmful Open Letter to the Industry In: *JOOP, Vol. 6, No. 4, pp. 8–9.*

MEYER, B. (1997): Object-Oriented Software Construction. 2nd Ed., Englewood Cliffs: Prentice Hall.

OBJECT MANAGEMENT GROUP (1996): Object Analysis & Design RFP-1, ad/96-05-01. URL: http://www.omg.org/library/public-doclist.html

OULD, M.A. (1995): Business Processes: Business Processes: Modeling and Analysis for Re-Engineering and Improvement. Chichester et al.: Wiley.

PLATINUM: Object Analysis and Design Facility Response to OMG/OA&D RFP-1. URL: http://www.omg.org/library/schedule/AD_RFP1.html

RATIONAL (1997a): UML Semantics. Version 1.0, 02-13-97, 1997. URL: http://www.rational.com

RATIONAL (1997b): UML Notation Guide. Version 1.0, 02-13-97. URL: http://www.rational.com

RATIONAL (1997c): UML Summary.0, 02-13-97. URL: http://www.rational.com

RATIONAL (1997d): UML Semantics. Version 1.1 alpha R6, 07-21-97. URL: http://www.rational.com

REENSKAUG, T. (1995): Working with Objects: The OORAM Software Engineering Method. Englewood Cliffs: Prentice Hall.

RUMBAUGH, J. et al. (1991): Object-Oriented Modeling and Design. Englewood Cliffs, N.J.: Prentice Hall.

SCHNUR, B. (1997): Objektorientierung in Versicherungsunternehmen. Die Branche gibt sich bislang noch zurückhaltend. In: *Informatik Spektrum, Vol. 20, No. 1, pp. 52–53.*

SCHWABE, D. and ROSS, G. (1995): The Object-Oriented Hypermedia Design Model. In: *Communications of the ACM, Vol. 38, No. 8, pp. 45–48.*

SOFTEAM (1997): Submission of the specification of Object Analysis & Design Facility OMG RFP response. URL: http://www.omg.org/library/schedule/AD_RFP1.html

SÜTTENBACH, R. and EBERT, J. (1997): A Booch Metamodel. Fachberichte Informatik, 5/97, Universität Koblenz.

TASKON (1997): The OOram Meta-Model—combining role models, interfaces, and classes to support system centric and program centric modeling. A proposal in response to OMG OA&D RFP-1. URL: http://www.omg.org/library/schedule/AD_RFP1.html

TAYLOR, D.A. (1995): Business Engineering with Object Technology. New York et al.: Wiley.

WAKEMAN, L. (1993): PCTE: The Standard for Open Repositories. Foundation for Software Engineering Environment. New York et al.: Prentice Hall.

WFMC (WORKGROUP 1) (1996): Interface 1: Process Definition Interchange WfMC TC-1016, Version 1.0 Beta, May 29, 1996. URL: http://www.aiai.ed.ac.uk/WfMC/

WHITE, I. (1994): Using the Booch Method—A Rational Approach. New York et al.: Benjamin Cummings.

WIRFS-BROCK, R.J., WILKERSON, B., and WIENER, L. (1990): Designing Object-Oriented Software. Englewood Cliffs, NJ.: Prentice Hall.

From a Semantically Irreducible Formulated Conceptual Schema to an UML Model

L. Kern-Bausch[1], M. Jeckle[2]

[1] University of application oriented science and research Augsburg
Department of Computer Science

[2] Daimler-Benz Research and Technology Ulm
Department of Process chain analysis and reengineering

Abstract: This paper presents an algorithm to derive class diagrams and consistency guaranteeing constraints formulated using the unified modeling language (UML) form a semantically irreducible formulated conceptual schema.

Originally a global sight to the universe of discourse can be modeled. All limiting assumptions arising from a special application view or implementation language could be taken into account as late as desired.

1 Motivation

Nowadays the object oriented paradigm is widely accepted in the industry. One first realized benefit of objects is the possibility to cut down the huge complexity of today's business applications to an overlookable level.

After having heard about the power of objects, people believe in the promises of their salesman or consultant, that design is not as important for the oo systems as it has been for its predecessors. It looks like we could forget all the stuff concerning design. Further the impression of nature is can be used as blueprint for the design. This is more or less true, at least theoretically.

Sure, the prevalent view of oo is the real world, and every developer (every human being, indeed) knows the nature. But, "subtle is the nature—not wily".

So they start to develop their application, enjoying the ease of doing it with objects and all the new stuff and load their new applications into production use. The result is often a severe disappointment, as this application software does not meet the requirements, performance or consistency needs at all. In this situation they try to tune the application by adding extra pieces of code neglecting the former intended oo principles like encapsulation (e.g., classes become friends...) by attenuating the design. Despite all efforts they often cannot reach the break through they really need.

The first reaction afterwards is usually to blame either the used language (e.g., C++ is not real oo) or the system environment (e.g., faster CPUs will give us the performance necessary for oo apps). Seldom the design is reevaluated as the source of the production bottleneck. When they realize that other companies apply oo technology quite successfully, then they try to investigate what was wrong with their approach. Let's dare to say: You can never get back the information you've lost by design.

In this paper we will present a modeling approach for oo applications dealing with that kind of problems. Not a toolbox of sophisticated workarounds or exemplary good design pieces like patterns our approach is intended to provide for every modeler the possibility to create stable class structures including the necessary constraints. The presented approach is directed to the oo experienced developers as well as to end users of the later application i.e., the domain expert involved in the analysis process because he knows the requirements.

2 Semantically Irreducible Formulated Conceptual Schema

The basis of the approach is the conceptual schema (CS) semantically irreducible formulated with information analysis (IA). The conceptual schema describes the information structure of an application, which is not subject to change as the application evolves. In addition, various rules (meta information) about the relationships of modeled information, could be expressed. All these facts are expressible with the information analysis language delivering both a graphical and a textual notation called Information Analysis Structure Description Language (ISDL).

Why do we start with the CS, and why do we insist on semantically irreducible formulation, and do not start with one of the UML diagrams from the very beginning?

First, the CS contains the global information structure and not only information viewed through the glasses of a later implementation (regardless if oo or not). Besides, application specific views could be brought in later.

Second, existing algorithms are able to generate optimal database structures (e.g. highest possible normal (5NF) form for relational data bases; this could be guaranteed by semantically irreducibility).

In addition to the static information structure various rules could be applied to the schema. Let us provide a handy definition of "semantically irreducible": It is not possible to decompose a fact expressed in the CS in two or more others without the loss of information.

Semantic irreducibility supports the completeness and contradiction freeness of the modeled information. On the other hand the semantically irreducible formulation allows the easier modeling of complex contexts.

Furthermore, changes to the information structure grounded by the application may normally lead to serious problems. But, due to the semantically irreducible expressed basic facts changes to the problem domain could be applied easy. The changes happen only to the few directly involved facts—hence due to the semantically irreducibility side effects on other information are excluded or recognized.

Based on a semantic datamodel, the information analysis describes the information structure of an application and allows the automatically derivation of an UML model (see section 4). Information structure means more precisely spoken the atomic parts of information and their interrelations.

3 Information Analysis

This papers focus on the algorithm to derive a static oo model including the necessary constraints expressed in UML from the semantically irreducible formulated CS. The key principle of IA is the object role modeling method, which is based on the semantics of the natural language. Sure every method developed by human being is at least based on the natural language, more or less. But the information analysis allows it to express the semantic of the natural language by simple sentences visualized by simple graphic elements that also could be notated using a formal language of the same expressivity. So it helps bridging the gap between the abstract world of the experienced modeler and the usual domain expert. Due to this is the IA radically new? Yes and No.

Yes, because IA emphasizes an entire description of information as well as it supports the relevant application specific views which could be brought in later. No, because the IA was developed in early days of information modeling, and as shown in Figure 1 the information analysis integrates well-recognized methods.

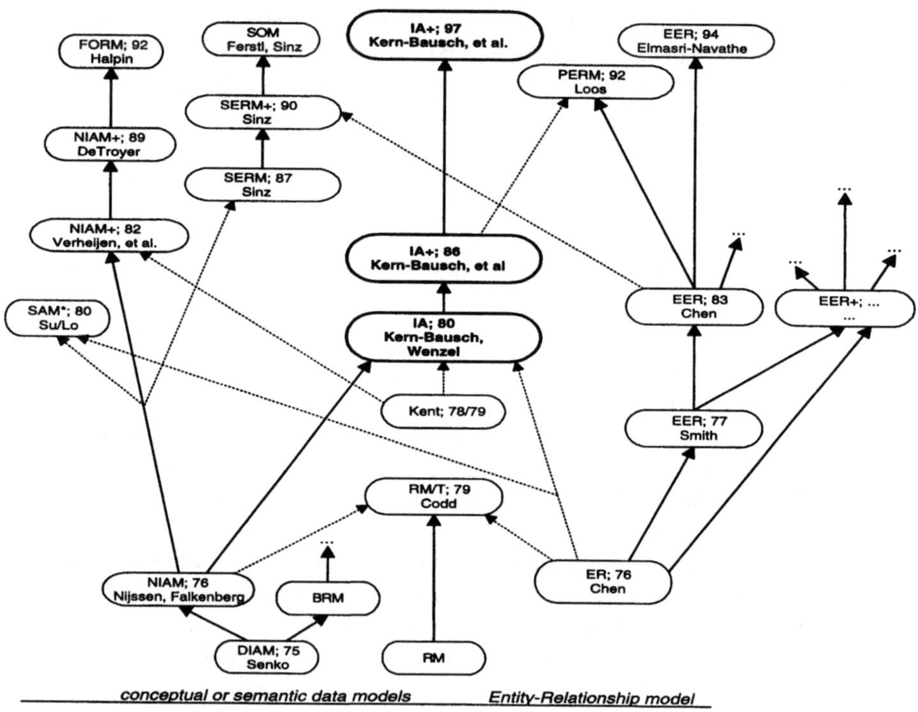

The first word indicates the name of the method followed by the year founded or published
the second information represents the author(s).
Dotted lines represent explicit or implicit influence between models on development and normal lines mark direct extensions of a model.
A plus after the method name indicates a extension to the method without changing the name

Figure 1: Evolution of data modeling methods

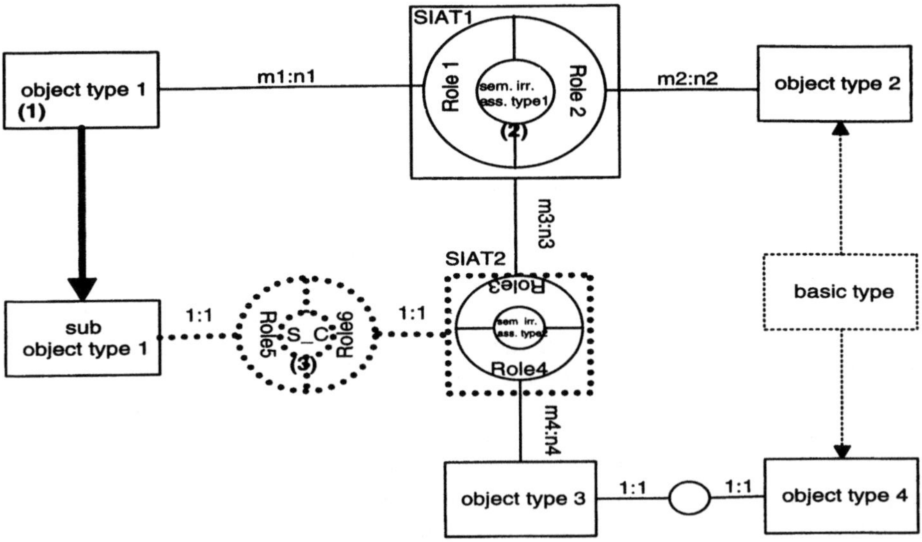

Figure 2: Information analysis elements

3.1 The Structural Elements of the Information Analysis

3.1.1 Object Types

The elements of the information analysis are object types, association types and dependence types. An object type is a class of things (real or abstract), which is interesting in the context of the application area.

In the environment of object orientation the word "object" is well known, and often misunderstood. Every oo guru who has provided a different oo method in the past provided a different definition of the term "object" as well. Hence it is obviously that the expression needs more clarification. The understanding of the object type within the area of the information analysis is according to Webster's Dictionary a thing that has a real and individual existence in reality or in mind. Nevertheless, the object type definition is very similar to that of the object in the oo environment, and so it could be as simple or as complex as the oo definition. But, the definition does not include an object type in sense of an abstract data type (ADT). Common feature of both is the emphasis on the concrete instance of something.

Using the graphical notation for the results of information analysis, object types are represented by rectangles (see Figure 2).

A special kind of object types are the basic types (e.g. number) they represent the data type (the physical representation) of an object type. Only lexical object types are represented by a basic type (e.g., object type "birthdate" is represented by date). The other kind of object types, non lexical object types needs a representation (directly) either or at least one unique identifier (see chapter about 3.1.2).

As shown in Figure 2 a represented-by relationship is drawn as a dashed arrow line from the basic type to the object type 2.

3.1.2 Semantically Irreducible Association Types

An association type is a class of information about objects of given types. It can be considered as a pattern of a natural language.

To avoid instabilities to the information structure, the association types have to be semantically irreducible. This means as mentioned before, that it mustn't be possible to decompose an association type into two or more others without loss of information. Consequently, the association type represents the semantically irreducible relationship between the modeled information. In our graphical notation the circular constructs represent association types.

Since an association type depicts a relationship between two or more object types, it is possible to model all kinds of relationships from binary up to n-ary kinds. A role within an association type is connected to exactly one object type which means that an object type can only play distinct roles within exactly one association type, but it could play the same role in different association types (e.g. (see Figure 4) the object type "person" plays the role "contributor" within the association type "done work" and plays within association type "leadership" the role "project leader" twice against the same object type "project").

Along this connection line the lower and upper bounds of the corresponding membership interval (i.e., multiplicity) are placed. An unlimited upper bound is denoted by an asterisk. It has to be read from the object type (rectangle) to the role. The lower bound tells, in how many occurrences of the association type any occurrence of the corresponding object type at least has to be found playing this role. The upper bound represents the maximum. Inside of the inner cycle the name of the semantic irreducible association type is placed.

It is important to mention, that an association type itself may be used as an object type in another association type (objectified relationship or structured object).

Figure 2 shows the SIAT1 which plays as an object type role Role3 as an object in SIAT2.

One special kind of relationship is the naming convention. As mentioned earlier, non lexical object types do not need a representation (see the person example in the previous section). In order to persistently store these object types they have to be made lexically. This means nothing more than they have to get an unique identifier. For doing so the IA provides the naming convention construct. It's semantically equal and graphically similar to the association type; the only difference is that roles and the naming of the association could be omitted. An object type that is identified by another object type plays always the role "has name", and vice versa the object type serving as the identifying one plays the role "is name". Both have the membership intervals with maximum 1. In Figure 2 object type 3 is identified by object type 4 and the unnamed little circle visualizes the naming convention.

3.1.3 High Level Information Elements

IA allows also to specify all kinds of relationships between information like sub/super relations, further constraining meta information i.e. information about already modeled information as well as business processes resp. similar complex operations. Only the first and second one are considered in this paper.

INHERITANCE HIERARCHY
A special form of relationship is the is-a predication or generalization/specialization. The semantics behind this kind of relationship is that one object type called sub object type is always a specialization of another one. Vice versa the other object called super object type is the generalization of another one. Implicitly the sub object type is always an instance of its super type. The relationship is denoted by a bold directed arrow from the super type to the connected sub type(s). A sub type may have multiple super types i.e., multiple inheritance is allowed. As depicted in Figure 2 object type 1 is the super type of sub object type 1.

Since every sub type instance is also an instance of its super type(s), it should only be constructed in case of a true specialization. Creating inheritance hierarchies only for propagating associations without the is-a semantics leads to a lack of model clearness. No need to say that circular inheritance—the sub type is directly or transitive its own super type is prohibited.

Furthermore, additional precising semantics on the hierarchy could be expressed. E.g. it's possible to distinguish between "one-of" and "and/or".

Due to the object type definition abstract super object types could not be modeled. Although they could be brought in the model after the transformation to class structures without loosing quality to the resulting model (see 4.4).

META INFORMATION AND DEPENDENCE TYPES
The Information Analysis allows it to apply constraining meta information formally on three different levels.

First, it is possible to put it on one single object type, without any side effects. In fig. 2 the "(1)" can mark a constraint concerning the domain of object type 1.

Second, a constraint could be placed on the level of a single association type. As depicted in Figure 2 the "(2)" can mark a constraint which determinds the compatible instances of object type 1 and object type 2.

Constraints on both levels could be formulated using plain text in any language or using formal or mathematical notations.

The third level of meta information describes correlations between association types. In IA this last kind is annotated as the dependence type. A dependence type looks formally like an association type (see Figure 2 the bold dotted element "S_C" is a dependence type) but always constrained by a rule. The "S" in the name of the dependence type implies that this element is an IA-S dependence type i.e. meta information formulated between already modeled structures only.

Additional modeling of business processes (IA-P dependence type) enforces the creation of new parts of information which is also expressed as object types and association types.

3.2 The Information Analysis Structure Description Language (ISDL)

As mentioned earlier, the IA uses the formal textual notation ISDL as well as the graphical one described before. ISDL allows various syntactical checks and serves as input for an algorithm processor like the one described in this paper (see next section) or as output for drawings. The following schema example (ISDL notation of Figure 2) is shown to give a short impression of ISDL.

```
CONCEPTUAL_SCHEMA (Figure2 / Version, 1.3);
#doc
  schema description
  ============
doc#
OBJECT (TYPE object_type_1, constrained_by (1));
#doc
  *** additionaly description for a object ***
doc#
OBJECT (TYPE object_type_2, represented_by basic_type);
OBJECT (TYPE object_type_3, named_by object_type_4);
OBJECT (TYPE object_type_4, represented_by basic_type);
OBJECT (TYPE sub_object_type_1, subtype_of object_type_1);
ASSOC (TYPE SIAT1,
      comp (object_type_1 Role1 interval (m1,n1),
      comp (object_type_2 Role2 interval (m2,n2),
      constrained_by (2)
      );
#doc
 *** additionally description for a semantically irreducible association type ***
doc#
ASSOC (TYPE SIAT2,
      comp (SIAT1 Role3 interval (m3,n3),
      comp (object_type_3 Role4 interval (m4,n4)
      );
#doc
 *** SIAT1 is used as object type ***
doc#
DEPEND (TYPE S_C, S_dep,
      comp (sub_object_type_1 Role5 interval (1,1),
      comp (SIAT2 Role6 interval (1,1)
      );
#doc
 *** additionally description for a dependence type ***
doc#
END_SCHEMA;
```

Note: In this case an ISDL parser will note that object type 1 has neither a representation nor a naming convention.

4 The Transformation Algorithm

4.1 Overview

After all information about the problem domain is formulated in IA and all the necessary dependencies are brought in the model various algorithms could be applied to derive the intended structures (e.g. oo class structures, data base structures). In the following sections we will only present the derivation of UML modeled class structures.

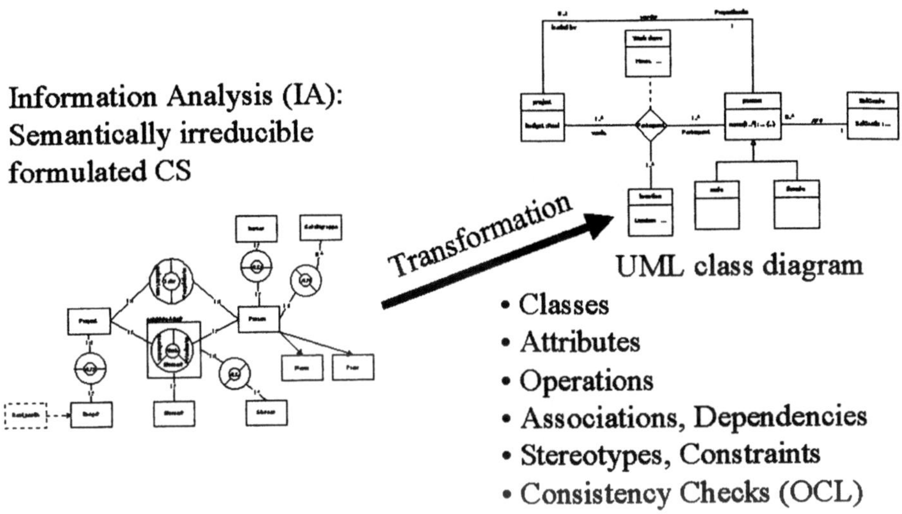

Figure 3: Tranformation form conceptual schema to UML

The semantically irreducibility allows it to derive classes with its attributes on a high level of cohesion. Since the basic facts i.e., associations between object types are expressed semantically irreducible within the conceptual schema there are no implicit relationships that force a special complex treatment. Through the transformation algorithm special relationships (property relationships) among the association types could be detected and converted in classes and their attributes.

This technique is fair more sophisticated than simple approaches of an (E)ER to oo transformation. The problem of these ideas is the one to one transformation of entity types and their attributes into classes and their attributes, since this is only a transformation without focusing on the information semantics itself.

Further, associations between the resulting classes and special dependencies among them could be derived.

The last step is the formulation of consistency checks using the object constraint language (OCL) provided since UML V1.1. The necessary conditions (pre-, post-condition and invariants) could also be derived from the conceptual schema (mainly based upon the meta information). IA-S dependence types are mapped into stereotypes or OCL conditions whereas IA-P dependence types like business processes and similar complex operations could be transferred into class methods.

4.2 Building Compositions

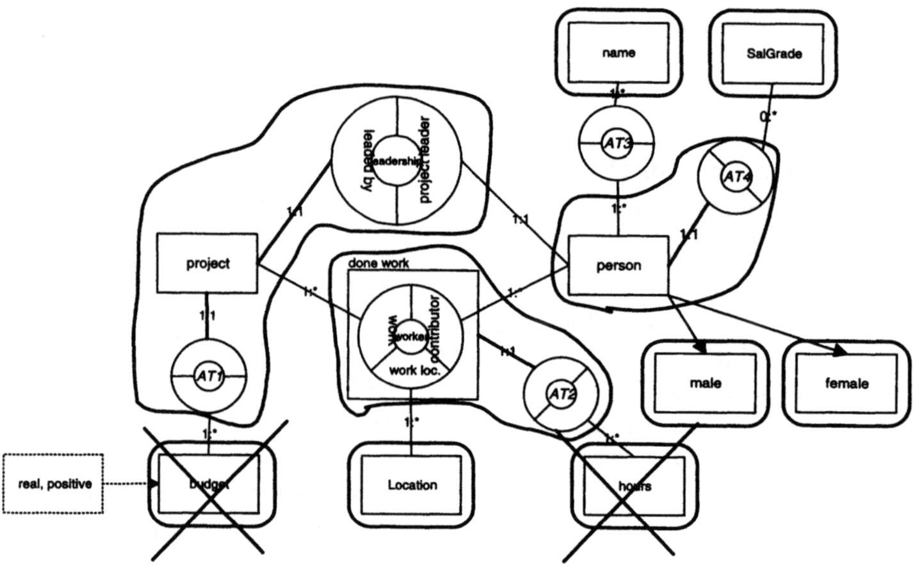

Figure 4: Building compositions of association types and object types

The Figure 4 (zoomed IA part of Figure 3) graphically aggregates the following transformation steps together.

First, mark every line denoting a relationship with 1:1 membership interval.

Second, group all elements along previously marked relationships together into one compositions. We could regard compositions as raw classes.

Third, build compositions around all remaining object types and cross them out if their information is already contained in another composition. Remaining association types remain unchanged, yet.

Additionally, we want to emphasize on a further step creating classes which obey to the principle of encapsulation. In other words the separation into objects with an own identity. The reason why we stress this topic is that there is often no clear idea about doing this nor a formal algorithm serving this problem has been presented yet.

As shown in Figure 4 all one to one relationships are marked, except the one between "person" playing the role "project leader" in the connected association type "leadership". In that case the algorithm detects, that even person and project possess an own identity and so the two must be separated into distinct compositions.

4.3 Deriving Class Structures

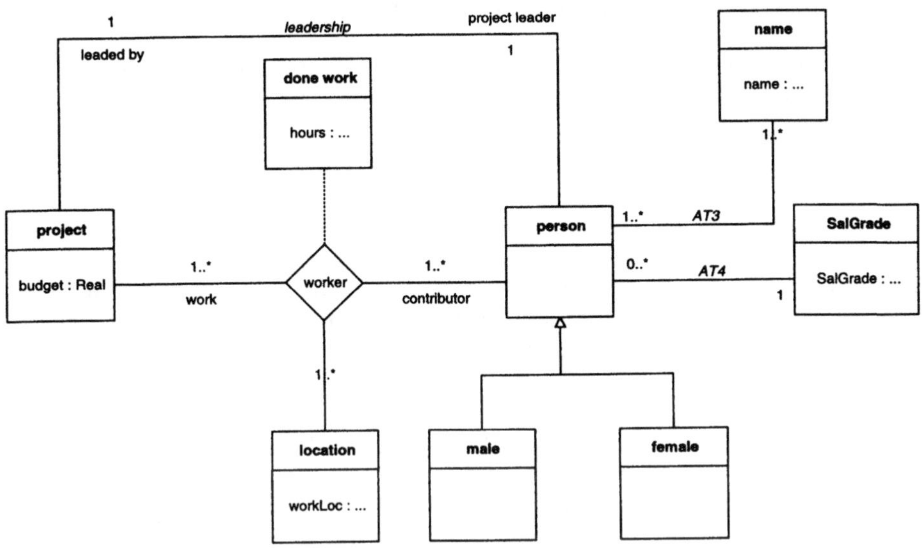

Figure 5: Derived class structures

The structure diagram in Figure 5 illustrates the main steps of the algorithm. The automatically derivation of classes with its attributes, association between classes including n-ary associations and association classes if necessary and inheritance hierarchies.

First we will check if all information modeled in the CS is completely transformed into the UML class diagram. Hence this is true—all object types representing the basic pieces of information are transformed—no information is lost.

Secondly we consider the relations between the basic information pieces originally expressed as semantically irreducible association types in the CS—the class diagram seems to have less associations. The reason for this is that some formerly explicitly expressed relationships are now implicitly expressed e.g. the association type "AT1" in Figure 4 is now implicitly expressed through the relationship of the attribute "budget" and its containing class "project". Taking this into account no association types and so no information of CS is lost—it all have been converted into the semantically corresponding UML model elements.

Concentrating further on the associations we detect the UML association class as a container for the properties of an association itself (e.g. "hours" in Figure 5). The semantics behind the association class as the association itself—in other words the class modeling the association is far more language depended and therefore not taken into account here. The object type representing the hours one employee at one location has contributed to the specified project was transformed into an attribute of the UML class linked as association class to the relationship.

4.4 Applying the Intended Application View

The steps up to now are completely reversible. This means that the class diagram even if it's not created with the presented algorithm could be transferred back into a semantically irreducible formulated CS.

In order to incorporate the intended application view several manual operations have to be done now.

By applying one application specific point of view all the other possible previously existing views are faded out. This procedure intentionally neglects information—but even those information which isn't interesting for the intended application use. As shown in Figure 6 the class "name" is transformed into a set of "names" owned by a instance of the class "person".

Another point finally to take into account is the specific implementation language and its possibilities and limitations. Before this step we modeled pure object oriented concepts without the limiting focus on a specific oo language, concerning stuff like multivalued attributes, multiple inheritance and so on e.g. as mentioned before class "person" has now a multivalued attribute "name".

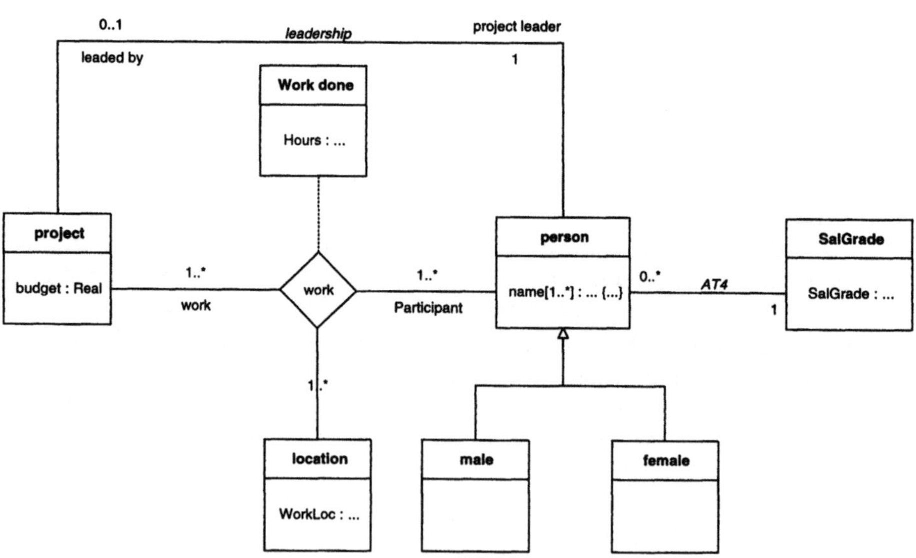

Figure 6: Class structure with applied application view

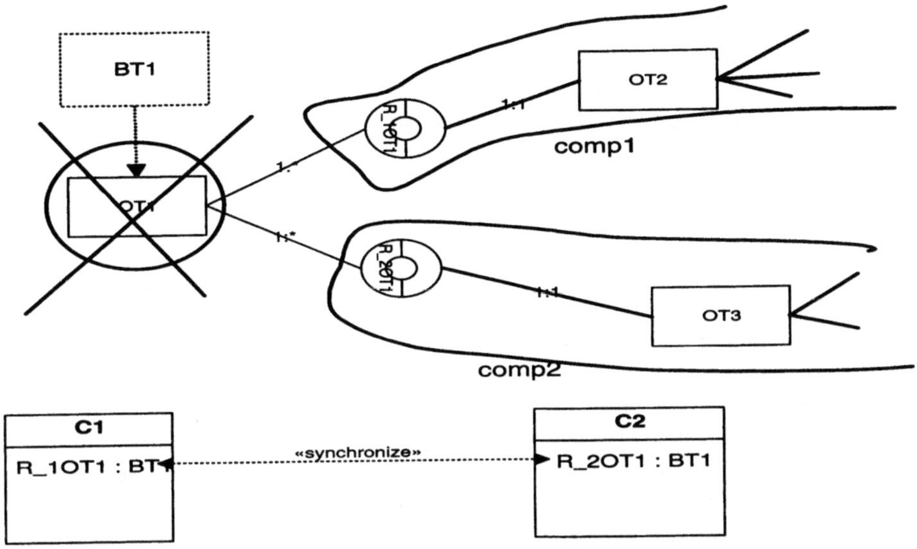

Figure 7: Synchronize constraint

4.5 Constraints Arising Form Membership Intervals

Neglecting meta information the CS indeed still contains more information then transformed until here especially membership intervals are often bearing constraining information not handled yet. Figure 7 depicts a typical situation of a constraint derived directly from the conceptual schema without using meta information.

Class C1 results from composition comp1 and class C2 from composition comp2. The situation leads us to the following semantic rules, expressed as semantic irreducible sentences:

1. Every instance of OT1 is connected to at least one instance of OT3
2. Every instance of OT1 is connected to at least one instance of OT2
3. Every instance of OT3 is connected to exactly one instance of OT1
4. Every instance of OT2 is connected to exactly one instance of OT1

Explicitly modeled, an instance of OT1 is shared between the two resulting classes. First, the creation of a new value for OT1 within an instance of class C2, in order to enforce the semantic rules the set operation must ensure that the intended value is valid by querying all instances of class C1, and vice versa.

On the other hand by deleting i.e., nullifying an instance of OT1 that serves as attribute within the two classes leads also to a deletion of the attribute in the other object that uses the same attribute. Generally spoken, the two attributes

are connected together on a meta level in order to synchronize their content (i.e. domain constraint) over lifetime.
This can explicitly expressed using a restrictive stereotype "synchronize" between the attributes resulting from OT1 within the two classes.

5 Resume

Based on the information analysis method (IA) that empowers the modeler to formulate all requirement of the problem domain in an easy as well as expressive way we presented a transformation to UML.
As mentioned earlier the modeling and transformation of business processes is similar to handle but scope of another paper (to appear).
We allow the claim that the same result had could been produced as a output of the knowledge of an experienced oo modeler, too. But taking the presented way which is not a detour at all has at least the following significant advantages.
First, the derivation of class structures on the basis of a semantically irreducible formulated CS provides assuredness in the way that all derived class structures reflect the semantics of the requirements.
Second, our approach provides "information independence" that means, applying a new application view may require new class structures. But, the former classes could be kept in order to guarantee the executibility to former application software.
Third, the presented method serves as source of arguments for modeling these exactly class structures and no other. It's as a methodical foundation on which applications could be built and provides an answer to the question "how do I find the fitting classes?".
But, it must be kept in mind that the IA modeling technique doesn't support all kind of active behavior of the oo system, hence no state nor activity diagrams could automatically be derived without explicitly modeling these dynamic processes.

References

KERN-BAUSCH, L., WENZEL, B. G. (1980): Informationsanalyse *Leibniz-Rechenzentrum Munich, internal paper.*

KERN-BAUSCH, L., WENZEL, B. G. (1986): Database Design for Relational Systems: Why, Who, How? *European ORACLE Users Group Newsletter, No. 10.*

BOOCH, G., RUMBAUGH, J. and JACOBSON, I. (1997): Unified Modeling Language, Version 1.1. Rational Software Corporation, 2800 San Thomas Expressway, Santa Clara, CA 95051-0951 (USA), URL:http://www.rational.com

On Mapping Between UML and Entity-Relationship Model

Yongzhen Ou

Fakultät für Mathematik und Informatik,
Universität Konstanz, Fach D188, 78457 Konstanz, Germany

Abstract: Nowadays, the Entity-Relationship Model (ERM) is the most important and widely used method for modeling data and designing databases. On the other hand, the Unified Modeling Language (UML) is expected to become more and more popular in object-oriented analysis and design (OOA/OOD). As a by-product of OOA/OOD, a database design can be derived by mapping of objects to entities. The purpose of this paper is to define a mapping between UML and ERM. The translation of a UML class diagram to and from an ER diagram is also elaborated. This work is part of a multi-model multi-tool database application engineering framework that is being designed and prototyped at University Konstanz.

1 Motivation

Since its introduction by Chen (1976), the Entity-Relationship Model (ERM) has found its wide acceptance in the area of database design and related fields. In the ER model, all data are viewed as stating facts about entities and relationships, i.e., connections or associations between entities. These simple and clear structuring concepts allow users to naturally model the "things" in real world. As a result, most of the existing databases are first designed conceptually using some variant of ERM and then got their conceptual schemata translated into logical schemata of the target system (Batini (1992), Elmasri and Navathe (1994)).

In the beginning of this year, the Unified Modeling Language (UML), which unifies the Booch (1994), OMT (Rumbaugh et al. (1991)) and OOSE (Jacobson et al. (1992)) methods and incorporates ideas from other methods and industry practice, was submitted to OMG (Object Management Group) for adoption as a standard. That means the UML may become a standard modeling language for object-oriented development soon. For UML is meant to be applicable to the modeling of all types of systems, it can also be applied to conceptual database design. How to map the constructs between UML and ERM? Is it possible to automate the translation of a UML class diagram to an ER diagram? This paper tries to answer these questions. A good solution to these problems is very useful for forward engineering and reverse engineering of database design.

In forward engineering, a software application can be developed by using the UML notations. The persistent classes underlying the application can then be stored in an object-oriented database or in a relational database. In the latter case, a mapping from the object model to the relational model is required. The ER model is the best choice to represent the relational model visually. Moreover, many database designers and database users have been using ER model for a long time and have mastered all the modeling techniques of ER models. They prefer viewing database schemata as ER diagrams. Furthermore, it can also happen that some preexisting parts of the UML class diagrams have originally been modeled as entities and relationships in some ER diagrams. If the UML class diagram can also be shown as ER diagram, it would be a useful first step towards schema integration and database integration (Batini (1992)). In all these cases, it is desirable to transform UML class diagrams to ER diagrams automatically. Even though almost all OO design tools -including Rational Rose- provide some mapping of their class diagrams to database schema definitions (e.g., in SQL), these transformations are typically very limited in functionality (coverage of integrity constraints) and for flexibility (e.g., choices for representing generalization hierarchies). Therefore, the goal of our work is to develop a multi-model, multi-tool design platform that allows the use of different analysis/design/implementation tools, possibly based on different models (such as UML and ER variants). Such an environment will give the designer a broad choice of models and tools to use for the individual tasks during the forward and also reverse engineering tasks for database applications.

In reverse engineering, if an existing ER diagram can be viewed as a UML class diagram, one can easily change, update, or enhance the existing database design under the OO paradigm. Showing the ER diagrams as UML diagrams also make it possible to integrate the existing database designs with other OO designs. In these cases, the mapping of ER model to UML is needed. The automatic transformation of ER diagrams to UML class diagrams is useful.

The layout of this paper is as follows. Section 2 gives an overview of UML, Section 3 discusses the mapping of UML to ERM. In Section 4, the translation of a UML Class Diagram to an ER Diagram is elaborated. Section 5 briefly discusses the mapping of ERM to UML. Finally Section 6 concludes this work.

2 The Unified Modeling Language (UML)

What is the UML? As its designers pointed out, the UML is a language for specifying, visualizing and documenting the artifacts of an object-oriented system under development (Booch et al. (1997)). It was developed jointly by Grady Booch, Ivar Jacobson, and Jim Rumbaugh at Rational Software Corporation, with contributions from other leading methodologists, software vendors, and many users. It provides the application modeling language for business process modeling with use cases, class and object modeling, component modeling, distribution and deployment modeling (Booch et al. (1997)). The UML semantics defines model elements, relationships among the model elements, mechanisms organizing the model elements, and diagrams showing the projection of model elements. The UML also defines notations for its various types of diagrams. These notations provide a very convenient way to describe the various modeling aspects. The diagrams supported by UML are:

- Class diagram and object diagram
- Use case diagram

- Interaction diagram
  - Sequence diagram
  - Collaboration diagram
- State diagram
- Implementation diagram
  - Component diagram
  - Deployment diagram

In the process of object-oriented analysis and design, a model and a few diagrams can be produced. The model contains all of the underlying elements of information about a system under consideration, while diagrams capture different perspective, or view, of the system model. A class diagram shows types, classes, and their relationship; it shows the building blocks of the model. An object diagram describes instances and their relationship; it shows the sample data structure. Both class diagram and object diagram project the static structure of a system model. A use case diagram encompasses actors, use cases, and their relationship. It provides a natural high-level view of the intended functionality of the system. Interaction diagrams, including sequence diagram and collaboration diagram, display instances and their relationships (including messages), organized either by space (collaboration diagram) or by time (sequence diagram). A state diagram shows states and their relationships, organized by state, and is used to specify the overall behavior of a type. A component diagram encompasses components and their relationships; it reveals the dependencies among software units. A deployment diagram depicts components, nodes, and their relationships; it shows the distribution and interaction of components and objects on computational nodes.

In this paper, we concentrate on the UML semantics and notations describing the static structure aspects of a model, namely, types, classes, associations, etc., and the class diagram visually presenting these aspects.

3 Mapping of UML to ERM

The class diagram is core to a UML model. It presents the important abstractions in a system and shows how they relate to each other. This section will discuss the concepts underlying the class diagram and their mappings to ER model. As there exist many variations of ER model, we take the one presented in (Elmasri and Navathe (1994)) as our ER model. This ER model has the following concepts: entities and attributes (include composite attributes and multivalued attributes), primary key; regular and weak relationships (they can also have attributes), roles, and cardinality; and weak entities. The graphical notation of the ER model is the same as that in the DB-MAIN CASE tool (Hainaut (1994)), which uses rectangle to represent entity type and hexagon to represent relationship type. Weak entity type is represented by double rectangles and its identifying relationship by double hexagons. If we do not explicitly indicate, we mean an entity an entity type and a relationship a relationship type in the following discussion.

3.1 Classes, Attributes and Operations

According to the UML semantics, a class is the descriptor for a set of objects with similar structure, behavior, and relationships. A class is the implementation of type. A class can have attributes defining its structure and operations defining the behaviors of instances of the class. Obviously, an object is essentially an entity in ER model. Therefore, a class is mapped to an entity type in ERM. Attributes of the class are mapped to attributes of the resultant entity type. Mapping of operations is the future research. In UML, it is assumed that each object (instance of a class) is uniquely identified by its object identifier (OID). In the ER model, an entity is distinguished from other entities by the value of its key attribute. To accommodate this, a surrogate key is added to the resultant entity type which has a name of the entity type name concatenating "-ID" (such as window-ID). For example, Figure 1 shows the mapping of a class Window to an entity Window.

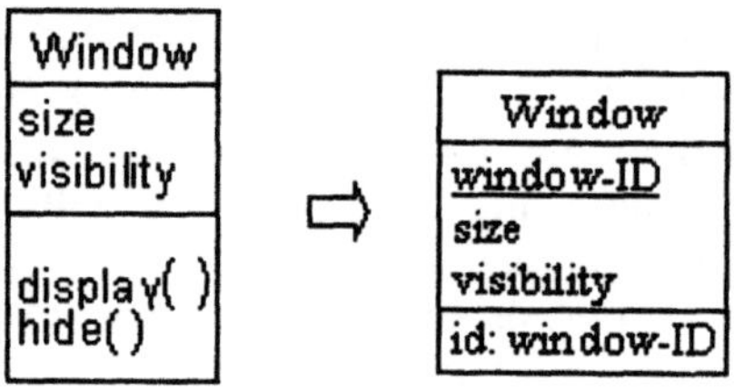

Figure 1: The mapping of a class to an entity

3.2 Relationships

A relationship is a semantic connection among classes. There exist several different kinds of relationships in UML, namely the bi-directional association, uni-directional association, dependency, aggregation association, inheritance and template instantiation.

Association

An association is used to represent a structural dependency among objects. A bi-directional association indicates that the involving objects are mutually dependent on each other, while a uni-directional association indicates the one directional dependency. Both bi-directional and uni-directional associations are mapped to relationships in the ER model, though the relationship in ER model has more mathematical sense. The UML supports n-ary (n > 2) associations, so does ER model. Therefore, an n-ary association is mapped to a n-ary relationship in ER model. Some associations may have association classes. An association class is just an association that has class properties (such as attributes) as well. Therefore, an association class is also mapped to a relationship with attributes. For example, in Figure 2, the association class Job in UML is mapped to the relationship Job in ER model.

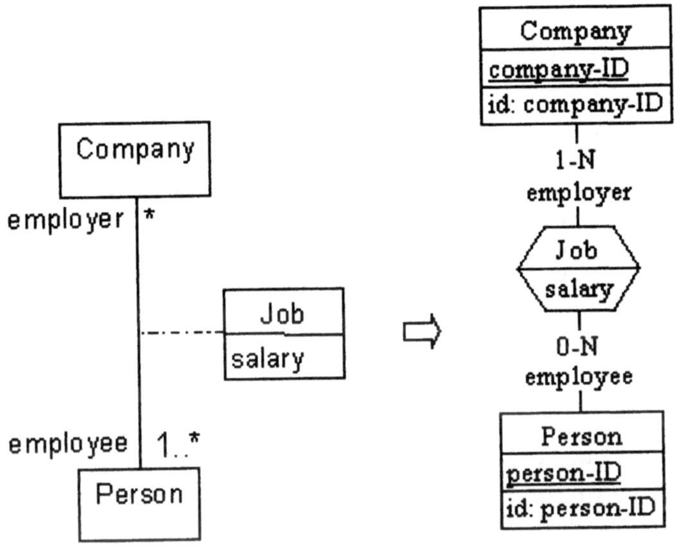

Figure 2: The mapping of an association class to a relationship

Qualified Association

A qualifier is sometimes used to qualify an association and reduces the effective multiplicity of an association. Usually only one-to-many and many-to-many associations may be qualified. The qualifier separates the objects on the "many" side into some subsets. A qualified association is also mapped to a relationship in ERM, just like the normal associations. However, depending on the multiplicity, the multiplicity and primary key of the resultant relationship are different.

For example, Figure 3 shows the mapping of an one-to-one qualified association to an one-to-many relationship. In this example, the qualified association indicates that a company may have one or more departments with each having a unique dept-name. A department belongs to only one company while departments from different companies may have the same dept-name. Here the qualifier "dept-name" happens to be an attribute of the class Department. Consequently, the resultant relationship R is an one-to-many relationship, and the key of this relationship can be the key of entity type Department (department-ID) or the combination of the key of entity type Company and dept-name (company-ID, dept-name).

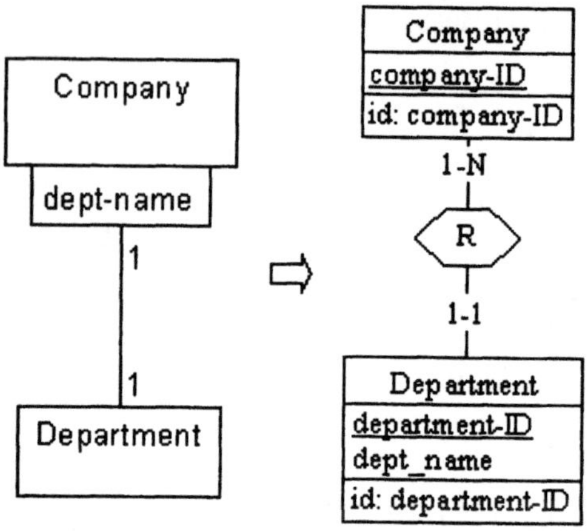

Figure 3: The mapping of a qualified association to a relationship – 1

Figure 4 shows an one-to-many qualified association. In this example, a bank may have many persons as their customers with each uniquely identified by his account#. A person may have zero or more accounts in zero or more banks. Therefore, the resultant relationship has the multiplicity of many-to-many. The qualifier "account#" becomes the attribute and part of the key of the relationship. The primary key of the relationship is then the combination of the key of bank and "account#" (bank-ID, account#).

Figure 5 illustrates the mapping of a many-to-many qualified association to a many-to-many relationship. In this example, a company may have employed many persons and a person may be employed by many companies. Each company may possess many offices with each headed by one or more officers (persons). The qualifier "office" divides the persons into a few subsets with each attaching to an office. Therefore, the resultant relationship has the multiplicity of many-to-many. The qualifier "office" becomes the attribute and part of the key of the relationship. The primary key of the relationship is "office" combined with the keys from entity type Company and entity type Person (company-ID, person-ID, office).

Aggregation

Aggregation is a special form of association that specifies a whole-part relationship between the aggregate (whole) and a component part. There are two kinds of aggregation depending on the containment of the parts in its whole: one is by reference (shared aggregation), the other is by value (composite aggregation). The composite aggregation is equivalence to the attribute composition.

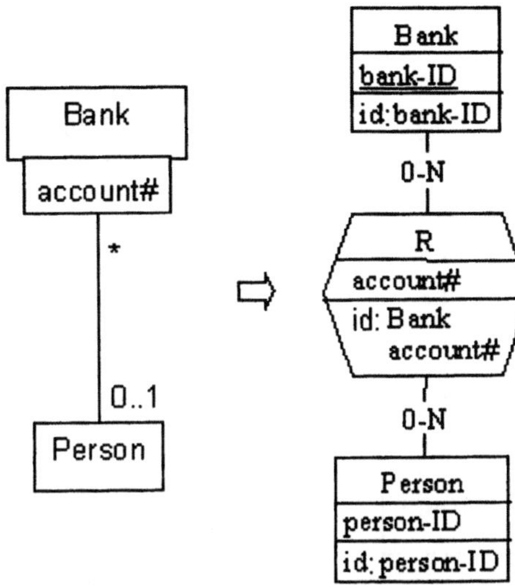

Figure 4: The mapping of a qualified association to a relationship – 2

Aggregation indicates that the existence of the parts is dependent on the whole. This existent dependency leads to the mapping of an aggregation to a relationship in the ER model with a total participation constraint on the entity representing the component part. For example, in Figure 6, the aggregation Contains is mapped to relationship Contains. There is no mapping for the UML adornment ordered. In such cases, a note or a comment can be added to the ER diagram or to its attaching documentation to accommodate the constraint definitions.

Inheritance

Inheritance is used when a more specific class is to incorporate structure and behavior of a more general class. The more specific class (the subclass) is a specialization or extension of the more general one (the superclass). The original ER model does not directly support the concept of inheritance. However, an inheritance can be simulated by an isa relationship in the ERM, which indicates that the entity representing the subclass "is-a" kind of entity representing the superclass. For example, Figure 7 shows the mapping of a generalization in UML to some isa relationships in ER model.

Dependency

Dependency is a relationship between two classes, in which one of them (the client class) depends on some service(s) of another class (the supplier class).There are four kinds of predefined Dependency: *trace*(Trace), *refine*(Refinement),

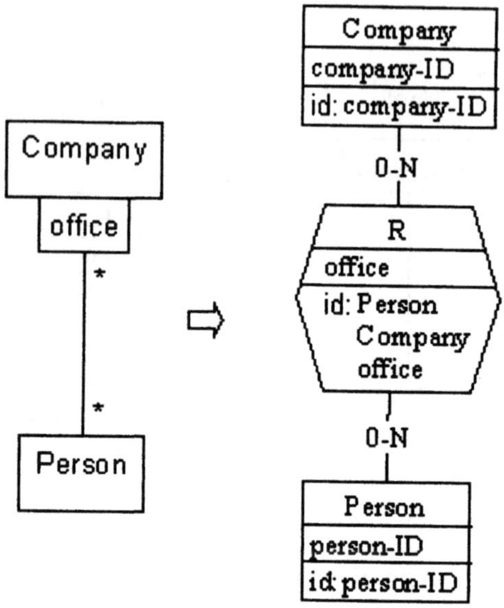

Figure 5: The mapping of a qualified association to a relationship – 3

uses(Usage), and *bind*(Binding). The ER model has no direct representations for these concepts. However, the dependencies between model elements (the trace, refine and uses dependencies) in a UML class diagram can be documented and attached to the resultant ER diagram. The bind dependency is the same as the instantiates relationship and is discussed below.

Instantiates

An instantiates relationship between two classes indicates that one of them (the instantiated class) is created as a result of instantiation of the other class (the parameterized class, or the template class). The parameterized class has a formal parameter and the instantiated class replaces the formal parameter with an actual one. The instantiates relationship is actually a kind of inheritance as well. Therefore, an instantiates relationship is also mapped to an isa relationship in ERM. Moreover, the identification and existence of the entity type representing the instantiated class depends on the entity type representing the parameterized class. Therefore, the former entity type should be a weak entity and should totally participate in the relationship. For example, Figure 8 shows the mapping of an instantiates relationship to isa relationships.

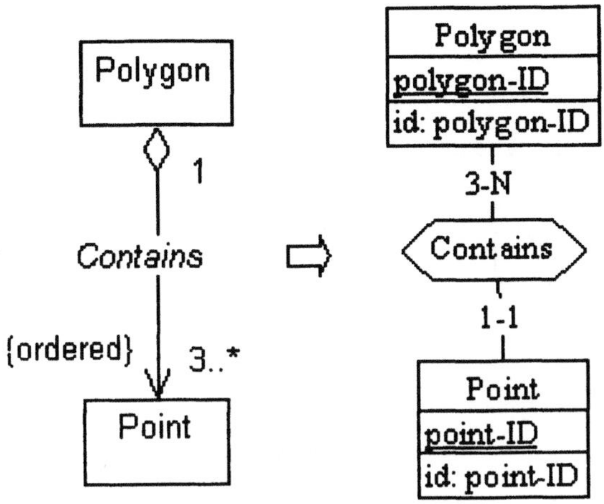

Figure 6: The mapping of an aggregation to a relationship

4 Translation of a UML Class Diagram to an ER Diagram

The translation of a UML class diagram to an ER diagram requires the following steps:

1. For each regular class (not association class) in the class diagram, create a corresponding entity type. The name of the entity type is directly taken over from the class. The attributes of the original class are all carried over to the resultant entity type as well. An attribute with the name of the class name plus "-ID" is added to the entity type and is marked as the primary key. If the class is an instantiated class, mark the resultant entity type as a weak entity type. See Figure 1 and Figure 8 for examples.

2. For each inheritance relationship, create an isa relationship type between the resultant entity types of the two participating classes. See Figure 7 for an example.

3. For each instantiates relationship, create a weak isa relationship type between the resultant entity types of the two participating classes. See Figure 8.

4. For each aggregation relationship, create a relationship type between the resultant entity types of the two participating classes. Add the cardinality constraints to the resultant relationship properly. See Figure 6.

5. For each association, draw a relationship type among the entity types representing the participating classes. The association name is the name of the

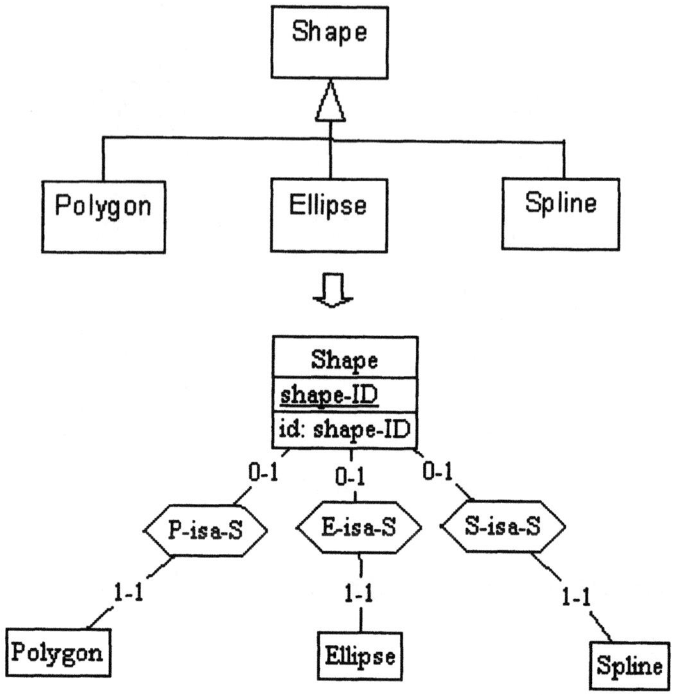

Figure 7: The mapping of generalization to isa relationships

resultant relationship. If the association possesses an association class, add all the attributes of the association class to the resultant relationship type. See Figure 2.

6. For each association, do:
   - If there are any role names, then carry them over to the resultant relationship type. See Figure 2.
   - If there is any cardinality specified and the association is not qualified, then put the specification on the resultant relationship type but exchange the positions of the specification. See Figure 2 and Figure 6.
   - If a qualifier is defined for the association, depending on the cardinality specification of the qualified association, put the proper specification and attributes on the resultant relationship type and define the primary key for the relationship type. See Figure 3, Figure 4, Figure 5 for examples.

After these steps, an ER diagram equivalent to the original UML class diagram is created. However, some refinement must be done by the designer. For instance, the names of the relationships should be added if missing.

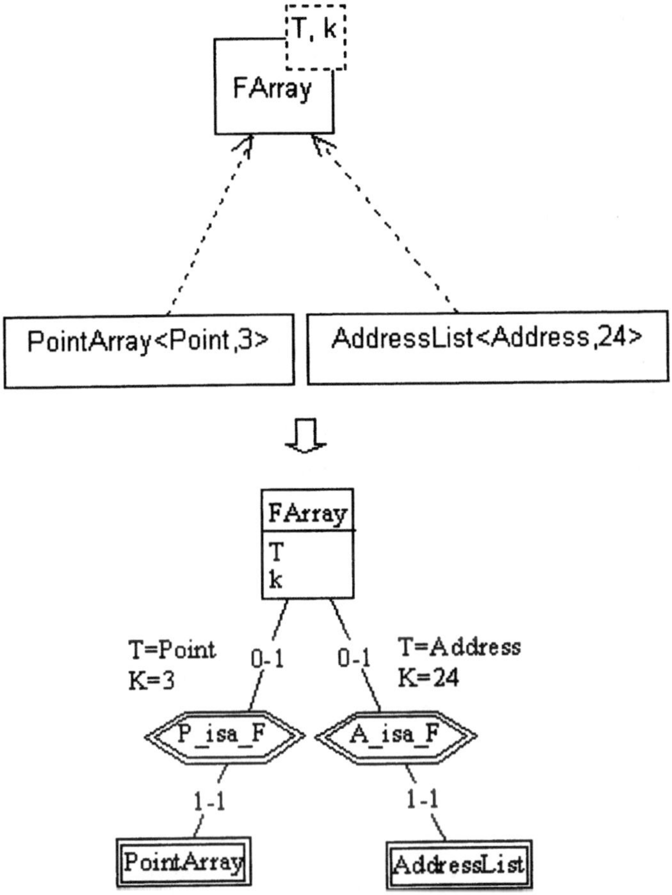

Figure 8: The mapping of instantiates relationship to isa relationships

5 Mapping of ERM to UML

As Rumbaugh et al. (1991) pointed out, the OMT (Object Modeling Technique) is an enhanced form of ER that includes some new concepts (such as qualification). The UML is an enhanced form of OMT and thus an enhanced form of ER model. Therefore, the mapping of ER model to UML is quite straightforward. An Entity type can be mapped to a class. The attributes of the entity type are then carried over to be the attributes of the resultant class. A relationship type is mapped to an association. More accurately, the isa relationship type should be mapped to a generalization, an identifying relationship type to an uni-directional association. A relationship type with attributes must mapped to an association class. The role names of the relationship type become role names of the resultant association.

The cardinality definitions in ERM are mapped to the multiplicity definitions in UML, but the specification positions are exchanged (cf. Figure 2).
In another words, to translate an ER diagram to a UML class diagram, the following steps are needed.

1. For each entity type in the ER diagram, create a corresponding UML class with the same name. The attributes of the entity type become attributes of the resultant class.

2. For each relationship type:

   - If it is an isa relationship, create a generalization between the classes representing the participating entity types.
   - If it is an identifying relationship type, create a uni-directional association between the classes representing the participating entity types.
   - Otherwise, create an association among the classes representing the participating entity types.

3. For each relationship type:

   - If there are any role names specified, add the role names to the resultant generalization/association as well.
   - If there are any cardinalities specified, add the specifications to the resultant association properly.

6 Conclusion

The UML is a semantically rich and expressively powerful modeling language. Many CASE tools will soon support it. The ER model is essentially *the* model used in database design, especially in relational database design. This paper has tried to define the mapping between the UML and the ER model. Due to the simplicity of the ER model, some of the UML concepts and notations, like operations, visibility of classes and some adornments attached to an association role, are ignored during the mapping. One solution to amend this is to map these concepts into constraints, comments or notes in ER model, so that the semantics of the UML model can be more or less preserved. Nevertheless, the essences of a UML class diagram can be sufficiently represented by an ER diagram. The translation of a UML class diagram to and from an ER diagram is very useful in database forward and reverse engineering.

More complete mappings will have to take advantage of dynamic features of relational DBMS, such as constraints, triggers, and stored procedures. These are, however, not easily represented in an ER context. This is another indication for the usefulness of a multi-model database design framework.

A CASE tool to automate the translation process is under construction. This CASE tool is intended to incorporate at least Rational Rose from the OO CASE tool area and the ER tools Erwin (Logic Works) and DB-MAIN. Our first goal is to provide automatic import and export facilities for UML diagrams to and from ER diagrams. Further work will have to deal with extensions of the ER-based representations to account for dynamic aspects (such as triggers and procedures). In parallel to that, we are also looking at target DBMS platforms different from SQL, namely ODMG's object databases (ODL, OQL).

References

BATINI, C., CERI, S., and NAVATHE, S. (1992): Conceptual Database Design: An Entity-Relationship Approach. The Benjamin/Cummings Publishing Company, Inc., California.

BOOCH, G., RUMBAUGH, J., and JACOBSON, I. (1997): Unified Modeling Language, Version 1.0. Rational Software Corporation, 2800 San Tomas Expressway, Santa Clara, CA 95051-0951 (USA), URL: http://www.rational.com

BOOCH, G. (1994): Object-Oriented Analysis and Design with Applications, Second Edition. The Benjamin/Cummings Publishing Company, Inc., California.

CHEN, P. P. (1976): The Entity-Relationship Model – Toward a Unified View of Data. *ACM Transactions on Database Systems, Vol.1, No.1, 9-36.*

ELMASRI, R. and NAVATHE, S.B. (1994): Fundamentals of Database Systems, Second Edition. The Benjamin/Cummings Publishing Company, Inc., California.

HAINAUT, J.-L., ENGLEBERT, V., HENRARD, J., HICK, J.-M., ROLAND, D. (1994): Database Evolution: the DB-MAIN Approach. In: P. Loucopoulos (Ed.): *Proceedings of the conference on the ER Approach – ER'94.* LNCS, Springer-Verlag, Germany, 112-131.

JACOBSON, I., CHRISTERSON, M., JONSSON, P., and OVERGAARD, G. (1992): Object- Oriented Software Engineering. Workingham, England, Addison-Wesley Publishing Company.

RUMBAUGH, J., BLAHA, M., PREMERLANI, W., EDDY, F., and LORENSEN, W. (1991): Object-Oriented Modeling and Design. Englewood Cliffs, New Jersey, Prentice-Hall.

Evaluation of Object-Oriented Modelling Languages: A Comparison Between OML and UML

Michael Prasse

Institut für Wirtschaftsinformatik
Universität Koblenz-Landau, D-57075 Koblenz, Rheinau 1, Germany

Abstract: The following article is motivated by the current efforts of the Object Management Group (OMG) to standardize object-oriented modelling languages. In the face of the great economic importance of such a standardization, a careful consideration of possible requirements for modelling languages is necessary. The development of suitable criteria and measures is, however, a delicate task. One reason for this is that the various tasks during the software engineering demand different, partly contradictory, requirements. Beyond this the valuation of quality is not independent from individual preferences and patterns of perception.

In this article, we will give a framework for evaluating modelling languages. We will consider different levels of requirements—from subjective ones, like clarity of notation, to technical ones, like completeness and correctness of the language description. Finally we will use this framework for the comparison between OML and UML. An extended version of this comparison can be found in Frank and Prasse (1997).

1 Introduction

The development of software requires an adequate coverage and description of chosen properties of the current problem domain. In general, not only software engineers but also users and domain experts take an essential part in the development of such a description. For such teams, programming languages are not suitable because they are implementation-oriented. Furthermore, they are not easily understood by all team members. But on the other side, natural language is neither an alternative. So, descriptions of domains should provide guidelines and directions for the implementation. Therefore, some formal, unambiguous language aspects are required. Driven by this conflict, conceptual modelling was born. The aim is to provide a representation of an application domain which is understandable for all persons involved in the software engineering process. This representation, called model, only shows the essential parts of the planned system. In addition, implementation details should be supported, too. To realize this claim, a suitable modelling language is necessary.

We expect that object-oriented conceptual modelling solves the sketched conflict between clarity and software engineering requirements at the same time. Object-oriented modelling is subject to intensive research. Consequently, there is a large number of related approaches with different tool support and modelling languages (cf. Frank (1997)). The large number of different approaches increases the uncertainty of potential users, because it is difficult to select and apply the appropriate language. There are also considerable risks for the necessary investment.

In this article we attempt a contribution to the important evaluation of object-oriented modelling languages. Our work was triggered by the current efforts of the OMG, to establish a standard for object-oriented modelling languages. At the moment, the most promising candidate is the "Unified Modeling Language" (UML). There are hints that economic considerations will have some influence on the standardization process. This is a further reason to examine requirements of modelling languages from a scientific point of view. Therefore, we suggest a framework which contains important evaluation criteria. Some of these criteria need a careful interpretation. In particular, the framework is not a set of metrics which allow to quantify automatically the quality of a modelling language. To evaluate our ideas, we apply the framework to OML and UML.

2 Some Aspects of Object-Oriented Modelling Languages

Contrary to natural language, modelling languages are artificial languages. In contrast to the artificial languages which are interpreted by machines or used by experts of a small domain, modelling languages have in common with natural languages that they are used by persons of different professions. A modelling language is a language for describing models. We call a modelling language object-oriented if it is based on the object-oriented paradigm. A modelling language can contain different kinds of diagrams and models to describe a complex system with different abstractions.

A modelling method is a method which supports the development of a class of similar models. It includes one or more modelling languages and a strategy for the development process. We do not question the importance of the development process, but we doubt whether it is possible to standardize it. The most promising solution seems to be the use of a uniform notation with separate instances of the development process. Often, not the different strategies are the problem but the diverse kinds of documents which are created in the single activities. A unification of the documents and the notation allow a uniform vocabulary. This improves clarity and helps comparing the different approaches. For this reason we concentrate on modelling languages.

There are various ways to describe a language. Firstly, you can define only the syntax of a language. This can be done using grammars. Then, a language is a set of words over an alphabet which is defined by the corresponding grammar. Secondly, you can additionally consider the semantics of the single words. Axiomatic and operational semantics for the specification of programming languages are an example for this (Kowalk, p. 372 ff. (1996)). Beside the separation of syntax and semantics, there is a further step in which you can abstract fundamental concepts from their concrete representation. This leads to a third way, the separation from abstract concepts and concrete representations. This alternative is quite useful if different languages are to be investigated which base on a common paradigm like object orientation. The concepts of the common paradigm form the abstract skeleton for these languages.

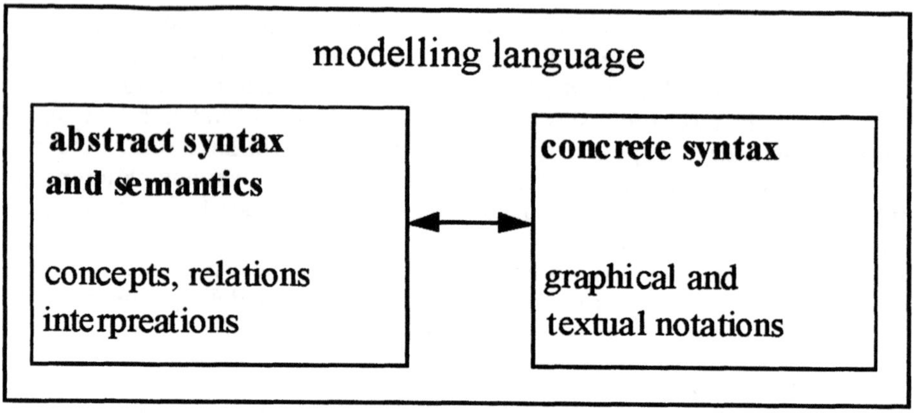

Figure 1: Ideal Structure of Object-Oriented Modelling Language

In this sense, OML, UML and other object-oriented modelling languages show the same principal structure (Figure 1). The abstract syntax and semantics define the concepts of the language elements and the syntactical configuration. Furthermore, they deliver an interpretation—the semantics—and form the more or less formal foundation for the language. They describe the meaning of the language and determine their expressive power. Therefore, many evaluation aspects correlate to the abstract syntax and semantics. The concrete syntax describes the textual and graphical notation based on the abstract concepts. In the case of object-oriented modelling languages, mainly graphical representations form the concrete syntax. The main task of the concrete syntax is representation. The model is described in terms of the abstract syntax and semantics but represented by the concrete syntax. Each language concept contains, in general, abstract and concrete aspects. The abstract aspects embody the essence or logical meaning independent from the current representation. The concrete aspects deal with the current representation. The advantage of this separation between abstract and concrete aspects is a better (formal) representation of the language. On the other hand the representation or notation can be decoupled from the application and it can be developed separately. So, experiences from semiotics can be taken into account more readily. Following this approach, the notation is easily exchangeable and modifiable. So, deficits in the notation can be fixed without side effects on the concepts.

3 A Framework to Evaluate Object-Oriented Modelling Languages

There is a large number of surveys comparing different object-oriented notations and approaches[1]. Often, these surveys concentrate on listing the language features.

[1] cf. Arnold et al. (1991), Biggs (1997), Cribbs et al. (1992), De Champeaux and Faure (1992), Frank (1993), Hewlett Packard (1991), Hong and Goor (1993), Hsieh (1992) and Monarchi and Puhr (1992).

There, the more comprehensive languages achieve good results. Other characteristics like integration, unambiguity or adequacy are often ignored. Therefore, these characteristics should be taken into account, too, although it is difficult to find suitable measures and interpretations for these features. There are different opinions concerning the importance of single features like formalization or multiple inheritance, too. In many cases, we can only give a subjective judgement. This judgement often needs a critical interpretation.

The evaluation framework provides a short characterization and evaluation of the investigated object-oriented modelling languages. With this framework, we do not aim at comparing object-oriented modelling languages quantitatively. We do not suggest an "algorithm" which leads automatically from a set of modelling languages to the "optimal" language. There are too many influencing factors which exclude this possibility presently and perhaps even in general. Rather, we want to provide a comprehensive but short characterization of the language to support the selection and inspection of object-oriented modelling languages. The framework is by no means to be considered complete. In particular, the provision of suitable measures and criteria needs further research. In the framework, we use a table with three columns. The first column contains the identifier of the property, the second the value and the last the evaluation results.

To examine a modelling language, the subject and the general criteria of investigation have to be considered. In the field of modelling languages, the subjects are the language itself, its application and its description. The general criteria can be applied to the language, the language concepts, the metalevel, language design and, finally, the artefacts of the language. It is important to note that all these aspects are relevant for the investigation. This partitioning was done to structure the different aspects more strongly. Single aspects can be assigned to the different areas mentioned. Between these areas exist interactions and, accordingly, antagonisms. So, there is a conflict between expressive power and simplicity. Greater expressive power tends to cause more special language constructs while simplicity implies less.

3.1 Subject of Investigation

The subject of investigation can be subdivided further (Table 1). In addition to the language, we consider its application and its description. It is our opinion that both factors influence the language directly. The separate subdivisions can be refined further.

3.1.1 Description

The description presents the language to the user. It should contain a definition and a user documentation. The description of a modelling language should be both informal and formal. The informal parts make it easier to understand the basic ideas. The exact formal parts secure unambiguity. The description language of a language—the metalanguage—should in particular be unambiguous since otherwise unambiguous interpretation of the language itself can hardly be

language	application	description
abstract syntax and semantics concepts ***concrete syntax*** notation diagrams and annotations	***application purpose*** ***perspectives*** user perspective meta perspective ***activities*** analysis and design implementation verification and validation	***definition*** language specification grammar metamodel ***documentation*** user documentation

Table 1: Subject of Investigation

guaranteed. This can be achieved by a formalization of the metalanguage or by the elimination of ambiguities. The quality of the description is an important criterion for the learnability and intelligibility of the language. However, it plays a subordinate role in the evaluation of the language.

3.1.2 Language

The specification of a modelling language contains the representation of the basic concepts as well as the definition of syntax and semantics. It can be divided into abstract syntax and semantics and concrete syntax.

The abstract syntax and semantics defines the concepts of the language. An object-oriented modelling language should provide object-oriented, process-oriented and concurrent concepts as well as concepts for dynamical behaviour and modularization. It is important that all these different kinds of concepts have to be integrated to form a homogeneous overall picture. Furthermore, all concepts have to be described unambiguously. Sometimes an object-oriented modelling language is compared to an object-oriented programming language. In particular this requires the detailed and complete determination of syntax and semantics of the language like in programming languages.

Object-oriented concepts are of great importance for object-oriented modelling languages. They form the skeleton of object-oriented modelling and the basis for the integration with other concepts. Unfortunately, there is no commonly accepted definition. This makes it difficult to determine a definition. However, an exact definition is a necessary requirement to interpret models unambiguously. For these reasons, the provided concepts of a modelling language have to be carefully inspected with respect to quality and completeness of their definition. Moreover, without a standardization of object-oriented concepts there is no standardization of object-oriented modelling languages.

The concrete syntax defines the currently used notation. Usually it consists of textual annotations and diagrams. The combination of textual and graphical notation can ensure formalism, clarity and understandability. Unfortunately, this combination is not a common practice. Many known object-oriented modelling languages lack textual annotations which could provide a formal basis for the diagrams. For an example of the combination of formal specification and graphical notation see Achatz and Schulte (1996).

Almost all object-oriented modelling languages use diagrams. Diagram techniques can improve the clarity, understandability and learnability of the language. Furthermore, they are intended to support and improve the communication between the team members. The clarity of a notation can be increased by considering the following hints and criteria (cf. Rumbaugh (1996)):

- unambiguous mapping between concepts and notation
- common and uniform mapping rules
- no overloading of notation elements
- little similarity between notation elements
- simple notation for the concepts used most
- easily drawable and printable notation
- easily learnable and memorizable notation

3.1.3 Application

Under this heading, the application perspective of modelling languages is described. Object-oriented modelling languages are used for supporting conceptual modelling and software development using the object-oriented paradigm. They should support all phases of the software development and describe all important aspects of software. This support mainly refers to the modelling activities. Other tasks, like project management, are usually not supported by modelling languages. The expressive power of a modelling languages is mainly determined by their application purposes. The size of the language defines the ways in which models can be described. At the same time, the size of the language also determines the aspects which are expressible by the language. The language used has direct influence on the kind of modelling. The language concepts are selected arbitrarily. This selection often evolves over time and favours language concepts having proved to be effective in practice or possessing a good theoretical foundation. Many object-oriented modelling languages consists of a large number of different diagrams and concepts. Another, and perhaps better, approach would be the concentration on the object-oriented concepts and the provision of defined interfaces to other concepts, like state machines or flow charts. This would improve the integration with other paradigms.

There are two application views of a modelling language. Firstly, you can look at a modelling language from an application perspective. This view is the most common one and it is described above. Secondly, you can look from a metaperspective. This is the perspective of language design. The aim of this view is to

User-Relevant Criteria	Model-Relevant Criteria	Economic Criteria
Usability	Unambiguity	Reusability
Clarity	Consistency	Extensibility
Understandability	Formalization	
Adequacy	Integration	
Verification		
Power		

Table 2: Criteria of Investigation

extend, adapt and specify the language concepts. With respect to the continuous progress in software engineering, this view gains increasing importance.

One of the advantages of object-oriented modelling is the seamless connection between single activities. The different models should cover the whole software life cycle. A modelling language for all development activities has to provide corresponding concepts for analysis, design, implementation and testing. The aims and requirements concerning the degree of detail and formalization of a model are different in the individual phases. The transition from one activity to another should be possible without loss of semantics. Furthermore, modelling decisions should be traceable.

3.2 General Criteria of Investigation

For evaluating modelling languages, we introduce general criteria. These are properties of object-oriented modelling languages and their corresponding values. They can be applied to the whole language or to individual parts. In many cases, close relations exist between different properties. Depending on the part of the language considered, different measures can be applied during the judgement. For many of the measures introduced, no exact evaluation procedures exist to determine if the property holds.

The different criteria help to investigate the subject. In the field of object-oriented modelling languages these criteria can be subdivided into three categories (Table 2).

3.2.1 User-Relevant Criteria

Modelling languages offer the possibility to exchange ideas and thoughts about models. They are primarily languages for humans and not for machines. The user-relevant criteria reflect this circumstance.

In this context, clarity and understandability are always mentioned. They are two inherent requirements of a modelling language. A model is called clear if it corresponds directly to recognition patterns of the user. Recognition patterns vary largely from user to users. Therefore, these criteria are very subjective. It is determined by experience, knowledge and perception. The familiarity with the concepts and notation is an additional factor influencing clarity and understandability. Understandability could be further divided into conceptual and notational understandability. This separation maps that of semantics and syntax. The conceptual understandability deals with the properties of the language concepts and their adequacy for modelling. Notational understandability examines the notation concerning ergonomic aspects.

Adequacy and expressive power are two related criteria. Both criteria should be considered relative to the application purpose. Together, they offer the possibility to examine if a languages provides only the concepts necessary for modelling and no superfluous concepts. In particular, in the case of very specific language constructs, one must examine whether these constructs are really necessary or whether they only lead to an increase of complexity. The decision, however, whether a concept is appropriate or not, cannot be drawn objectively, but depends strongly on the preferences of the user. In general, each new construct always implies both advantages and disadvantages. Therefore it should be examined if a modelling concept is important or not for the application purpose. The expressive power of a modelling language is measured by determining in how far essential facts of the problem domain can be expressed in a clear and natural manner.

A model is a simplified and idealized description of a problem domain. Such descriptions are fallible in principle. Therefore, a model always requires a verification and validation on the problem domain. Its representation should support this. The term problem domain is used for actual and planned reality but also for specifications and models. On the one hand, the problem domain can be expressed very vaguely, and on the other hand already formally. The evaluation of the adequacy of the model takes place relative to the modelling purpose because models abstract from unimportant details. In general, the relationship between model and domain cannot be expressed directly. Therefore, it has to be examined whether the model corresponds to its problem domain. Exact and precise models simplify this task because they can be interpreted more unambiguously. On the other side, there are sometimes facets of a model which cannot expressed objectively. In such situations, the evaluation is guided by the subjective judgement of the user.

3.2.2 Model-Relevant Criteria

The model-relevant criteria concern the artefacts of a modelling language. These criteria can be evaluated more objectively than the user-relevant ones because they are more independent from the user.

A model should leave as little room for interpretation as possible. The final aim is that a sentence of the description language should be clearly interpretable concerning abstract semantics. The unambiguity of a model always refers to the abstract syntax and semantics. In this way, the abstract syntax and semantics become a basis for common understanding. By the unambiguous interpretation of the language concepts and of the combining rules, the user can check whether his model corresponds to the requirements. The language cannot guarantee in principle that the customer constructs a model representing his problem. However, unambiguity can secure that the model is interpreted unambiguously.

Many object-oriented modelling languages do not define exactly the semantics of their concepts. The language elements then only appear as templates whose real meaning is determined by using them. This means that the concepts and their representation are indeed known, but not the real semantics of the concepts whose interpretation can be different from observer to observer. Consequently, an imprecise determination of the semantics allows different interpretations and applications which can lead to misunderstandings. For this reasons, the semantics should be determined exactly. This has the advantage that one not only speaks the same language but also associates the same meaning with it.

Yet another reason leads to the requirement of unambiguity. Often the result of object-oriented modelling is to implement the modeled systems in a programming language later on. But, programming languages require the representation of the domain as program code which only allows one interpretation.

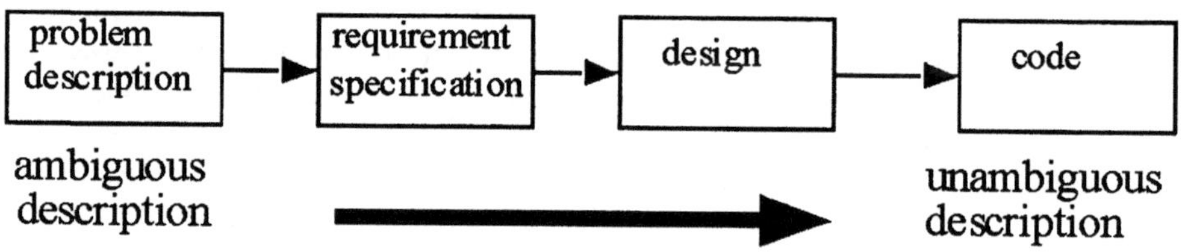

Figure 2: Reduction of Ambiguity during Software Engineering

If you consider the different documents of Figure 2 which result from software development, you find that a step-by-step reduction of ambiguity occurs in these documents. Programs which are clearly interpretable can be found at the end of this chain. If a modelling language does not support the generation of clearly interpretable documents, then the transition from ambiguous to unambiguous descriptions must take place after modelling.

Unambiguity is a good foundation for consistency. Consistency refers to the model and not to the relationship between model and modeled domain. In this way, consistency is a technical quality relating to the different concepts. Consistency is closely related to integration. Formalization is one way to guarantee unambiguity and consistency but it often reduces the clarity of a language. Therefore, the challenge we face is to associate informal and formal techniques to support detection of ideas and testability.

There are three different aspects concerning integration. Firstly, most modelling languages contain a large number of different concepts which have to be integrated to a homogeneous whole. Secondly, the modelling language itself could be integrated with other paradigms. Thirdly, the language could be integrated into the development process (called process integration). This requires the usability in all phases and a seamless transition of modelling documents.

3.2.3 Economic Criteria

Economics of modelling depends on a lot of factors. They include factors which are directly connected to a modelling language, but also external factors like tool support, process support, protection of investment, acceptance of the language and availability of developers familiar with this language.

The reuse of existing artefacts can increase the economic efficiency. There, reuse is not limited to single concepts. Reuse can be applied to the modelling language itself and to the models. In the first case, reuse refers to the metalevel. The language definition uses general principles and concepts. In the other case, the language definition provides the concepts for reusing components in models. There are two ways of reuse. Firstly, you can reuse existing components. Secondly, you can derive new components from existing ones. Reuse is supported in principle if the modelling concepts offer generalization/specialization and components. Besides, a modelling language can support "abstract" artefacts like *design patterns*.

Extension of the modelling language measures the extent to which the language can be enriched with additional concepts. Both, extension and reuse are employed to extend existing components. At the same time, extension is associated with flexibility and adaptability. The definition of new language concepts should follow formal rules and is part of the metaperspective of modelling languages. Concerning the interchangeability, the extension of a language should not change the structure of the metamodel.

4 Comparison Between OML and UML

OML and UML are two object-oriented modelling languages. They are based on previous modelling languages. With regard to unification of object-oriented modelling languages, both play an important role.

OML (Open Modeling Language) is part of OPEN (Object-oriented Process, Environment, and Notation) (Firesmith et al. (1996))(Figure 3). OPEN is an effort to develop a homogeneous method for the object-oriented software and system development which is intended to lead to a standardization of process and notation. OPEN is derived from the COMMA project (Common object meta modelling architecture) in which Henderson-Sellers examined different object-oriented notations and approaches (Henderson-Sellers and Bulthuis (1996)). In our comparison, we will focus only on the modelling language OML. OML consists of COMN (Common Object Modeling Notation) and a metamodel that describes the individual language elements and their relationships.

UML (Unified Modeling Language) is the result of the standardization efforts of Booch, Rumbaugh and Jacobson. The ultimate goal of UML is a language for specifying, constructing and documenting software systems of any complexity from all domains (Rational, p. 4 (1997c)). Booch, Rumbaugh and Jacobson concentrated on the development of a homogeneous modelling language because standardization of the development process is difficult. The current version 1.1 of UML (Figure 4) is documented in a set of papers (Rational (1997c-f)).

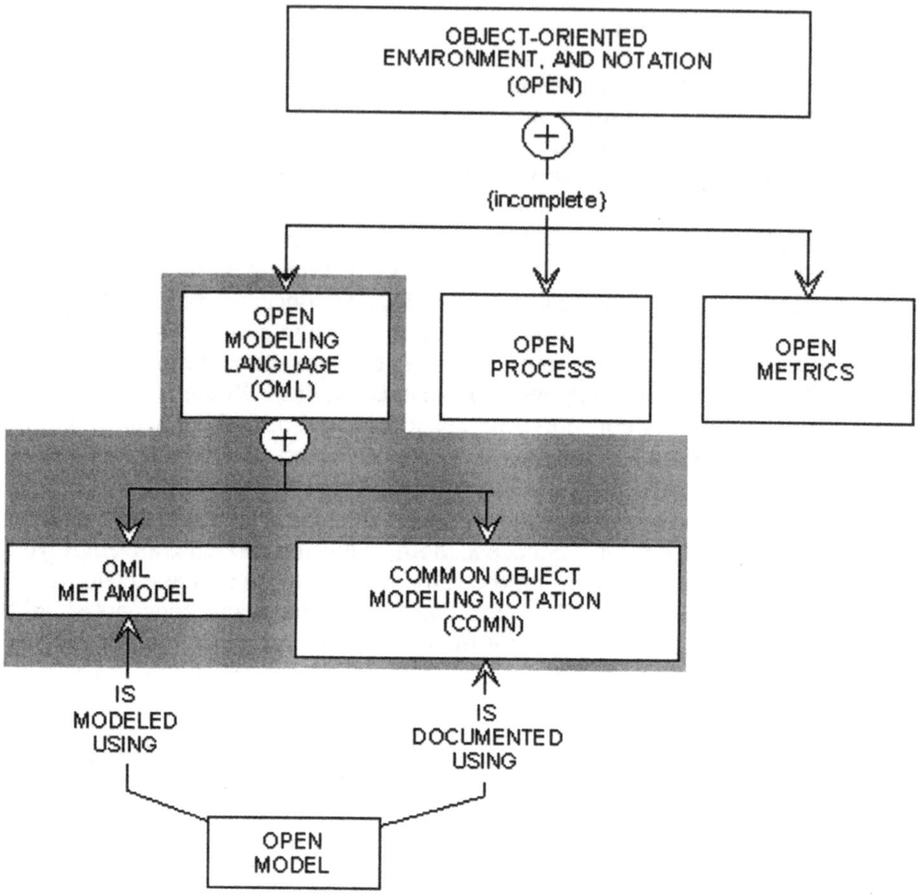

Figure 3: Structure of OPEN (Firesmith et al., p. 5 (1996))

UML and OML use the same basic pattern for their language description which is characterized by a metamodel as well as the separation of language concepts and graphical representation. This structure corresponds to the ideal structure of an object-oriented modelling language (Figure 1).

4.1 Size of the Language

OML and UML are very powerful modelling languages and provide a large number of different concepts. Both support the same application domains and are suitable for the object-oriented modelling of software systems. In this respect, they refer to the same abstract syntax and semantics. They are similar concerning the expressive power and the provided language constructs. Table 3 shows the language design concepts, which are applied to OML and UML. The number of corresponding principles in both languages is remarkable. UML supports an

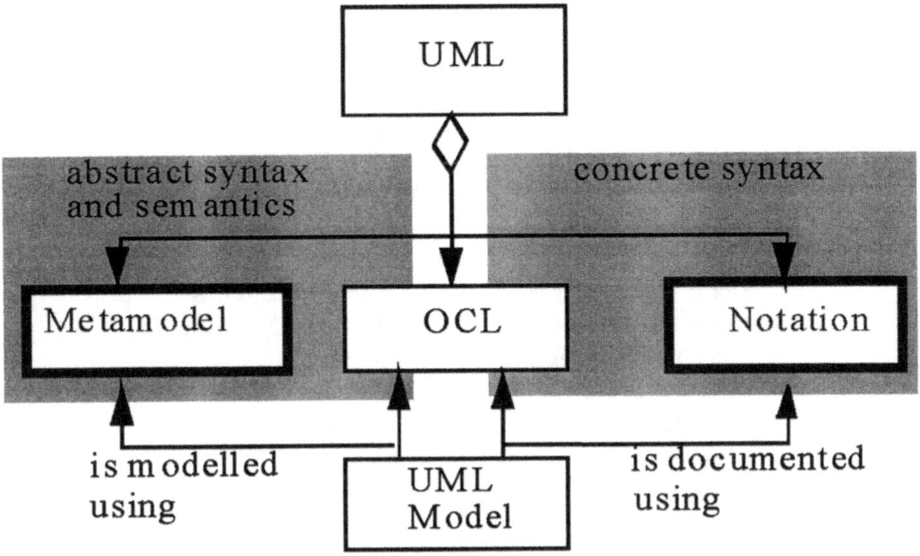

Figure 4: Structure of UML, Version 1.1

Object Constraint Language (OCL) which allows a more formal expression of constraints (Rational (1997d)).

Many of the provided modelling concepts are similar, too. Both languages support object-orientation, modularization, state machines and process-orientation. This allows the modelling of the dynamic and static aspects of a system.

UML and OML make available a large number of diagrams for the current views of object-oriented approaches. In general, both languages provide the same diagrams. That means, each diagram has a more or less corresponding equivalent. Each language defines its own notation different from that of the other. In this sense, the selection of the diagram symbols is different and mainly a result of incorporating known symbols of former notations.

OML	UML
type/instance dichotomy separation of type and implementation structural and functional models stereotypes role concept definitional and referential relations drop-down-boxes	type/instance dichotomy separation of type and implementation structural and functional models stereotypes classification of language concepts by common abstract one OCL

Table 3: Language Design Concepts

OML	UML
Semantic Nets	***Static Structure Diagrams***
Context Diagrams	Class Diagrams
Layer Diagrams	Object Diagrams
Configuration Diagrams	***Behavior Diagrams***
Cluster Diagrams	Use Case Diagrams
Inheritance Diagrams	Interaction Diagrams
Deployment Diagrams	Sequence Diagrams
Scenario Class Diagrams	Collaboration Diagrams
Mechanism Diagrams	State Diagrams
Task Script Diagrams	Activity Diagrams
Use Case Diagrams	***Implementation Diagrams***
Interaction Diagrams	Component Diagram
Collaboration Diagrams	Deployment Diagram
Sequence Diagrams	
State Transition Diagrams	
State Diagrams	

Table 4: Diagrams

However, they also have striking differences. In particular, this holds for the determination of individual language elements. In spite of the same abstract semantics formed by the object-oriented concepts, they already differ in the determination of language elements. Furthermore, the modelling conception of both languages is different. For example, the role concept is more important for OML than for UML. On the other hand, UML stresses structural modelling of objects more strongly.

4.2 Abstract Syntax and Semantics

OML and UML apply a number of general concepts leading to a unification and simplification of the language. One of these is the type/instance dichotomy.

OML uses the type/instance dichotomy for same concepts, namely *Class/Object, Cluster class/Cluster instance, Scenario class/Scenario instance* and *Association/Link*. In UML the type/instance dichotomy is a fundamental mechanism, too: "The separation of Type and Instance constitutes the essence/manifestation dichotomy of the UML" (Rational, p. 29 (1997a)). It seems a good idea to apply typing not only to abstract data types, but also to systems, functions and relationships. In particular, systems and objects have a lot in common. Therefore, system types can also be introduced in analogy to classes. So, characteristic properties can be determined and similar entities can be grouped together. A further advantage is that type relations like inheritance can be applied to these components then.

But since types and instances for systems or scenarios have no analogy on the programming language tier, it must be specified how these constructs are used in the individual stages. For this, concrete declarations are missing both in OML and in UML. Unfortunately, in both languages the terms *type, role* and *generalization* are not defined exactly. Therefore the advantages of the type/instance dichotomy cannot be utilized completely.

4.3 Concrete Syntax

The concrete syntax of both languages is dominated by a graphical notation. OML and UML define a large number of different diagram types (Table 4, p. 13). Some of these diagrams, like state diagrams, use-case diagrams or system structure diagrams, are not object-oriented. They can be applied without the object-oriented paradigm. As a rule, the diagrams have been derived from former notations.

The intended purpose of some diagrams (cluster diagram, inheritance diagram in OML; object diagram, class diagram, collaboration diagram in UML) overlaps quite strongly so that the choice of the defined diagram types does seems arbitrary. Some diagram types provide a very large amount of diagram elements. The diagrams of UML and OML show a certain degree of redundancy in their entirety. Their application is not always simple and intuitive. The large number of different diagrams complicates its application additionally. In both notations, there are no guidelines, which diagram should be applied at which time. The syntax of the individual diagrams is not defined formally, too. In particular, the meaning of nested diagram elements and duplicates is not elaborated completely.

There are some rules which can be applied to the notation. One of these rules says that graphical symbols should not be overloaded. UML introduces the construct *note* as: "a comment placed on the diagram" (Rational, p.5 (1997b)). Notes are used for the representation of *comments, conditions, procedure bodies* and *tagged-value pairs*. Unfortunately, the different variants cannot be distinguished. Therefore there is a decision problem for the user because the representation is not unambiguous. Figure 5 shows note symbols which are used for representing conditions. Firstly, there is an inconsistency in the representation. In the right symbol, the parentheses miss. Secondly, you cannot decide whether these notes represent comments or conditions. Both interpretations are valid. In our opinion, this is a misuse of the note symbol. A note symbol represents an additional information which can be ignored. A condition is an important modelling element and not a comment! Using notes for conditions, UML does not obey the rule of avoiding overloading. A better solution would be a separate notation or stereotyping notation elements. UML Version 1.1 suggests stereotypes for the different types of information. However, UML does not use these stereotypes (Figure 5). Therefore, we recommend a truly distinguishable notation.

A further rule states that diagram elements should not resemble each other. Otherwise they might confused. Controversy, related language concepts should be represented in similar ways. These facilitates application through simplifying and unifying the notation. However, the danger is that individual notation elements cannot be distinguished sufficiently.

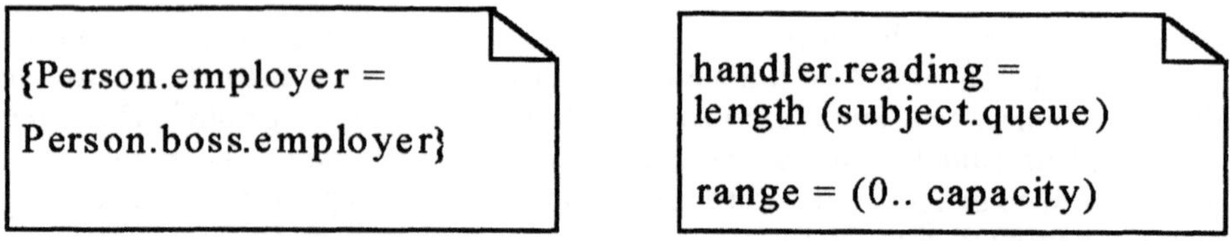

Figure 5: Note Symbols for Conditions (Rational, p. 17, 91 (1996e))

OML and UML attempt to support the type/instance dichotomy by a suitable choice of notation. The use of similar symbols for types and instances is useful because it reduces the number of employed symbols. In OML, types[2] are only characterized by a "*C*" which stands for "*Class*". The distinction between cluster and cluster instance is drawn only through this "*C*". Figure 6 shows an example by Firesmith et al. (1996) and demonstrates how easily the "C" can be forgotten (*Customer "is an instance of" Customer*). Omitting this detail, no wrong symbol results but one which is still valid, but applied wrongly. Therefore, there should be no symbols in a view, which could be confused easily.

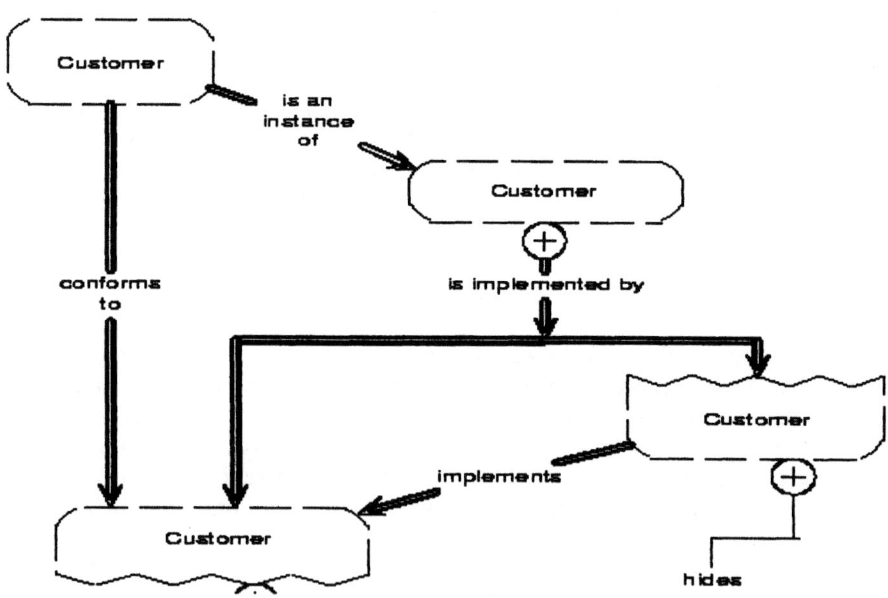

Figure 6: Customer "is an instance of" Customer? (Firesmith et al., p. 78 (1996))

A more detailed discussion of OML and UML can be found in Frank and Prasse (1997).

[2]Only class and object have different symbols.

5 Summary

The selection of a modelling language suggests a careful comparison of essential properties. In our article, we showed that this matter is complicated. So, some properties like adequacy are not independent from the respective point of view and therefore more or less subjective. Moreover, there are properties like understandability or clarity whose evaluation recommends empirical studies in the field of cognitive psychology. As long as there are no extensive research results in this field, a judgement of such properties is based on subjective assumptions. Therefore it is important to mention that our framework is no procedure, which allows the evaluation of object-oriented modelling languages by easy understandable rules. Instead, it is a mental framework that shows essential criteria and, if necessary, the inherent problems. A reasonable application of the framework presumes a qualitative and critical interpretation of the evaluation criteria.

The inspection of OML and UML shows some positive results. Clear improvements are recognized compared to earlier modelling approaches like Booch (1994), Jacobson et al. (1992) or Rumbaugh et al. (1991). They provide a more precise description of the language constructs, the integration of extension mechanisms and the correction of a number of discrepancies of earlier approaches. Nevertheless both proposals show clear inadequacies. There is still a lack of formality and correctness in the description of diagrams and language constructs. In particular, the semantics of the object-oriented concepts is not complete. In addition the large diversity of partly redundant kinds of diagrams complicates the application of both languages.

From a scientific point of view there is another problem regarding this standardization. Science suffers under economic pressure arising from the, mostly commercial, standardization efforts. In this situation, the following statement from the UML consortium lacks a scientific validation and has primarily marketing character: “(to) bring some stability to the object-oriented marketplace, allowing projects to settle on one mature modelling language and letting tool builders focus on delivering more useful features” (Rational, p. 12 (1997c)). This position is hold by the authors of the OML, too: “It is our professional opinion that OML COMN is currently the best available notation for object-oriented modeling” (Firesmith et al., p. 200 (1996)). Given circumstances that many questions are insufficiently answered, such statements are not adequate. Even if a fast standardization makes sense for economic reasons, too many problems remain open from a scientific point of view. This holds for the redesign of object-oriented modelling languages and for the corresponding empirical research. Moreover the interaction between requirements and evaluation criteria needs further research.

References

ACHATZ, K. and SCHULTE, W. (1996): Formale objektorientierte Softwareentwicklung. In: *Beiträge der GI-Fachtagung Softwaretechnik ‘96. Koblenz. p. 24–32.*

ARNOLD, P., BODOFF, S., COLEMAN, D., GILCHRIST, H., and HAYES, F.(1991): An Evaluation of Five Object-Oriented Development Methods. Report No. HPL-91-52, June 1991 Bristol

BIGGS, P. (1997): A Survey of Object-Oriented Methods. URL:http://www.dur.ac.uk/~dcs3pjb/survey.html

BOOCH, G. (1994): Object-oriented Analysis and Design with applications. 2nd ed., Redwood/CA.: Benjamin Cummings

CRIBBS, J., ROE, C., and MOON, S. (1992): An Evaluation of Object-Oriented Analysis and Design Methodologies. New York: SIGS Books

DE CHAMPEAUX, D. and FAURE, P. (1992):A comparative study of object-oriented analysis methods. In: *Journal of Object-Oriented Programming (JOOP), Vol. 5, No. 1, pp. 21-33*

FIRESMITH, D., HENDERSON-SELLERS, B., GRAHAM, I., and PAGE-JONES, M. (1996): OPEN Modeling Language (OML). Reference Manual. Version 1.0. 8 December 1996. URL: http://www.csse.swin.edu.au/OPEN/comn.html

FRANK, U. (1993): A Comparison of two Outstanding Methodologies for Object-Oriented Design. Arbeitspapiere der GMD, No. 779, Sankt Augustin

FRANK, U. (1997): Towards a Standardization of Object-Oriented Modeling Languages? Arbeitsberichte des Instituts fuer Wirtschaftsinformatik, Nr. 3, Koblenz. URL: http://www.uni-koblenz.de/~iwi/

FRANK, U. and PRASSE, M. (1997): Ein Bezugsrahmen zur Beurteilung objektorientierter Modellierungssprachen—veranschaulicht am Beispiel von OML und UML. Arbeitsberichte des Instituts für Wirtschaftsinformatk, Nr. 6, Koblenz 1997. URL: http://www.uni-koblenz.de/~iwi/

HENDERSON-SELLERS, B. and BULTHUIS, A. (1996): The COMMA Project: Final Report (First draft for limited circulation to methodologists and collaborators) nr. 95/36, pp. 1-45, 1996. Swinburne University of Technology. Sydney, Australia. URL: http://www.csse.swin.edu.au/cotar

HEWLETT PACKARD (1991): An Evaluation of Five Object-Oriented Development Methods. Software Engineering Department, HP Laboritories. Bristol

HONG, S. and GOOR, G. (1993): A Formal Approach to the Comparison of Object-Oriented Analysis and Design Methodologies. In: Nunamaker, J.F.; Sprague, R.H. (Ed.): Information Systems: Collaboration Technology, Organizational Systems, and Technolgoy. Proceedings of the 26th International Hawaii International Conferenc on System Sciences. Los Alamitos, pp. 689-698

HSIEH, D. (1992): Survey of object-oriented analysis/design methodologies and future CASE frameworks. Menlo Park, Ca.

JACOBSON, I., CHRISTERSON, M., JONSSON, P., and OVERGAARD, G. (1992): Object-Oriented Engineering. A Use Case Driven Approach. Reading, Mass.: Addison-Wesley

KOWALK, W.P. (1996): System—Modell—Programm. Heidelberg, Berlin, Oxford: Spektrum

MONARCHI, D.E. and PUHR, G. (1992): A Research Typology for Object-Oriented Analysis and Design. In: *Communications of the ACM, Vol. 35, No. 9, 1992, pp. 35-47*

RATIONAL (1997a): UML Semantics. Version 1.0. 13.01.1997. URL: http://www.rational.com

RATIONAL (1997b): UML Notation Guide. Version 1.0. 13.01.1997. URL: http://www.rational.com

RATIONAL (1997c): UML-Summary. Version 1.1. 01.09.1997. URL: http://www.rational.com

RATIONAL (1997d): OCL. Version 1.1. 01.09.1997. URL: http://www.rational.com

RATIONAL (1997e): UML-Notation Guide. Version 1.1. 01.09.1997. URL: http://www.rational.com

RATIONAL (1997f): UML-Semantics. Version 1.1. 01.09.1997.

RUMBAUGH, J., BLAHA, M., PREMERLANI, W., EDDY, F., and LORENSEN, W. (1991): Object-Oriented Modeling and Design, Englewood Cliffs: Prentice Hall.

RUMBAUGH, J. (1996): Notation notes: Principles for choosing notation In: *Journal of Object-Oriented Programming (JOOP), Vol. 8, No. 10, Mai 1996, pp. 11–14*

Part 2

Technical Aspects and Concepts

A Critical Look upon UML 1.0

K. Bergner, A. Rausch, M. Sihling

Lehrstuhl IV, Institut für Informatik,
http://www4.informatik.tu-muenchen.de
Technische Universität München,
D-80290 München, Germany

Abstract: The Unified Modeling Language consists of a set of mostly graphical description techniques for the specification, modeling, and documentation of object-oriented systems. Based on the experience gained in using UML 1.0 for the development of a medium-sized, distributed Java program, we comment on its strengths and weaknesses. Furthermore, some proposals for extensions and changes are made.

1 Introduction

The Unified Modeling Language has been proposed by Grady Booch, Ivar Jacobson, and James Rumbaugh as a standard notation for object-oriented analysis and design (Booch et al. (1997)). UML version 1.0 incorporates and improves the successful methods OOA/OOD (Booch (1994)), OMT (Rumbaugh et al. (1991)), and OOSE (Jacobson (1992)) developed by the same authors, and adds some new contributions.

This evaluation of UML 1.0 is based on a case study in which we have developed a medium-sized, distributed Java system for planning break supervision schedules in large schools. The application example was provided originally in Roock et al. (1996) for the evaluation of programming paradigms and tools by the DACH group (DACH Group). The system can be roughly categorized as a graphical, distributed editor; it offers simple edit functions and requires neither specialized algorithms nor complex concurrency management.

One of the goals of the case study was to examine the individual description techniques as well as their interrelationships and use as a whole in the context of a complete and self-contained example. To do that, we tried to apply each technique as recommended in Booch et al. (1997), showing all its possible application areas. An example are activity diagrams, which were used for modeling business processes during analysis and also for describing the control flow of operations during design.

Most of the comments and proposals in the following sections are directly motivated by concrete problems during the development of the break planner application. We did not try to cover the aspects and possible problems of other application areas systematically. Due to the restricted space, we do not treat the software engineering process, but refer to the detailed case study report for that purpose (Bergner et al. (1994)). As this report includes the complete UML development documents and provides methodical guidelines and hints, it can be used as a tutorial for UML 1.0 and object-oriented development in general.

The rest of this paper mainly consists of sections covering the individual description techniques of UML, assuming that the reader is familiar with their presentation in Booch et al. (1997). At the end, a short conclusion is given.

2 Use Case Diagrams

Use case diagrams model the users and their interactions with the system at a very high level of abstraction. Hence, use case diagrams are very useful for early requirements analysis because they enforce the identification of the different users and uses of a system and can be easily understood by customers.

In the so-called "semantics definition" of Booch et al. (1997), it is "the responsibility" of a use case to "specify a set of use case instances, where a use case instance represents a sequence of actions a system performs that yields an observable result of value to a particular actor".

Seen as an isolated description technique, use case diagrams are not a very powerful formalism. They contain hardly any information about the functionality of a system, but are useful mainly as a structuring aid for other kinds of diagrams that describe the action sequences of a system in more detail, like sequence diagrams, collaboration diagrams, and activity diagrams.

In the meta-model provided by the UML authors the concept of a use case is derived from the "Type" concept. A somewhat strange effect of this derivation is that use cases inherit some properties that we cannot make sense of. As expressed in Section 7 of the semantics document (Booch et al. (1997)), they have attributes and operations, but it is not explained what these attributes and operations should be. In our eyes their presence conflicts with the semantical definition of a use case as a set of action sequences.

Another unclear point concerns the semantics of the ≪uses≫ and ≪extends≫-relations. Apart from informal descriptions where both relations are equally described as a sort of "inclusion" or "extension", the UML 1.0 semantic definition documents provide no useful information on this issue.

A possible interpretation of A ≪uses≫ B is given by the following conditions, according to Coleman (1997):

- A incorporates B as a sub-flow of events. It must be specified where B is inserted.
- The details of use case B are hidden from A.
- B is a fully fledged use case and may involve some or all of A's connections.

With respect to the corresponding sequences, this can be interpreted as: One or more sequences of A's sequence set contain sequences of B's sequence set as contiguous subsequences at certain locations in time. Note that although this situation resembles a procedure call in programming languages, one cannot assume the presence of a "runtime connection" or a procedure call between two

use cases because use cases are only conceptual modeling constructs usually not directly implemented in a system.
In contrast to this, the situation B ≪extends≫ A can be defined by other conditions, again following Coleman (1997):

- B is a variation of A. It contains additional events (e.g. for a failure or to deal with an extra complexity) for certain conditions.
- It has to be specified where and how B enhances A.
- B is not a fully fledged use case.

With respect to the corresponding sequences, this can be interpreted as: B contains all action sequences of A and furthermore adds own sequences that contain sequences of A as (possibly non-contiguous) subsequences.
Other questions left open by Booch et al. (1997) are:

- Is it possible to have a use case without a connection to an actor?
  Such a use case would in some way contradict with the purpose of a use case as a modeling concept for the usage of a system by external actors, but could be handy for modeling internal system tasks that can be handled automatically and do not need external interaction.
- If a use case A is extended by a use case B, does B have to be connected with all actors of A?
  We think the answer is negative, considering the example of a hypothetical use case Edit Data extended by Edit Confidential Data, which contains additional functionality for authorization. In this example, there may well be (classes of) actors associated exclusively with only one of these use cases.
- If a use case A is extended by a use case B, must B have ≪uses≫-connections to the same use cases as A?
  According to the sequence interpretation of use cases given above, the answer must be yes. However, it is questionable whether such obligatory and, therefore, redundant connections should be represented in a use case diagram. Our recommendation is to draw them only if the extended use case introduces own functionality that ≪uses≫ the concerning use case, too, and to leave them out otherwise.

UML 1.0 does not make a proposal for the structure and the contents of a textual use case dictionary. Besides informal textual descriptions, we added items for the estimated number, the experience level, and the location of each actor group, and the frequency and the required security level of each use case, respectively. Later on, information like this can be used for various purposes, for example, to design an adequate GUI and a help system, or to estimate the performance of a design.
To strengthen the connection to class diagrams, we also included entries listing the classes concerned by a use case. By comparing the actions of a use case's

action sequences with the attributes and operations of the assigned classes, one can check whether the classes contain all functionality needed (and not more than needed) and get hints about what data is shared among which actors. A better way to visualize the correlation between classes and use cases could be provided by a tool that highlights the classes belonging to a certain use case in the class diagram.

In total, we think that UML use cases are a valuable tool for requirements analysis. A clear definition of their syntax and semantics seems to be possible, but is missing in Booch et al. (1997).

3 Class and Instance Diagrams

UML's so-called *static structure diagrams* mainly model the data aspect of an object-oriented system, but contain also information about the operations of the data items. Static structure diagrams exist in two variants: *Class diagrams* show the classes of the program code, their attributes and operations, and the relationships and dependencies between them. *Object diagrams* or *instance diagrams* show graphs of object instances that may arise during runtime of a system. Class diagrams may be seen as a special kind of E/R-diagrams (Chen (1976)) and are very common in object-oriented development methods (Shlaer and Mellor (1998), Rumbaugh et al. (1991), Booch (1994), Coleman et al. (1994)). They are used for data modeling in the early development phases and are later refined and enriched with additional attributes and operations. Finally, they can be translated into class skeletons.

Semantics of Associations Although class diagrams are a well-known formalism in many object-oriented development methods, their semantics is not totally clear with respect to associations. Some of the possible implementations for associations are:

- Reference attributes or—in the case of 1-to-n- or m-to-n-associations—containers with references can be embedded into the associated class. If the association must be bidirectional, both concerned classes have to be adapted, and the consistency of the two directions has to be ensured.
- Associations can also be implemented by a dedicated association class containing references to the associated objects. The main advantage of this implementation scheme is the possibility to store the association instances between all objects in a container and to enumerate them quickly. Furthermore, one can add additional attributes easily.
- In Java, associations to a so-called "singleton class" with exactly one instance can be implemented in a special way by an "implicit class reference". To allow for associations to the singleton class S, for example, S can be given a static variable S.theInstance that is instantiated once during the initialization of class S. This would make it possible to access this variable's object with the Java idiom S.theInstance in the code of other classes.

However, one could principally also think of implementing an association via a network socket or via explicit object names. An unambiguous, abstract characterization of the semantics of associations together with some common implementation schemes could help to automate the generation of association implementations by means of tools.

Boundary Concept Class diagrams as used in UML lack the concept of a system scope, making it hard to distinguish entities that must be implemented from entities in the environment of the system. This is in general true for all description techniques of UML except for use case diagrams where this boundary is represented by the rectangle enclosing the use case ellipses. The addition of a system boundary concept, as, for example, in Fusion (Coleman et al. (1994)), would fill this gap.

Instance Diagrams In general, class diagrams do not constrain the possible object graphs that may occur during the runtime of a program. For the description of object graphs, UML additionally offers instance diagrams. They show a snapshot of the runtime objects and their interconnections in a certain situation.

Instance diagrams are not suitable for the description of large object configurations, as they do not scale well and get too large and too complicated even for small examples. Because they can only describe snapshots, they can also not be used to specify dynamic object graphs with changing associations and objects.

In order to deal with complex, dynamic object graphs, more powerful description and specification formalisms than instance diagrams are needed, like, for example, component diagrams as introduced in Bergner (1996).

Refinement During the development of a system, one usually constructs a series of class diagrams from the analysis class diagram, until a detailed, refined implementation class diagram is reached. Although UML contains notations to represent refinement steps, we could not use them in our case study because the proposed notation for "refinement *within* a given model" would have led to a huge, incomprehensible model containing all the classes of the different development phases together with their refinement relations (see Booch et al. (1997), Notation Guide, Section 4.26, and left side of Figure 1). In our opinion, this variant should be restricted to the special case in which one wants to demonstrate the refinement of a single entity explicitly.

The notation for "refinement *between* models" is based on "an invisible hyperlink supported by a dynamic tool" and is, therefore, not a suitable notation for a paper-based presentation. We think that a simple and general notation for the representation of refinement relations between models should be introduced that is usable also for a paper-based presentation. We propose a special symbol for this purpose, reminiscent of a back-reference as well as of a generalization arrowhead (see right side of Figure 1).

The semantics of refinement relations is left entirely open in UML—there are no rules clarifying which refinement steps exist and when they can be applied. A

Figure 1: Representation of Refinement Within and Between Models

more formal treatment would allow the implementation of tools that support or maybe even automate the execution and validation of refinement steps. Note that although we have restricted our discussion to class diagrams, it applies also to other kinds of diagrams, like, for example, sequence diagrams.

Responsibilities UML lacks a notational construct for grouping operations and attributes of classes together to so-called "responsibilities", a concept introduced by Wirfs-Brock (Wirfs-Brock et al. (1990)).

We propose to use a simple, tree-like notation, where responsibilities are represented in bold font above the indented names of their contained elements (see Figure 2). A tool could then be used for switching between folded and unfolded views.

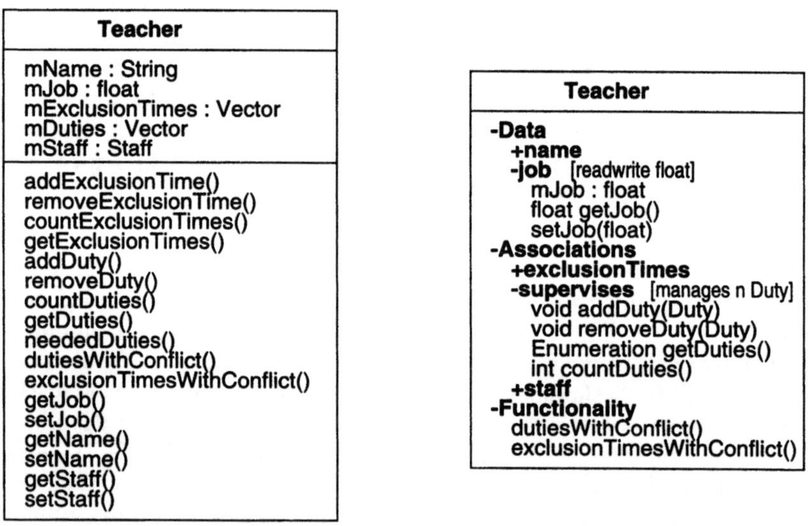

Figure 2: Grouping of Class Features with Responsibilities

Even in the context of relatively small class diagrams like the ones of the break planner, responsibilites would allow to comprehend the structure of classes with many features much faster. The use of equally named responsibilities in different classes could furthermore help in understanding mechanisms implemented by collaborating classes. An example would be the use of MVC responsibilities, grouping together the collaborating operations in various model, view and controller classes.

Responsibilities can first be introduced during requirements analysis to specify the data and functionality of a class informally, leaving open the final names and signatures of its operations and attributes. During design and implementation, responsibilities can then be refined stepwise by adding attributes, operations, and also other responsibilities. Specialized documentation tools like javadoc (SUN Microsystems (1997)) could also use responsibilities to present class features in a structured way.

Another possibility is the use of standardized responsibility schemes that could be unfolded automatically with the help of a tool. This would for example be useful for the handling of associations or data attributes, where the same patterns of attributes and access operations appear over and over again in a detailed class diagram. An example for a responsibility schema is a scalar attribute, like job in Figure 2. It is usually implemented by the attribute itself and two access methods getJob and setJob for reading/writing the attribute's value. Another example are managed 1-to-n associations that are usually implemented by a special pattern of operations (see also the paragraph above on associations).

Interfaces According to UML, an interface should be represented as a little, named circle next to the class implementing the interface. The advantage of this notation is that it needs less diagram space and fewer lines in comparison to a class-like representation. The disadvantage is that one cannot see the operations of an interface in the class diagram. There is also no notation for representing subtype relations between interfaces.

The notation should therefore only be used for standard interfaces with known functionality that are not subtyped. A good example in the context of Java is the standard interface Serializable.

If the operations of an interface are important or an interface is subtyped, we recommend to use a class-like notation where interfaces are marked with the special stereotype ≪Interface≫.

4 Sequence Diagrams

Sequence diagrams, a variant of the well-known message sequence charts (ITU-TS (1993), Loidl et al. (1997)) and extended event traces (Schätz et al. (1996), Broy et al. (1997)), show example communication histories between users or objects. The UML variant is extended with constructs for the creation and deletion of objects as well as for synchronous and asynchronous communication.

It is out of question that sequence diagrams are a useful description technique. In our experience, they are—together with class diagrams—one of the predominant description techniques in design meetings. Furthermore, sequence diagrams can be given a precise semantic, as, for example, shown in Broy et al. (1997).

UML enhances sequence diagrams with a notation for modeling the message flow between "entire sets of objects" instead only between single objects. It is, however, not clear what the semantics of this construct is—is a message related to all or only some of the objects in the set? If the latter is true, how is the subset specified? If there is an arrow from a set of objects to a single object, how many messages does the single object receive?

Sequence diagrams can be used as test cases for an existing implementation of a system. For this purpose, additional information like preconditions, input data, and test instructions should be provided for sequence diagrams, and there should be methodical guidelines on the usage of sequence diagrams for testing.

In addition to "exemplary" sequence diagrams, the UML variant contains features like conditional subsequences that make sequence diagrams useful also for the specification of behavior. However, there exists no notation to distinguish sequence diagrams meant as comprehensive specifications from sequence diagrams showing just exemplary interactions. It is also not clear for which object configurations a sequence diagram specification is valid—does the sequence diagram imply that only certain configurations appear during the runtime of a system or does it apply only in certain situations?

5 Collaboration Diagrams

Collaboration diagrams resemble sequence diagrams in most respects. However, they emphasize the relationships between objects and show the flow of time only implicitly using sequence numbers. An automatic translation between sequence diagrams and collaboration diagrams is, therefore, possible with one exception: Connections not used for communication can only be represented in collaboration diagrams. Apart from this rather unimportant issue, it seems just a matter of personal style which of both techniques one wants to use.

The authors of Booch et al. (1997) also propose the usage of "before-after conditions" for declarative specifications of the behavior of a type's instances (Booch et al. (1997), Section 7.3). However, it is left unclear how this formalism is related to the other description techniques for the specification of a system's dynamics, what formalisms are admissible in before-after conditions, and how the "context" of a type should be defined.

Another collaboration diagram notation is used for design patterns which would otherwise not be visible in a class diagram. This notation has proved valuable to describe the presence of the observer pattern in our case study (Bergner et al. (1997)). However, it is doubtful whether more complex design patterns can be integrated into a class diagram at all—the different components of the microkernel pattern in Buschmann et al. (1996) represent, for example, rather subsystems than classes, so that mapping them to simple classes makes no sense.

6 Class State Diagrams

Class state diagrams can be used to model the *data state* and its changes during the lifecycle of the objects of a certain, single class. The data state of an object consists of the actual attribute values of the object, its references to other objects, and possibly also the data states of referenced objects. A special notation is provided for state transitions that trigger the sending of messages to other objects.

State transition diagrams are a universal and well-known formalism for specifying the state space and the state transition relation of entities. However, most questions about their methodical use and about their semantics in the context of object-oriented modeling are left open in the UML specification. Consistency criteria and methodical guidelines for the simultaneous use and the transition between activity diagrams, state diagrams, sequence diagrams, and collaboration diagrams are urgently needed.

A similar problem concerns the consistency between different, but related documents of a single dynamic description technique. Classes related by inheritance should inherit not only attributes and operation signatures, but also dynamic behavior as specified by the class state diagrams of their base classes (Rumpe (1996)), and refined versions of classes should have a suitably refined behavior. Also needed is the possibility to assign a state diagram to a compound component and to break it down into subordinate state diagrams.

7 Activity Diagrams

Activity diagrams are a special kind of state transition diagrams used to specify *control state*. They can be used on different abstraction levels for business process modeling of user interactions as well as for modeling the control flow of single operations.

Although the use of activity diagrams for business process modeling during the analysis phase seems like a simple and natural concept, their implementation and translation to source code is not trivial. In principle, the following possibilities exist:

Explicit Control: Activity diagrams serve as an explicit, operational specification for a specialized workflow engine controling the functionality of components of a system. Using a workflow engine seems to become a common architecture for the integration of legacy components (which may be also whole programs) into a larger system.

Implicit Control: Activity diagrams serve as a specification for the interaction of components. This approach is common with user interfaces, where the control flow will likely not be implemented by a centralized workflow component, but will be integrated in the callbacks and operations of the GUI classes. When used to specify the interactions of GUI elements, activity diagrams resemble the so-called "interaction diagrams" of Denert (Denert (1991)).

To facilitate the translation to source code or to even allow an automated implementation via tools, the semantics of activity diagrams must be clearly defined. This would also help the user to understand the connection between action states and actual programs or GUI prototypes.

Another critical point is the lack of methodical guidance for the transition from exemplary sequence diagrams to prescriptive activity diagrams. In general, it is not trivial to identify the common characteristics of a set of possible sequences and to build suitable activity diagrams that allow all these sequences. This is particularly difficult because a single action sequence can in principle be the result of the interleaved execution of more than one use case.

UML states that an activity diagram is "a special form of a state diagram". As such, it should use the syntactical constructs introduced in the section on state diagrams. However, that seems not to be the case with so-called "complex transitions", especially when the "swimlane" notation is used.

First, there is a minor inconsistency in Figure 50 of Booch et al. (1997): The surrounding complex transitions are missing and concurrency is represented there by short heavy *horizontal* bars instead of short heavy *vertical* bars, as specified in section 8.6.2 of Booch et al. (1997).

Second, the diagram in Figure 53 of Booch et al. (1997) contains action states like Pay in swimline Customer and Take order in swimlane Sales that are meant to run concurrently, but it does not have any surrounding complex transition. The correct representation should have additional complex transitions after Request service and before Deliver order.

Although activity diagrams are intended to specify the dynamic behavior of a system, they cannot deal with changing object graphs properly. This can be seen from diagram 3: It contains two swimlanes, namely Break and Teacher. While the action Break::hasConflict belongs to a special, single object, the action Break::overlaps is executed for all instances of Break that are connected to its supervising Teacher object. However, there is no notation to discern actions concerning a single object from actions concerning a whole set of objects in the same swimlane.

During design, activity diagrams can be used to specify the control flow of methods. When used for this purpose, they are very similar to well-known techniques like Nassi-Shneidermann charts or flowcharts. However, most operations in object-oriented programs are very simple and creating an activity diagram for them would not introduce additional clarity.

8 Implementation Diagrams

Implementation diagrams exist in two variants. *Component diagrams* show the structure of the source code and its partitioning into components, and *deployment diagrams* show the run-time implementation structure and the distribution of objects and components on physical computing nodes.

However, UML seems to neglect the difference between component and deployment diagrams and allows combined diagrams containing both aspects. This is

Break::hasConflict

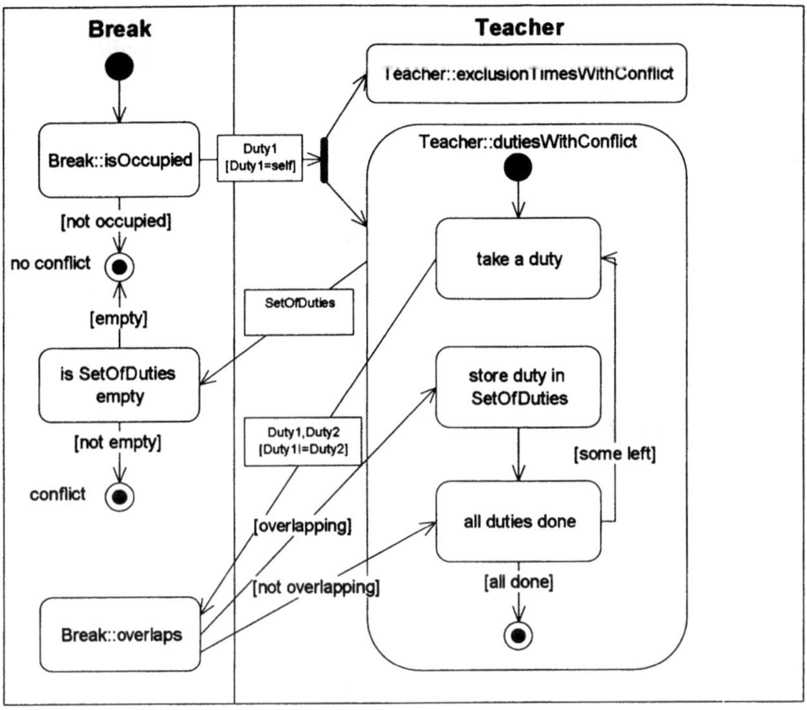

Figure 3: Activity Diagram for Method Break::hasConflict

shown in Figure 4 which contains Figures 56 and 57 of Booch et al. (1997): The component diagram on the right contains the program component Scheduler that accesses the component instance meetingsDB. In a semantically correct diagram, the Scheduler component should be marked as instance with underlined text, similar to the component instance meetingsDB.

The notation provided seems also overly simple. It does, for example, not contain concepts for inheritance and recursive containment of component instances, and it allows only the representation of static configurations consisting of a fixed number of hard-wired component instances. To overcome these limitations, more powerful formalisms like the one proposed in Bergner (1996) are needed.

Finally, UML says nothing about the relation of implementation diagrams with the other description techniques. This would be necessary especially for instance diagrams, sequence diagrams, and collaboration diagrams because these diagrams also refer to object and component runtime configurations.

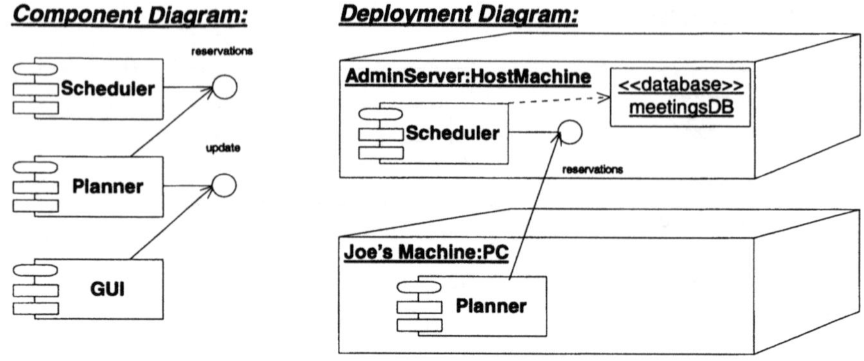

Figure 4: Component and Deployment Diagrams in Booch et al. (1997)

9 Conclusion

All in all our experiences with UML in the case study were not totally negative—we could overcome all problems and were able to model most aspects of the break planner system. However, this does not imply that UML is a mature modeling language that can be used for real projects without problems. Our main criticisms are:

- UML provides a wealth of description techniques, but defines neither their syntax nor their semantics precisely and unambiguously Breu et al. (1997). This makes modeling sometimes deceptively easy because one is allowed to draw all kinds of diagrams that have no useful meaning for the subsequent implementation.

- The missing semantic foundation is also problematic with respect to the relationships between the various development documents, especially when it comes to describing the dynamic behavior of a system: Because there exist no consistency criteria between description techniques it is hard to check whether all of their requirements can be combined and fulfilled by the implementation. Consistency criteria and methodical guidelines could also make the production of development documents easier because they restrict the possibilities of the developers and force them to consider only meaningful diagrams.

- The same considerations apply to UML's concept of refinement—it is not defined when a development document is a refined version of another document and what development steps are admissible for refining documents.

- UML's description techniques cannot deal sufficiently with complex, changing object graphs and hierarchical composite objects. The existing notations for so-called "multi-objects" in sequence and collaboration diagrams seem very ad-hoc and leave many questions open, as well as the whole description technique of component diagrams.

- UML lacks abstraction techniqes for large class diagrams with many attributes and operations.
- Some of the techniques of UML aim at the implementation of a CASE tool and cannot be presented on paper. An example are most relationships between development documents which shall be represented by "invisible hyperlinks" according to UML's definition.
- The UML Notation Guide and the UML Semantics Document (Booch et al. (1997)) do not contain sufficient examples and are not very readable, if not to say confusing. This is especially true for the Semantics Document: Large parts of it seem to be machine-generated English, the index is nearly unusable because it contains too many references for each entry, and the definitions contained are informal and unclear.

References

BERGNER, K. (1996): Spezifikation großer Objektgeflechte mit Komponentendiagrammen. PhD thesis, Technische Universität München.

BREU, R., HINKEL, U., HOFMANN, C., KLEIN, C., PAECH, B., RUMPE, B., and THURNER, V. (1997): Towards a formalization of the unified modeling language. Technical Report TUM-I9726, Technische Universität München.

BROY, M., HOFMANN, C., KRÜGER, I., and SCHMIDT, M. (1997): A graphical description technique for communication in software architectures. Technical Report TUM-I9705, Technische Universität München.

BUSCHMANN, F., MEUNIER, R., ROHNERT, H., SOMMERLAND, P., and STAL, M. (1996): Pattern-Oriented Software Architecture—A System of Patterns. Wiley & Sons.

BOOCH, G. (1994): Object-Oriented Analysis and Design with Applications. Benjamin/Cummings, 2 edition.

BOOCH, G., RUMBAUGH, J., and JACOBSON, I. (1997): Unified Modeling Language, Version 1.0. Rational Software Corporation, 2800 San Tomas Expressway, Santa Clara, CA 95051-0951 (USA), 1997, URL: http:/www.rational.com

BERGNER, K., RAUSCH, A., and SIHLING, M. (1997): Using UML for modeling a distributed Java application. Technical Report TUM-I9735, Technische Universität München, Institut für Informatik.

COLEMAN, D., ARNOLD, P., BODOFF, S., DOLLIN, C., GILCHRIST, H., HAYES, F., and JEREMES, P. (1994): Object-Oriented Development—The Fusion Method. Prentice Hall.

CHEN, P. P. S. (1976): The entity-relationship model—toward a unified view of data. ACM Transactions on Database Systems, 1(1).

COLEMAN (1997): Slides on UML use case modeling.

DACH Group. Universität Hamburg, FB Informatik, AB Softwaretechnik; Johannes-Kepler-Universität, Linz, Austria, Institut für Wirtschaftsinformatik, Doppler-Labor für Software Engineering; GMD Bonn, Schloß Birlinghoven, St. Augustin; UBS Information Technology Laboratory, Zürich, Switzerland.

DENERT, E. (1991): Software Engineering. Springer-Verlag.

ITU-TS (1993): ITU-TS Recommendation Z.120: Message Sequence Chart (MSC). ITU-TS, Geneva, September 1993.

JACOBSON, I. (1992): Object-Oriented Software Engineering—A Use Case Driven Approach. Addison-Wesley.

LOIDL, S., RUDOLPH, E., and HINKEL, U. (1997): MSC'96 and beyond—a critical look. In A. Cavalli A. Sarma, editor, *SDL Forum 97.* Elsevier.

RUMBAUGH, J., BLAHA, M., PREMERLANI, W., EDDY, F., and LORENSEN, W. (1991): *Object-Oriented Modeling and Design.* Prentice Hall.

ROOCK, S., SYLLA, K.-H., LILIENTHAL, C., and MÜLLER-LOHMANN, A. (1996): Der Pausenplaner—Szenario, CRC-Karten, Systemvision, URL: http://set.gmd.de/~sylla/dachpap-aufgabe.html

RUMPE, B. (1996): Formale Methodik des Entwurfs verteilter objektorientierter Systeme. PhD thesis, Technische Universität München, 1996.

SCHÄTZ, B., HUSSMANN, H., and BROY, M. (1996): Graphical development of consistent system specifications. In James Woodcock Marie-Claude Gaudel, editor, *FME'96: Industrial Benefit and Advances In Formal Methods*, pages 248–267. Springer. Lecture Notes in Computer Science 1051.

SHLAER, S. and MELLOR, S. J. (1998): Object-Oriented Systems Analysis. Prentice Hall.

SUN MICROSYSTEMS (1997): javadoc—the Java API Documentation Generator, URL: http://java.sun.com/products/jdk/1.1/docs/tooldocs/ win32/javadoc.html

WIRFS-BROCK, R., WILKERSON, B., and WIENER, L. (1990): Designing Object-Oriented Software. Prentice Hall.

Systems, Views and Models of UML

R. Breu, R. Grosu, F. Huber, B. Rumpe, W. Schwerin

Technische Universität München,
Arcisstr. 21, D-80290 München, Germany
email: {breur,grosu,huberf,rumpe,schwerin}@informatik.tu-muenchen.de

Abstract: In this paper we show by using the example of UML, how a software engineering method can benefit from an integrative mathematical foundation. The mathematical foundation is given by a mathematical system model. This model provides the basis both for integrating the various description techniques of UML and for implementing methodical support. After describing the basic concepts of the system model, we give a short overview of the UML description techniques. Then we show how they fit into the system model framework and sketch an approach to structure the UML development process such that it provides methodological guidance for developers.

1 Introduction – Why Formalization?

"The nice thing about graphical description techniques is that everyone understands them, the bad thing, however, is that everyone understands them in a different way." This often heard quote captures a main property of modeling techniques using semi-formal, mostly graphical notations, beginning with the early structured modeling techniques and prevalent until today's object-oriented methods. The diagrammatic notations used here seem easily comprehensible for everyone dealing with software development. Experience shows, however, that, except from obvious properties, these notations do in fact bear a great number of possible divergent interpretations. To gain a deeper and more exact understanding of the notations used, the need for providing a stringent formal foundation for them has long been recognized and has lead to considerable advances in the recent past. Many of these efforts aim at providing a formal semantics for single notations. Considering the different aspects of a system, described by different notations, captured in a system development process, providing isolated semantics, possibly even using diffent models as a basis, does not seem to be adequate. The complete description of such a system is given only by the assembly of all different views. It is therefore desirable to have a common semantic basis for *all* notations used in a development method. This allows both to provide an exact interpretation for diagrams in a single notation and to inter-relate diagrams in different notations on a common basis.

The SysLab method (Breu et al. (1997b)) builds upon such an integrated semantic framework, which we call the *System Model*. The foundations and the basic mathematical concepts of this system model will be introduced in Section 2. The SysLab method, just like the Unified Method, is a view-oriented, integrated, and object-oriented development method. Its description techniques are deliberately similar to those used in the UML. Thus it seems worthwile to apply SysLab's system model to the UML in order to embed its description techniques into the system model's mathematical framework. What can be gained by this effort is, quite obviously, a deeper understanding of the single notations and, as outlined above, the possibility to more tightly intergrate the UML description techniques on a sound mathematical basis. The benefits hereof can be enormous, especially for tool developers, resp. tool vendors, and methodologists. Tool developers are enabled to provide a much larger set of precise consistency conditions than currently possible by using just the UML *Meta Model* which basically represents only the abstract syntax of UML's description techniques. Using the semantic properties of diagrams produced in different stages of a development project and their inter-relationships, transformation tools can be provided, which tranform, either automatically or with a human developer's assistance, documents from one notation into another. On this basis, methodological guidelines for software developers can be elaborated and eventually implemented in CASE tools.

The rest of the paper is organized as follows. In Section 2 we present the basic concepts of the SYSLAB system model and in Section 3 we give a brief overview of the UML description techniques. We then outline methodological aspects in Section 4, where we define general properties of a software development method and show how a development process using UML description techniques can be structured and supported by a tool. Finally, an outlook on further steps in formalization and tool support is given in Section 5.

2 Models of Systems

In general, a *system* is a technical or sociological structure consisting of a group of elements combined to form a whole and to work, function or move interdependently and harmoniously. A *system model* represents certain aspects of systems in a certain way, using certain concepts, e.g. OO-concepts, such as classification, encapsulation etc. . One way to formulate system models is to use mathematical techniques (e.g. sets, functions, relations, predicates). This leads to the notion of *mathematical* system models.

In the following we first motivate the use of a system model and then describe the one on which the SYSLAB method is based and which is also appropriate for UML.

2.1 Motivation of the System Model

In the introduction we have motivated, *why* a formalization of UML description techniques is useful. We argued that a precise semantics is important not only for the developer, but also for tool vendors, methodologists (people that create the method) and method experts (people that use the method and know it in detail). We get the following requirements for a formalization:

1. A formalization must be complete, but as abstract and understandable as possible.

2. The formalization of a heterogeneous set of description techniques has to be integrated to allow the definition of relations between them.

This does not mean that every syntactical statement must have a formal meaning. Annotations or descriptions in prose are always necessary for documentation, although they do not have a formal translation. They may however eventually be translated into formal descriptions or even into code in the course of a software development process.

As soon as one uses description techniques with a fixed syntax and semantics, one no longer describes systems in general but models of systems. Using UML, for example, one models systems in terms of objects, classes etc. To manage the complexity of formalization, we introduce a layer between the syntactic description techniques and pure mathematics as shown in Figure 1.

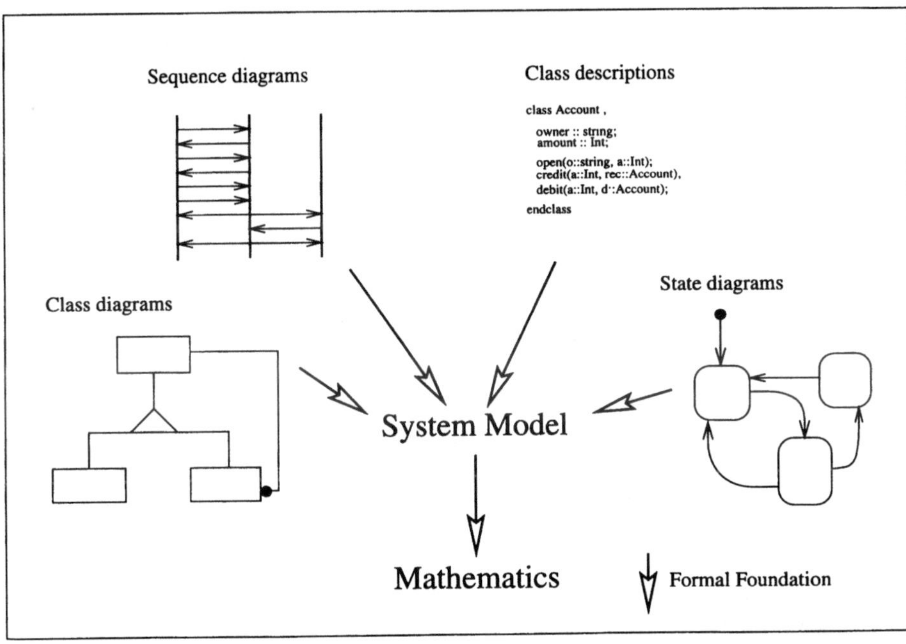

Figure 1: Layered formalization of description techniques

This intermediate layer is the mathematical system model. On this layer, various aspects of systems such as structure, behavior and interaction are formulated by mathematical techniques. We call the representation of a system, formulated solely in terms of the system model, a *model* of a system. Furtheron, the set of all models that can be described in terms of a certain system model is called the *universe* of this system model. Figure 2 illustrates the ideas that are explained below.

Description techniques offer syntactical elements that allow the specification of certain views, i.e., certain aspects, of systems. One way to define a semantics is

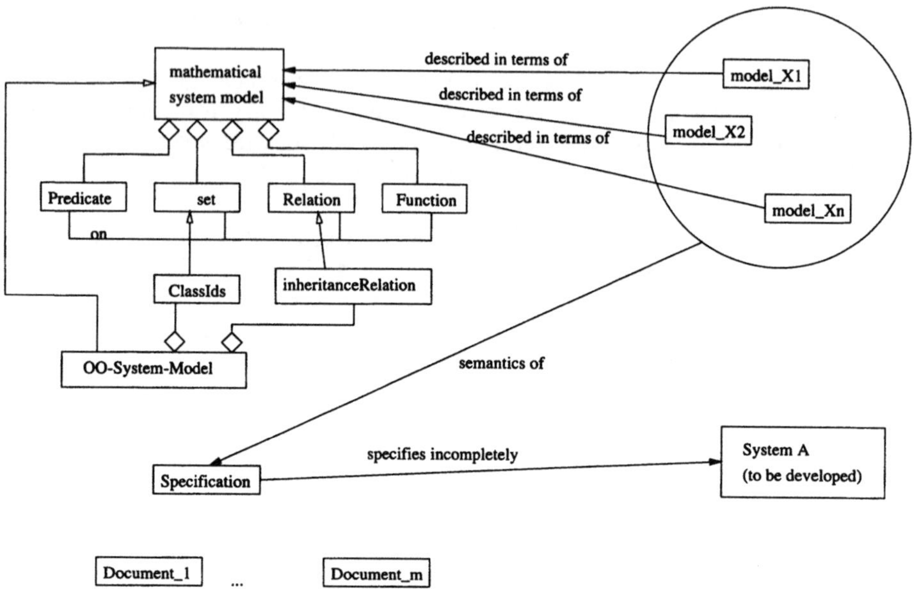

Figure 2: System model, models and specification

to express the meaning of syntax in terms of a system model. Using a unique system model for a set of description techniques results in an integrative semantics for the different techniques. An integrative semantics allows reasoning about interrelations between different views expressed by different techniques. Notions like *refinement*, *consistency* and *completeness* can be precisely defined.

A *mathematical* system model provides terms with a formal semantics, e.g. functions, and can therefore serve as a basis for a *formal* semantics for a set of description techniques.

With the above definitions, one can define the semantics of a *document* (which is a kind of a module on the syntactical level) of a given description technique as the set of all those models, that have the properties that are expressed in the document.

Using a set of models and not a single one as the basis of the proposed semantics has several advantages. For example, refinement of documents corresponds to set inclusion. Furthermore, we get the meaning of different documents modeling different aspects of the system by intersection of their respective semantics. But the main reason is that, in contrast to fully executable programming languages, description techniques allow *underspecification* of system properties in many different ways. A proper semantics cannot be therefore captured by a single model. For the same reason, it is not possible to give an operational semantics in the sense that a document specifies a single abstract machine that "executes" it.

2.2 Definition of the System Models

The system characterisation given below is a refinement of the SYSLAB system model as presented in Klein et al. (1996) and Grosu et al. (1996), and it is rather similar to the one used in Breu et al. (1997b). Each document, for instance an object diagram, is regarded as a constraint on the system model's universe.

The system model introduced below is especially adapted for the formalization of UML. Thus, relevant aspects of UML like classes, objects, states, messages etc. are explicitly included. A precise formalization of our UML system model is currently under development.

Our system model is very general, covering various kinds of object-oriented systems such as conventional object-oriented software systems, systems including hardware components, embedded systems and real-time systems. For the formalization of the current set of UML notations, we will only need a specialized version of the system model, which is briefly presented below.

In the following, we describe the most important elements of our system model.

The structure of a system is, according to object-orientation, given by a set of objects, each with a unique identifier. Therefore, we regard the enumerable set *ID* of object identifiers as an element of each model.

In any system objects interact by means of *call message passing*. By this term we express that objects on the one hand communicate via a sequential call-return mechanism, but on the other hand have the possibility to send messages asynchronously, which means that the receiver may neither deny messages nor block the sender of a message. Both communication mechanisms are treated within one framework in detail in Paech and Rumpe (1997).

Asynchronous communication models provide the most abstract models for systems with message exchange, since deadlock problems as in synchronous systems do not occur. To model communication between objects we use the theory of timed communication histories as given in Broy et al. (1993). The notion of explicit time in the system model allows us to deal with real time, as proposed in UML.

We regard our objects as spatially or logically distributed and as interacting in parallel. As described in UML, sequential systems are just a special case, where always exactly one object is "active".

Interaction between objects occurs through the exchange of messages, as shown in Figure 3. Let *MSG* be an element of the system model, denoting the set of all possible messages in a system. An object with identifier $id \in ID$ accepts a unique set of messages. Its input interface is defined by

$$msg_{id} \subseteq MSG$$

The *behavior* of an object is the relationship between the sequences of messages it receives and the sequences of messages it emits as a reaction to incoming messages. We allow our objects to be nondeterministic, such that more than one reaction to an input sequence is possible.

According to Broy et al. (1993); Broy and Stølen (1994), the set of timed communication histories over M is denoted by $M^{\overline{\omega}}$. A communication history is basically an infinite sequence containing (possibly only a finite number of) messages and time stamps inbetween, that mark time progress. Thus the messages occurring

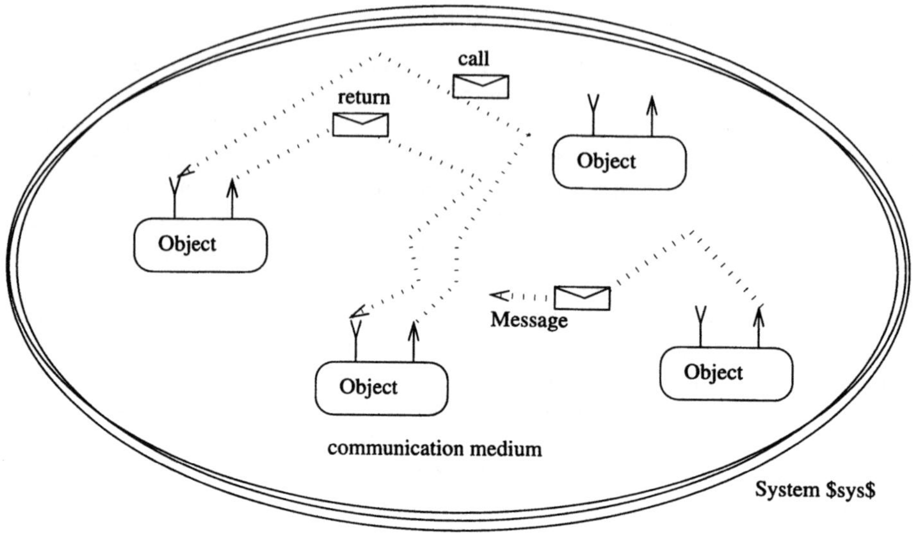

Figure 3: Objects in the UML system model

in a communication history are in linear order. A communication history models the observable sequence of incoming or outgoing messages of one object. The behavior of a nondeterministic object id is then given by the mapping of its input stream to the set of possible ouput streams. Using relations, the behavior of an object id is given by the relation between its input and output streams

$behavior_{id} \subseteq msg_{id}^{\overline{\omega}} \times MSG^{\overline{\omega}}$

Objects encapsulate data as well as processes. *Encapsulation of data* means that the state of an object is not directly visible to the environment, but can be accessed using explicit communication. *Encapsulation of process* means that the exchange of a message does not imply the exchange of control: each object can be regarded as a separate process. Note, that this view on object controls also works in conventional sequential programs. Objects get active when receiving a message and fall asleep after emitting a message. Given the set of possible states *STATE* of objects in a system, the function *states* assigns a subset of possible states to every object id:

$states_{id} \subseteq STATE$

Furthermore, a state transition system is associated with each object, modeling the connection between the behavior and the internal state of an object. We use a special kind of automata (Grosu and Rumpe (1995)) for this purpose.

An automaton of an object with identifier *id* consists of a set of input messages msg_{id}, a set of output messages *MSG*, a set of states $states_{id}$, and a set of initial states $states_{id}^0 \subseteq states_{id}$. The nondeterministic transition relation δ_{id} defines the behavior of the automaton. From the state-box behavior, given for the automaton in terms of state transitions, the black-box behavior in terms of the *behavior*-relation can be derived (Grosu and Rumpe (1995)).

Messages are delivered by a *communication medium*, which is an abstraction of message passing as it is done in real systems by the runtime system of the programming language in combination with the operating system. The communication medium buffers messages as long as necessary. Each message contains the receiver's identifier, so that the communication medium contains of a set of message buffers, one for each object. The order of messages between two particular objects is always preserved by the communication medium. The contents of messages are not modified. Messages cannot be duplicated or lost. No new messages are generated by the communication medium. This is formalized in Grosu et al. (1996).

Each system allows a possible set of system runs. A system run is characterized by the messages exchanged between all the objects and the sequence of their states. We thus characterize a system run by the following three functions:

$input : ID \to MSG^{\overline{\omega}}$
$output : ID \to MSG^{\overline{\omega}}$
$state : ID \to STATE^{\overline{\omega}}$

associating with each object identifier the stream of messages the object receives in a run, the stream of messages the object emits in a run, and the stream of states the object has during the run. Of course, this trace like view on a system is strongly interconnected with the automaton based view given previously. The use of this trace like view is only possible, if objects are regarded as process capsules and therefore each computational step equals one step of an automaton (of the above characterized type) for exactly one object. Furthermore, as objects don't share common variables, computational steps of different objects cannot interfere and can therefore be serialized.

Objects are grouped into classes. We assume that each system owns a set *CN* of class names. *CN* may, for instance, be derived from UML class diagrams. In object-oriented systems, each object identifier denotes an object that belongs to exactly one class. This fact is represented by the function

$class : ID \to CN.$

Classes are structured by an inheritance relation, which we denote by $. \sqsubseteq .$ (read: "subclass of"). The inheritance relation is transitive, antisymmetric and reflexive, as usual. With every class $c \in CN$ a signature Σ_c is associated, containing all attributes and methods together with their argument and result types. The signature induces a set of input messages and a set of states for each object of the class. One impact of inheritance is that signatures are only extended: $c \sqsubseteq d \Rightarrow \Sigma_d \subseteq \Sigma_c$.

Another concept of object-orientation is the dynamic creation of objects. Deletion need not be modeled, as we assume that our objects are garbage collected in the usual way. However, we may define a special *finalize*()-method that may be used to clean up objects, as, for instance, in Java.

Initially, a finite subset of objects (usually one main-object) exists and is active. We regard all other objects to be created in the course of a system run and to be active after having received a first message. Thus, the creation of a new object essentially consists of a message transmission from the creator to the created object. To allow this, each object is equipped with a sufficiently large (usually infinite) set of object identifiers denoting the set of all object identifiers the object may create:

$creatables : ID \rightarrow \mathcal{P}(ID)$

To prevent multiple creation, these sets of identifiers have to be pairwise disjoint, and objects that are initially active are not creatable at all.

3 Views

In the following section, we explore the meaning of a "view". Afterwards, we briefly explore which UML notation describes which aspects of a system.

3.1 Views and Projections

A view of a system is a projection of the system on one of its relevant aspects. Such a projection emphasizes certain aspects and ignores others. Therefore it is useful to have different views of a system. This also allows each stage of the development to concentrate on relevant aspects and to delay others, that are at the moment less important. In general different kinds of projections can be found, that are rather orthogonal and therefore constitute different dimensions:

- Projection on development phases: The same "thing" may have different appearances during analysis, design and implementation phases, and therefore described by different notations, or even not appear at all.
- Projection on structural, behavioral, interface and data aspects.

In general a projection can be any combination of the above mentioned kinds.
A document describes such a projection. As each document is of a certain kind, it projects certain aspects of the system, that can be described within the document. UML therefore uses multiple notations, that focus on different aspects, therefore exhibiting different "views" of the system.
Basically there are four main views:

- The *structural view* focuses on the structure of a system. It describes layout between objects and classes, their associations and their possible communication channels.
- The *behavioral view* focuses on the behavioral aspect of the system components. It describes how they interact, and characterizes the response to external system operations.
- The *data view* focuses on the data aspects of the system. It describes the state of the system units (objects), as well as their relationships.
- The *interface view* focuses on the encapsulation of system parts, and the possible usage from outside, e.g., through characterizing signatures.

Although these four views focus on different aspects, there are close relationships between them. Therefore it can be expected, that the notations, describing these views are also related, and that there are context conditions between them. This is currently one of the major problems of UML.

3.2 Notations of UML

UML currently has as many as eleven different and partly overlapping notations, which constitute different views of UML designs. In the following, we will discuss briefly, which notation can be used to describe certain aspects, without introducing the notations (this can be found in one of the various UML books, e.g. Burkhardt (1997); Booch et al. (1996)).

Class diagrams are the central notation for structural aspects. They define classes, their associations and how they are aggregated. However it is also possible to add data information, as each class can have an attribute section. Furthermore the connection to behavioral aspects is given by a method signature section, that can also be attached to classes.

Besides defining structural aspects, a class diagram may be used as source of data information, when transforming it into a database schema definition.

Object diagrams describe the actual layout of a part of the system within a certain situation. They clearly focus on structure, partly on contained data, and have to be compatible with the class diagrams. They can serve as a basis for behavioral descriptions.

Packages group classes (resp. their implementations) together. Their main focus is the definition of interfaces. They also define structure, but on a different level than class or object diagrams do: A package structures interfaces and implementations and is important during development. Relationships between packages are usually rather independent from the relationships between their included classes. Also due to the dynamics of object-orientation, this is again, to some extent, independent of the structure of the instantiated objects. Therefore we have different levels of structural views to be served.

Use case diagrams show the relationships among actors and use cases within a system. Although the concept of use cases seems to be very helpful, the actual use of this notation is to some extent unclear and will heavily depend on the method, which is still in development. However, use cases deal with interface and behavioral aspects at the border of the system. They exhibit possible actions to be taken, and who is allowed to undertake these actions. This means that there is also some structural aspect within the current UML use case notation.

Sequence diagrams describe a pattern of interaction among objects. Interactions between participating objects are arranged in timed sequences similar to Message Sequence Charts (MSC). Sequence diagrams therefore clearly define behavioral aspects but are based on structural and interface views.

Object lifelines are somewhat similar to sequence diagrams, but focus more on the control structure of an object and its related thread. They deal with the lifetime of a single object. They are used for describing behavioral aspects of a single object and are therefore more implementation oriented than ordinary sequence diagrams.

Collaboration diagrams are based on object diagrams, exhibiting a certain (numbered) flow of messages between objects in order to describe interaction between the participants. Collaboration diagrams and sequence diagrams are very similar in content, and it seems it is to some extent a matter of taste, which notation is to be preferred. Collaboration diagrams therefore also focus on behavior pattern.

Design patterns as introduced in UML comprehend a compact notation for collaboration patterns and are incorporated into class and object diagrams.

State diagrams are the central notation for describing behavior of a single object. This behavior description is based on the state space the object has, and it is also related to the message interface. State diagrams are therefore the central notation to relate data aspects and behavioral aspects of objects. It was therefore natural to enhance state diagrams with many features for different purposes. Examples are hierarchical structuring of the state space, state activities, entry and exit actions, state dependent attributes, or the history mechanism. Also hierarchical structuring of the event set and complex transitions have been defined. However, these newly added concepts interact with each other in ways, that have not yet been fully explored, and it seems advisable not use them too much.

Activity diagrams are defined as "a special case of a state diagrams" (Booch et al. (1996)), where the occurring states are named as "action states". However, there are serious doubts about that. It could be wise to regard activity diagrams as a form of data flow diagrams with additional components for control flow. Therefore activity diagrams could be useful for describing internal processing of operations (or use cases). Thus they clearly focus on behavioral aspects of individual components, but more on its functional decomposition into different actions.

Swimlanes in activity diagrams, furthermore allow the decomposition and regrouping of a series of actions for implementation by different objects.

Other notations exist, that are more implementation oriented, and thus mainly deal with the physical structure of a system. These notations only partly deal with some of the above mentioned views:

Component diagrams show the dependencies among software components.

Deployment diagrams show the configuration of runtime processing elements, processes and the objects that live on them.

4 Methodological Aspects

At the current stage, UML is not more than a syntactic framework for system specification. What is missing to make UML to a full-fledged software engineering method is what the word "method" is characterizing: a set of rules that guide the designer to obtain a runnable and correct system implementation.

In this section we will discuss in more detail what aspects a method should cover and identify three kinds of methodological rules (subsection 4.1). Subsection 4.2 sketches our view of the design process and its interconnection with the methodological rules. We give an idea of document graphs documenting design decisions and the dependencies between the specifications developed during design.

4.1 What a Method Is

It is not easy to define what a method is and we do not want to give an exact definition here. It is however certain that a method consists, apart from the notations themselves, of a set of rules and steps guiding through the *design process*. The design process is generally defined to be the sequence of specifications developed during the lifetime of the software system (including documents specifying extensions and modifications of the system).

The design process for large systems is very complex and thus the methodological rules deal with many different aspects and activities during design. In order to come closer to the kernel aspects of a method, we distinguish rules at three levels of abstraction,

- process models
- procedural guidelines and
- technical steps.[1]

Process Models. Rules on a high level of abstraction structure the design process as a whole. Typically they define *design phases* and the kind of documents that have to be produced in these phases. We call a set of such rules a *process model.* Examples of process models are the classic waterfall model or the spiral model (cf. Boehm(1994)). A characteristic of these models and of process models in general is that they are independent of notations and even independent of the underlying system view (function oriented or object oriented).

Nevertheless it can be observed that process models in an object oriented setting follow a different design philosophy than the classic models and support a more activity oriented design process than a phase oriented design process. Such activities during the development are analysis, implementation and testing, but also prototyping and reuse. In this way, the design process becomes more flexible and adaptable to particular needs.

[1] The latter two terms have been taken from Hussmann (1994), however with a slightly different meaning

Procedural Guidelines. Process models are mainly concerned with the question of *when* particular specifications have to be produced. In addition, rules at a lower level of abstraction support the designer *how* to produce a specification. These kinds of rules are in most cases of a heuristic, informal nature. They are formulated in the terminology of the underlying system view but independently of particular notations (e.g. types of diagrams). In the sequel we will call these rules *procedural guidelines*.

As an example, many object oriented methods give procedural guidelines to support the designer in identifying objects, methods and attributes in the application domain. Moreover the paradigm of design with use cases also comes along with a set of procedural guidelines.

Technical Steps. Rules at the lowest level of abstraction are both dependent of the system view and of the notations used. We call them *technical steps*.

Technical steps deal with the transformation of documents during the design process and with the interrelation of different notations. As an example, technical steps give rules for the refinement of diagrams or rules that ensure the consistency of a specification. Technical steps thus support the designer's understanding of the use of the description techniques and the production of a sound and complete system specification.

In contrast to their importance, technical steps are the most neglected kind of rules in today's methods, since they require a deep understanding of both the system view and the description techniques. While process models and procedural guidelines are less amenable to a formal treatment due to their heuristic nature, a formal foundation of the system view and the notations like our model is an eminent basis for studying technical steps in a systematic way.

In subsection 4.2 we sketch our view of the design process and clarify the semantic treatment of technical steps within the semantic model. Before, table 1 summarizes the concepts discussed in this section.

4.2 A View of the Design Process

A system specification in UML consists of a set of documents like sequence diagrams, class diagrams or free text. In order to support the effective management of a large number of documents, we extend this simple view and consider a system specification to be a *document graph* containing the following kind of information.

- The nodes of the document graph are UML documents.
- Each document in the graph has a *state* documenting its stage of development.
- A set of *relationships* between nodes describe dependencies between documents.

Document state. The document state is intimately connected with the notion of a document lifecycle. Apart from information, by whom and when some document has been created or updated, the document state reports whether the document has been *validated* (in case of informal and formal documents), *verified* (in case of formal documents) or *tested* (in case of programs).

Further attributes determining the state of a document are the *redundancy* of a document or its *consistency*. A document is redundant if all the properties of the system it describes can be derived by other documents in the graph.

Document relationships. Documents in UML have been syntactically decoupled as far as possible in order to support a flexible use during design. Thus, it is the meta level that has to document the structure of specifications. There are two main kinds of relationships in the document graph.

The first one is a kind of import or clientship relation. We call it the **refers to** relation. The **refers to** relation is directed and relates a document with the set of documents that have to be known in order to understand the document. For instance, a sequence diagram always has to refer to some class diagram in order to understand the labels of the object lifelines. As a further example, a state diagram may refer to a class diagram or to a method specification.

The second kind of relationship between documents is the **transform** relation. Also the **transform** relation is directed and relates specifications that are involved in some transformational step during design. A document A transforming a document B is the result of some technical step and describes some aspect of the system in more detail than document B. More generally, a technical step and the **transform** relation, respectively, may be based on more than one document and may produce several documents.

In our semantic framework, the **transform** relation has its counterpart in a semantic refinement relation on the semantic domain of documents. The refinement relation guarantees that the system properties specified in earlier stages are preserved during the development. Hence the technical steps formulate conditions at the syntactic level of UML that ensure that the refinement relation holds at the semantic level. The rules of the technical steps have to be formulated for every kind of document and have to be proved correct with respect to the semantic refinement relation.

In the current stage of development we have developed technical steps for the development of class diagrams and state diagrams (Rumpe (1996)). Rules concerning the interrelation between sequence diagrams and state diagrams are currently under investigation (Breu et al. (1997a)). Table 1 sketches the main idea of these technical steps. Figure 4 depicts a sample document graph. It has to be stressed again that the depicted diagram is *not* an UML document itself but a concept at the meta level, e.g. produced and administrated by a tool. Moreover, document graphs are rather used as a paradigm for managing the design process than as a kind of document suitable for graphical representation.

Integrating the transform relation, a document graph does not only represent a system specification at a single stage of development but represents the whole design process. Compared to the traditional view of the design process as a sequence of system specifications the document graph view is advantageous for several reasons.

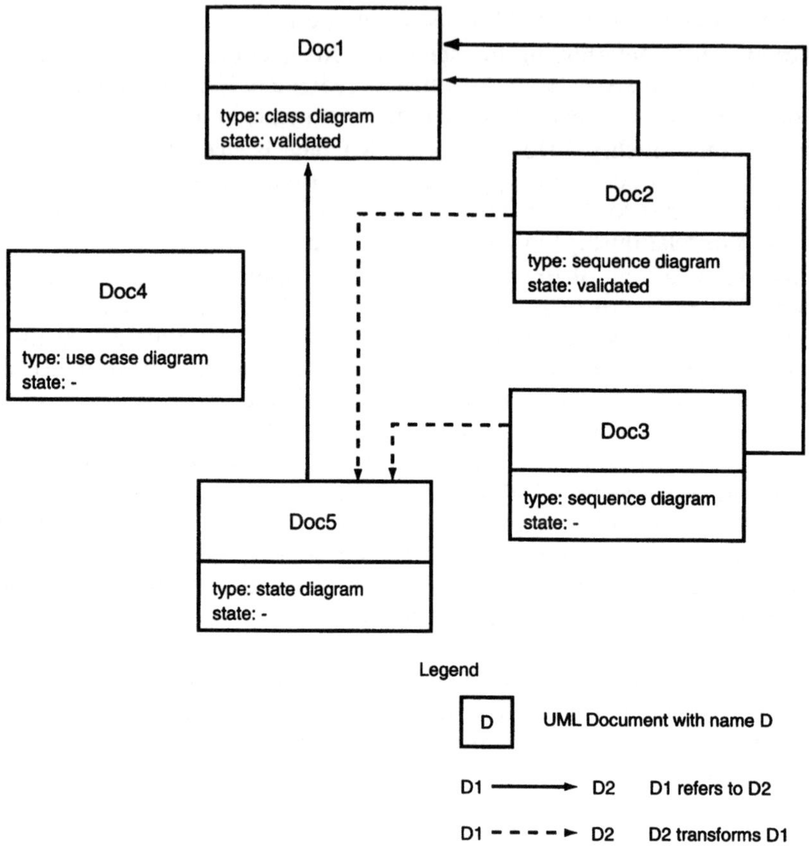

Figure 4: A sample document graph

First, the notion of document graphs supports a design which does not have to be strictly phase oriented and homogeneous but enables the prototyping of subsystems and the reuse of documents. In this respect, the notion of document graphs is particularly suitable in an object oriented design environment.

Second, a system specification in any case consists of documents at different levels of abstraction (e.g. for documentation or communication purposes). Thus, the representation of the whole design process in the document graph is only a matter of consequence. It is clear that an explicit versioning concept for documents is not needed in our framework since the sequence of design steps is represented by a sequence of transform relations in the document graph.

Source of transformation: Class diagram(s)
Produced documents: Class diagram **Description** Allowed activities for the design of class diagrams are the introduction of new classes, attributes and methods, the introduction of new associations and inheritance relations, the strengthening of invariants and the integration of several class diagrams.
Source of transformation: State diagram **Produced documents**: State diagram **Description** Allowed activities for the design of state diagrams are the introduction of new states, the refinement of states, the introduction of new transitions under certain conditions, the deletion of transitions. The exact rules can be found in Rumpe (1996).
Source of transformation: Sequence diagram(s) **Produced documents**: State diagram(s) **Description** Sequence diagrams describe exemplary event traces that may be synthesized to complete descriptions in state diagrams. Sequence diagrams roughly correspond to paths in the synthesized state diagram.

Table 1: Technical steps for UML documents

5 Outlook and Further Work

In this paper, we have outlined directions for a stronger integration of the description techniques provided by the Unified Modeling Language. The underlying basis used for the integration is a mathematical model developed in the SYSLAB method, the *system model.*

This setting provides a rich field for future research activities. As a start, precise mappings of the UML description techniques onto the mathematical system model have to be defined. Based on them, notions of consistency between development documents of the same or different description techniques can be defined. Consequently, a further step of research would be to use the interrelationships between the UML description techniques defined on the basis of the system model to soundly integrate them methodically, particularly on the level of the technical steps introduced in Section 4.1. The last step, building upon such an integration framework, would be to develop appropriate tools that support these techniques and the methodology.

References

BOEHM, B.W. (1994): A spiral model of software development and enhancement. *Software Engineering Notes, 11(4).*

BOOCH, G., RUMBAUGH, J., and JACOBSON, I. (1996): The Unified Modeling Language for Object-Oriented Development, Version 1.0.

BREU, R. GROSU, R., HOFMANN, CH., HUBER, F., KRÜGER, I., RUMPE, B., SCHMIDT, M., and SCHWERIN, W. (1997a): Describing Object Interaction: From Exemplary to Complete Descriptions. TUM-I9737. Technische Universität München

BREU, R. GROSU, R., HUBER, F. RUMPE, B., and SCHWERIN, W. (1997b): Towards a Precise Semantics for Object-Oriented Modeling Techniques. In: KILOV, H., and RUMPE, B. (eds): *Proceedings ECOOP'97 Workshop on Precise Semantics for Object-Oriented Modeling Techniques.* TUM-I9725.

BROY, M. and STØLEN, K. (1994): Specification and Refinement of Finite Dataflow Networks - A Relational Approach. Tech. rept. TUM-I9412. Technische Univerität München.

BORY, M., DEDRICH, F. DENDORFER, C., FUCHS, M., GRITZNER, TH., and WEBER, R. (1993): The Design of Distributed Systems - An Introduction to FOCUS - revised version -. Tech. rept. SFB-Bericht 342/2-2/92A. Technische Universität München.

BURKHARDT, R. (1997): UML - unified modelling language - objektorientierte Modellierung für die Praxis. Addison Wesley.

GROSU, R. and RUMPE, B. (1995): Concurrent Timed Port Automata. Tech. rept. TUM-I9533. Technische Univerität München.

GROSU, R., KLEIN, C., and RUMPE, B. (1996). Enhancing the SysLab System Model with State. TUM-I9631. Technische Univerität München.

HUSSMANN, H. (1994): Formal Foundations for SSADM. Technische Universität München, Habilitationsarbeit.

KLEIN, C., RUMPE, B., and BROY, M. (1996): A stream-based mathematical model for distributed information processing systems - SysLab system model - . In NAIJM, E., and STEFANI, J.-B. (eds): *FMOODS'96 Formal Methods for Open Object-based Distributed Systems, 323-338.* ENST France Telecom.

PAECH, B. and RUMPE, B. (1997): State Based Service Description. In: DERRICK, JOHN (ed): *Formal Methods for Open Object-based Distributed Systems.* Chapman-Hall.

RUMPE, B. (1996): Formale Methodik des Entwurfs verteilter objektorientierter Systeme. Herbert Utz Verlag Wissenschaft. PhD thesis, Technische Universität München.

On Constraints and Queries in UML

M. Gogolla, M. Richters

Arbeitsgruppe Datenbanksysteme,
Fachbereich 3, Mathematik und Informatik,
Universität Bremen, D-28334 Bremen, Germany

Abstract: The UML has recently been extended by an Object Constraint Language (OCL). This formal language can be used for specifying constraints on a model in order to restrict possible system states. We present some examples for illustrating main concepts of OCL. Problems with the current definition of OCL resulting from imprecise or ambiguous definitions are investigated. A comparison of OCL with a language for specification of queries and integrity constraints in an Extended Entity-Relationship model shows similarities between both approaches. This comparison could lead to a better understanding of OCL.

1 Introduction

Many languages and methods for object-oriented analysis and design (OOAD) have been developed during the last decade. Although these methods share many concepts, differences in terminology and notation makes it quite difficult to directly compare or reuse design models. A promising approach in this situation is the development of the *Unified Modeling Language* (UML), which is a concerted effort to provide a single standardized language for object-oriented modeling (Rational (1997a)). It integrates and enhances concepts from three of the most popular OOAD methods, namely Booch (Booch (1994)), OMT (Rumbaugh et al. (1991)), and OOSE (Jacobson et al. (1992)).

The process of standardization is organized by the Object Management Group (OMG), which issued a Request for Proposals in 1996. A first version of UML was submitted to OMG in January, 1997. The review process and feedback from a broader public audience exposed several deficiencies concerning clearness and consistency of the UML definition. In particular, it proved difficult to interpret the *UML Semantics* document (Rational (1997b)) in an unambiguous way. The given description in form of diagrams and English text was not precise enough for a complete and consistent understanding of the UML metamodel. In fact, the authors expected other individuals to express the UML semantics more precisely by using formal techniques.

The problem has been recognized and a new version (UML 1.1) with many improvements has been published recently. A major extension in this version is the introduction of an *Object Constraint Language* (OCL) (Rational (1997c)). This language is intended to facilitate specification of model properties in a formal yet comprehensible way (Warmer et al. (1997)). For example, the semantics document has been completely restructured by replacing large parts of textual descriptions of constraints on the UML metamodel by equivalent OCL expressions.

Besides the aforementioned application of OCL to formalizing the UML metamodel, there is also benefit for users of UML. Since the constraint language is also a *part* of the metamodel, it can be used to express constraints on concrete system models. Previously, UML support for describing constraints was limited to annotations in form of uninterpreted textual comments. The introduction of a formal constraint language is an important step towards proper formalization of complex models. It should also facilitate the development of methods for simulation, validation and verification of system models. In the information systems field we are particularly interested in data models and their query languages. With respect to its use as a query language, the relationship of OCL to object-oriented query languages like OQL (Cattell (1997)), to (E)ER models like the original ER model (Chen (1976)), the data type based approach (dos Santos et al. (1979)), INCOD (Atzeni (1981)), ECR (Elmasri et al. (1985)), BIER (Eder et al. (1987)), ERC (Parent and Spaccapietra (1987)), or ORAC (Wei and Teorey (1991)) should be investigated.

The structure of the paper is as follows. Section 2 introduces the concepts of OCL and Section 3 gives some examples of constraint expressions. In Section 4 we report on some problems with the current definition of OCL. Section 5 compares OCL with a language for specification of queries and integrity constraints in an Extended Entity-Relationship model, and Section 6 gives some final remarks.

2 Concepts of OCL

The main purpose of the Object Constraint Language is to specify restrictions on the possible system states with respect to a given model. An OCL expression is declarative in the sense that an expression says *what* constraint has to be maintained, not *how* this is accomplished. Therefore, specification of constraints is done on a conceptual level, where implementation aspects are irrelevant.

Evaluation of an expression always results in a value without changing the system state of a model. With respect to its evaluation strategy, the language resembles functional programming languages, and considering its use as a constraint language, there is an obvious connection to logic based languages. In fact, Sect. 5 will reveal a strong similarity to a query and constraint language for an EER model based on predicate calculus.

There are several places where OCL expressions can be used within a UML model. According to the metamodel described in Rational (1997b), any kind of ModelElement can be associated with a Constraint (ModelElement and Constraint both being classes of the UML metamodel). A Constraint has an attribute 'body' of type Expression. Any legal OCL expression may be used as a body of a constraint. For example, an attribute 'age' of a class Person may be restricted to hold only positive integer values. This may be achieved by attaching the expression `self.age >= 0` to the Person class. In general, constraints may also be related to a group of model elements, allowing to specify relationships among elements. Path expressions can be used to navigate various kinds of associations, e.g. a "recursive" children association of a class Person can be constrained to allow only unique forenames for children of a given person.

OCL expressions are not only used to define invariants on classes and other types, they also allow specification of pre- and postconditions on operations. If an operation has no side effects (i.e. the operation has the property "isQuery"), its meaning can usually be specified with an OCL expression. Examples of these can be found in the *UML Semantics* document where OCL is used extensively to define static well-formedness rules of the metamodel. Frequently needed operations are named and defined separately, thus reducing the overall length of rules.

Besides its application for improving the UML metamodel, OCL can also be utilized in concrete application models. UML users may add constraints to their models in order to restrict the possible set of system states. Because of the descriptive nature of constraints, OCL expressions can also be used for specifying queries. Since any expression is evaluated to a value of a certain type, constraints can be considered a special case where the result has to be a truth value. Queries can be very useful to validate models in the early phases of design. Tools supporting simulation or animation of models are powerful only if they provide means for querying the simulated state of a system (Richters and Gogolla, 1997).

3 OCL Examples

Let us take a closer look now at some examples of OCL expressions. The following expressions refer to Fig. 1, which shows a class model for a simple airline domain.[1]

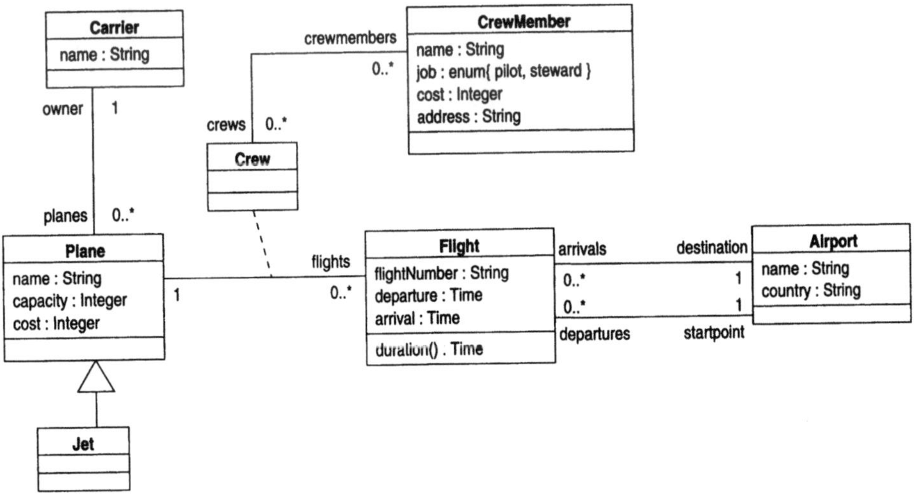

Figure 1: Class Diagram for Airline Example

The first example expresses an invariant on Plane instances, stating that their attribute capacity must have positive values.

[1]This example has been used to illustrate some OCL features in a preliminary version of the OCL specification document, but has been dropped from the final version.

(1) "The Capacity of each plane must be positive"

```
Plane
  self.capacity > 0
```

Evaluation of an expression always requires a contextual instance of a specific type. In the example, the expression self refers to an object of type Plane. Properties like attributes (e.g. 'capacity') may be referenced by using a dot notation. The term "property" is also used for association ends and side effect-free operations. To determine the names of all planes owned by a given carrier (see next example), we first have to follow the association between carrier and plane objects. The expression self.planes results in a set containing all elements of type Plane owned by a given carrier instance. Next, the predefined operation collect applies the expression name to every single element of this set. Generally, application of collect on a set results in a multiset with same cardinality but possibly duplicate values.

(2) "Return the names of all planes owned by a given carrier"

```
Carrier
  self.planes->collect(name)
```

If an expression denotes a collection (e.g. the set of planes), it is accessed by using an arrow -> (instead of a dot) followed by a feature name. The next examples demonstrate further useful collection features. The select feature can be used to retrieve subsets of collection. A boolean expression given as argument is evaluated for each element of a collection, thus deciding whether an element has to be included in the result set. Similarly, a forall feature applies its argument expression to each element of a collection, making the whole expression true, only if the argument yields true for each element.

(3) "A carrier owns at least two planes with less than 100 seats"

```
Carrier
  self.planes->select(capacity<100)->size >= 2
```

(4) "Each plane of a carrier has a cost below 500.000"

```
Carrier
  self.planes->forall(cost<500000)
```

(5) "All planes owned by a carrier have unique names"

```
Carrier
  self.planes->forall(p1, p2 |
    p1.name = p2.name implies p1 = p2)
```

While example (2) is a query with result type Bag(String), all other expressions are constraints (i.e. their result type is boolean) that must be true in all valid system states. We consider these constraints for demonstration purposes only. They are not intended to be a complete realistic constraint set for the given class model.

4 Some Problems of OCL

In this section we investigate some aspects of OCL in more detail. We look at the type system, the concept of value and object, rules for various forms of polymorphism, rules for handling complex values and the undefined value, and some technical issues like notation and different ways of interpreting expressions. As it will turn out, there are some aspects, which are not sufficiently defined in the OCL specification to give a precise idea of their meaning.

4.1 Types

Each OCL expression has a type that belongs to one of the following groups.

- Basic types are Integer, Real, Boolean, and String.
- Collection types are Collection, Set, Sequence, and Bag.
- Special types are OclAny, OclType, and OclExpression.
- Additional types are introduced by classes, interfaces, associations and enumerations as part of a UML model.

Type hierarchy. A subtype relationship induces a hierarchy on these types (see Fig. 2). The type OclAny is the supertype of all other types. All OCL types have a set of predefined operations that can be applied to instances of a type. These operations are also called "features". For example, the type Integer provides features for arithmetic operations (addition, multiplication, etc.), and the type Set has features for common operations on sets like union, intersection, difference, etc.

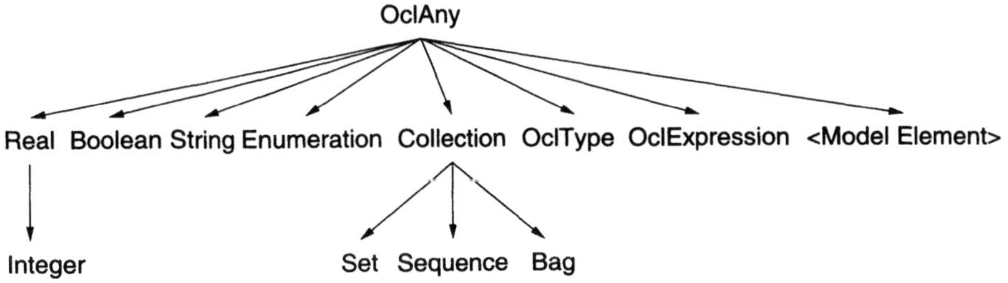

Figure 2: OCL Type Hierarchy

Features of a specific type are also available for any of its subtypes, e.g. to determine the size of a Set, Sequence, or Bag the feature 'size' defined for the Collection type can be applied. An expression is only valid, if it complies to certain rules for *type conformance*. These rules say, that an instance of type B can be used where an instance of type A is expected, if B is a (direct or indirect) subtype of A.

There are several problems with the current definition of types in OCL. First, it is not clear whether a conceptual distinction is made between data values and object instances. We consider data values to be immutable whereas object instances have a mutable state (Beeri, 1990). The terms value/object and subtype/subclass are not used consistently throughout the OCL specification document. The type hierarchy as shown in Fig. 2 has been derived from the textual description of OCL types. It is not clear whether the basic data types (Real, Integer, Boolean, String) are really (or should be) subtypes of OclAny. For example, comparison of an Integer value with a String value should be prohibited by typing rules. However, both being a subtype of OclAny, this would perfectly satisfy the type conformance rules. Consider the following feature defined for type OclAny.

```
object1 = (object2 : OclAny) : Boolean
```

Equality is a feature ("=") defined on values of type OclAny (object1) expecting as argument another value of type OclAny (object2). According to the type conformance rules any subtype of OclAny can be used in place. Since Integer and String are subtypes of OclAny, the expression 5 = "five" should be type correct which certainly is not the intended behavior.

Polymorphism. The language introduces various kinds of polymorphism. We classify these according to Cardelli and Wegner (1985).

- Inclusion polymorphism: A subtype relationship induces a partial order on OCL types.
- Parametric polymorphism: Collection types are parameterized by their element type, e.g. Set(String).
- Ad-hoc polymorphism: Overloading of operations allow their application to different argument types.

In the current language definition, there is no precise information about how these concepts are applied correctly. For example, there are no rules defining how to select a specific operation from a set of overloaded ones.

Meta types. The OCL defines special types OclAny, OclType, and OclExpression. OclAny is the supertype of all other types and provides features that are available to all subtypes. These include operations for reflective inspection of values. For example, in OCL it is possible to query the type of any value. Evaluation of the expression 3.oclType results in Integer which is an instance of OclType. Applied repeatedly, the result of Integer.oclType is OclType. But what is the result of OclType.oclType? There is no statement about this in the OCL specification.

Expression type. The type OclExpression is a higher-order construct used for expressions that are passed as arguments to Collection operations like select, collect, forall, etc. To evaluate any of these operations, the argument expression has to be evaluated for every element of a collection. Again, OclExpression being a subtype of OclAny we can ask for the meaning of equality between values of type OclExpression. Does 2 + 2 = 1 + 3 hold, if the terms on both sides are considered to be values of OclExpression? This would presume a notion of syntactic equality.

4.2 Flattening

There are also some serious restrictions on the way types can be combined for the construction of new complex types. We have already seen that the Collection types are actually type operators, which are parameterized with a type argument. The expression Set(T) where T may be replaced by an OCL type, should yield a new set type with elements of type T. However, OCL currently does not allow usage of Collection types for T. This means that one can not create nested collections, e.g. Bag(Set(T)) is not allowed. The problem with this restriction is, that occurrences of nested values can not be completely avoided in non-trivial models. For example, the following expression determines all flights for each plane owned by a carrier (see Fig. 1).

```
Carrier
  self.planes->collect(flights)
```

The result type should be Bag(Set(Flight)). However, according to the OCL specification the result gets "automatically" flattened into a value of type Bag(Flight). The process of flattening is not described precisely. Consider the next example.

```
Sequence{ Set{1,2}, Set{3} } ⇒ Sequence{ 1,2,3 }
Sequence{ Set{2,1}, Set{3} } ⇒ ?
```

What is the result of flattening the second expression? The naive rule of removing all inner Collections and just repeating the elements in order of their appearance in the source expression leads to the different result Sequence{ 2,1,3 }, which is not correct, since the expressions on the left side are equal. In order to achieve a deterministic flattening semantics, and therefore equal results in the previous example, one would have to induce an order on the set elements, which is not a priori defined on all types.

4.3 Undefined Value

Another problematic field concerns the undefined value, which is introduced in order to have it, for example, as the result of an attribute application to an object instance when the attribute is not set or for incorrect operation applications like division by zero. The general OCL rule is that, if one or more parts in an expression are undefined, then the complete expression will be undefined (with two exceptions being that true or-ed with anything is true and false and-ed with anything is false). There are however cases when this strict propagation rule seems to be too strong, for instance undefined = undefined should yield true and if true then 1 else undefined endif should result in 1. Also it is not clear how undefined is handled in a context where a boolean value is expected. Is undefined then treated as false or as true? Is it always the case that not(undefined) = undefined holds? How is undefined related to the universal and existential quantifier? Consider the following terms.

```
collection->exists( expression)
collection->forall( expression)
```

What happens in either case if each application of *expression* to the elements of the collection yields undefined?

4.4 Structured Values

For the construction of new types, the OCL provides Set, Sequence, and Bag, all of which are restricted to only one level of nesting. In general, the minimal set of type constructors in most object-oriented data models with query languages also include a tuple type, a "struct" or a similar facility for structured aggregation of values (Butterworth et al., 1991), (Deux, 1991), (Lamb et al., 1991), (Cattell, 1997). This is necessary for delivering structured or aggregated query results, e.g. for querying the departure *and* arrival times for all flights (see Fig. 1). Currently, this kind of query is not supported by OCL.

4.5 Notation

The syntactical structure of OCL constraints is mainly characterized by path expressions. Expressions are read left-to-right, where, in general, operations are applied to a value resulting from evaluation of an expression on its left side. This way, deep syntactical nesting of function application is avoided. Function definitions thus are grouped by one of their arguments—in OO terms the "receiver" of a message causing a function to be evaluated. The disadvantage of this approach is, that functions with irrelevant ordering of arguments—such as most commutative mathematical functions—have to be defined for each single argument type. For example, the union of a bag and a set is defined in different places, once for the Bag type and once for the Set type.

```
aBag.union(aSet)
aSet.union(aBag)
```

Hence, with an increasing number of arguments, feature definitions are scattered over several locations. While the previous issue may be a matter of style, some aspects of the OCL notation lead to more serious problems. Rules for a shorthand notation allow rewriting of frequently needed expressions containing collect terms as the following example shows.

```
Carrier
 self.planes->collect(name) ⇒ self.planes.name
```

Again, we can find a case, where application of this shorthand notation leads to an ambiguity.

```
Set{1,2}->collect(oclType) = Bag{Int, Int}
Set{1,2}.oclType = Set(Int)
```

Naive evaluation of these expressions yields different values. The result of the first expression is of type Bag(OclType), while the second expression has type OclType. However, the shorthand rule postulates equivalence of both expressions.

The previous examples demonstrated that the Object Constraint Language has some interesting but problematic features. At first sight, these features offer flexibility and expressiveness. However, it seems that not all consequences of some design decisions have been considered in all details. A lack of orthogonality in the language makes it possible to construct examples where the semantics of evaluation is not given or is questionable.

5 Comparison of OCL with an EER Approach

As a preparation for the comparison of OCL and an EER calculus (Gogolla and Hohenstein, 1991) we shortly demonstrate how the presented UML example of an airline domain (Fig. 1) looks like in the EER approach. One equivalent EER schema (other solutions are possible) is pictured in Fig. 3. Attributes are omitted in the diagram for brevity.

In the following EER formulations of the five OCL expressions from Sect. 3 we make use of one derived schema component serving as a shorthand for the set-valued rule-navigating UML expressions. From the relationship 'owns' we derive a set-valued attribute

$$\text{planes} : \text{CARRIER} \rightarrow \text{set(PLANE)}$$

by defining

$$\text{planes(c:CARRIER)} := \text{BTS -[p} \mid \text{(p:PLANE)} \land \text{owns(c,p)]-.}$$

Thus the derived attribute 'planes' represents the relationship 'owns' from the viewpoint of a carrier (analogously we could do for the other side of the relationship, but this is not needed for the following examples). The definition of the derived attribute 'planes' involves a query term retrieving all planes connected via the relationship 'owns' to a given carrier. As in OCL, generally the result of a query is a multiset which is converted in the given definition to a set by the function 'BTS' which stands for 'Bag To Set'.

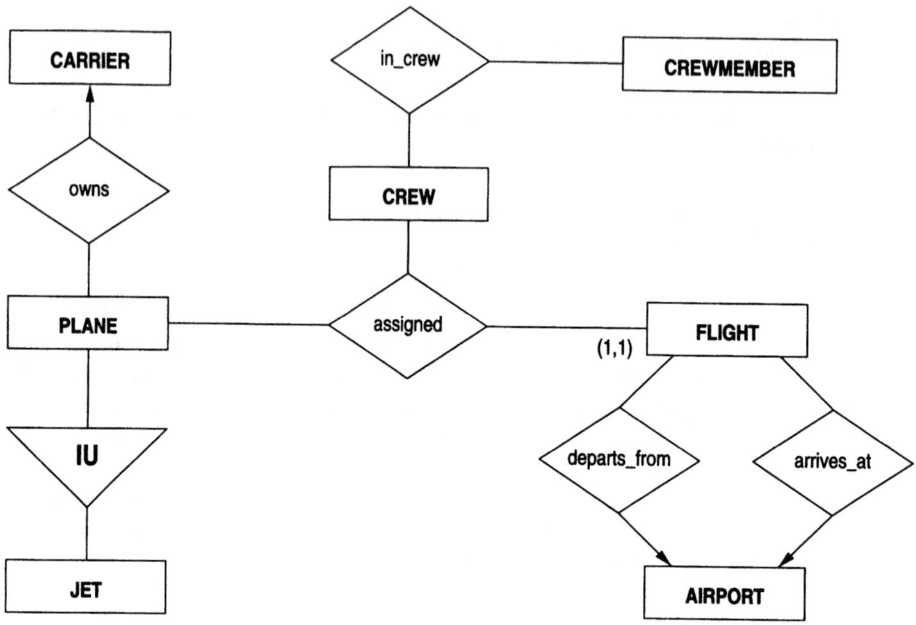

Figure 3: EER Diagram for Airline Example

(1) "The Capacity of each plane must be positive"

∀ (p:PLANE) capacity > 0

(2) "Return the names of all planes owned by a given carrier"

-[name(p) | (p:planes(c))]-

(3) "A carrier owns at least two planes with less than 100 seats"

∀ (c:CARRIER)
CNT -[p | (p:planes(c)) ∧ capacity(p)<100]- ≥ 2

(4) "Each plane of a carrier has a cost below 500.000"

∀ (p:planes(c)) cost(p) < 500000

(5) "All planes owned by a carrier have unique names"

∀ (c:CARRIER) (p1,p2:planes(c))
name(p1)=name(p2) ⇒ p1=p2

The main difference between the OCL formulations and the EER calculus can be summarized as follows ($\delta = v : s$ is a declaration binding a variable v to a set s, φ is a formula, and τ is a result term).

1. Query expressions frequently are given by explicit SQL-like terms: -[$\tau \mid \delta \wedge \varphi$]- is a short notation for SELECT τ FROM δ WHERE φ
2. Quantifiers are used in a more traditional way in the form $\forall/\exists(\delta)\varphi$.

Let us now compare both OCL and EER calculus by means of some selected topics.

Purpose: Both the EER calculus and OCL are intended to specify declarative constraints in order to restrict the possible system states to desired ones. Both also allow to query the current state of a system in the same language framework.

Semantics: The EER calculus has a completely worked out formal semantics based on set theory, and equivalence rules for EER calculus expressions are known. OCL deserves yet a theoretic foundation.

Safeness: The EER calculus is proved to be safe in the sense that all expressions and therefore in particular all query expressions yield a finite result. In the present version of OCL this is not true, for example, Integer.allInstances returns the infinite set of all integer values.

Computational power: Due to its structuring mechanisms the EER calculus is able to represent the result of a query in various forms. In contrast to this, OCL flattens collections of collections automatically. Flattening can also be achieved in the EER calculus but this is done by explicit formulations.

Notation: OCL directly allows to navigate through a class model in a path expression-like style. This enhances in certain cases the readability of expressions in comparison to the respective logic-based EER calculus formulations with its SQL-like query notation. However, by employing derived attributes, especially for relationships, EER calculus expressions become more user-friendly.

Orthogonality: The EER calculus is completely orthogonal, i.e. a concept can be applied if the syntactical context fits. In contrast to this, certain OCL language elements need to be restricted to special situations in order to be applied meaningfully, e.g. allInstances should be applied only to finitely interpreted object classes and finitely interpreted data types and oclType should be applied only to direct model elements.

6 Conclusion

OCL offers with respect to UML modeling advantages both in giving a better understanding of UML itself (because OCL is used for making precise the UML semantics) and in giving developers the possibility to sharpen their models. However, the present concepts and their semantics of OCL could be improved because its interpretation is partly incomplete and in some cases inconsistent.

On the other hand there are similar well-developed approaches like the EER calculus which have a precise mathematical semantics but which are with respect to notation a bit more elaborate and perhaps not so close to programming languages notation as OCL. The concepts of OCL however improve the UML modeling facilities and can be employed in a successful manner for various purposes. Most of the OCL semantics could be explained in a way analogously to, for instance, the way the EER calculus semantics is defined.

References

ATZENI, P., BATINI, C., LENZERINI, M., and VILLANELLI, F. (1981): INCOD: A System for Conceptual Design of Data and Transactions in the Entity-Relationship Model. In P. P. Chen (ed.): *Proc. 2nd Int. Conf. on the Entity-Relationship Approach (ER'81).* North Holland, 375–410.

BEERI, C. (1990): A Formal Approach to Object-Oriented Databases. *Data & Knowledge Engineering, 5(4), 353–382.*

BOOCH, G. (1994): Object-Oriented Analysis and Design with Applications. Benjamin/Cummings.

BUTTERWORTH, P., OTIS, A., and STEIN, J. (1991): The GemStone Object Database Management System. *Communications of the ACM, 34(10), 64–77.*

CARDELLI, L. and WEGNER, P. (1985): On Understanding Types, Data Abstraction and Polymorphism. *ACM Computing Surveys, 17(4), 471–522.*

CATTELL, R. G. G. (1997): The Object Database Standard: ODMG 2.0. Morgan Kaufmann Publishers, Inc.

CHEN, P. P. (1976): The Entity-Relationship Model—Toward a Unified View of Data. *ACM Trans. on Database Systems, 1(1), 9–36.*

DEUX, O. (1991): The O2 System. *Communications of the ACM, 34(10), 34–48.*

DOS SANTOS, C. S., NEUHOLD, E. J., and FURTADO, A. L. (1979): A Data Type Approach to the Entity-Relationship Approach. In P. P. Chen (ed.): *Entity-Relationship Approach to Systems Analysis and Design. Proc. 1st International Conference on the Entity-Relationship Approach. Los Angeles, California, USA.* North Holland, 103–119.

EDER, J., KAPPEL, G., TJOA, A. M., and WAGNER, R. R. (1987): BIER—The Behavior Integrated Entity-Relationship Approach. In S. Spaccapietra (ed.): *Entity-Relationship Approach: Ten Years of Experience in Information Modeling, Proceedings of the Fifth International Conference on Entity-Relationship Approach, Dijon, France, November 17-19, 1986.* North-Holland, 147–166.

ELMASRI, R., WEELDREYER, J., and HEVNER, A. (1985): The Category Concept: An Extension to the Entity Relationship Model. *Data & Knowledge Engineering, 1, 75–116.*

GOGOLLA, M. and HOHENSTEIN, U. (1991): Towards a Semantic View of an Extended Entity-Relationship Model. *ACM Trans. on Database Systems, 16(3), 369–416.*

JACOBSON, I., CHRISTERSON, M., JONSSON, P., and OVERGAARD, G. (1992): Object-Oriented Software Engineering: A Use Case Driven Approach. Addison-Wesley.

LAMB, C., LANDIS, G., ORENSTEIN, J., and WEINREIB, D. (1991): The ObjectStore Database System. *Communications of the ACM, 34(10), 50–63.*

PARENT, C. and SPACCAPIETRA, S. (1989): Complex Objects Modeling: An Entity-Relationship-Approach. In: S. Abiteboul, P. C. Fischer, and H.-J. Schek, (eds.): *Nested Relations and Complex Objects, Papers from the Workshop "Theory and Applications of Nested Relations and Complex Objects", Darmstadt, Germany, April 6-8, 1987*, Vol. 361 of *Lecture Notes in Computer Science*, 272–296.

RATIONAL (1997a): Unified Modeling Language, Version 1.1. Rational Software Corporation, 2800 San Tomas Expressway, Santa Clara, CA 95051-0951 (USA), URL: http://www.rational.com.

RATIONAL (1997b): UML Semantics. Published as part of RATIONAL (1997a).

RATIONAL (1997c): Object Constraint Language Specification. Published as part of RATIONAL (1997a).

RICHTERS, M. and GOGOLLA, M. (1997): A Web-based Animator for Validating Object Specifications. In: B. C. Desai and B. Eaglestone (eds.): *IDEAS'97: International Database Engineering & Applications Symposium, Montreal, Canada, August 25–27, 1997*, 211–219.

RUMBAUGH, J., BLAHA, M., PREMERLANI, W., EDDY, F., and LORENSON, W. (1991): Object-Oriented Modeling and Design. Prentice-Hall, Englewood Cliffs (NJ).

WARMER, J., HOGG, J., COOK, S., and SELIC, B. (1997): Experience with Formal Specification of CMM and UML. In: H. Kilov and B. Rumpe, (eds.): *Proceedings of the ECOOP'97 Workshop on Precise Semantics for Object-Oriented Modeling Techniques, Jyväskylä, Finland, 10 June 1997.* TU München, TUM-I9725.

WEI, G. and TEOREY, T. (1991): The ORAC Model: A Unified View of Data Abstraction. In: T. J. Teorey, (ed.), *Proc. 10th Int. Conf. on Entity-Relationship Approach (ER'91). ER Institute, Pittsburgh (CA)*, 31–58.

Modeling Java Threads in UML

M. Schader, A. Korthaus

Lehrstuhl für Wirtschaftsinformatik III,
Universität Mannheim, D-68131 Mannheim, Germany

Abstract: Modern programming languages such as Java facilitate the use of concurrent threads of control within computer applications. Considering concurrency is an important prerequisite for the adequate realization of object-oriented ideas, since real world objects usually operate in parallel. This brings up the requirement to be able to express concurrency issues already in design models, which precede implementation activities. The paper examines the possibilities of modeling Java threads using the Unified Modeling Language (UML). UML is the official industry standard for object-oriented modeling as defined by the Object Management Group (OMG).

1 Standardization of the UML

In order to cope with the complexities of modern software products, today's software development methodologies propagate a model-based approach. Graphical models of the system's structure and behavior are built and serve as a high-level, easy-to-understand means of communicating requirements and analysis/design concepts to software developers, management, end users, and customers.

With Object Management Group's adoption of the Unified Modeling Language (UML) as the official industry standard in Nov. 1997, a consolidation of software design notations has been achieved in the field of object technology. The UML does not prescribe a process and thus is no methodology, but just a modeling language. It is often referred to as a general-purpose "language for specifying, visualizing, constructing, and documenting the artifacts of software systems, as well as for business modeling and other non-software systems" (Rational Software Corp. (1997c)). Its proponents claim that the UML is well-suited to address current software technology problems such as component technology, patterns, frameworks, distribution, and last but not least concurrency.

2 Modeling Concurrency

The set of basic concepts supported by OO-methods is influenced by the capabilities of the programming languages used for implementing software systems and the operating systems on which the software is executed. The growing popularity of Java, a language which enables and encourages the use of interfaces and threads, has led to the integration of these concepts in analysis and design methodologies formerly lacking support of such concepts (Coad and Mayfield (1997)). In particular, the modeling of concurrency is an aspect often neglected by current object-oriented analysis and design methodologies, but it becomes more and more important as operating systems support multitasking/-threading and programming languages such as Java integrate language elements for writing code to implement multiple threads of control.

Concurrency denotes the occurrence of two or more activities during the same time interval. In computer-based systems, concurrency can be achieved by interleaving (i.e., concurrency is simulated) or simultaneously executing two or more threads of control, which are single execution paths through a program (Rational Software Corp. (1997b)). In the area of object-oriented analysis, most of the methodologies found in literature support either none (e.g. OOA, Coad and Yourdon (1991)) or only very few rudimentary mechanisms of expressing concurrency issues within analysis models (e.g. MAOOAM, Schader and Rundshagen (1996)). Only a very small number of specialized methods, such as MORE/RT (Stein (1995)), integrate concepts of concurrency. In object-oriented design methods such concepts can be found more frequently, e.g. in Booch (1994), ROOM (Real-Time Object-Oriented Modeling, ObjecTime (1997)), and CODARTS (Concurrent Design Approach for Real-Time Systems, Gomaa (1993)). Allowing for the latest requirements of object-oriented software development and profiting from the experience with existing methods, the UML as a language for building analysis and design models integrates the concepts of concurrency, as we will show in section 3.

In concurrent object-oriented systems, a distinction between *active* and *passive objects* is made. Active objects (belonging to active classes) model the concurrent behavior of real world objects and serve for improving the efficient use of system resources. Active objects own an execution thread and can initiate control activities. Passive objects (belonging to passive classes) on the other hand generally wait for messages from other objects to arrive in order to perform an operation, and execute only within the thread of an active object (or the main program thread) (Rational Software Corp. (1997b), Eriksson and Penker (1998)). Active classes can be implemented by heavyweight processes with their own address space or by lightweight threads sharing the same address space. We will focus on Java threads in this paper, so the latter interpretation is relevant to us here.

Programming with concurrent execution paths is a difficult task. As Booch (1994) puts it: "Indeed, building a large piece of software is hard enough; designing one that encompasses multiple threads of control is much harder because one must worry about such issues as deadlocks, livelock, starvation, mutual exclusion, and racc conditions." A concurrent system is a system where different components execute independently of one another, but often have to communicate with each other and therefore have to synchronize (Stein (1995)). Communication and synchronization are the most important issues to be considered when designing a concurrent system, so the minimum requirement for a modeling language to support the design of concurrent systems is to provide some means of expressing different kinds of communication among active and passive objects as well as their synchronization. Before we will go into detail describing how UML supports this, it should be explained further what is meant by communication and synchronization.

In order to communicate, two objects exchange messages across a link. In programs that contain only one thread of control, message passing leads to simple method calls: control flow is sequential and the caller waits for the supplier to complete the invoked method. In a concurrent system, a sender might for example be able to send an asynchronous message, which means, that it does not have to wait for the receiver to finish the execution of the method called, but may go on with its own execution immediately after sending the message. (Different kinds of communication supported by the UML are introduced later.) Synchronization is a mechanism needed to avoid that different active objects acting simultaneously on the same object interfere with its state and may corrupt it in the worst case. If there are no means of ensuring that some resources can only be used by one thread at a time, inconsistent system states can be the result. Booch (1994) describes the purpose of synchronization by saying: "In the presence of concurrency, it is not enough simply to define the methods of an object; we must also make certain that the semantics of these methods are preserved in the presence of multiple threads of control."

The modeling elements for expressing concurrency issues provided by the UML will be introduced in the remainder of this paper, focusing on examples of multi-threaded code snippets in Java. Modeling a system with the UML is done by modeling different views of the system. Therefore, the UML contains a number of different diagram types, all of which serve a certain purpose and emphasize different aspects of the system. The UML's set of diagrams consists of use case diagrams, static structure diagrams (class and object diagrams), dynamic diagrams (state diagrams, activity diagrams, and interaction diagrams, i.e. sequence diagrams and collaboration diagrams), and implementation diagrams (component diagrams and deployment diagrams) (Rational Software Corp. (1997a)). As can be inferred from the names of the diagrams, there is no special diagram for expressing concurrency. Each diagram may contain information relevant for the modeling of parallel activity, but especially the dynamic diagrams have expressiveness with respect to concurrency.

3 Modeling Java Threads in UML

The exponential growth of the internet, the development of the World Wide Web, and the features of the programming language itself (portability, robustness, security, object-orientation, dynamics, ease-of-use, etc.) have made Java[1] very popular at present. Two of the main advantages of Java are that it has been designed from scratch based on experience gained with existing languages, and that it takes advantage of the features of modern operating systems (e.g. preemptive multitasking/-threading). While many programming languages don't support concurrency at all or require the use of separate packages or libraries which are hard to use, Java integrates multithreading mechanisms directly into the language. The use of threads in Java still requires the use of classes provided by the standard Java package, but thread synchronization is included at the language level.

[1]For a Java language reference, see Sun Microsystems, Inc. (1997); introductory descriptions are provided, for example, by Boon (1996 and 1997) and Ritchey (1995); for concurrent programming with Java, see, for example, Lea (1997).

In Java, concurrency is introduced through the use of class Thread of package java.lang. Thread extends Object, which is the root class of the Java class hierarchy (see Figure 2). In Java, threads of control can be created either by declaring a class to be a subclass of class Thread and overriding the run method, or by declaring a class that implements the interface Runnable, which means to implement the run method and to pass an instance of that class as a parameter to a new Thread. The use of the second option is compulsary, if the user class is already a subclass of some other class, because Java does not support multiple inheritance. For the purpose of this paper, there are no important differences between the two possibilities, so we will only declare subclasses of Thread.

In order to introduce the semantics of Java threads, we fall back on statechart diagrams provided by the UML as a means of modeling the lifecycles of objects in a certain class. These lifecycles are visualized in the form of state machines which show the different states an object may go through during its lifetime and the transitions between those states which model the reaction to received stimuli. Figure 1 shows a simplified statechart, which depicts the lifecycle of objects of class Thread in Java. It shows the thread lifecycle states Created, Alive (with substates Runnable and Not Runnable), and Terminated. It can be seen how composite states may be composed of sequential substates in UML statechart diagrams. Composite state Alive, which is refined by substates Runnable and Not Runnable, is meant to indicate that the thread will respond to the message isAlive() by returning true, and that the thread may be terminated by the stop event at any time, no matter in which substate it is.

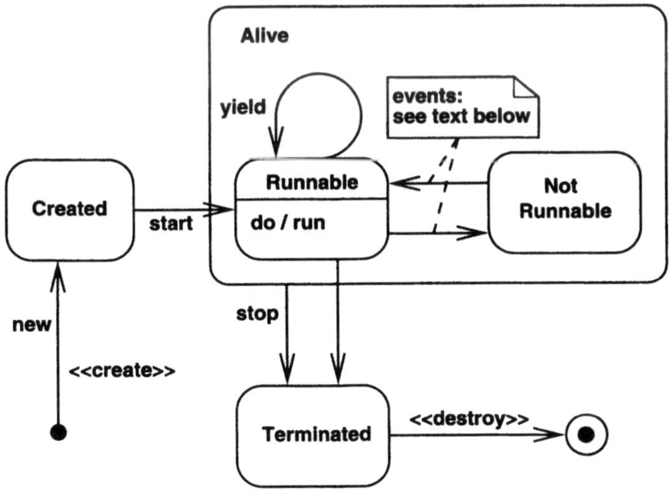

Figure 1: Simplified statechart of Java class Thread

Threads executing statements on a CPU are called active. Immediately after its creation a Thread object is not active; first, its operation start() has to be invoked. The object then shifts to state Runnable, which means that it can become active at any time, provided a CPU is available. The note symbol in Figure 1 (the rectangle with a bent corner) indicates that there are several possible events leading to transitions between the two states Runnable and Not Runnable, which are left out in the diagram for the sake of simplicity. Examples of events that may cause a runnable thread to become Not Runnable are that the object calls sleep for itself, that its method suspend is invoked, that it sends a join message to another thread or that method wait is called. A thread in state Not Runnable cannot become active, i.e. cannot execute statements. But, analogously, there are a number of events which may cause the transition of the thread object back into state Runnable. For example, if the period of time specified as an argument of sleep is over, if method resume is called, if the thread who was sent a join has terminated, or if notify or notifyAll is being called. By calling yield a thread indicates that it is ready to become inactive while keeping its state (i.e. Runnable).

The string 'do' '/' machine-name (argument-list) in the lower compartment of a state symbol indicates, that the object performs an activity while in the current state, which can be represented by a nested state machine. The activity a thread performs is defined in its method run. Completion of the activity triggers the unlabeled transition leaving the state, i.e. completion of run results in the normal termination of the thread. The initial state (shown as a small solid filled circle) and the final state (shown as a bull's eye) are called pseudostates, because objects cannot be in such a state. Transitions from the initial state and to the final state may be labeled with stereotypes ≪create≫ and ≪destroy≫. Stereotypes are an extensibility mechanism of the UML, which will be explained below.

Every Java class with thread functionality owns the above state machine, but may provide additional states, depending on its structure. UML statecharts offer some advanced features for specifying state machines of active objects. In addition to the decomposition of composite states into sequential substates, concurrent substates may be defined, which are usually associated with concurrent execution. It is often the case, that the substates execute their own threads, but this is not necessarily so. The regions for the concurrent substates are separated by dashed lines. The same notation may be used for decomposing composite states into mutual exclusive substates, where only exactly one of the substates can be active at a given instant (i.e. sequential execution). Which interpretation has to be chosen is specified by the attribute isConcurrent of class CompositeState in the UML metamodel. In the model of the system the value of isConcurrent can be shown as a property string (e.g. {isConcurrent = true}). Furthermore, it is possible to specify complex transitions which indicate the forking or joining of control flows. We will use complex transitions in our example activity diagrams, which are a special case of statecharts (Eriksson and Penker (1998), Rational Software Corp (1997b)).

3.1 Modeling a Simple Example of Multithreading

Our first example describes a Java program consisting of three parallel threads of execution. The main thread first leads to the creation of an object test and the invocation of method beginTest() of that object. Within this method, two new thread objects of class ThrEx1 are created and the threads are started. From that point on the execution of these threads occurs in parallel. Each thread performs its run method, where a loop is executed, whose upper bound has been passed—together with the thread's name—as an argument to the constructor of class ThrEx1. Within the body of the loop the thread simply prints out its name and the value of the iteration counter i, and calls method work(). The busy waiting implemented in this method is used instead of an invocation of sleep, because this guarantees, that the thread will not change its state. The Java Virtual Machine (JVM) finally exits, when all three threads (i.e. thr1, thr2 and main) have terminated.

This simple example may serve to present some more basic modeling elements of the UML in general and for expressing concurrency in particular. Figure 2 shows a class diagram representing the static design of the program as it could have been developed before the implementation. Figure 3 is a dynamic view of the program modeled as a sequence diagram, and Figure 4 expresses similar information within a collaboration diagram. These diagrams are discussed in the following subsections.

Listing 1:

```
// ThrEx1.java

import java.io.*;

class ThrEx1 extends Thread {
   static PrintWriter out = new PrintWriter(System.out, true);
   int num;
   ThrEx1(String name, int num) {
      super(name);
      this.num = num;
   }
   public void run() {
      for (int i = 0; i < num; ) {
         out.println(getName() + ": " + ++i);
         work();
      }
   }
   void work() {
      long t = System.currentTimeMillis() + 500;
      while (System.currentTimeMillis() < t)
         ;
   }
}
```

```
// ThrTest1.java

class ThrTest1 {
   private ThrEx1 thr1, thr2;
```

```
    public void beginTest() {
        thr1 = new ThrEx1("Thread 1", 4);
        thr2 = new ThrEx1("Thread 2", 6);
        ThrEx1.out.println("Ready to start two Threads");
        thr1.start();
        thr2.start();
        ThrEx1.out.println("Started two Threads");
    }
    public static void main(String[] args) {
        ThrTest1 test = new ThrTest1();
        test.beginTest();
    }
}
```

3.1.1 Visualizing Static Aspects in Class Diagrams

Like many other OO-methods, the UML uses class diagrams to show the static structure of the system under construction, containing classes and types, their relationships to each other, and their internal structure. Although dynamic diagrams are more important regarding the modeling of concurrency, some basic information may be placed in class diagrams also.

Figure 2 shows the structure of the program in Listing 1. In the center of attention is class Thread, which is not defined in the listing, but originates from the Java class library. It extends class Object (the generalization relationship is shown as a line with a hollow triangle), which is the root of all Java classes, and implements the Java interface Runnable (the implementation relationship is shown as a dashed line with a hollow triangle). We have restricted ourselves to show only the most relevant attributes and operations of Thread and Object in the diagram. Thread is extended by class ThrEx1, which is defined in Listing 1. Likewise, class ThrTest1 is shown, which contains the entry point to the program, the static function main. Note that class-scope attributes and operations are underlined in UML diagrams. The arrow from ThrTest1 to ThrEx1 and the multiplicity 2 indicate, that each object of ThrTest1 knows exactly two objects of class ThrEx1, whereas these objects do not know their counterpart.

In UML, active classes and objects are shown as symbols with heavy borders. They are often shown as composites with embedded parts, which is not the case in Figure 2. The heavy border is a notational convenience which may be seen as the graphical representation of a stereotype for classes, indicating that they are active. Stereotypes are a built-in extensibility mechanism of UML, because they introduce new classes of modeling elements to the set provided by UML at modeling time. Stereotypes have to be applied to existing modeling elements in the metamodel of UML and represent subclasses of them with probably additional constraints. The standard notation for a stereotype is a string in guillemets. In Figure 2, the stereotype ≪thread≫, which is predefined in UML, indicates, that the active class Thread is implemented as a thread, and not as a process. Analogously, ≪interface≫ classifies Runnable as an interface, and not a class.

Optionally, a stereotype may be associated with a graphic icon or marker, and the representation of the base modeling element may even be replaced completely by the associated stereotype symbol. Another way of indicating that a class or an object is active, is to use the property keyword {active}, which specifies, that the class attribute isActive of metamodel class Class holds true. We used all these mechanisms in the class diagram, although at least the use of heavy borders and the use of the property string {active} are redundant.

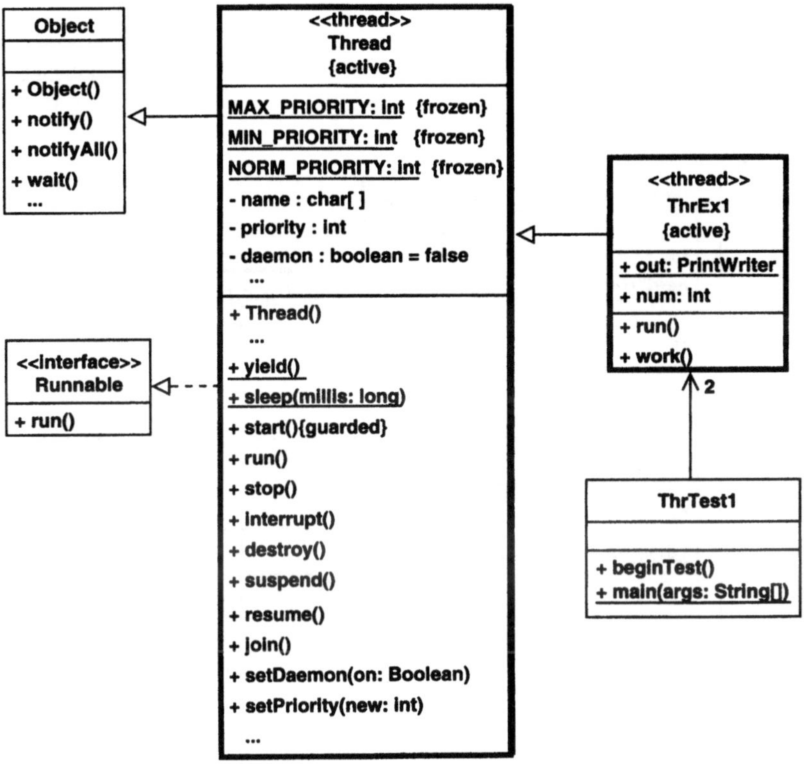

Figure 2: Simplified class diagram for Listing 1

3.1.2 Visualizing Dynamic Aspects in Sequence Diagrams

Sequence diagrams enable us to show the interaction of objects, i.e. the messages they exchange, arranged in time sequence. Figure 3 shows the objects created by the program in Listing 1 and the message flow between them, which has to be read from top to bottom. The vertical dashed lines below the object rectangles represent the lifelines of the objects, which indicate the existence of the object at a particular time. Message arrows creating an object end right next to the object rectangle. The thin, vertical rectangles show activations of the respective object. Activations represent the period of time during which an object performs an action or, in the case of procedural code, a subordinate method is active, which may belong to some other object. Concurrent objects often have execution control during their whole lifetime, performing their run activity while both sending and receiving messages. In the case of concurrency, operations of other objects are not relevant to the activation of an object and the entire lifeline may be shown as an activation, if the distinction between direct computation and indirect computation (by a nested procedure) is unimportant.

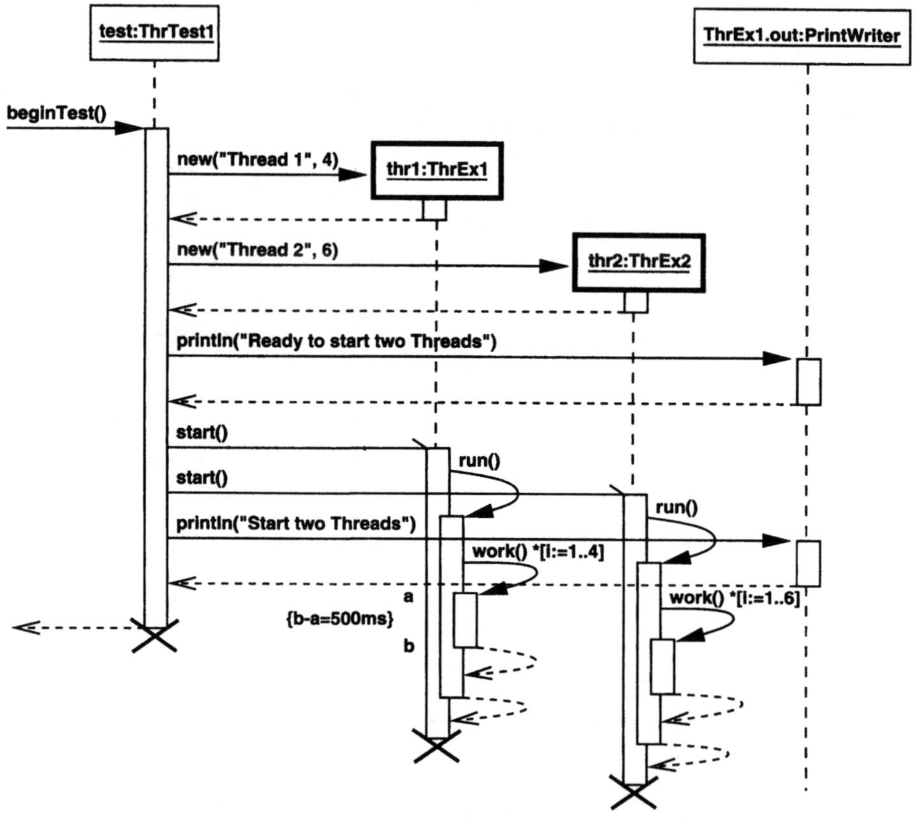

Figure 3: Sequence diagram for Listing 1

The physical location of the arrows in the sequence diagram shows the relative sequences of messages. In the presence of concurrent threads of control, sequence numbers may be used to identify those threads. We do not use sequence numbers in Figure 3, but use them in the corresponding collaboration diagram (see Figure 4). As mentioned before, the UML supports different kinds of communication between objects in a system. For example, messages can be implemented as procedure calls, as the sending of signals between active objects, as the raising of a specific event, and so on. In UML, different kinds of communication are distinguished by the use of different types of arrows for messages. The filled solid arrowhead predominating in Figure 3 stands for a method call or nested flow of control. In the case of concurrently active objects, it indicates wait semantics, i.e. an object sends a signal and waits for a nested sequence of behavior to complete. Half stick arrowheads, like the ones used in our example for the start() messages, stand for asynchronous flows of control where the sender does not wait for the receiver to deal with the message. Stick arrowheads should be used to express a flat flow of control without describing any details about the communication. Returns may be shown by dashed arrows with stick arrowheads. They may be omitted when purely procedural flow of control occurs, but for parallel processing and asynchronous messages they should be shown explicitly.

In Figure 3, the procedural call of method beginTest() is shown, which leads to an activation of object test. The sequential creation of two thread objects and the printing of a string follow; return arrows indicate the completion of the respective operations. The sending of start() messages to the thread objects is asynchronous, and test continues its own execution by printing the Started two threads info and destroying itself after the completion of the printing (indicated by a bold cross). At the same time, the threads execute their run() method, which calls work() several times. The staggered activations indicate the resulting stack frame. *[i:=1..n] is an iteration clause which simplifies the presentation of the sequential execution of method calls in an iteration. In addition, UML offers the opportunity to specify that the methods invoked are executed concurrently. In that case, the star would have to be followed by a double vertical line for parallelism: *||.

Another feature of UML sequence diagrams, which is important for modeling real-time systems, is the possibility to label the diagram with timing marks and timing constraints. In our example, the constraint {b-a=500ms} prescribes the duration of the execution of method work(). A feature not shown in the example is branching. Branches are labeled by guard conditions and are shown as multiple arrows leaving a single point. This may be used to visualize concurrency, but only if the guard conditions are not mutually exclusive. In the latter case, conditionality is expressed in the sequence diagram, so that it takes a general form instead of an instance form.

A very important task in modeling is to ensure that the diagrams expressing different system views are consistent and integrated. There are a number of consistency rules to be followed. For example, the objects shown in the sequence diagram of Figure 3 need to have corresponding classes in the class diagram of Figure 2, and, if the classes are active, the objects in the sequence diagram need to have heavy borders just like their corresponding classes in the class diagram. Furthermore, messages arriving at an object lifeline in a sequence diagram must correspond to operations declared for that object's class in the class diagram. The adherence to these kinds of consistency rules may best be supervised by a case tool used for modeling and system development.

3.1.3 Visualizing Dynamic Aspects in Collaboration Diagrams

Collaboration diagrams are another kind of dynamic diagram in the UML. Although they express information similar to that expressed by sequence diagrams, they lay emphasis on the inclusion of structural aspects of an interaction, whereas the time sequence is no dimension of its own in collaboration diagrams. This is the reason why the use of sequence numbers in collaboration diagrams is indispensable for determining the message sequences and multiple threads of control. Figure 4 shows a collaboration diagram for Listing 1, showing the collaboration of the four objects involved in order to execute beginTest(). The message labels placed near the object links are specified according to the following template: predecessor guard-condition sequence-expression return-value := message-name argument list. Predecessors and guard conditions are not shown in the example, but they can be important for modeling concurrency. If predecessors are specified, the message flow cannot continue until all of the preceding message flows have occured and the guard condition is satisfied. The specification of a list of predecessors therefore represents a means of thread synchronization. The sequence-expression consists of terms of the form [integer | name][recurrence], separated by dots and ended by a colon. The terms represent levels of procedural nesting, which do not occur, if the control flow is solely concurrent. In that case, all the sequence numbers are at the same level. A message sequence is expressed by ascending integer numbers at the same level of nesting depth. In Figure 4, message println(...) with sequence number 3 follows message new("Thread 2", 6) with sequence number 2. Names, on the other hand, represent concurrent threads of control. In our example, 4a and 4b indicate the starting of the parallel execution of two threads. With the help of a recurrence string, conditional or iterative execution can be specified (see Figure 3). The types of arrows used to distinguish different kinds of communication are the same as those used in sequence diagrams. Additionally, model consistency considerations similar to those mentioned in section 3.1.2 arise.

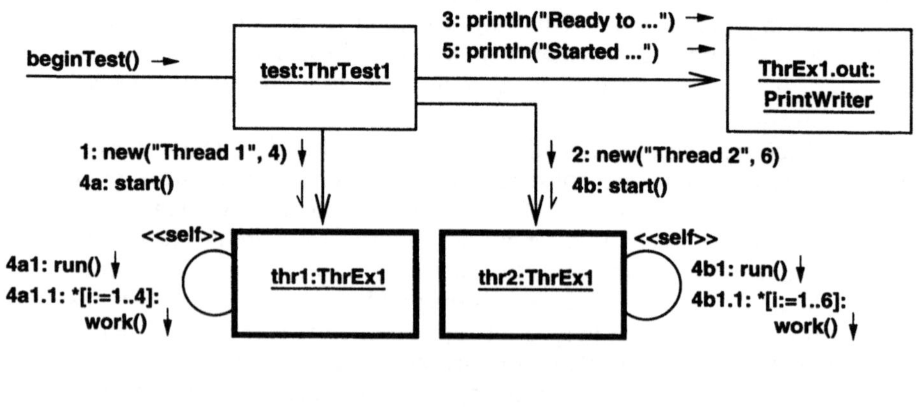

Figure 4: Collaboration diagram for Listing 1

3.2 Characteristics of Daemon-Threads

Java distinguishes between user threads and daemon threads. The difference is that the JVM does not wait for daemon threads to terminate before exiting, whereas it cannot exit as long as any user threads are still running. A thread should be set as a daemon or user thread when it is created. The kind of thread an object represents is stored in its private instance variable daemon of type boolean, which is false by default (see Figure 2). Via the public method setDaemon(boolean on) the daemon-feature of a thread object can be set and isDaemon() returns the state of the feature.

The following listing is identical with Listing 1 except for the statement making thr2 a daemon thread object (thr2.setDaemon(true);). The effect is, that the program might stop before thr2 has counted up to 6, because thr1 and the main thread have already terminated, causing the JVM to stop.

In UML design models, daemon threads should be marked as daemon threads explicitly by using one of UML's built-in extension mechanisms. For example, in object or collaboration diagrams daemon objects could be emphasized by a property string using a tagged value (e.g. {kind=daemon}). The tagged value mechanism can be used to define new model element properties in order to permit arbitrary information to be attached to models (Rational Software Corp. (1997a)).

In the sequence diagram presented in Figure 3 the modification in Listing 2 would show in two places: first, the setDaemon-message would have to be added, and second, the lifeline of thr2 would have to stop in accordance with the termination of the last user thread (here probably thr1).

Listing 2:

```
// ThrTest2.java

class ThrTest2 {
   private ThrEx1 thr1, thr2;
   public void beginTest() {
      thr1 = new ThrEx1("Thread 1", 4);
      thr2 = new ThrEx1("Thread 2", 6);
      ThrEx1.out.println("Ready to start two Threads");
      thr2.setDaemon(true);
      thr1.start();
      thr2.start();
      ThrEx1.out.println("Started two Threads");
   }
   public static void main(String[] args) {
      ThrTest2 test = new ThrTest2();
      test.beginTest();
   }
}
```

3.3 Thread Priorities

In a concurrent Java program, a scheduler decides which thread should run next, if several threads are in state Runnable. Usually, some time-slicing algorithm is used to allocate a CPU to threads in order to simulate parallel execution. Programmers may take influence on scheduling by setting thread priorities using the method setPriority(), since the scheduler prefers threads with high priorities. The range of permissible priority numbers for threads lies between Thread.MIN_PRIORITY and Thread.MAX_PRIORITY, and by default the priority is set to Thread.NORM_PRIORITY. Listing 3 gives an example of setting priorities for threads.

There is no built-in modeling element for specifying priorities of active objects in UML, but the extensibility mechanisms of UML can come to assistance again. The modeler should simply define a new property for active classes in the form of a tagged value priority which can be assigned the appropriate priority values in UML diagrams (Eriksson and Penker (1998)). Since it is normally impossible to rely on priorities in regard to the actual scheduling dynamics, the impact of priorities on the running times of the threads involved cannot and should not be shown in dynamic diagrams.

Listing 3:

```
// ThrTest3.java

class ThrTest3 {
   private ThrEx1 thr1, thr2;
   public void beginTest() {
      thr1 = new ThrEx1("Thread 1", 4);
      thr2 = new ThrEx1("Thread 2", 6);
      thr1.setPriority(Thread.MIN_PRIORITY);
      thr2.setPriority(Thread.MAX_PRIORITY);
      thr1.start();
      thr2.start();
   }
   public static void main(String[] args) {
      ThrTest3 test = new ThrTest3();
      test.beginTest();
   }
}
```

3.4 Modeling Synchronization with Activity Diagrams

One of the main tasks in designing concurrent systems is to coordinate multiple threads with each other in such a way that the system remains consistent and the intended semantics are preserved. For example, different active objects have to be prevented from trying to modify or access a shared resource simultaneously. UML's mechanisms for expressing synchronization semantics are presented in this and the following subsection.

The first example of synchronization (Listing 4) shows the simplest form of coordination between concurrent threads: A thread creates other threads and waits for their termination before it continues its own execution. In Java, this can be achieved by having the creator thread send join() messages to its child threads.

Listing 4:

```
// ThrTest4.java

class ThrTest4 {
   private ThrEx1 thr1, thr2;
   public void beginTest() throws InterruptedException {
      thr1 = new ThrEx1("Thread 1", 4);
      thr2 = new ThrEx1("Thread 2", 6);
      ThrEx1.out.println("Ready to start two Threads");
      thr1.start();
      thr2.start();
      thr1.join();
      thr2.join();
      ThrEx1.out.println("Started two Threads");
   }
   public static void main(String[] args) {
      ThrTest4 test = new ThrTest4();
      test.beginTest();
   }
}
```

The effect of joining can be illustrated very well with the help of activity diagrams (Fowler (1997)). Activity diagrams are a special kind of state diagram, containing so-called action states and transitions which are (usually) triggered by completion of the actions in the source action states. Activity diagrams have to be associated with a class, an operation or a use case (Rational Software Corp. (1997a)). In Figure 5, the implementation of method beginTest() of class ThrTest4 is shown with actions expressed in Java language code (alternatives are natural language or pseudo code). The three areas, divided by dashed lines, are called swimlanes, which are a kind of package for organizing responsibility for activities. They are used here to show the responsibilities of the different threads created during program execution.

To show the splitting and joining of control flow, we need complex transitions. A complex transition, drawn as a synchronization bar, either splits control into simultaneously executed threads or unifies concurrent threads into a single one. There is a correspondence between parallel parts of control flow in activity diagrams and concurrent substates in normal state diagrams. "The dynamic semantics of activity models can be expressed in terms of state machines. This means that the process structure of activities formally must be equivalent to orthogonal regions (in composite states)." (Rational Software Corp. (1997b))

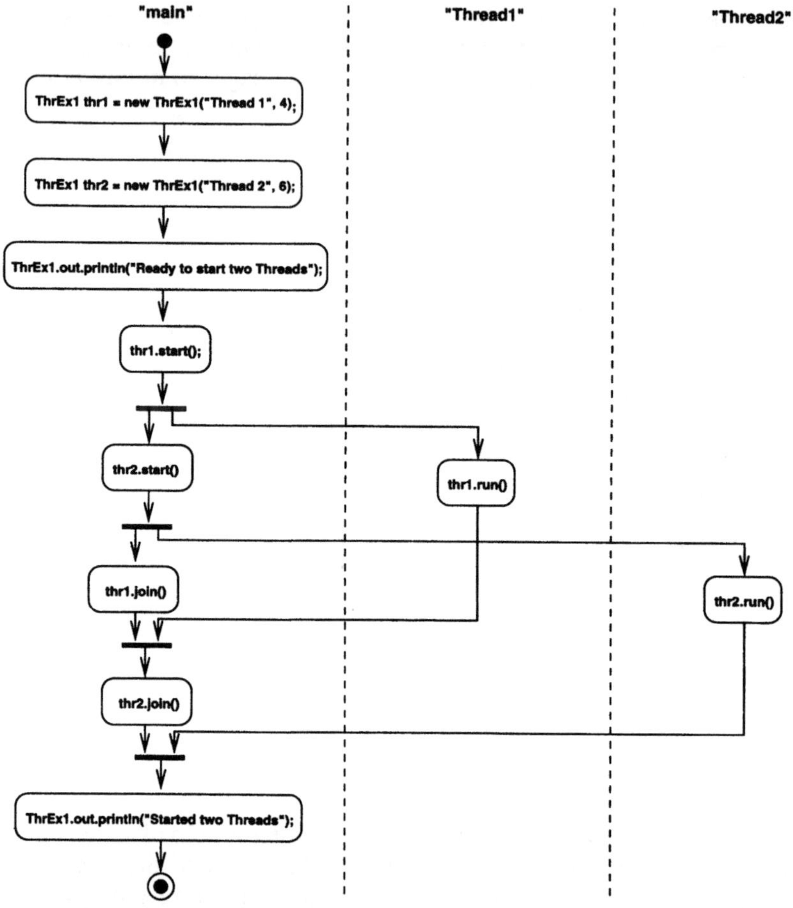

Figure 5: Activity diagram illustrating forks and splits in Listing 4

The diagram illustrates how the thr1.start() message leads to the splitting of control flow and the parallel execution of thr1.run() and thr2.start(). The same happens again with the starting of the second thread. After performing thr1.join(), the main thread becomes Not Runnable until thr1.run() is complete, i.e. the thread named Thread 1 has terminated (which leads to a state transition back to Runnable, see Figure 1). Analogously, the main thread waits for the termination of the second thread. After it has become Runnable again and a CPU has been assigned to it (i.e. it has become active), the final output is made.

3.5 Object-Level and Class-Level Thread Synchronization

Java integrates a means of synchronizing multiple threads at the language level by providing the synchronized modifier. This modifier may be used to mark some portion of code (usually class or instance methods) which needs a lock in order to run. Locks (or monitors) are owned by classes or objects in order to keep sections of code from running at the same time as others. A thread can take temporary ownership of a lock and release it later so that another thread can become the owner of the same lock. By owning a lock, a thread hinders all other threads from invoking other synchronized methods defined for an object or class that the lock belongs to. Listing 5 shows an example of using a lock at the object level.

The UML metamodel predefines a property concurrency for operations, which may take the values sequential, guarded, or concurrent in order to specify the concurrency semantics of a class-scope or instance-scope operation. The property has to be shown as a tagged value in UML diagrams (see Figure 6 as an example). The value sequential specifies that the integrity of the class/object cannot be guaranteed if simultaneous calls occur, i.e. active clients calling the same sequential operation of a passive class/object have to ensure by themselves, that only one call is outstanding at any time. With the value guarded, the semantics of Java's synchronized modifier can be expressed: Guarded operations allow multiple calls from concurrent threads simultaneously, but block all threads as long as another thread executes the operation. In Java, this means that an active thread trying to invoke a synchronized method which is already occupied by another thread stays Runnable, but becomes inactive. In this situation, the programmer has to take care of avoiding deadlocks due to simultaneous blocks. Specifying an operation as concurrent indicates, that multiple threads may safely work in parallel on that object/class without corrupting its state (Rational Software Corp. (1997b)).

Listing 5:

```
// Worker1.java

class Worker1 {
   synchronized void work() {
      long t = System.currentTimeMillis() + 500;
      while (System.currentTimeMillis() < t)
         ;
   }
}
```

```
// ThrEx2.java

import java.io.*;

class ThrEx2 extends Thread {
   static PrintWriter out = new PrintWriter(System.out, true);
```

```
    int num;
    Worker1 worker;
    ThrEx2(String name, int num, Worker1 worker) {
        super(name);
        this.num = num;
        this.worker = worker;
    }
    public void run() {
        for (int i = 0; i < num; ) {
            out.println(getName() + ": " + ++i);
            worker.work();
        }
    }
}
```

```
// ThrTest5.java

class ThrTest5 {
    public static void main(String[] args) {
        Worker1 w = new Worker1();
        ThrEx2 thr1 = new ThrEx2("Thread 1", 4, w),
            thr2 = new ThrEx2("Thread 2", 6, w);
        thr1.start();
        thr2.start();
    }
}
```

3.6 A More Complex Example: Producer, Mediator and Consumer

Our last example will combine a considerable number of the concepts described before in this paper. We discuss the implementation of a simple Producer/Consumer-Pattern, where a producer supplies a consumer with an integer value via a shared mediator object. To allow efficient execution, both producer and consumer block (i.e. become Not Runnable) if the resource is not available and wake up (i.e. become Runnable again) when being notified by their counterpart. Furthermore, the mediator object uses synchronized methods to avoid interference of the two threads when its methods are called.

Figure 6 shows the class diagram corresponding to Listing 6, containing the active classes Producer and Consumer and the passive class Mediator. Mediator's methods are guarded, which indicates that they will be implemented as synchronized in Java code. The synchronization mechanisms in this example are quite complex, so we have visualized them with the help of an activity diagram (see Figure 7). Amongst pseudo states, action states, transitions and complex transitions we have made extensive use of another UML feature for activity diagrams (and state diagrams in general): decisions. Decisions are used to indicate different possible transitions to successor states in dependency of a boolean guard condition. The presence of decisions can be made explicit by the use of diamond shaped icons with one or more incoming arrows and at least two outgoing arrows, each labeled with distinct guard conditions. If complex transitions have to be represented, decisions may even be chained. In that case, all the segments may have guard expressions, but only the first may contain an event trigger label, because decisions are not states in their own right. In Figure 7, chaining of decisions is used to model the sequence of checking the lock and the availability of val in Mediator's methods put(int i) and get.

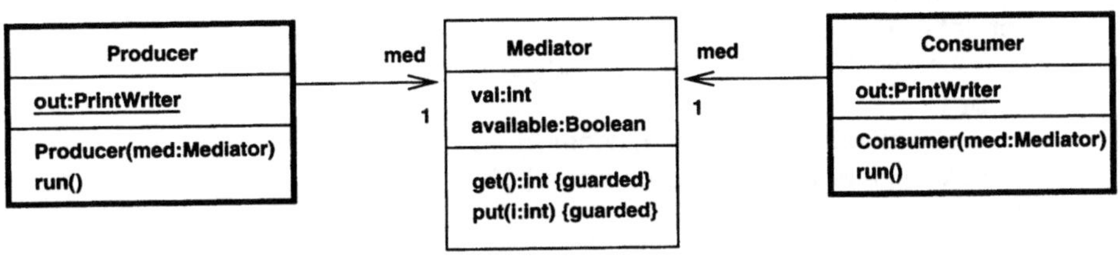

Figure 6: Class Diagram for Producer/Consumer-Listing

Listing 6:

```
// Producer.java

import java.io.*;

class Producer extends Thread {
   static PrintWriter out = new PrintWriter(System.out, true);
   Mediator med;
   Producer(Mediator med) {
      this.med = med;
   }
   public void run() {
      for (int i = 0; i < 10; i++) {
         med.put(i);
         out.println("Producer put: " +i);
         try {
            sleep((int)(100.0*Math.random()));
         } catch (InterruptedException ignore) { }
      }
   }
}
```

```
// Consumer.java

import java.io.*;

class Consumer extends Thread {
   static PrintWriter out = new PrintWriter(System.out, true);
   Mediator med;
   Consumer(Mediator med) {
      this.med = med;
   }
   public void run() {
      for (int i = 0; i < 10; i++) {
         out.println("Consumer got: " + med.get());
         try {
            sleep((int)(1000.0*Math.random()));
         } catch (InterruptedException ignore) { }
      }
   }
}
```

```
// Mediator.java

class Mediator {
   int val;
   boolean available;
   synchronized int get() {
      while (!available)
        try {
            wait();
        } catch (InterruptedException ignore) { }
       notify();
       available = false;
       return val;
   }
   synchronized void put(int i) {
      while (available)
        try {
            wait();
        } catch (InterruptedException ignore) { }
       notify();
       val = i;
       available = true;
   }
}
```

```
// ThrTest6.java

class ThrTest6 {
   public static void main(String[] args) {
      Mediator med = new Mediator();
      Producer prod = new Producer(med);
      Consumer con = new Consumer(med);
      con.start();
      prod.start();
   }
}
```

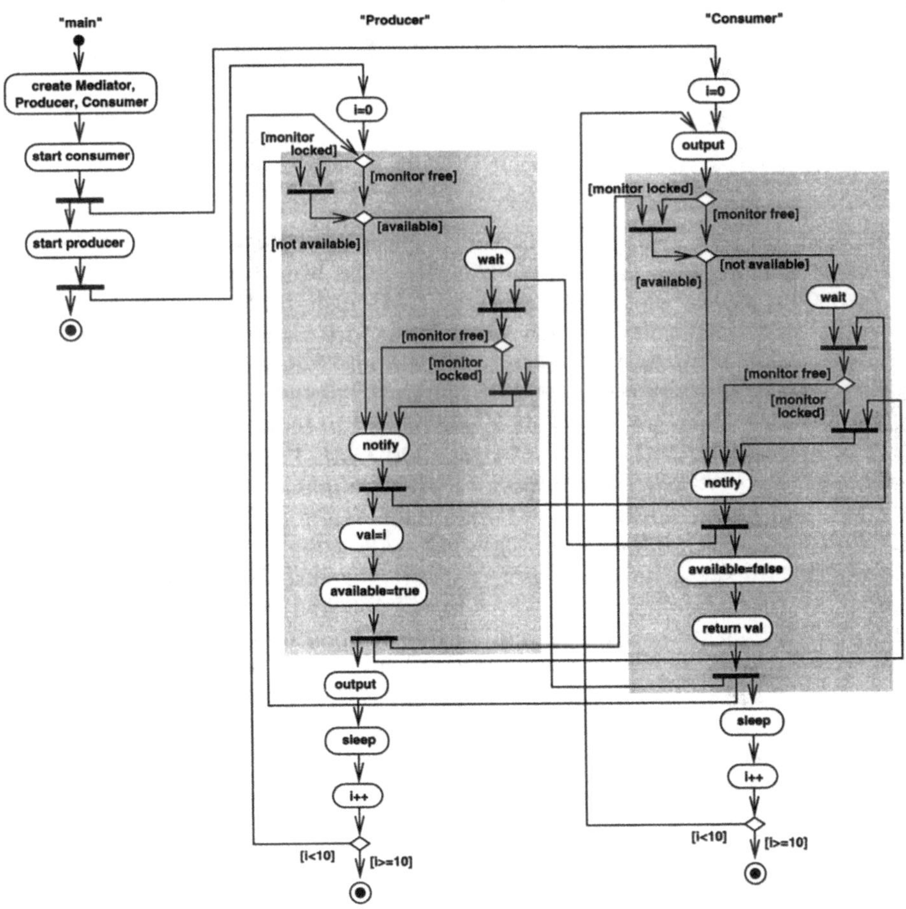

Figure 7: Activity diagram of consumer/producer problem with pseudo code

The example activity diagram uses pseudo code to describe the actions in the control flow of the Producer/Consumer-Pattern. Again, the different threads can be identified by different horizontal regions (the dashed lines are left out here). In order to be able to show the complex intertwining of the threads, we decided to reveal the internal flows of methods run(), put(int i), and get(). The light grey regions depict the run() method's control flow, and the dark grey regions show the control flows of put(int i) and get(), respectively. put(int i) and get() are responsibilities of the mediator object, which are not separated into a distinct swimlane here in order to show the intertwining more directly. When analyzing the code of Listing 6 and in particular the implementation of method put(int i), the reader may at first be surprised at the fact, that notify() is called before a value is assigned to val, because notify() leads to changing the state of the consumer thread to Runnable, so that it tries to read the new value. As can be seen from the activity diagram, the consumer thread may of course not execute method get() until the producer thread has released the lock of object med, and this is not done until the producer thread completes put(), leaving behind a correct state of med for the consumer thread to continue.

4 Conclusion

This paper has provided the reader with a basic understanding of Java threads and their modeling with the help of the UML. It has been shown that, in contrast to many other current modeling languages, UML includes the basic mechanisms for expressing concurrency, which are sufficient for standard applications with a small number of threads of control. Nevertheless, it has to be stated clearly that the **UML is a general-purpose modeling language which,** of course, **has its limitations.** Therefore, the UML camp agreed to build specialized, domain-specific variants of UML (UML Variants and UML Extensions: see Rational Software Corp. (1997c)) to serve special purpose domains. **One important variant of UML under devolopment is UML-RT (ObjecTime (1997)), which is based on ObjecTime's ROOM methodology and adds value for modeling real-time domain-specific applications requiring concurrency, distribution, high reliability, availability, serviceability, and so forth.** In order to analyze and design industrial strength real-time systems with a high degree of parallelism and other real-time requirements, such as timing constraints, reliability, performance etc., one has to consider using UML-RT which might fit the purpose better than the standard version of UML. On the other hand, this kind of UML variant will further increase the level of complexity inherent in the modeling language—a problem, even the UML core suffers from—and, at the same time, will decrease its ease of use and its understandability for non-experts.

References

BOOCH, G. (1994): Object-Oriented Analysis and Design with Applications. 2nd edn. Benjamin/Cummings, Redwood City, California.

BOONE, B. (1996): Java Essentials for C and C++ Programmers. Addison-Wesley, Reading, Massachusetts.

BOONE, B. (1997): Java Certification for Programmers and Developers. McGraw-Hill, New York.

COAD, P. and MAYFIELD, M. (1997): Java Design – Building Better Apps & Applets. Yourdon Press Computing Series, Prentice Hall, New Jersey.

COAD, P. and YOURDON, E. (1991): Object-Oriented Analysis. 2nd edn. Prentice Hall, Englewood Cliffs, New Jersey.

ERIKSSON, H.-E. and PENKER, M. (1998): UML-Toolkit. Wiley Computer Publishing, New York.

FOWLER, M. and SCOTT, K. (1997): UML Distilled – Applying the Standard Object Modeling Language. Addison-Wesley, Reading, Massachusetts.

GOMAA, H. (1993): Software Design Methods for Concurrent and Real-Time Systems. SEI Series in Software Engineering. Addison-Wesley, Reading, Massachusetts.

LEA, D. (1997): Concurrent Object Models – Design Principles and Patterns. Addison-Wesley, Reading, Massachusetts.

OBJECTIME (1997): URL: http://www.objectime.com/new/uml-rt/index.html

RATIONAL SOFTWARE CORP. (1997a): UML Notation Guide. Version 1.1, 1 September 1997, Rational Software Corp. et al.

RATIONAL SOFTWARE CORP. (1997b): UML Semantics. Version 1.1, 1 September 1997, Rational Software Corp. et al.

RATIONAL SOFTWARE CORP. (1997c): UML Summary. Version 1.1, 1 September 1997, Rational Software Corp. et al.

RITCHEY, T. (1995): Programming with Java! New Riders Publishing, Indianapolis, Indiana.

SCHADER, M. and RUNDSHAGEN, M. (1996): Objektorientierte Systemanalyse – Eine Einführung. Springer-Verlag, Heidelberg.

STEIN, W. (1995): Objektorientierte Analyse für nebenläufige Systeme: Die Methode MORE/RT. Reihe Forschung in der Softwaretechnik, Band 2, Herausgeber: H. Balzert. BI Wissenschaftsverlag, Mannheim.

SUN MICROSYSTEMS, INC. (1997): URL: http://www.javasoft.com/docs/

Formal Definition of UML's Package Concept

A. Schürr, A. Winter[1]

Lehrstuhl für Informatik III,
RWTH Aachen, Ahornstr. 55, D-52074 Aachen

Abstract: UML is the first OO modeling language with a useful modularization and information hiding concept. It supports nesting, import, and refinement of so-called packages. This paper translates UML's informal package definition into predicate logic formulas and solves some open problems concerning the visibility of exported and imported modeling elements.

Furthermore, the formulas will be transformed into a specification based on PROgrammed Graph REwriting Systems. We will very briefly sketch how a graphical UML editor can be generated from this PROGRES specification.

1 Introduction

After about 20 years of research and development, object-oriented (OO) modeling methods and notations have reached a certain degree of maturity and acceptance. They are no longer the occult science of a small number of OO gurus, but the widely accepted approach for analysis (OOA) and design (OOD) of software (hardware) systems. Popular OO methods—like Booch (1994), OMT (Rumbaugh et al. (1991)), or OOSE (Jacobson (1994))—are nowadays used to develop systems of continuously increasing size and complexity. As a consequence, produced analysis or design documents may consist of hundreds or even thousands of elements (classes, relationships, etc.). Keeping these documents in a consistent state or reusing generic parts of one analysis or design document within another one is a nightmare without the existence of any module concept.

These problems should be familiar for software developers of the late 60ies. Well-known software engineering concepts like "abstract data types" (Parnas (1972)) and "programming-in-the-large" (DeRemer and Kron (1976)) have been invented to overcome these problems. They lead to the development of modular programming languages like Modula-2 or Ada (Wiener and Sincovec (1984)) and software design languages like HOOD (Robinson (1992)) or EMIL (Börstler (1994)).

For a long time these ideas did not have any significant impact onto the development of OOA/OOD notations. The first generation of OO methods simply ignored the problem. Later on developed approaches offered more or less ad hoc solutions for partitioning analysis and design documents (diagrams) into surveyable pieces. OMT (Rumbaugh et al. (1991)) offers for instance so-called "modules", which allow to decompose unmanageable diagrams into a number of related diagrams. But there are no means to construct exports or imports of modules. As a consequence, any two elements in two different diagrams with the same name have to be identified. And even more elaborate concepts like categories in Booch (1994),

[1]This work has been supported by APPLIGRAPH.

collaborating subsystems with their contracts in Wirfs-Brock et al. (1990), or subsystems with well-defined interfaces in ADM3 (Firesmith (1993)) do not study the interactions between information hiding, module boundary crossing associations and inheritance.

The proposal of a Unified Modeling Language (UML) presented in Rational (1997) as a successor of Booch, OMT, and OOSE, is in our opinion the first OO notation which addresses all facets of a state-of-the-art module concept. Its modules, called packages, build shells around arbitrary types of diagrams (static structure diagrams, collaboration diagrams etc.). They provide a grouping mechanism for their elements. Within packages, an element can be used as source or target in relationships if it is either owned by the package or if the package references the element from another package. In order to be able to reference elements from another package, the client package must have a corresponding dependency to the package which makes the target element accessible. This dependency on package level can either be an import or a generalization dependency.

In the following section we describe the concept of packages in more detail and we show some examples for ambiguous and even contradictive statements concerning the semantics of packages in the UML description. Then, we translate the natural language definition of UML's module concept into predicate logic formulas which give precise answers to the problems raised before.

In Schürr and Winter (1997a) we have already presented formulas for UML 1.0 very briefly. In this paper we deal with UML 1.1 and motivate our reservation with respect to UML semantics with some examples. Finally, we transform the formulas into a formal specification based on graph rewriting systems. The PROGRES specification language, environment and prototyping machinery (cf. Schürr et al. (1995)) allows to generate a graphical UML (class diagram) editor from the specification which "recognizes" inconsistent diagrams to some degree.

2 Informal Description and Problems

The UML package concept offers an information hiding concept which was heavily influenced by the design of C++ (cf. Ellis and Stroustrup (1994)). There may be relationships between elements contained in the same package, but not a priori between an element in one package and an element outside the package. All elements inside a package are featured with a visibility value from the ordered set $\{\text{public} > \text{protected} > \text{private}\}$[1].

There are two ways of making elements outside a package available inside the package:

- Explicit *import* relationships have to be used to access public elements of one package within another package,
- *Refinement* (generalization) relationships provide additional access to protected elements.

[1]Please note that both, the friend relationship and the implementation visibility introduced in version 1.0 of UML, do not belong to the core concepts in UML 1.1 anymore.

Furthermore, UML allows nesting of packages. This concept is rather similar to nested scopes in programming languages à la Modula-2 or Ada.

All concepts are essentially defined in natural language. Although the semantic description for UML 1.1 is accompanied by the UML meta model and Object Constraint Language expressions, there are still many statements which lack the precise definition. We will now sketch our main problems with UML's module concept together with some examples.

In some cases the introduced terms are described in an ambiguous way. This makes it sometimes really difficult to determine their precise semantics. Consider, for instance, a sentence like

> *"Elements made available to another package by the use of generalization ... have the same visibility in the heir as they have in the owning package."*

on page 135[2]. This statement appears to be rather clear on the first sight. But even small examples raise questions which are hardly answered by sentences like this.

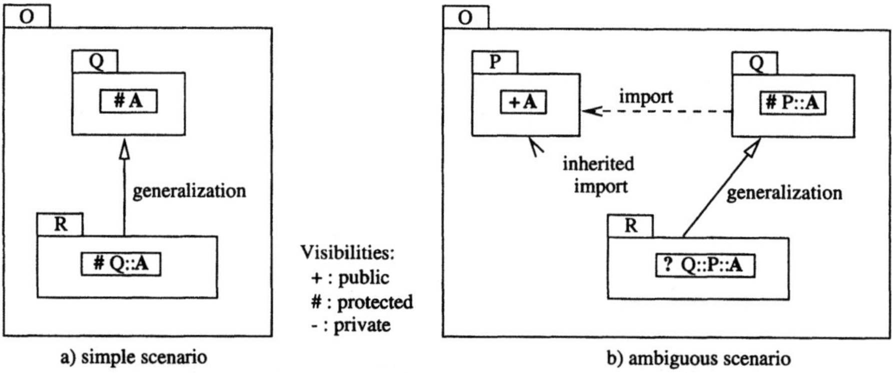

Figure 1: Problem with ambiguous UML semantics.

On the left side of Figure 1 we have depicted a situation, where a package R uses the element A, e.g. a class, made available by generalization from package Q. In UML Q is called the *owner* of A, whereas R *references* A. Local references of elements are used to avoid package crossing dependencies to elements located in different packages whenever an element is used in a new context, e.g. to establish a new association to a class defined somewhere else. References carry the path (of packages) to the their source which is Q::A for the reference A in R. All elements must be owned by exactly one package[3]. The package O serves this purpose for Q and R. Note that every element is featured with a visibility attribute. In diagrams

[2]Page numbers refer to Rational (1997).

[3]Obviously the toplevel package in the model is an exception from this rule.

the feasible visibility values are represented by single characters ('+' for public, '#' for protected, and '-' for private visibility). If not present, visibilities default to *public*; this is also true for dependencies.

Taking the scenario in Figure 1a alone, the sentence above states that the visibility of reference A in package R should be the same as in Q which is protected.

In 1b) the situation is slightly more complex. Here, Q is not the owner of the element A. It is imported from another package P. Package P owns the element A with public visibility. The reference in Q has restricted the visibility of A to protected.

Read the sentence above once more with the new situation in mind. Now, it is not clear which visibility is feasible for the reference A in R (expressed by the question mark). In the example on the left side we were quite convinced that it makes sense to give the visibility in the heir the same value as in the target of the generalization dependency. But, in this case, we have to take into account that the target of the generalization dependency and the owner of the regarded element are not the same package. Taking the sentence above literally, we would have to decide that the visibility of A in R has to be the same as in its owning package P, which is public.

In order to solve this problem, it would be necessary to distinguish that a package does not only make available its own elements by generalization, but also imported elements from other packages.

Until now, we have not even considered the fact that dependencies between packages are also elements and, therefore, carry a visibility attribute themselves. For showing the ambiguity in the UML semantics we did not exploit this feature, yet.

In Figure 2 we almost have the same situation compared to Figure 1a. According to the previous discussion, we would expect the visibility of the reference A in package R to inherit the visibility property from package Q. In this case Q is both, provider of its elements for heir R and, at the same time, owner of these elements. Therefore, we do not have the problem mentioned above.

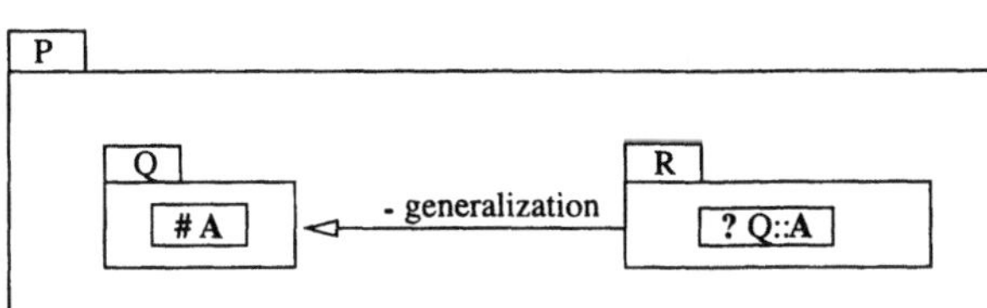

Figure 2: Contradicting UML semantics.

The difference of the two Figures 1a and 2 is the visibility attribute of the generalization dependency itself. Import and generalization relationships between packages are indirect subclasses of the UML top-level class Element and inherit its property to possess a visibility attribute. We have changed its value from the default public to private. The purpose is to hide the generalization for the outside world. We did not find a single line that explains the consequences of dependency visibilities for connected packages, although the usage of import and generalization relationships with varying visibility values makes sense from the software engineering point of view.

Concerning visibility, a look at page 142 of the UML semantics description revealed the following statement about the issue of private generalization giving us a new source of confusion.

> *"Private inheritance (generalization) ... hides the inherited features of a class (package) ...."*

Although this statement is made for classes, statements concerning generalization should hold for both, classes and packages. Obviously this sentence forces elements which are made available by a private generalization to be visible at the same level as the generalization itself. This means that, whenever the dependency is private and, therefore, not at all visible to the outside world, the elements made available by the generalization should also be hidden. Nevertheless, both citations from the UML semantics report contradict each other in an obvious way.

We have found even more contradictions in the semantics description of UML and we are sure that some more lurk in its over 150 pages. Some of them are obvious remainders of former versions and some of them are not really critical. But, anyway, the aim of a semantics description document should be to make things more precise, not to spread confusion among its readers.

Moreover, we were not able to find some strictly necessary constraints like "*a client A of another (imported/referenced) package B should not add (own) an import relationship from B to another package C*". They are either too obvious to be part of the UML semantics definition itself or carefully hidden in one of its paragraphs.

Consequently, we introduce predicate logic formulas explained in the following which are our attempt to give precise answers to problems outlined above. Furthermore, we suggest five additional formulas that address still missing restrictions.

Within all these formulas we use the following (all-quantified) variables which correspond directly to the UML semantics description:

$$
\begin{aligned}
P, P', P'' &\in \textsf{Package is\_a Element}, E \in \textsf{Element} \\
\textsf{dep} &\in \{\textsf{imports}, \textsf{generalizes}\} \\
\omega, \omega', \omega'' &\in \{\textsf{public} > \textsf{protected} > \textsf{private}\}
\end{aligned}
$$

3 Aggregation of Elements and Packages

Any UML document contains a number of top-level packages which represent the regarded system model. Each package defines a visibility shell around a number of elements, which are either

(a) basic constructs of a certain type of diagrams or

(b) nested packages or

(c) dependencies between nested packages.

A package A contains an element E, if it owns or references (uses) E, which belongs to another package B. In the latter case, where A references E, E must be visible inside A. Depending on the relationship of A and B on package level, A can "see" elements in B. An import relationship from A to B reveals the public elements in B. A generalization makes available the protected elements from B in A in addition to the public elements. This situation is captured by the following five predicate logic formulas. The interactions between visibility of elements and (explicit) import relationships as well as generalization are the subject of sections 4 and 5, respectively.

We do hope that almost all of them are self-explanatory as soon as the role of ω variable is clear. Terms like

$$P \text{ owns } \omega\ E \text{ or } P \text{ references } \omega\ E \text{ or } P \text{ contains } \omega\ E \text{ or } \ldots$$

have to be interpreted as "Package P owns/references/contains/... the element E with the visibility $\omega \in \{\text{public} > \text{protected} > \text{private}\}$".

(1) The owner of any element is unique:

$$P \text{ owns } \omega\ E \ \wedge\ P' \text{ owns } \omega'\ E \Rightarrow P = P' \ \wedge\ \omega\ =\ \omega'$$

(2) Elements (from other packages) may be referenced if visible. The visibility of the reference may be restricted:

$$P \text{ references } \omega\ E \Rightarrow P \text{ sees } \omega'\ E \ \wedge\ \omega\ <\ \omega'$$

(3) The contains relationship comprises owns and reference relationship:

$$P \text{ contains } \omega\ E :\Leftrightarrow P \text{ owns } \omega\ E \ \vee\ P \text{ references } \omega\ E$$

(4) The offers relationship is the transitive closure of contains relationship:

$$\begin{aligned} P \text{ offers } \omega\ E \quad :\Leftrightarrow \quad & P \text{ contains } \omega\ E\ \vee \\ & \exists P' : P \text{ contains } \omega\ P' \ \wedge\ P' \text{ offers public } E \end{aligned}$$

(5a) Visibility of elements (of nested packages) is determined as follows:

$$P \text{ sees } \omega\ E :\Leftrightarrow P \text{ offers } \omega\ E \ldots$$

The first two formulas establish requirements on the concepts of *owns*, *references* concerning the correctness of UML diagrams. Furthermore, the new terms *contains*, *offers*, and *sees* are introduced in order to keep the formulas as simple as possible. Please note that formula (2) uses the definition of (5a) which only considers visibility of nested package elements. We will extend the rather complex definition of the sees relationship step by step. Note that these extension have again impact on the validity of references in formula (2). This makes it necessary to take all formulas into consideration.

The most important consequence of the definitions above is that a package sees all public elements of contained packages with the visibility of the containership itself. This is also true for packages which are transitively nested. Elements which are contained within several layers of nested packages can also be offered to the outside world as long as the element is made available to the top-level package as public element.

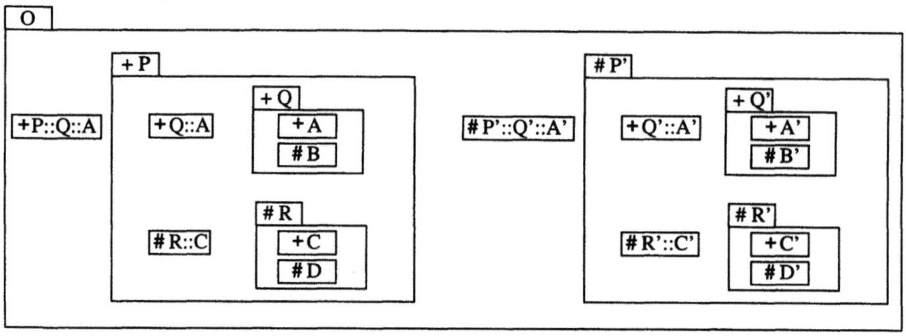

Figure 3: Visibility in nested package.

In Figure 3 package O contains two packages P and P'. P has public visibility, the visibility of P' is protected. P (P') contains two packages Q and R (Q' and R'). The visibility of Q and Q' (R and R') is public (protected). Each of the packages Q, Q', R, and R' contain two elements, one of which is public, the other one is protected. In this example we can observe how elements of different visibilities propagate upward through nesting levels. The main rule is that only public elements are visible one package level higher. The (new) visibility of the referenced element can be restricted by the package itself. Here, e.g. the protected element B in package Q is not visible for P. But element C is of course visible for P, even though the reference R::C is restricted by the visibility of R, which is protected. Eventually, from all elements A-E and A'-E' only A and A' are visible in O. Note the different visibilities of the elements which have impact, either for the owner of O or an importing client, which will only see public elements in O.

Technically, the requirement of Q::A being public in P, in order to be visible from O, is due to the fact that nesting establishes an *implicit import* of the nested packages. We will consider the explicit import relationship between packages in detail in the next section.

4 Export/Import of Packages

We have seen that nesting of packages gives surrounding packages access to the public elements of enclosed packages. Therefore, UML states that nesting establishes a kind of implicit import. Using implicit imports only, a package would never be able to reference elements at the (public) interface of sibling packages. Therefore, UML introduced the concept of explicit import as a dependency relationship between packages that belongs to the common surrounding package of the related client (source) and server (target) package.

These import dependencies even have their own visibility attributes. A *public import*, on one hand, represents a kind of interface import, which is visible for all clients of the surrounding package. A *private import*, on the other hand, is an always hidden import, representing local analysis or design decisions.

The following four formulas are our attempt to formalize imports and exports of packages. Please note that packages do not have any means to define sets of *exported elements*, explicitly. Their public/protected exports are always implicitly determined by their sets of public/protected visible elements. As a consequence, packages do not only export own elements, but also referenced elements from other packages. This takes from client packages the cumbersome burden to import all those elements of other packages which are used in the interfaces of already imported packages.

(6a) Implicit import exists to nested packages and to transitively imported packages (will be extended in the following section):

$$P \text{ imp\_imports } \omega\ P' :\Leftrightarrow P \text{ contains } \omega\ P' \lor \exists P'' : (P \text{ contains } \omega\ P'' \lor P \text{ exp\_imports } \omega\ P'') \land P'' \text{ imports } \omega\ P'$$

(7) Import is the union of the explicit package import dependency and implicit import):

$$P \text{ imports } \omega\ P' :\Leftrightarrow \text{exp\_imports } \omega\ P' \lor P \text{ imp\_imports } \omega\ P'$$

(8) Export is set of all offered nonprivate elements:

$$P \text{ exports } \omega\ E :\Leftrightarrow P \text{ offers } \omega\ E \land \omega > \text{private}$$

(5b) Visibility of elements across packages is extended as follows:

$$P \text{ sees } \omega\ E \;:\Leftrightarrow\; P \text{ offers } \omega\ E \lor (\exists P' : P \text{ exp\_imports } \omega\ P' \land P' \text{ exports public } E)$$

We distinguish explicit import between packages and implicit import. The former is defined in UML whereas the latter needs more explanation. The implicit import comprises both, nested packages contained in a package together with their public contents, and the public contents of explicitly imported packages. Note that we used "contained in a package" and not only "owned in a packages". That means that packages themselves—being elements anyway—can be referenced in other packages. Figure 4 gives an example of some packages showing all implicit imports resulting from the nesting structure and two explicit imports.

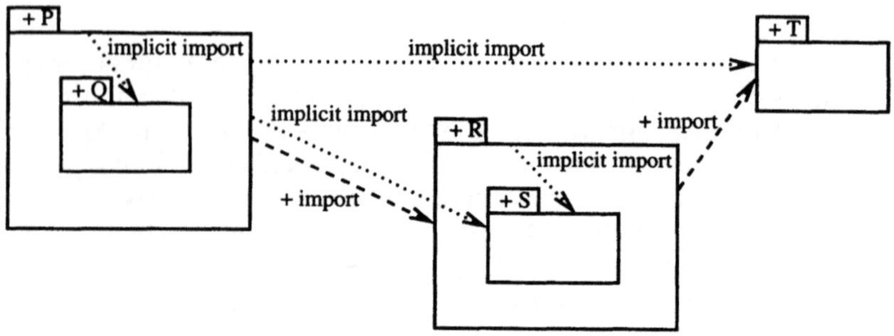

Figure 4: Explicit and implicit imports.

5 Refinement of Packages

The previous two sections introduced the "classical" modularization concepts of programming languages like Modula-2 (as defined in the ISO/IEC 10514-1 standard by Schoenhacker and Pronk (1996)), i.e. the construction of export interfaces for packages (with varying degrees of visibility inherited from C++), nesting of (local) packages, and the establishment of visible or hidden import relationships between packages. These import relationships permit access to public interface elements of server packages, only. The remaining visibility value (for interface elements)—protected—is only useful in combination with refinement (generalization) relationships between packages. The concept of refining/generalizing packages will be explained here.

Note that we give preference to the term *refinement* over *generalization* which is used in UML, because it expresses directly the relationship that we are interested in and—in most cases—helps to simplify the formulas. That means, that whenever the package P is source of a generalization dependency to package Q, P *refines* Q. The main motivation for introducing the refinement relationship between packages is that the important OO concept of inheritance should not only be available for defining single classes, the basic elements of static structure diagrams, but also for defining and refining arbitrarily complex subdiagrams.

(9) Refines* relationship is transitive closure of refinement relationship:

$$P \text{ refines* } P' :\Leftrightarrow \\ \exists P'', \omega : P \text{ refines } \omega \; P'' \wedge (P'' = P' \vee P'' \text{ refines* } P')$$

(10) Refinement relationship is acyclic:

$$\neg(P \text{ refines* } P)$$

(11) Public export of refining package has refined package's export:

$$P \text{ refines public } P' \wedge P' \text{ exports public } E \Rightarrow P \text{ exports public } E$$

(5c) Visibility across package boundaries is extended as follows:

$$\begin{aligned}&P \text{ sees } \omega\, E :\Leftrightarrow P \text{ offers } \omega\, E \vee \\ &\quad (\exists P' : P \text{ exp\_imports } \omega\, P' \wedge P' \text{ exports public } E) \vee \\ &\quad (\exists P', \omega', \omega'' \geq \text{ protected } : P \text{ refines } \omega'\, P' \wedge P' \text{ exports } \omega''\, E \\ &\qquad\qquad \wedge\, \omega = \min(\omega', \omega''))\end{aligned}$$

(6b) Implicit import is extended along the generalization relationship:

$$\begin{aligned}&P \text{ imp\_imports } \omega\, P' :\Leftrightarrow P \text{ contains } \omega\, P' \vee \\ &\quad \exists\, P'' : (P \text{ contains } \omega\, P'' \vee P \text{ exp\_imports } \omega\, P'' \vee P \text{ refines } \omega\, P'') \\ &\qquad \wedge\, P'' \text{ imports } \omega\, P'\end{aligned}$$

Please note that formulas (5c) and (6b) above are just an extension of formulas (5b) and (6a) of the previous section, resp. For visibility refinement relationships with different degrees of visibility are taken into account, ranging from a kind of public subtype inheritance to pure implementation inheritance. That means, that a refining package sees all public elements of the refined package as public elements (if the refinement relationship is public, too). Furthermore, a refining package sees all protected elements of the refined package as $\omega \geq$ protected visible elements (if the refinement relationship is ω visible, too). It is an open question, whether it makes sense to have three different visibility cases for refinement relationships, instead of the usual distinction between interface preserving subtype inheritance and the hidden inheritance of implementations.

It is not at all difficult to come up with a precise definition of the consequences of refinement (generalization) relationships for the visibility of package elements as well as with a formal definition of the constraint "generalization relationships do not build cycles". It is far more difficult to translate the meaning of sentences like "... an instance of the subtype is substitutable for an instance of the supertype". The latter constraint cannot be defined for packages in general, but must be studied for each language of UML diagrams, separately. Such a precise definition of the term "substitutability" is not part of UML. Therefore, our formulas will only take the consequences of public refinement relationships for the visibility of (public) interface elements of related packages into account. For further details concerning the formal treatment of subtyping from an algebraic point of view the reader is referred to Breu (1991) and from a type-theoretic point of view to Palsberg and Schwartzbach (1994). It is an open question whether similar constraints have to be added for the case of non-public refinement relationships and interface elements.

6 Further Consistency Constraints

The developed formal definition of the basic UML package concept shows that on one hand, the original natural language definition seems to contain some contradictions, and, on the other hand, is not at all complete. As a consequence, we add a number of own assumptions, without knowing (until now) whether these add-ons respect the original intentions of the three amigos Booch, Jacobson, and Rumbaugh. These add-ons were kept as minimal as possible within the previous sections, thereby postponing the definition of a number of important additional constraints to this section. All these constraints, which will presented below, are—in our opinion—not a matter of debate, but should be part of UML. It is for instance useless to see a dependency without seeing its source or target package (13). Furthermore, a package should never be able to define additional server packages or generalizing packages for not locally defined packages (14). Otherwise, it would be possible to extend and modify the implementation of imported packages, thereby violating the very principle of information hiding. Last but not least it makes no sense that a package refines one of its locally defined packages (15) or that a package which is a generalization depends on one of its refining packages (16, 17).

(13) Visibility of import/refines dependency is less equal visibility of related packages:

$$P \text{ dep } \omega\ P' \Rightarrow \exists P'', \omega', \omega'' : P'' \text{ owns } \omega \text{ dep} \wedge \\ P'' \text{ offers } \omega'\ P \wedge P'' \text{ offers } \omega''\ P' \ \wedge\ \omega\ \leq\ \min(\omega', \omega'')$$

(14) Source of import/refines dependency belongs to owner of dependency:

$$P \text{ dep } \omega\ P' \Rightarrow P'', \omega' : P'' \text{ owns } \omega \text{ dep } \ \wedge\ P'' \text{ owns } \omega'\ P$$

(15) A package should neither import nor refine its offered (own) packages:

$$P \text{ dep } \omega\ P' \Rightarrow \neg\exists\, \omega' : P \text{ offers } \omega'\ P'$$

(16) DependsOn relationship is transitive closure of imports and refines:

$$P \text{ dependsOn } P' :\Leftrightarrow \quad \exists P'', \omega : \quad (P \text{ refines } \omega\ P'' \ \vee\ P \text{ imports } \omega\ P'') \\ \wedge\, (P'' = P' \ \vee\ P'' \text{ dependsOn } P')$$

(17) Package may not refine a package which is an (in-)direct client of itself:

$$P \text{ refines } P' \Rightarrow \neg(P' \text{ dependsOn } P)$$

7 Generating UML Diagram Editors

The last sections have been dedicated to giving the UML package concept a precise semantics. Why did we bother with predicate logic formulas, as one of the pros of UML is the intuitive clearness of diagrams? In fact, playing around with packages and the visibility of their elements raised many questions. It was a tedious task to find the relevant pages in Rational (1997) and many details remained unanswered.

This was our motivation to suggest predicate logic formulas. They reflect parts of the static semantics of the UML package concept given by meta model, OCL expressions, and natural language description. In order to study the rules concerning packages and visibility in more detail for different diagrams and situations, we wanted to "play" with the formulas and their effects on the diagrams. For that purpose we have translated the formulas into a *PROgrammed Graph REwriting Systems specification*.

The PROGRES language is a logic-based executable specification language (Schürr et al. (1995)). It not only permits to model the static structure of graphs with a *graph schema* very similar to the UML meta model, but furthermore, allows to describe *transformations* on these graphs with declarative graph rewrite rules. The specifications can be executed either with an interpreter, which is an integral part of the PROGRES environment, or by generating C code from the specification, which can compiled and linked together with a Tcl/Tk user interface. While the former is very useful for debugging a specification, the latter establishes a tool for working with the specification interactively.

For the UML specification the generated tool can be considered as a *UML editor* which allows the user to call typical diagram editing operations like, for instance, AddPackage or AddGeneralization. These operations have been specified in PROGRES and perform transformations on the underlying internal graph structure ensuring the consistency according to the given graph schema (meta model). This means, the actually executed graph transformations are written in a way to respect the formulas introduced above. In Figure 5 we present the PROGRES environment showing the so-called *production AddGeneralization* that inserts a new generalization dependency between two packages.

A PROGRES production consists essentially of its left hand side and its right hand side. Its operational semantics is, that a match for the graph in the left side is searched in the underlying working graph. If a matching subgraph can be found, it is replaced by the right hand side of the rule. Nodes and edges which are present on the left hand side, but not on the right are deleted, whereas elements of the right side not appearing on the left are newly created. It is also possible to identically replace nodes which are identified on the left and right side. That means, the nodes are not actually deleted and reinserted, but they are retained during the application of the rule.

The example in Figure 5 shows the production AddGeneralization. It takes two nodes as input parameters Src, Trg which are of type Package. The intention is, to establish a new generalization dependency from the package Src to the package Trg. Here, we demand that both packages are contained in a common package '3. Furthermore, according to rule (17) we require that the target of the generalization does not depend on the package which is about to become its refinement in this rule. This fact is expressed by the crossed dependsOn path. This path itself is a derived graph navigation defined in the sense of rule (16).

During the execution of the rule, the three package nodes of the left side are retained (e.g. 1' = '1) and the new Generalization dependency (node 4') is inserted

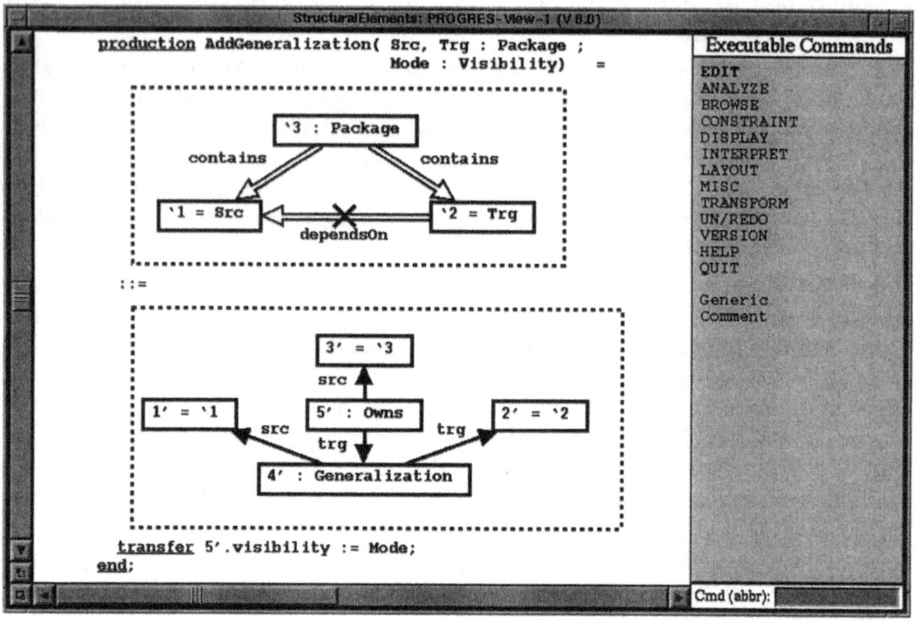

Figure 5: PROGRES production adding a generalization dependency.

and attached to its source and target. The generalization will get a visibility attribute (transfer part) which has also been passed as parameter Mode. The Owns node (5') which is also created, denotes the ElementOwnership of UML's meta model. In this case, the package which contained the source and the target package of the new dependency will also be its owner.

We have seen in this example production, in which way the formulas of this paper can influence the PROGRES specification. Here, we would reject the execution of the production if no match for the left side of the rule can be found. But this is not an adequate reaction for all the rules suggested above. For example, if a user wants to use an element from another package if the required import dependency is missing (formula (5a-c)), it is not necessary to reject the operation. Instead, we have realized this error situation with the help of an error message attribute in the used element itself. This means, that the operation is executed and an error message requests the diagram modeler to add the missing import in order to get a consistent diagram.

In Figure 6 we present a view of a UML diagram within a generated UML editor which also reveals internal dependencies, e.g. ElementOwnership, explicitly, in order to explain the situation sketched above. This is of course not the normal editor view. Normally, the user of the editor would only see the UML diagram with the elements that he has inserted, not the internal dependencies. Nevertheless, the view shown here is especially useful for debugging sessions.

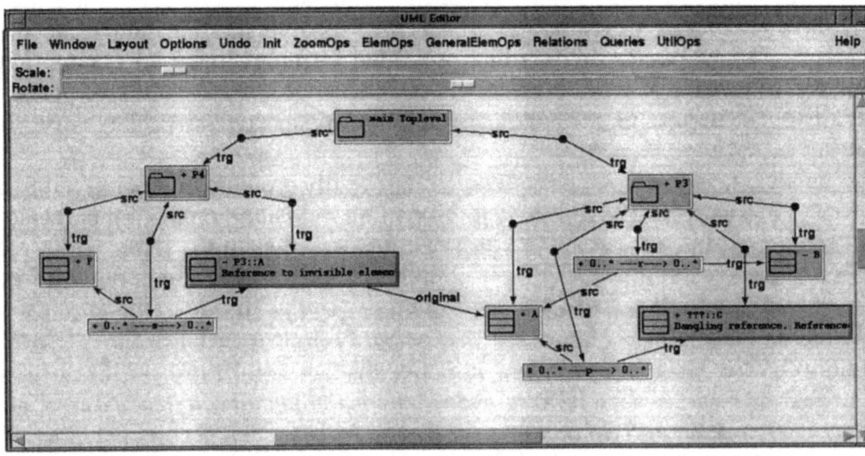

Figure 6: Session with the PROGRES generated UML editor.

In this screen shot of the generated UML editor, we have three packages, two of them, namely P3 and P4, are contained in package main. Package P3 contains a class element A which is also used in package P4. But, the reference P3::A in P4 does not "see" its origin anymore, e.g. due to the deletion of the import dependency from P4 to P3. We could have forbidden the deletion because of the resulting inconsistency. But, instead, the reference node carries an error message attribute saying *"Reference to invisible element"* which demands to add the missing import in order to re-establish a consistent UML diagram.

8 Summary

This paper presented a very compact definition of the UML notation's modularization concept and suggested a number of useful extensions. These extensions compensate the obviously incompleteness of UML's natural language definition in Rational (1997) or represent additional policies for the definition of import and refinement relationships between packages. Furthermore, we gave a very short impression of translating predicate logic formulas into a PROGRES specification which allows to generate an editor automatically, corresponding to the semantics given in the formulas. On one hand, this is very useful, if further formulas are developed. In that case the new editor is able to check the constructed diagrams against the new formulas. On the other hand, experiences with the editor can give valuable information about constellations which have not been considered adequately in the formulas to this moment.

To summarize, neither UML's module concept itself nor the considerations presented here concerning its formal definition and necessary modifications are restricted to a single object-oriented analysis and design method. On the contrary, the presented module concept may be added to other analysis, design, or specification languages or it may even build the basis for a separate module interconnection language. This is due to the fact that presented formulas make no assumptions about the semantics of basic elements in packages. It is their exclusive purpose to explain the impact of packages and relationships between packages on the visibility of package elements.

As a consequence, this paper complements the rapidly growing number of publications which have either the formal definition of module interconnection languages (architecture styles) or certain OO diagram types as their main topic. Both categories of papers assume either very simple visibility rules (compared with the visibility rules introduced here) or neglect this aspect at all due to the absence of a module concept. Examples of the first category are for instance the VDM-SL definition of the Modula-2 standard in Schoenhacker and Pronk (1996) or the Z definitions of various data flow or event based architecture styles (Abowd and Garlan (1995), Rice and Seidman (1994)). Examples of the second category are formal definitions of (subsets of) OMT (Jonckers et al. (1996)) and Fusion (Bates et al. (1996)).

References

ABOWD, G. and GARLAN, D. (1995): Formalizing Style to Understand Descriptions of Software Architecture. *ACM Transactions on Software Engineering and Methodology, 4(4), 319-364.*

BATES, B., BRUEL, J., FRANCE, R., and LARRONDO-PETRIE, M. (1996): Guidelines for Formalizing Fusion Object-Oriented Analysis Models. In *Proc. CAiSE'96*, LNCS 1080, Springer Verlag, Berlin, 222-233.

BOOCH, G. (1994): Object-Oriented Analysis and Design. Benjamin Cummings Series in Object-Oriented Software Engineering. Benjamin Cummings, Redwood City, CA.

BÖRSTLER, J. (1994): Programming-in-the-Large: Languages, Tools, Reusability. Dissertation (RWTH Aachen), TR UMINF 94.10, Department of Computer Science, Umeå University, Sweden (in German).

BREU, R. (1991): Algebraic Specification Techniques in Object-Oriented Programming Environments. LNCS 562, Springer Verlag, Berlin.

DEREMER, F. and KRON, H. (1976): Programming-in-the-large versus Programming-in-the-small. *IEEE Transactions on Software Engineering, 2(2), 80-86.*

ELLIS, M. and STROUSTRUP, B. (1994): The Annotated C++ Reference Manual. Addison-Wesley, Reading, MA.

FIRESMITH, D.G. (1993): Object-Oriented Requirements Analysis and Logical Design: A Software Engineering Approach. John Wiley, New York.

JACOBSON, I. (1994): Object-Oriented Software Engineering: A Use Case Driven Approach. Addison-Wesley, Reading, MA, fourth edition.

JONCKERS, V., VERSCHAEVE, K., WYDAEGHE, B., CUYPERS, L., and HEIRBAUT, J. (1996): OMT*, Bridging the Gap between Analysis and Design. In *Proc. FORTE '95*. Chapman & Hall, 39-55.

NAGL, M. (1990): Software Engineering: Methodological Programming-in-the-Large. Springer Verlag (in German).

PALSBERG, J. and SCHWARTZBACH, M. (1994): Object-Oriented Type Systems. John Wiley, New York.

PARNAS, D. (1972): A Technique for Software Module Specifications with Examples. *Communications of the ACM, 15, 330-336.*

RATIONAL ROSE SOFTWARE CORPORATION (1997): UML Semantics, Version 1.1, September 1, URL:http://www.rational.com

RICE, M. and SEIDMAN, S. (1994): A Formal Model for Module Interconnection Languages. *IEEE Transactions on Software Engineering, 20(1), 88-101.*

ROBINSON, P.J. (1992): Hierarchical Object-Oriented Design. Prentice Hall, Englewood Cliffs, MA.

RUMBAUGH, J., BLAHA, M., EDDY, W., and LORENSEN, W. (1991): Object-Oriented Modeling and Design. Prentice Hall, Englewood Cliffs, NJ.

SCHOENHACKER, M. and PRONK, C. (1996): ISO/IEC 10514-1, The Modula-2 standard: Changes, Clarifications, and Additions. *ACM SIPGPLAN notices, 31(8), 84-95.*

SCHÜRR, A. (1996): Logic Based Programmed Structure Rewriting Systems. *Fundamenta Informaticae, XXVI(3/4).*

SCHÜRR, A. and WINTER, A. (1997a): Formal Definition and Refinement of UML's Module/Package Concept. In Kilov H., Rumpe B. (eds.): Proc. ECOOP '97 Workshop on Precise Semantics for Object-Oriented Modeling Techniques, TR TUM-I9725, Technical University Munich, also to be published in LNCS, Springer Verlag.

SCHÜRR, A. and WINTER, A. (1997b): Modules and Updatable Graph Views for PROgrammed Graph REwriting Systems. Technical Report AIB 97-3, RWTH Aachen, Germany.

SCHÜRR, A., WINTER, A., and ZÜNDORF A. (1995): Graph Grammar Engineering with PROGRES. In Schäfer W., Botella P. (eds.): *Proc. 5th European Software Engineering Conf. (ESEC '95), LNCS 989.* Springer Verlag, Berlin, 219-234.

WIENER, R. and SINCOVEC, R. (1984): Software Engineering with Modula-2 and Ada. John Wiley, New York, NY.

WIRFS-BROCK, R., WILKERSON, B., and WIENER, L. (1990): Designing Object-Oriented Software. Prentice Hall, Englewood Cliffs, NJ.

UMLscript: A Programming Language for Object-Oriented Design

J. Seemann, J. W. von Gudenberg

Lehrstuhl für Programmiersprachen und Programmiermethodik
Universität Würzburg, 97074 Würzburg, Am Hubland
email: {seemann | wolff}@informatik.uni-wuerzburg.de

Abstract: In this paper we describe the UML class diagrams by means of a programming language we call *UMLscript.* This language has the advantage that it presents a concise graphic independent definition of one of the cornerstones of the UML. The language may be used to exchange UML models among different tools and projects. It is suitable as input language for automatic layout algorithms, as output language from reverse engineering tools, as data format for repositories as well as maintenance tools. UMLscript provides a concrete syntax for class structure diagrams. After a short introduction we give an ELL(1) grammar of the language presented as a set of commented, easy to read syntax diagrams. We also point out some flaws or inaccuracies of the original UML language definition.

1 Introduction

1.1 Modeling Diagrams with Grammars

A model of a large software system consists of various parts, the static structure, dynamic aspects, coordination of activities, description of use cases etc.

The UML (Booch et al. (1997)) provides an abstract syntax for the static structure of a model and specifies a concrete graphical notation: the class structure diagrams. These are the fundamental sources for the implementation.

In this paper we present a concrete textual notation for those diagrams by means of an attributed grammar. Classes, packages, templates, and objects as well as their relations like association or inheritance are design items and therefore are represented as attributed non-terminals. They can be organized in a symbol-table-like dictionary. The keys are mainly derived from the corresponding names and visibility scopes. This emphasizes the importance of significant names in a design.

The nodes of the diagram or graph, i. e. classes and packages etc., are denoted like structured data types whereas links or edges are given as triples *(node, binary relation, node)* or $(n+1)$-tuples for higher order relations.

The semantic value of a class is a domain that is obtained by the disjoint sum of all domains given by the attributes, methods or relations of the class. The meaning of an attribute is just the domain of the given type and the meaning of a method is a function from the input domain to the output domain. Since associations may have attributes themselves their domains are registered separately, whereas

inheritance or refinement information is incorporated in the domain of the classes directly.
The semantic value of a package or complete diagram is the sum of all domains of all contained classes and associations.

1.2 Example

The following example shows a small UML model and its representation in UMLscript.

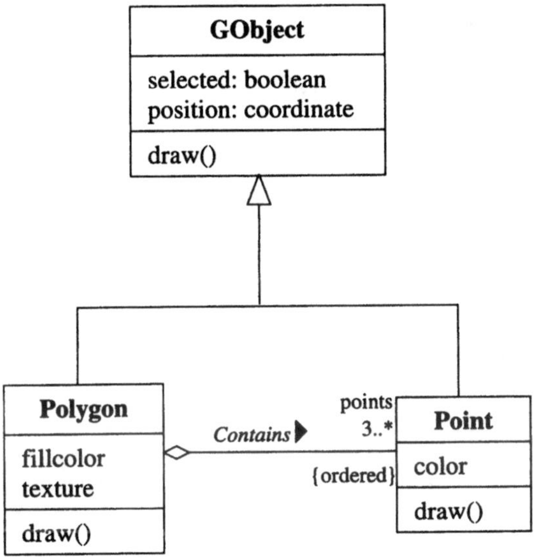

Figure 1: Example

1.3 Applications

The language may be used as

- a textual representation of class structure diagrams.
- an input language for automatic layout algorithms.
- an output language from reverse engineering tools.
- an internal format for repositories.
- an input for conventional text based maintenance tools such as versioning or automatic documentation.
- a data format or protocol to exchange data between various CASE tools or across different systems.

```
DIAGRAM
    CLASS Polygon
        ATTRIBUTES fillcolor, texture
        METHODS draw
        RELATIONS
            ASSOC aggregate ROLE Contains > TO [3..*]
                ROLE points CONSTRAINT ordered
                CLASS Point
                    ATTRIBUTES color
                    METHODS draw
        END
    CLASS GObject
        ATTRIBUTES position: coordinates, selected: boolean
        METHODS draw
        RELATIONS
            GENERALIZE Polygon, Point
        END
END DIAGRAM
```

Figure 2: UMLscript code

2 UMLscript Syntax

2.1 Language Architecture

Since any graph can be defined by the set of its edges and isolated nodes, we represent a diagram as a list of relations and definitions of templates or stereotypes.

UMLscript

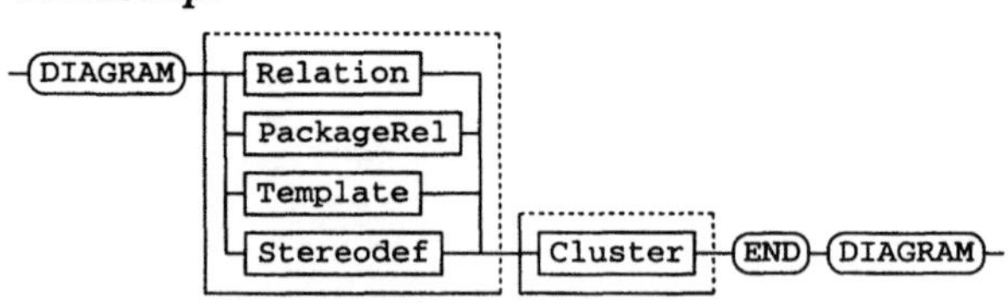

We distinguish between class and package relations. Templates are isolated nodes, since they are not considered as 'first-class citizens' of the design (see below). In this context a package is a named subdiagram defining a nested namespace.

Package

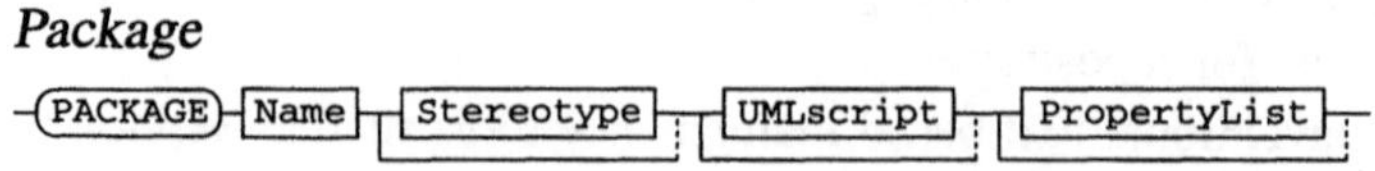

A name is a string beginning with a letter. The name of the surrounding package implicitly belongs to each class name or package name inside the package.

ClassName

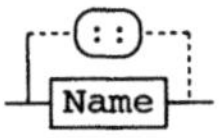

Having this in mind all classnames have to be unique. Sometimes the qualified class name is necessary, e.g. in import dependency relations.

A cluster or collaboration is a loose collection of classes and relations, which groups related parts of the design. Clusters are not an element of the original UML class structure diagram, but they are very useful for applications like the annotation of design patterns in a model.

Cluster

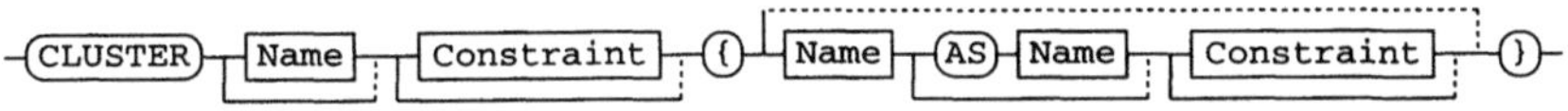

An alias name may be given to each class denoting its role in this specific cluster. A class may belong to several clusters. Clusters need not be disjoint. All relations between the listed classes belong to the cluster by default.

Although part of the UML we do not include instance relations between objects and their corresponding classes, but we separate the instance diagrams completely.

We do not prescribe a strict definition usage order. We allow to use class names without having defined the class, and it is possible to walk through the diagram from class to class via the given relation edges. Hence our graph need not be given as a dull list of single relations although this may be the favorite internal format.

Relation

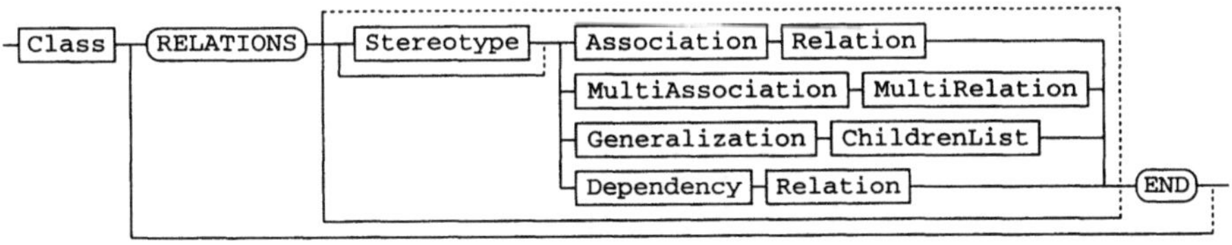

PackageRel

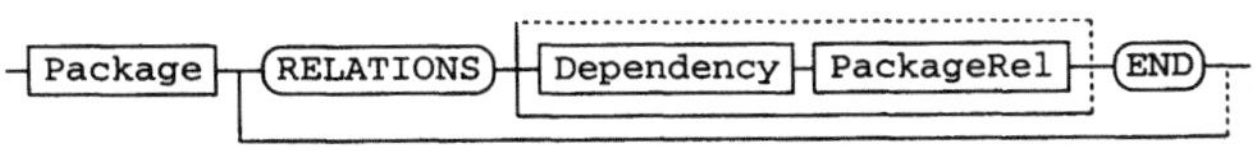

The key to identify a relation includes the name of the relation as well as the names of its two adjacent classes. It has to be unique in its scope.

2.2 Classes and Templates

ClassDef

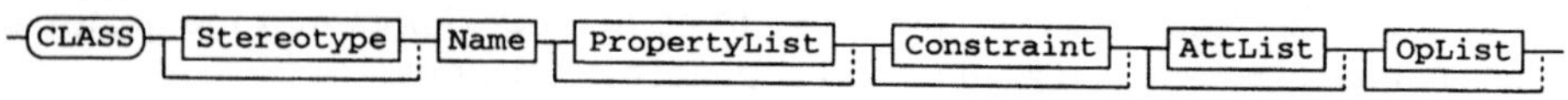

A class definition introduces the new class name and optionally the lists of attributes and operations. Stereotypes are used for further classification and property lists specify additional features (see below). A constraint attached to a class states some conditions that have to be fulfilled by the attributes of an object.

Template

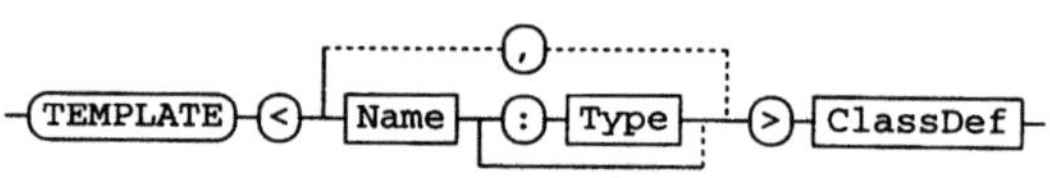

A template is a parameterized class. It cannot be used in an ordinary relationship, cannot be subclassed or associated to other templates. This rule restricts the use of templates in an UML design to the mere fact that a class is instantiated from a template.

In such an instantiation the full name including the actual types or values may be replaced by a more convenient class name.

Class

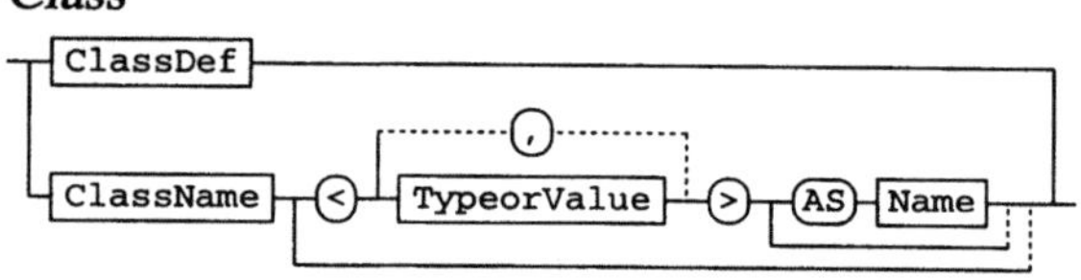

AttList

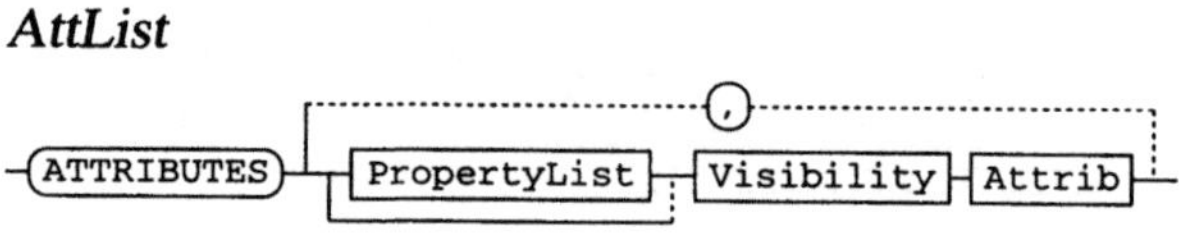

Attrib

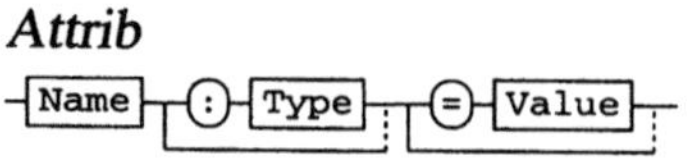

All identifiers of the attributes of a class have to be unique in the namespace which is obtained by joining the namespace of the class with those of its ancestors. A multiplicity constraint (see association) for each attribute is specified via an appropriate type. If default values are given, they have to match the corresponding types. But usually values will be specified when objects are created. Types may be omitted meaning that they are not yet specified. Specific properties inserted in the list are applied to all succeeding attributes.

Type

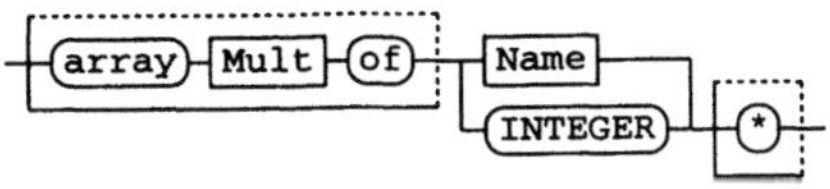

A type represents a domain as a data structure including a specification of multiplicity.

OpList

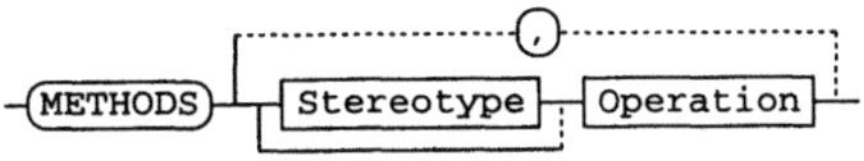

Operation

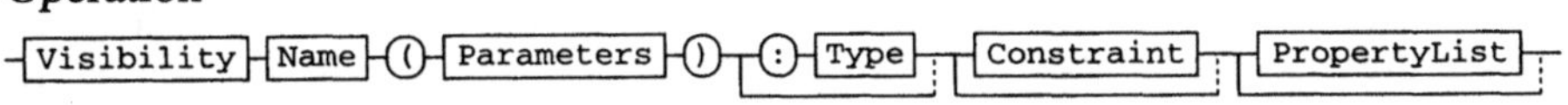

Parameters

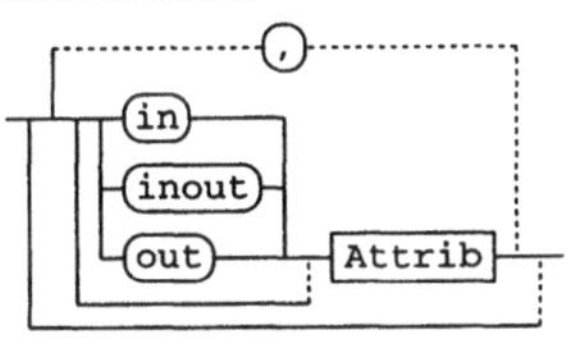

Like an attribute name the name of an operation has to be unique in its namespace. If no result type is specified, the method does not return a result. Parameter types need not be given. The signature of the operation or method is determined by the name, its number and types of parameters. A constraint may give some implementation information.

Further properties of the operation like concurrency information may also be given as constraints.

The interspersed stereotypes that groups methods into categories can invoke the checking of constraints.

Visibility

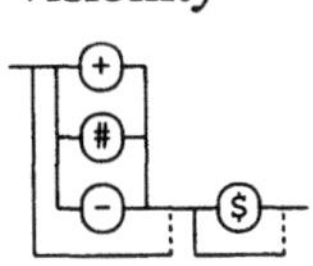

There is public, protected, or private visibility, each one can optionally be valid for class scope.

2.3 Relations

Each relation can be further specified by a stereotype.

2.3.1 Binary Associations

An association relates two classes. It cannot be reused for a second relation.

Association

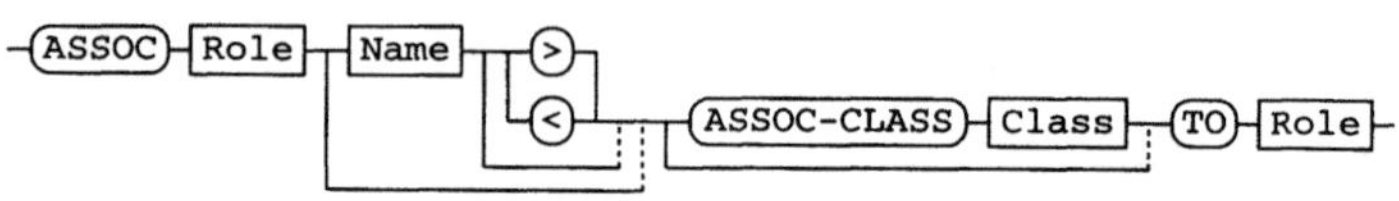

The optional name of the association may be followed by an arrow indicating how to read the name. If the association itself has attributes or methods they are given in the association class. Its name must coincide with the association name, if both are present.
The ends of an association carry the main information about it.

Role

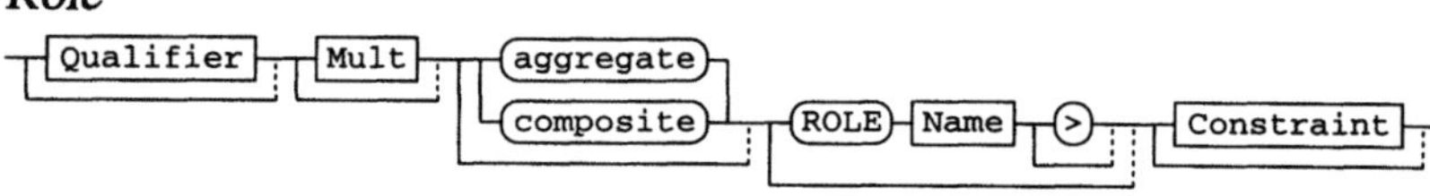

Role names must be specified, if the association is reflexive. The '>' indicates that the edge shall be directed towards this end.
One of the roles of an association can indicate an aggregation by independent components or the composition of unsharable, life-time dependent attributes.
Changeability, ordering or target scope may be specified as constraints. The predefined constraint |or| is noted in the role of the common class.

Mult

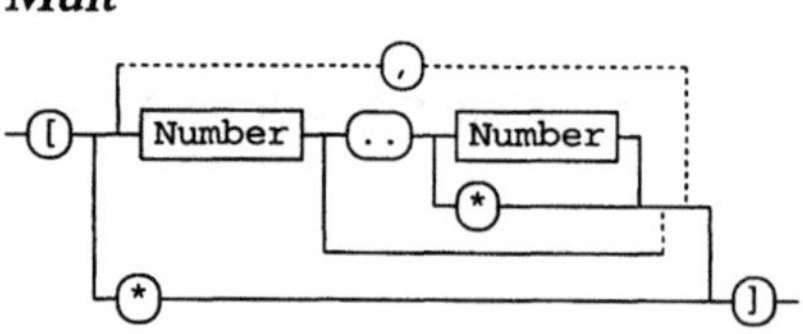

The multiplicity is given as a list of proper intervals with integer endpoints, where an asterisk means arbitrarily many.
Qualifiers reduce the multiplicity. They allow a unique selection of a specific object by using an attribute for the selection.

Qualifier

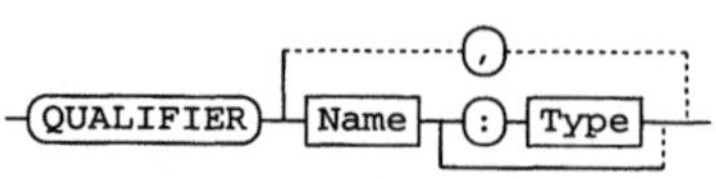

2.3.2 High Order Associations

A ternary or higher order association is to be considered as pairwise $m : n$ relation.

MultiAssociation

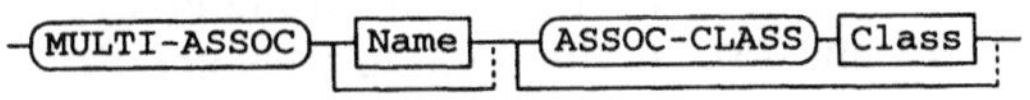

MultiRelation

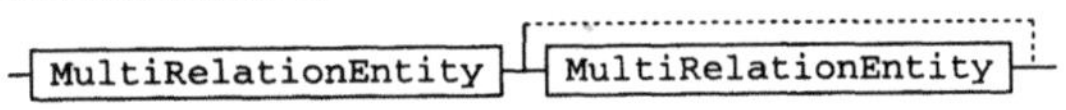

MultiRelationEntity

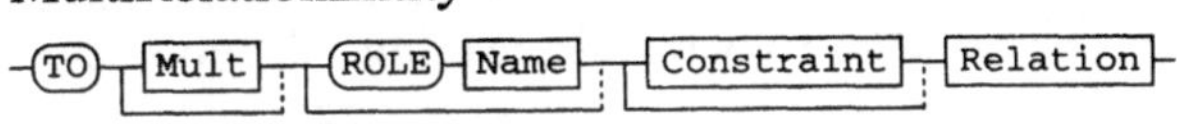

2.3.3 Generalization

Generalization is an inheritance, i. e. subtyping, relationship. There must be no cycles built only from inheritance relations.

Generalization

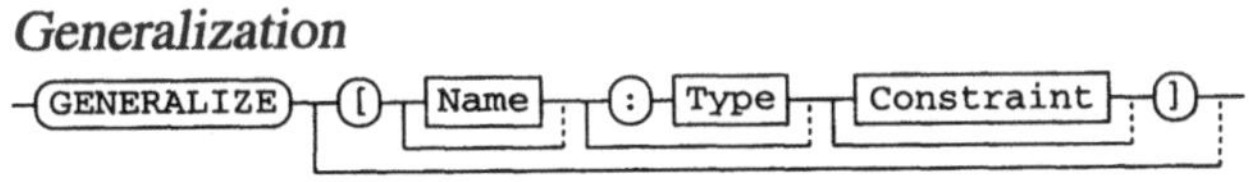

ChildrenList

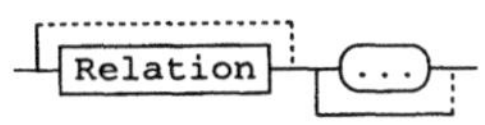

Multiple inheritance is possible, but a re-unification of two branches from one source is only possible, if these are marked with the constraint `overlapping`. The discriminator identifies a partition of the supertype into subtypes.

2.3.4 Dependency

Two or more packages or classes may depend on each other.

Dependency

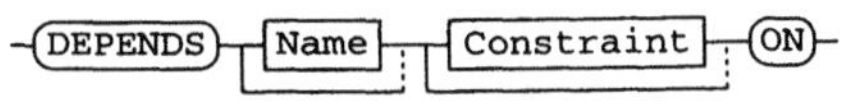

There are predefined stereotypes (see below) for this relation like ≪refine≫, ≪uses≫, ≪trace≫ or ≪bind≫.

2.4 Meaningful Text

2.4.1 Stereotypes

Not all aspects of a design can be anticipated and included in the language as keywords or attributes. Tool dependent and user defined extensions should be possible. The UML provides several such mechanisms which we also use in UMLscript to specify some of the original UML elements.

Stereotype

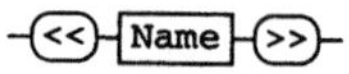

For classes UML provides predefined stereotypes like ≪type≫, ≪interface≫ and ≪implementation class≫. These have semantical meaning. A type corresponds to an interface in Java, or an abstract class. An interface represents parts of a type.
Some of the stereotypes used in a dependency relationship require some matching rules between the partners. A class implementing a type, or a subclass redefining some methods of its superclass must have corresponding signatures.
User defined stereotypes may be declared. They can be attached to a class, a relation, or a constraint.

Stereodef

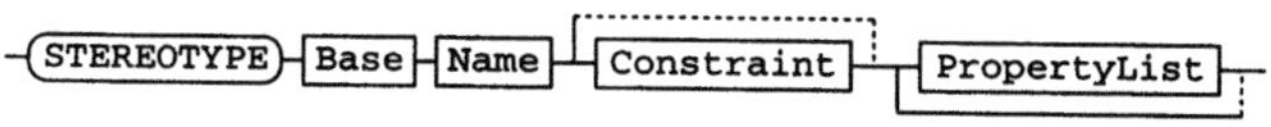

All elements that are marked by a stereotype must provide the tags of the property list and check all the constraints.

2.4.2 Constraints

Constraints can be used for a more detailed specification of the behavior of a class, method, package or relationship.

Constraint

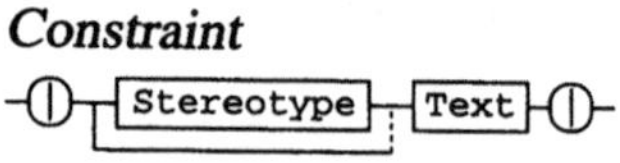

They may be expressed in natural language, as rules or equations in predicate logic or another appropriate language. They determine guidelines or requirements for the implementation of the design element. In UMLscript some attributes or elements of original UML are also given as constraints, e.g. association role is `|ordered|`, method is `|polymorphic|` or class is `|derived|`. Notes may specify a method body or another operation in a tool dependent pseu-

docode or in the implementation language. They are enclosed in quotation marks and can be considered as particular constraints.
Predefined stereotypes characterize constraints for invariants, pre- or postconditions, powertypes or metaclasses.

2.4.3 Property Lists

Each tag represents a property which can be applied to one or more elements. Properties are typically user defined entities that give additional information about an element. `Persistence` is such a standard flag.

PropertyList

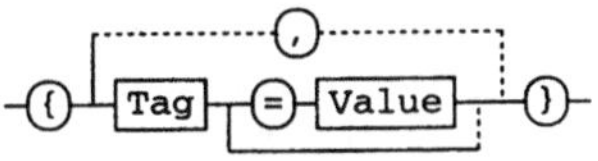

3 Discussion

We think that the UML in general as well as the class structure diagrams in particular are overspecified and contain far too much details.
Visibility and full specification of the parameters of a method is not possible during analysis and not necessary during design, neither is the body of a method. Such hints for implementation should better be annotated in the implementation language the developer uses. That means no new semantics and no new notation has to be introduced and learned.
For the same reason it could be better to formulate constraints in Prolog rather than in the OCL language.
Templates in the way presented in UML are useless. They only serve to illustrate that a class has been instantiated from a template, a simple implementation decision. C++ templates are far more powerful, since they can be used for association, inheritance or dependency.
The extensibility of the language by user defined stereotypes, keywords or property lists is an important and interesting feature of UML, but it has to be used with care.
Packages and collaborations of classes are two different ways to structure the model or highlight interesting parts of a diagram.
We tried to give a concrete syntax for the full language for static structure diagrams in this paper, but for our future work we will certainly neglect some of the constructs and will concentrate on a subset of the UML foundation package.

References

BOOCH, G., RUMBAUGH, J., and JACOBSON, I. (1997): Unified Modeling Language, Version 1.1. Rational Software Corporation, 2800 San Tomas Expressway, Santa Clara, CA 95051-0951 (USA). URL: http://www.rational.com

Ways of Handling and Interpreting Specialization in Object-Oriented Modeling

S. Strahringer

FB 1, FG Wirtschaftsinformatik II,
Darmstadt University of Technology, D-64289 Darmstadt, Germany
e-mail: susanne@bwl.tu-darmstadt.de

Abstract: Specialization is often considered being one of the crucial semantic operators in object-oriented modeling. Yet the ways of handling and interpreting this semantic construct differ highly from method to method. It is not only the lack of a precise definition the user of a method has to cope with, but also an in most cases missing discussion or simple indication of the implied consequences on the process of modeling, the resulting models, and the transformation into an implementation. In this respect even the Unified Modeling Language (UML) must not be considered an exception.

The following paper starts with a comparative look at different object-oriented modeling methods and the suggested ways of handling specialization. The differences can be partially explained by looking at the underlying basic classification approaches. These approaches are discussed with respect to consequences on modeling and implementing and correspondence to implementation technologies. The paper closes with a look at the UML while taking into account the previous results.

1 Ways of Handling Specialization in Different Object-Oriented Modeling Methods

Object-oriented modeling methods highly differ in various respects. Object-oriented modeling, therefore, is a popular topic for comparative studies. The following paper does not give a broad comparative survey but rather focuses on one simple aspect of an object-oriented modeling method: the way of handling specialization. In spite of its importance, this aspect is often not discussed with the necessary level of detail. Thus one often misses an awareness for the resulting consequences on the process of modeling and implementing. Before looking at the UML as a special case, other object-oriented modeling methods are discussed comparatively. The methods compared are:

- **OOA:** Coad and Yourdon (1991),
- **OMT:** Rumbaugh et al. (1991),
- **OSA:** Embley et al. (1992),
- **OOAD:** Martin and Odell (1992),
- **OOSA:** Shlaer and Mellor (1988), Shlaer and Mellor (1992).

The comparative analysis is a result of a metamodel-based comparison of the mentioned methods in Strahringer (1996). Table 1 summarizes the comparison results by showing different types of specialization and for each of the methods, whether it allows the use of such a form of specialization or not. The considered types of specialization are: multiple, overlapping and incomplete specialization, and multiple generalization (multiple inheritance).

	OOA	OMT	OSA	OOAD	OOSA
multiple specialization	not allowed	allowed	allowed	allowed	not allowed
overlapping specialization	not allowed	allowed	allowed	not allowed	not allowed
incomplete specialization	allowed	allowed	allowed	allowed	not allowed
multiple generalization	allowed	allowed	allowed	allowed	allowed
dynamic classification	not allowed	not allowed	allowed	allowed	allowed

Table 1: Types of specialization and their support in object-oriented modeling methods

Multiple specialization denotes that a class may be specialized on the basis of different independent criteria (discriminators) by creating groups of subclasses where each group represents an orthogonal dimension of specialization of the considered superclass. The association between the superclass and a set of subclasses which are derived according to the same criterion is said to be one specialization. Specialization thus is considered a directed n-ary association rather than the binary relationship between one super- and one subclass. It is important to remember that specialization is defined the mentioned way because this does not necessarily correspond to the terminology chosen by other authors. In the documentation of the UML, for example, the authors not only prefer using the inverse relationship, thus speaking of generalizations rather than specializations, but also define a generalization as a binary relationship. The grouping of subclasses according to a discriminator therefore has to be named differently and is called a partition.

In many methods the semantics of a specialization can be enhanced by defining constraints. Widely used constraints are the *overlapping* (inverse: disjoint) and the *complete* (inverse: incomplete) constraint. Note that theses constraints are considered to be properties of a specialization. Defining a specialization as overlapping allows objects to belong to more than on of the given subclasses (as a direct instance), defining it as complete implies that they must be an instance of at least one of the subclasses in the considered specialization. If multiple specialization is not allowed, completeness implies that the superclass has no direct instances at all and is said to be abstract.

Multiple generalization is often called multiple inheritance. Since inheritance is a mechanism supported by a programming language, the concept of multiple generalization is preferred as it focuses on the semantic relationship rather than the feature inherent in a programming language.

Dynamic classification indicates whether an object is allowed to change its class throughout its lifecycle. Dynamic classification may also be called dynamic or flexible typing, dynamic inheritance, reclassification, or object migration. The concept of dynamic classification is usually discussed in the context of specialization because one often considers the classes an object can belong to over a

period of time as subclasses of the same superclass, which in that case represents the structural and behavioral commonality between all the classes the object can belong to. Dynamic classification is not necessarily to be seen in the context of specialization but doing so is not an artificial restriction since it seems to be quite natural that there should be such a commonality.
Looking at Table 1 one finds it rather difficult to discover any pattern or an overly obvious logic in combining different forms of specialization. Multiple generalization, which is allowed in every method, can obviously not be used as a taxonomic criterion. Yet the other criteria, apart from completeness, which will be taken up later on, can be used as such even if it is not yet obvious. The following chapter predominantly reconsiders dynamic classification, multiple and overlapping specialization in order to discover combinations of these criteria which seem to be based on the same kind of classification approach. The basic forms of classification approaches considered are derived from the way of thinking that can be found in two different "worlds": the way of thinking in the world of entity relationship modeling and the way of thinking in the world of traditional object-oriented implementation technologies (programming languages, database systems).

2 Basic Classification Approaches

The results of reconsidering the criteria concerning the ways of handling specialization in the context of entity relationship modeling vs. traditional object-oriented implementation technologies are summarized in Table 2. It shows that the underlying classification approaches differ mostly in three criteria: whether multiple and overlapping specialization and dynamic classification are allowed or not. This can be explained by looking at the relationship between classes (types) and instances and at the correspondence of the latter to real world objects.

	entity relationship modeling	**object-oriented implementation technologies**
multiple specialization	allowed	not allowed
overlapping specialization	allowed	not allowed
incomplete specialization	allowed	indifferent
multiple generalization	allowed, but unusual and seldomly used	allowed, quite usual
dynamic classification	allowed	not allowed

Table 2: Types of specialization in entity relationship modeling vs. traditional object-oriented implementation technologies

Looking at specialization in terms of entity relationship modeling (which in the way it is used today is certainly influenced by relational modeling) does not necessarily lead to a concept called inheritance. The super-subtype-relationship in entity relationship modeling can be seen as a 1-to-1 relationship with predefined semantics, meaning that its semantics cannot be documented by attaching a relationship name or roles to it as in normal relationships. This is because the semantics are always the same and simply imply that an object of a subtype is a kind of object of the supertype. Inheritance has not to be mentioned at all. Thinking in terms of relational modeling one usually assumes that all entities in a specialization hierarchy are identified on the basis of the same primary key. A real world object therefore is represented by a set of entities, tied together by 1-to-1 relationships, i.e., a key attribute that is repeated in all entity types of the specialization hierarchy. This means an object is split into several "smaller" objects representing the aspects that are associated with exactly one entity type. The result is a high degree of flexibility in using multiple and overlapping specialization or dynamic classification. This flexibility is based on the fact that a real world object can be materialized as an instance of all the types it belongs to, as shown in Figure 1.

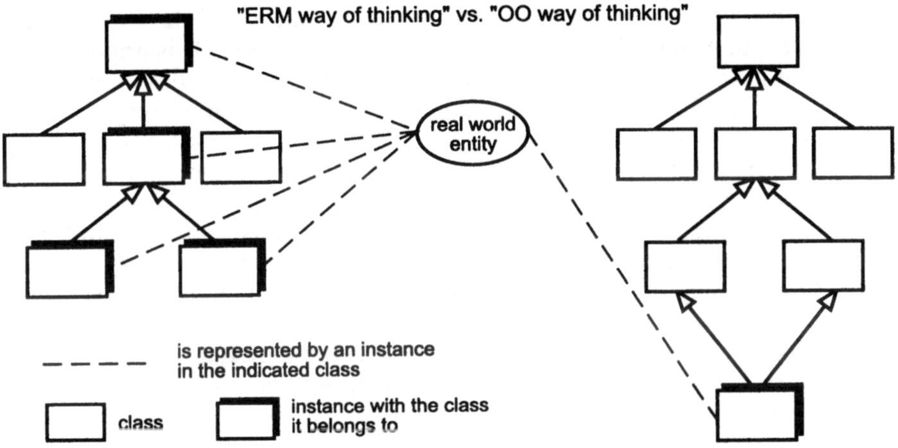

Figure 1: Real world entity and model correspondence

The way of thinking in the object-oriented community highly differs from this point of view. Palmer (1994a) characterizes the object-oriented way of thinking as strictly obeying a "one-to-one law" and even talks of a "oneness cult". The mechanism of inheritance makes the properties of a superclass available in the subclass so that an instance of the subclass fully describes a real world object, as shown in Figure 1. There is no necessity for splitting instances among classes. Since an instance is identified with no regard to any of its properties by a system wide and system controlled object ID, there is no way of instantiating different classes and making the instances look as if they represented the same object (or in other terms: making one instance belong to different classes as their *direct* instance (multiple classification)). Different instances always have different object IDs and thus different identity. Because of inheritance, creating instances in different subclasses of the same superclass will furthermore lead to a great amount of redundancy if those instances are to represent the same real world object.

Wegner (1990) makes it quite clear that this is only an implementation issue and cannot be considered a natural way of modeling: "The restriction that instances have precisely one base class may be understood in terms of considerations of implementation. Instances must know where to start looking for methods when they receive a message to be executed. Having pointers to more than one base class would make method lookup complex and possibly ambiguous. Allowing Jane to be both a student and a female ... would considerably complicate object-oriented semantics."

Even though most modelers and programmers are aware of this restriction Palmer (1994b) states that there still seems to be some confusion: "Many developers misunderstand inheritance. They think that new subclass instances are appended onto existing superclass instances. The reality is that instantiation creates a new subclass instance without any need to reference existing superclass instances."

The consequence of this restriction is that whenever subclasses are said to overlap, a specific class has to be created as the common subclass of the two previous classes to capture all the instances belonging to those classes. This implies usage of multiple generalization. The main difference to entity relationship modeling can be seen in the fact that object orientation enforces explicit modeling of classes, sometimes called intersection classes (Sciore (1989)) or join classes (Rumbaugh et al. (1991)), for those objects that seem to belong to more than one of the already existing classes. In some contexts this might lead to a class explosion and extensive usage of multiple generalization which in itself can lead to further problems. In entity relationship modeling there is no model-inherent reason for explicitly modeling such classes. (Sometimes there might be other reasons, for example, if the objects belonging to the intersection have additional properties.) The constraint "overlapping" already implies overlapping extensions. This is - as we have seen - not the case in the object-oriented way of thinking and therefore the reason why the integrity constraint "overlapping" is either not allowed, not supported or associated with different semantics. UML and OMT are examples for the latter case as will be discussed later on.

Multiple specialization leads to a very similar discussion. In entity relationship modeling multiple specialization implies that the same object can be instantiated in at least one of the subclasses of every specialization. Whether this can be more than one is a question of the integrity constraint (overlapping or disjoint) defined for each specialization. This means that subclasses belonging to different "parallel" specializations (dimensions) can always overlap whereas for subclasses belonging to the same specialization this depends on the constraints defined. In object orientation multiple specialization cannot be treated in a similar fashion.

Both problems can be reduced to the question whether multiple classification is supported or not. In entity relationship modeling it is, because objects are split along entity types, and in traditional object-oriented implementation technologies it is not, because instances are only allowed to have one base class. Although multiple classification does not imply that there will never be a need to model intersection classes, those will in some cases nevertheless be needed. This is the case if objects belonging to the intersection have additional properties, in entity relationship modeling those can only be structural properties, in object orientation also behavioral. This explains why one cannot totally ban multiple generalization from entity relationship modeling. Thus the difference in handling multiple generalization in ERM and OO, as mentioned in Table 2, is explained. It is also interesting to observe that the criterion how multiple generalization is handled has to be considered a result of the way the other criteria, especially multiple classification, are supported.

Coming back to Table 2, one can see that two criteria have not yet been discussed. One is the question of completeness which can only be understood in a context taken up later, the other is the support for dynamic classification.

Classification approaches can be looked at - as has been done up to now - from a purely static perspective. Taking the time dimension into account the topic should also be discussed from a dynamic point of view.

Dynamic classification cannot be considered much of a problem in entity relationship modeling. As before, the splitting of an object along types is a very convenient basis for allowing instances to move from one type to another as long as there is some kind of superinstance holding the partial instances together.

In object orientation, however, we cannot let an object move from one class to another if there is no direct support for this kind of operation, and usually there is no. Manually deleting an object and recreating it by instantiating a new class and initializing the new object with some of the former object's properties certainly is not a suitable way for aiming at dynamic classification. The main reason why this cannot be considered an appropriate way is to be seen in the object-oriented notion of identity. Each object has an inherent identity determined at object creation time which cannot be manipulated from outside. Of course clever programmers will always find a way to encompass such restrictions, e.g., Smalltalk programmers could use the message "become" to let objects change their identity (Goldberg and Robson (1989)), yet this is not what is meant by supporting dynamic classification, but rather a simple work-around.

The lack of semantic support for dynamic classification has been widely criticized. Wegner (1990), for example, states "that unique identifiers determined at object creation time do not completely capture the intuitive notion of identity". Gil and Lorenz (1996) draw an analogy to the environmental-heredity controversy and ask the widely discussed question of "Nature vs. Nurture". Although this basic philosophic/scientific question has been preoccupying minds of generations of thinkers the mainstream object-orientalist adheres to the fact that "the basic character of an object ... is determined at birth (instantiation), and not by the household".

Of course this kind of criticism has not been fully ignored by the object-oriented community. Over the years it has lead to many interesting suggestions in form of work-arounds, extensions of existing implementation technologies or new implementation technologies that are based on totally different premises. A few examples are to be discussed later on. Yet it can certainly not be seen a too narrow assessment if one eventually states that traditional object-oriented thinking disapproves of dynamic classification.

Summing up, one can differentiate two basic classification approaches that in themselves seem to be consistent. Looking at multiple vs. single classification from the perspective of a *point in time* and at dynamic vs. static classification from the perspective of a *period in time* it seems that on the one hand multiple and dynamic classification work together quite naturally requiring similar premises and on the other hand single and static classification. As pointed out in Figure 2, only two of four possible combinations seem to make sense and correspond to the way of thinking that can be found in the ERM- community (multiple/dynamic) vs. the way of thinking in the traditional OO world (single/static).

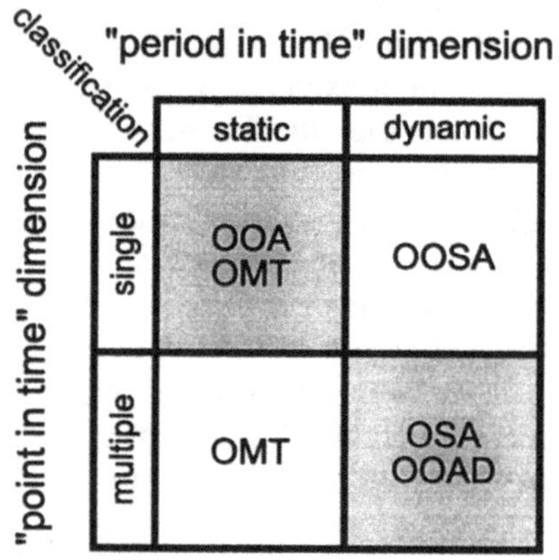

Figure 2: Assigning methods to basic classification approaches

Assigning object-oriented modeling methods to one of the four possible combinations is not always a simple task. Assigning OSA and OOA did not lead to major problems. OOAD seemed to be contradictory in the "point in time"-dimension, since multiple specialization is supported but no overlapping subclasses. OOSA has to be clearly assigned a combination which in itself seems inconsistent, yet the statements are quite clear: "In a subtype-supertype construct, one real world instance is represented by the combination of an instance of the supertype and an instance of exactly one subtype." (Shlaer and Mellor (1992)). One can see that the notion of classification corresponds to the ERM-way of thinking, yet there is the limitation to "exactly one subtype". Looking at the "period in time"-dimension, OOSA supports dynamic classification which is called migrating subtypes. The most problematic case is OMT. Although, according to Table 1, multiple specialization and the constraint "overlapping" are allowed, the associated semantics seem to differ from the introduced notion. Any form of overlap has to be explicitly modeled by introducing join classes (intersection classes). The integrity constraints defined, thus, simply indicate from which superclasses such join classes are allowed to inherit. This is why one could argue whether OMT should not be assigned to the single classification group. Looking at dynamics it seems quite clear that only static classification is allowed (Rumbaugh et al. (1991)). In Figure 2 OMT occurs in two fields to reflect this ambiguity.

The statement of Champeaux and Faure (1992) on object-oriented analysis methods that says, "an object belongs to at least one class and, in most methods can belong to at most one class. The class to which an object belongs is frozen in most methods", seems to be true for some of the methods looked at. Yet there are exceptions in form of methods that do allow multiple or dynamic classification. Doing so implies a mismatch with traditional object-oriented implementation technologies. The following chapter focuses on the consequences of such a decision.

3 Consequences on Modeling and Implementing

The previous results have shown that object-oriented modeling methods can support different classification approaches. The underlying approach has a strong influence on the resulting analysis models because of the implications on choosing classes. If multiple classification is not allowed then intersection classes have to be modeled or if multiple generalization is to be used carefully, other work-arounds have to be found to prevent its extensive use. If dynamic classification is allowed, one will tend to model states as subclasses, one thing one should by no means do otherwise. Different authors have suggested modeling solutions and patterns that can be used in such cases, like "object slicing" by Martin and Odell (1992), the "roles played pattern" by Coad (1992) or the state pattern by Gamma et al. (1994).

Assuming that most object-oriented modeling in analysis will be followed by an implementation in a traditional object-oriented implementation technology, there is a strong argument for using a matching modeling method. Only then, the widely emphasized seamlessness of the transition from analysis to design seems not to be endangered. Yet the price is that analysis results are technologically influenced.

The other approach can be seen in using one of the more flexible modeling methods allowing multiple and dynamic classification at the price of a potential need to re-model in design. This, of course, means giving up strict adherence to seamlessness. Yet, there is a small chance that the chosen implementation technology might support the same classification approach. This is not very likely in an industrial software project but should not be totally disregarded. The following chapter, therefore, takes a further look at object-oriented implementation technologies and shows that support for dynamic and multiple classification has not to be totally ruled out.

4 A Second Look at Object-Oriented Implementation Technologies

Taking a more detailed look at object-oriented implementation technologies makes clear that the assumptions made for traditional object-oriented implementation technologies are not always valid. There are implementation technologies, programming languages and more often database management systems, that are based on different classification approaches.

Looking at programming languages one has to mention prototypical languages like Self (Lieberman (1986), Ungar and Smith (1988), Stein et al. (1988), see also Malenfant (1995) on an overview on object- vs. class- centered programming). As shown in Figure 3 these languages are not based on classes but instead on prototypes. Prototypes themselves are to be considered simple objects that are used as standard examples with default behavior for other objects. Those other objects can be cloned from prototypes. Cloning can be considered a kind of copying process. Objects can be individually modified (in structure and behavior) over time. Prototypes seem to contain inheritance information since messages not understood by an object can be delegated to its prototype. This kind of prototype inheritance highly differs from class inheritance. Each object in a prototype-based system can have different prototypes and knows theses prototypes. As says Ungar (1988): "A prototype-based system places each object's inheritance information in the object itself. This means that an object can change its parents on-the-fly."

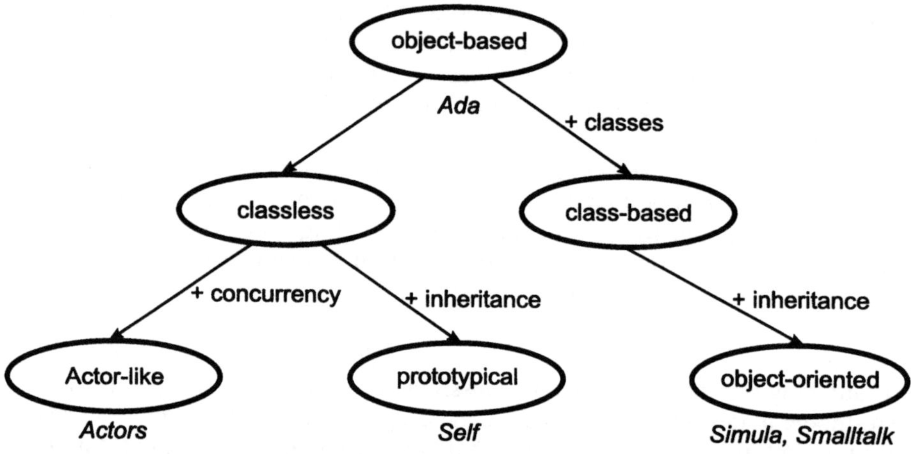

Figure 3: Classification of object-based programming languages (Wegner (1990))

Apart from this well known example much work has been done in the area of constructing work-arounds and of modifying or enhancing traditional object-oriented implementation technologies in order to gain some of the features of prototype-based systems. This usually leads to approaches aiming at more flexibility with regard to the relationship between an instance and its behavior and/or structure information. Examples for such work are: Hendler (1986), LaLonde et al. (1986), Sciore (1989), Pernici (1990), Augeraud and Freeman-Benson (1991), Ibrahim et al. (1991), Johnson and Zweig (1991), Davis (1992), Harrison and Ossher (1993), Taivalsaari (1993), Gil and Lorenz (1996).

In the area of object-oriented database systems this kind of flexibility is considered a more usual feature. One of the first and better known examples among OODBMS is IRIS as described in Fishman et al. (1989). Among the commercially available products C++/Versant has to be mentioned as an example of an

OODBMS supporting dynamic classification in a very straightforward manner. This is done by supplying the "migrateobject" command (Du and Wolfe (1997)). Willshire and Kim (1990) give a systematic overview on storage models used in object-oriented databases. Examples of such models are (Willshire and Kim (1990), Kim (1991)):

- Home Class Model

  An instance is completely stored in its home class, i.e., the most specific class it belongs to. The values of inherited instance variables are present in the instance along with the values of the instance variables particular to the subclass in which the instance occurs. Thus data is stored at the "lowest" level possible.

- Repeat Classes Model

  Data of an instance is repeatedly stored in each class an instance belongs to. Thus, in addition to the instances that would be stored according to the Home Class Model, instances are stored redundantly along the inheritance hierarchy from the lowest to the highest level possible.

- Split Instance Model

  In each applicable class, the unique OId is stored along with the values of the attributes particular to that class for the instance. Only the OId is duplicated down the hierarchy. Thus data is stored at the "highest" level possible. Elimination of redundancy is the difference to the Repeat Class Model.

- Leaf Overlap Model

  Instances can belong to several classes that are not directly related by the inheritance hierarchy, that is, no class is in the set of superclasses of the other classes.

The Home Class Model directly corresponds to the classification approach underlying traditional object- oriented implementation technologies whereas the Split Instance Model is in accordance with the ERM-way of thinking and therefore provides all prerequisites needed for multiple and dynamic classification. The fourth model (Leaf Overlap Model) directly supports multiple classification.

The relevance of the discussed technologies in industrial software development might be questioned. Yet, they show that the opinions and approaches in the area of object-oriented implementation technologies are not as homogenous as initially suggested. This can certainly be considered a reason why some of the authors of object-oriented modeling methods tend to be overly careful in committing themselves to one or other of the classification approaches. That even those who clearly allow for multiple and dynamic classification do not dwell long on the topic shows a lack of awareness for the consequences of supporting these mechanisms. That these classification approaches have to be thoroughly discussed and examined on how they influence other parts of a modeling method will be shown in the following chapter.

5 Influence of the Chosen Classification Approach on Dynamic Modeling

A widely used technique for modeling behavior is state transition modeling. In the context of object- oriented modeling this technique is usually used to model the behavior of a single class, which is also called modeling the intra-object behavior. The inter-object-behavior, for example the interaction between different objects along a thread of execution, is usually modeled using other techniques.

Allowing for dynamic and multiple classification highly complicates the semantics of these modeling techniques. Yet a thorough examination of this point cannot be found in methods supporting these mechanisms. A closer look at this aspect is intended to make clear that ignoring this point cannot lead to a satisfying situation.

Dynamic classification implies that an otherwise static relationship, meaning the one between object and class, is now modifiable. Thus the possible modifications of this relationship have to be somehow modeled and taken into account in the existing dynamic modeling techniques. Looking at state transition modeling this means that objects can somehow set foot into or leave the one class modeled in a state transition diagram. How are these migrating objects to be handled? It obviously comes to a diffusion of the inter-class perspective into the intra-class point of view. In literature a thorough examination of this point is difficult to find. Shlaer and Mellor (1992) are one of the few exceptions. They make the suggestion that the classes an object can belong to in time should be the subclasses of the same superclass. Thus they reduce the problem - as they call it - to migrating subtypes. As they demand specializations to be always complete, migration is limited to horizontal movements among the subclasses of one superclass. Disallowing multiple classification further simplifies the problem. Shlaer and Mellor (1992) eventually suggest a solution where object migration can be handled within state transition modeling, mostly from the point of view of the superclass. To a certain extent this explains the rather unusual way of handling specialization in OOSA that was pointed out in Chapter 2. It also makes clear how completeness of specializations can reduce complexity while allowing dynamic classification: vertical movements of objects between super- and subclasses can be totally ignored.

Yet one should not too harshly judge methods on the way they handle dynamic classification since methods can strongly differ in the approach taken to model behavior. According to Fowler (1994) there are at least two basic approaches, the predominant state-based approach using state transition modeling and the event-based that can for example be found in OOAD. Without going into much detail, handling dynamic classification in an event-based approach does not seem to lead to problems. That is why in a method like OOAD, dynamic classification is extensively used in modeling examples, yet not dwelled upon very long.

Before looking at the UML as one of the predominant approaches in the world of object-oriented modeling methods one final point, that is vigorously discussed among object-orientalists, is to be mentioned in the following chapter.

6 "A State of State Confusion"

Discussing dynamic classification usually leads to a point that Palmer (1993) has once aptly characterized as a "state of state confusion". With his statement he refers to the argument among object-orientalists whether one should model states as classes, which in turn raises the question of what is to be considered a state and what a class. Without looking at this argument in detail a few points shall be mentioned. A short overview on advantages and disadvantages of different approaches is, for example, given in Taivalsaari (1996). See also Odell (1992) and Palmer (1994a).

Rumbaugh et al. (1991) clearly point out: "A single object can have different states over time - the object preserves identity - but it cannot have different classes. Inherent differences among objects are therefore properly modeled as different classes, while temporary differences are properly modeled as different states of the same class." Although, at a first glance, this might seem quite clear and plausible, one has to admit that there is no reason why temporary differences should not be inherent at the same time. Temporary differences can, of course, lead to fundamental structural and behavioral differences requiring different classes.

Some authors (e.g. Pernici (1990)) try to solve this conflict by introducing a third term, such as role and by modeling roles in a specific way. It might be easy to give obvious examples for classes, states and roles, yet there will always be those cases where one is confronted with the properties of more than one of these concepts. Some authors (e.g. Embley et al. (1992)) even consider roles a short way of expressing specializations. It therefore seems to be an overly simplistic approach to assume that one can draw a clear distinction between class, state and perhaps a third concept one wishes to call role. Yet opinions differ on this point.

Without taking the previous discussion any further which would usually lead to the question of "naturalness" of the various approaches, it is sufficient to sum up that opinions on whether dynamic classification should be used or not highly differ. This paper does not aim at favoring one over the other of the approaches but at making clear that the approach taken with regard to classification has to be stated clearly and has to be given thorough consideration in static and dynamic modeling. In the following chapter UML is given a closer look from this point of view.

7 A Special Case: the UML

Because of the expected predominance of the UML in object-oriented modeling it deserves special attention. Looking at its latest two versions (1.0, 1.1) with respect to the way specialization is handled, it is interesting to state that differences between the two versions can be observed. However, the basic approach of the UML is to be as flexible and powerful as possible. This is a characteristic not surprising at all, it can be encountered in many areas of the language definition.

Version 1.0 takes the approach of defining default semantics and suggesting semantic variation points to be used when needed. The exact formulation is as

follows (UML1.0 (1997b)):
"These are some semantic variation points applicable to generalization:

> Multiple inheritance: Whether a class may have more than one superclass.
> Multiple classification: Whether an object may belong directly to more than one class.
> Dynamic classification: Whether an object may change class during execution.

The ordinary UML semantics assumes multiple inheritance, no multiple classification, and no dynamic classification, but most parts of the semantics and notation are not affected if these assumptions are change(!)."

It can be considered a major merit of UML, especially version 1.0, that the classification approach taken is stated so clearly. Yet the consequences of allowing variation are obviously underestimated. Recalling the previous discussion this is to be judged a great danger.

The latest version (1.1) takes a slightly different approach. The concept of default semantics seems to be banned in favor of the more flexible and powerful classification approach which implies allowing for multiple and dynamic classification. Again the consequences are underestimated (UML1.1 (1997b)): "The use of multiple classification (!) dynamic classification affects the dynamic execution semantics of the language but is not unusually apparent from a static model." Although a slight influence is admitted, this point is not revisited when talking about dynamics.

That the authors now clearly commit themselves to a more powerful - yet more difficult to handle - classification approach is stated quite clearly in the Semantics (UML1.1 (1997a): "An object may have multiple classes, i.e. it may originate from several classes. ... Moreover, the set of classes ... may vary over time. New classes may be added to the object and old ones may be detached." However, the given examples in the Notation Guide still seem to comply with the default semantics of the previous version. Besides, some aspects seem to be semantically vague, ambiguous or contradictory.

Before taking a look at these examples and the definitions in the Notation Guide the terminology of the UML which is different from the one chosen in this paper has to be introduced. In UML the term generalization is preferred over its inverse, the term specialization. It denotes a binary relationship between one super- and one subclass, not a group of such relationships being derived on the basis of the same discriminator. Yet the concept of discriminator is supported and the resulting grouping of classes is called partitioning.

There are two presentation options for generalizations: a solid-line path along each generalization (separate target style) or a grouping of generalization paths shown as a tree with a shared segment to the superclass (shared target style). (See the two examples taken from the UML in Figure 4 and 5.) As the authors point out, these two presentation options are "semantically indistinguishable" (UML1.1 (1997b)). Therefore, the notational grouping of subclasses into a tree does not necessarily correspond to partitioning. This is an important aspect to note,

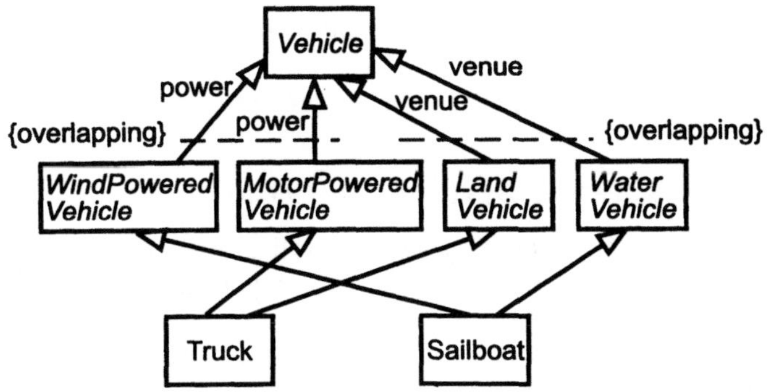

Figure 4: Example 1 with discriminator and constraints in separate target style (UML1.1 (1997b))

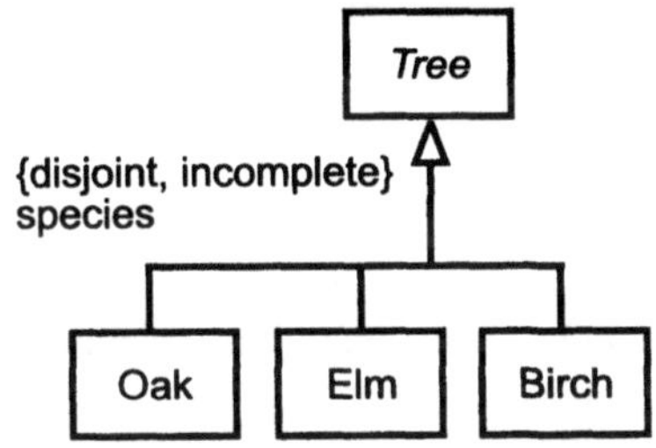

Figure 5: Example 2 in shared target style (UML1.1 (1997b))

since other methods usually tend to graphically express partitioning by collapsing generalization paths. In UML however, partitioning is visually expressed by labeling generalization paths with the same discriminator.

Partitioning also does not seem to have any semantic connection to constraints one can define among subclasses. Again, this is quite unusual. Yet, the examples imply a correspondence, which, however, is not mentioned explicitly. UML supports the constraints overlapping vs. disjoint and complete vs. incomplete. Although, the latter two are used in a quite unusual way, they shall be of no further interest in the following discussion focusing on the aspect of allowing overlaps among classes. Definitions for these constraints can be found in two places: in the Notation Guide and in Appendix 3 of the Semantics.

The formulation used in the Notation Guide is as follows (UML1.1 (1997b)):

"Predefined constraints may be used to indicate semantic constraints among subclasses. A comma-separated list of keywords is placed in braces either near the shared triangle ... or else near a dotted line that crosses all of the generalization lines involved. The following keywords ... may be used:

overlapping	A descendent may be descended from more than one of the subclasses.
disjoint	A descendent may not be descended from more than one of the subclasses."

Appendix 3 of the Semantics says (UML1.1 (1997a):

"Disjoint is a constraint applied to a set of generalizations, specifying that instance (!) may have no more than one of the given subtypes as a type of the instance. This is the default semantics of generalization. ... Overlapping is a constraint applied to a set of generalizations, specifying that instances may have more than one of the given subtypes as a type of the instance."

The major difference between these definitions is that the first works well in a world where multiple classification is not allowed and therefore intersection classes have to be explicitly modeled. This is why the formulation is based on descendants of the considered subclasses, meaning the subclasses of the subclasses among which the constraints are attached. A very strong similarity to the OMT-way of handling the overlap constraint can be noticed. The second definition, however, is rather formulated along the multiple classification line, allowing instances to have many types.

The confusion can be cleared up to a certain extent by considering that classes are allowed to be specialized into types and implementation classes (UML1.1 (1997b)). This differentiation, however, is not metamodel but stereotype based. Using it makes quite clear that objects are allowed to belong to several types and even change those types they belong to over time. A type, thus, is characterized as a changeable role an object can play, something that can be adopted and later abandoned. This flexibility does decidedly not hold for an object's implementation class, which is fixed over time and not legal for multiple classification.

Although, this differentiation might solve some of the mentioned problems, the way it is handled is not entirely satisfying. This can be attributed to two aspects. In most contexts the word class is used instead of the specializations implementation class or type, even in passages (as in the first definition) where it would be more useful to work with either of the specialized concepts or at least hint at this differentiation. The second aspect to mention is the relationship between the two concepts. An implementation class is said to realize a type, the relationship, therefore, is called "realizes" and can be explicitly modeled. Yet, rules for mapping the one concept into the other which would lead to suggestions on how to implement the notion of multiple and dynamic classification using technologies not supporting them are missing. This can be understood from the point of view that it is not the intention of the UML to pass on modeling expertise by formulating modeling rules and guidelines. But even then, one misses an indication that multiple and dynamic classification cannot be provided for in a trivial manner by simply differentiating between concepts allowing and disallowing them.

Taking the discussed concepts of type vs. implementation class into account the different perspectives used in the given definitions can be understood to a certain extent. Yet, there still remain some ambiguities on how generalizations and the depending concepts are to be handled and interpreted. Looking at the two definitions and the given example in Figure 4 still raises the following questions:

a. Is it a coincidence that in Figure 4 partitions and the groupings of subclasses formed through dotted lines coalesce?

b. Would it make any semantic difference if the two dotted lines in Figure 4 were substituted by one, since the constraints do not differ?

c. Does not drawing one single dotted line imply disjointness between classes coming from different groupings, since disjoint is assumed to be the default? (Of course, the classes Sailboat and Truck directly contradict this interpretation.)

d. Why do the chosen subclasses on the lowest level have superclasses coming from different groupings? Is this a coincidence? Would it not have been more appropriate according to the definitions to choose subclasses at the lowest level with superclasses belonging to the same grouping?

e. Assuming one of the constraints as disjoint, what combinations of superclasses would then be allowed?

f. Is a generalization path allowed to be trespassed by more than one dotted line? If so, which combinations of constraints are allowed and what are the semantics implied?

Most of these questions can be reduced to the point of clarifying the types of subclass groupings allowed and the interdependencies between these groupings. There are four types of subclass groupings:

1. groupings based on discriminators (partitions)
2. groupings based on constraints
3. groupings formed by dotted lines
4. groupings based on graphical formalisms when using shared target style

The ambiguity comes in when asking for the connections and dependencies between these groupings. As was mentioned before, according to the authors, the fourth grouping does not have any semantic implications. The second and third grouping certainly come together, yet as was formulated in question b) and c) it is not quite clear what differences can be expressed according to the way the dotted line is drawn. Taking a deeper look at the groupings based on the third criterion ("dotted lines") it is not quite clear whether a class may belong to more than one such group (question f)). The example implies a connection between grouping one and two (respectively three), yet there is no indication to be found in the text, that partitions and constraints are not to be considered wholly independent concepts.

Whatever the answers might be to the questions stated, the approach taken in the UML seems to be quite different from other approaches, where one usually finds more coalescence among the mentioned groupings. It is quite natural and usual (McGregor and Korson (1993), Embley et al. (1992), Martin and Odell (1992))

- to visually support partitions through a shared target style or a comparable graphical formalism,
- to let partitions be the groupings that can be labeled with constraints (usually implying disjoint semantics as a default within a partition or sometimes requiring disjointness within it) and
- to assume overlap among classes belonging to different partitions (i.e., using the semantics of multiple specialization as defined in the beginning of the paper).

It cannot be the intention of this chapter to answer the raised questions, it simply is to point out a few aspects. Summing these up, one has to state that there still is a great amount of vagueness and ambiguity concerning the way specialization is to be handled according to the UML. One does not feel that the multiple/dynamic classification approach is taken into account whenever it should be. On the contrary, one even senses fall backs to the default semantics of the previous version. The differences between the single/static vs. multiple/dynamic approach are underestimated. Therefore, consequences of using the one or the other approach are not discussed.

8 Conclusion

It was pointed out that specialization, which is usually considered a very crucial semantic construct in object-oriented modeling, can be handled and interpreted in different ways. There seem to be two basic classification approaches which in themselves are consistent: the single/static classification approach vs. the multiple/dynamic approach. The latter seems to correspond to a way of thinking that one is used to in the world of entity relationship modeling, whereas the former corresponds to a notion inherent in traditional object-oriented implementation technologies. Yet, the opinions and technologies in the OO community are quite heterogeneous and sometimes comply with the more flexible multiple/dynamic classification approach.

It follows that the classification approach underlying an object-oriented modeling method has to be stated clearly and be taken into account in different parts of the modeling method. Looking at existing methods shows that there is a danger of underestimating the consequences of using the one instead of the other way of thinking. This is also true for the UML. Yet, as the UML has changed from version 1.0 to 1.1 into now clearly favoring the more powerful and at the same time more complex approach over the other, it is to be expected that consequences not yet taken into account will penetrate other parts of the language in versions to come. Still other details concerning specialization seem quite ambiguous. Such ambiguity is quite unusual for a metamodel based language. As metamodeling enforces clearing ambiguity and disallows vagueness, one usually encounters a high degree of conceptual preciseness in such methods. Since the UML is designed as a very powerful language it is quite obvious that metamodeling can only address basics and must be very generic. Most of the points discussed cannot be encountered in any of the metamodels. This is also why the Semantics often lack in detail, and many important aspects can only be found in the Notation Guide. Thus, it remains to be seen, whether future versions of the language will clear some of the mentioned points and whether there will be a fundamental change in the level of detail metamodeling is taken to.

References

AUGERAUD, M. and FREEMAN-BENSON, B.N. (1991): Dynamic Objects. SIGOIS Bulletin, 12/2,3, 135-140.

CHMAPEAUX, D. DE and FAURE, P. (1992): A Comparative Study of Object-Oriented Analysis Methods. *Journal of Object-Oriented Programming, 5/1, 21-33.*

COAD, P. (1992): Object-Oriented Patterns. Communications of the ACM, 35/9, 152-159.

COAD, P. and YOURDON, E. (1991): Object-Oriented Analysis. Prentice Hall, Englewood Cliffs, New Jersey.

DAVIS, S.R. (1992): C++ objects that change their types. *Journal of Object-Oriented Programming, 5/4, 27-32.*

DU, T.C.-T. and WOLFE, P.M. (1997): An implementation perspective of applying object-oriented database technologies. IIE Transactions, 29/9, 733-742.

EMBLEY, D., KURTZ, B.D., and WOODFIELD, S.N. (1992): Object-Oriented Systems Analysis: A Model-Driven Approach. Prentice Hall, Englewood Cliffs, New Jersey.

FISHMAN, D.H., ANNEVELINK, J., CHOW, E., CONNORS, T., DAVIS, J.W., HASAN, W., HOCH, C.G., KENT, W., LEICHNER, S., LYNGBAEK, P., MAHBOD, B., NEIMAT, M.A., RISCH, T., SHAN, M.C., and WILKINSON, W.K. (1989): Overview of the IRIS DBMS. Technical Report HPL-SAL-89-15, Palo Alto, California.

FOWLER, M. (1994): Describing and Comparing Object-Oriented Analysis and Design Methods. In: A. Carmichael (ed.): Object Development Methods. SIGS Books, New York, 79-109.

GAMMA, E., HELM, R., JOHNSON, R., and VLISSIDES, J. (1994): Design Patterns: Elements of Reusable Object-Oriented Software. Addison-Wesley, Reading, Massachusetts.

GIL, J. and LORENZ, D.H. (1996): Environmental Acquisition - A New Inheritance-Like Abstraction Mechanism. In: OOPSLA96, Proceedings of the 11th Conference on Object-Oriented Programming Systems, Languages and Applications, 214-231.

GOLDBERG, A. and ROBSON, D. (1989): Smalltalk-80: The Language. Addison-Wesley, Reading, Massachusetts.

HARRISON, W. and OSSHER, H. (1993): Subject-Oriented Programming. In: OOPSLA93, Proceedings of the 8th Conference on Object-Oriented Programming Systems, Languages and Applications, 411-428.

HENDLER, J. (1986): Enhancement for multiple-inheritance. ACM SIGPLAN Notices, 21/10, 98-106.

IBRAHIM, M.H., BEJCEK, W.E., and CUMMINS, F.A. (1991): Instance Specialization without Delegation. *Journal of Object-Oriented Programming, 4/3, 53-56.*

JOHNSON, R.E. and ZWEIG, J.M. (1991): Delegation in C++. *Journal of Object-Oriented Programming, 4/7, 31-34.*

LALONDE, W.R., THOMAS, D.A., and PUGH, J.R. (1986): An Exemplar Based Smalltalk. In: OOPSLA86, Proceedings of the First Conference on Object-Oriented Programming Systems, Languages and Applications, 322-330.

LIEBERMAN, H. (1986): Using Prototypical Objects to Implement Shared Behavior in Object-Oriented Systems. In: OOPSLA86, Proceedings of the First Conference on Object-Oriented Programming Systems, Languages and Applications, 214-223.

MALENFANT, J. (1995): On the Semantic Diversity of Delegation-Based Programming Languages. In: OOPSLA95, Proceedings of the 10th Conference on Object-Oriented Programming Systems, Languages and Applications, 215-230.

MARTIN, J. and ODELL, J.J. (1992): Object-Oriented Analysis and Design. Prentice Hall, Englewood Cliffs, New Jersey.

MCGREGOR, J.D. and KORSON, T. (1993): Supporting dimensions of classification in object-oriented design. *Journal of Object-Oriented Programming, 5/9, 25-30.*

ODELL, J.J. (1992): Dynamic and multiple classification. *Journal of Object-Oriented Programming, 4/8, 45-48.*

PALMER, J. (1993): A state of state confusion. *Object Magazine, 3/4, 34-36.*

PALMER, J. (1994a): Inheritance Problems, Part 2: Dynamic Classification. *Object Magazine, 3/8, 77-79.*

PALMER, J. (1994b): O-O should show more class. *Object Magazine, 4/3, 81-86.*

PERNICI, B. (1990): Objects with Roles. SIGOIS Bulletin, 11/2,3, 205-215.

RUMBAUGH, J., BLAHA, M., PREMERLANI, W., EDDY, F., and LORENSEN, W. (1991): Object-Oriented Modeling and Design, Prentice Hall, Englewood Cliffs, New Jersey.

SCIORE, E. (1989): Object Specialization. ACM Transactions on Information Systems, 7/2, 103-122.

SHLAER, S. and MELLOR, S.J. (1989): Object-Oriented Systems Analysis: Modeling the World in Data. Prentice Hall, Englewood Cliffs, New Jersey.

SHLAER, S. and MELLOR, S.J. (1992): Object Lifecycles: Modeling the World in States. Prentice Hall, Englewood Cliffs, New Jersey.

STEIN, L., LIEBERMAN, H., and UNGAR, D. (1988): The Treaty of Orlando: A Shared View of Sharing. In: W. Kim, F.

LOCHOVSKY (eds.): Object-Oriented Concepts, Applications, and Databases. Addison-Wesley, Reading, Massachusetts, 31-48.

STRAHRINGER, S. (1996): Metamodellierung als Instrument des Methodenvergleichs: Eine Evaluierung am Beispiel objektorientierter Analysemethoden. Shaker, Aachen.

TAIVALSAARI, A. (1993): Object-oriented programming with modes. *Journal of Object-Oriented Programming, 6/3, 25-32.*

TAIVALSAARI, A. (1996): On the Notion of Inheritance. ACM Computing Surveys, 28/3, 438-479.

UML1.0 (1997a): Unified Modeling Language: Semantics, Version 1.0. Rational Software Corporation, 2800 San Toma Expressway, Santa Clara, CA 95051-0951 (USA), URL: http://www.rational.com

UML1.0 (1997b): Unified Modeling Language: Notation Guide, Version 1.0. Rational Software Corporation, 2800 San Toma Expressway, Santa Clara, CA 95051-0951 (USA), URL: http://www.rational.com

UML1.1 (1997a): Unified Modeling Language: Semantics, Version 1.1. Rational Software Corporation, 2800 San Toma Expressway, Santa Clara, CA 95051-0951 (USA), URL: http://www.rational.com

UML1.1 (1997b): Unified Modeling Language: Notation Guide, Version 1.1. Rational Software Corporation, 2800 San Toma Expressway, Santa Clara, CA 95051-0951 (USA), URL: http://www.rational.com

UNGAR, D. (1988): Are Classes Obsolete ? A panelists Perspective. In: OOPSLA88, Proceedings of the Third Conference on Object-Oriented Programming Systems, Languages and Applications, 358.

UNGAR, D. and SMITH, R.B. (1988): Self: The Power of Simplicity. In: OOPSLA88, Proceedings of the Third Conference on Object-Oriented Programming Systems, Languages and Applications, 227-242.

WEGNER, P. (1990): Concepts and Paradigms of Object-Oriented Programming. OOPS Messenger, 1/1, 7-87.

WILLSHIRE, M.J. (1991): How Spacey Can They Get ? Space Overhead for Storage and Indexing with Object-Oriented Databases. In: *Proceedings of the IEEE International Conference on Data Engineering, 14-22.*

WILLSHIRE, M.J. and KIM, H.-J. (1990): Properties of Physical Storage Models for Object-Oriented Databases. In: N.

RISHE, S. NAVATHE and D. TAL (eds.) (1990): PARBASE90, Proceedings of the International Conference on Databases, Parallel Architectures, and Their Applications. IEEE Computer Society Press, Los Alamitos, CA, 94-99.

Reuse of Models and Diagrams of the UML and Implementation Concepts Regarding Dynamic Modeling

W. Weber, P. Metz

Fachhochschule Darmstadt

w.weber@fbi.fh-darmstadt.de
p.metz@fbi.fh-darmstadt.de

Abstract: If the UML finally becomes a standard for a object-oriented notation we have a precise metamodel description for making the interchange of model data possible which allows the reuse of model elements of the OOA and OOD as well. The UML just offers a notation and does not impose a method. According to that the developer is free to combine the diagrams of the UML according to the metamodel to cope with the domain requirements. As an example, it is possible to assign state diagrams and activity diagrams to classes, operations and use cases - the mentioned interchange of model data involves sequences of diagrams and whole models, not just single diagrams. Now the developers problem is that based on missing methods for the UML there is a lack of consistency rules concerning the combination of its diagrams. The semantics for diagram assignments are not clearly defined. As a result the software developer gets no help for transferring the results of the OOD to an implementation. The UML does not solve the problem of the discontinuity between OOA, OOD and the level of implementation. The UML does not fill in the gaps of the given OO methods but widens these gaps. We want to demonstrate these problems regarding the association between a class and a state diagram: When a class A has a state diagram class B inherits the complete properties of class A for its behavioral description, the result is implicit inheritance of A's state diagram. We chose the correlation of classes and state diagrams because state diagrams are a very important means for detailed modeling of complex dynamics. At least the most important OO methods have state diagrams as its heart.

1 Content

The question is how we can adapt the inherited state diagram and supply additional information. Since in the object orientation the meaning of inheritance is fully defined only for classes, we propose an expansion of inheritance for state diagrams. These aspects becomes more difficult when we look at multiple inheritance. In this lecture, we want to develop basic concepts for dynamic conformity and concentrate on single inheritance. We will extend the ideas and concepts of Shlaer and Mellor (1992) and David Harel (1997) and try to establish semantics and consistency rules for the meaning of inheritance of state diagrams. In this context we will define the phrases 'polymorphic states' and 'abstract states'.

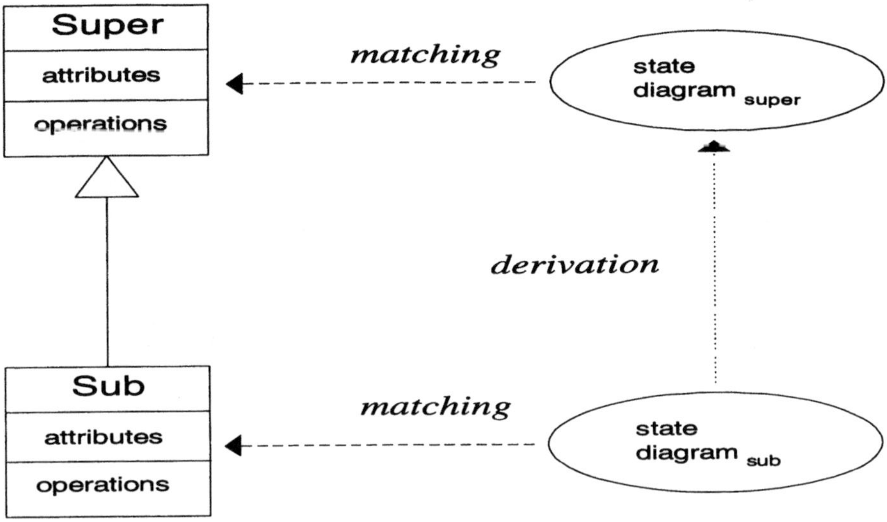

Figure 1: Inheritance of two classes with corresponding state diagrams

Fig. 1 shows the inheritance of two classes. Both the superclass and the subclass have state diagrams. That rises the question how does the state diagram of the subclass look like in comparison to state diagram of the superclass? At first we have to contemplate how a state diagram can be matched with operations and attributes of a class. After that we will propose modeling rules for deriving a state diagram of a subclass from the state diagram of a superclass. By showing examples we demonstrate the usefulness of these rules. Finally we will see, that the derivation of attributes and methods for class 'super'/'sub' from state diagram 'super'/'sub' corresponds to the common inheritance relationship between classes.

2 Transformation of State Diagrams

As an example for the transformation of state diagrams we consider a possible state diagram of a very simple compact disc player (Fig. 2). This state diagram serves as an explanation for the dynamic behavior for the class 'CD_player'. We consider that we have already identified an attribute 'price' and an operation 'adjust_volume()', which is independent from any state of the object and can be invoked in the object lifecycle any time. Such operations are not modeled by in state diagrams. The compact disc player can be started, paused and stopped. It stops playing when the total playtime is over.

The class having a state diagram is added with the attribute 'state'. The value of this attribute represents the current state the object is in. For each event and the activities of each state a method will be established. When an object receives a message the right event method is invoked. The event methods have to consult the attribute 'state' indicating whether the object can accept the message or not.

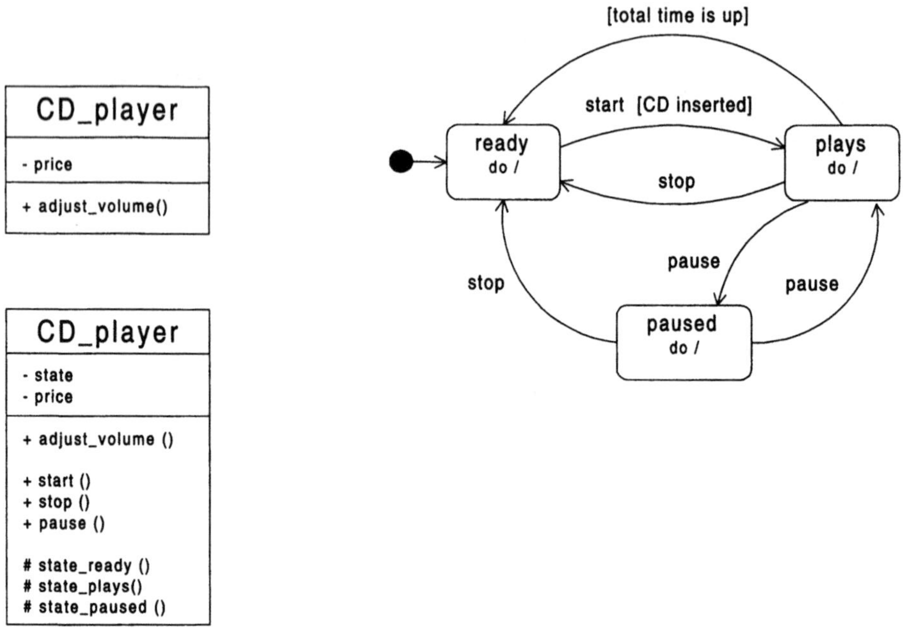

Figure 2: Matching state diagrams with attributes and methods of a class

If the message can be accepted the event method checks the condition, performs the actions and sends the messages of the underlying transition. Furthermore the event method sets the attribute 'state' to the value of the new state and calls the right state method.

The first reason for not simply concentrating the activities of a state in a single method with the name of the event is the following: The event 'pause' in Fig. 2 has a different reaction depending on the current state in which it is received. The reaction is either the activity of the state 'paused' or the activity of the state 'plays'. The second reason is possible source code redundancy: The events 'pause' and 'start' have the same reaction thus the event methods would have the same body.

Automatic Transitions are transitions that have no external event. These transitions fire as soon as the activity of the source state is completed. In Fig. 2 the state of the object changes from 'plays' to 'ready' when the CD is played to the end. As the state activities are responsible for firing automatic transitions we can integrate them within the state methods. The method of the source state calls the method of the target state after having updated the attribute 'state'.

This solution differs from the design pattern 'state' (Gamma et al. (1996)) and the proposal of Shlaer and Mellor (1992). The design pattern 'state' encapsulates state activities in classes. The object references one instance of the class 'state' and delegates the execution of activity to it. The state transition is represented by setting the reference to the instance of the following state. Each of the state classes implement methods for all events that can be send to the active class. The method body may be empty or throws an exception if the event is ignored in that state. The advantage is that the state machine can be changed on runtime by referencing a state instance of another state machine. This is a possibility to support the change of an object's class on the level of implementation. The disadvantage is that there is no distinction between a state activity and an event. State activities and events are the same method so that code redundancy may be the result. Another disadvantage is that state classes are friend classes of the class having a state machine. This is necessary because state activities are encapsulated in their own classes but at the same time they need to have access to the instance attributes and associations. Friend classes should be avoided to preserve the concept of encapsulation and suppress side effects. Shlaer/Mellor distinguish state activities and events by establishing event and state methods which are member functions of the class. Transitions are encapsulated in classes having two attributes, one for the state number of the source state and one for the target state. The event methods traverse a list of transition instances to check if the event is valid in the current state and which state is the next.

Both the state pattern and the proposal of Shlaer/Mellor have proved to be inefficient concerning runtime in real-time systems because of referencing many instances.

3 Derivation of State Diagrams

In the following we present senseful modeling techniques to derive state diagrams for subclasses from the state diagrams of their superclasses.

The most simple case is that the state diagram of the subclass remains the same as the one of the superclass (Fig. 3). We just add attributes and some functions which are independent from the state of the object and can be invoked at any time in the object's lifecycle. We extend the example of the CD player in Fig. 2 by adding a record out interface for digital output (attribute 'digital_rec_out'). Therefore we need a state-independent operation to select the record out signal.

3.1 Redefinition of State Activity

The CD player shows the total time of the CD when it is in the state 'ready'. The next generation of the CD player aditionally shows the name of the CD. To achieve this we must expand the state activity of state 'ready'.

The redefinition of state activity is not restricted to a change of the code or pseudocode sequences. A state activity can also be redefined by modeling substates for this state.

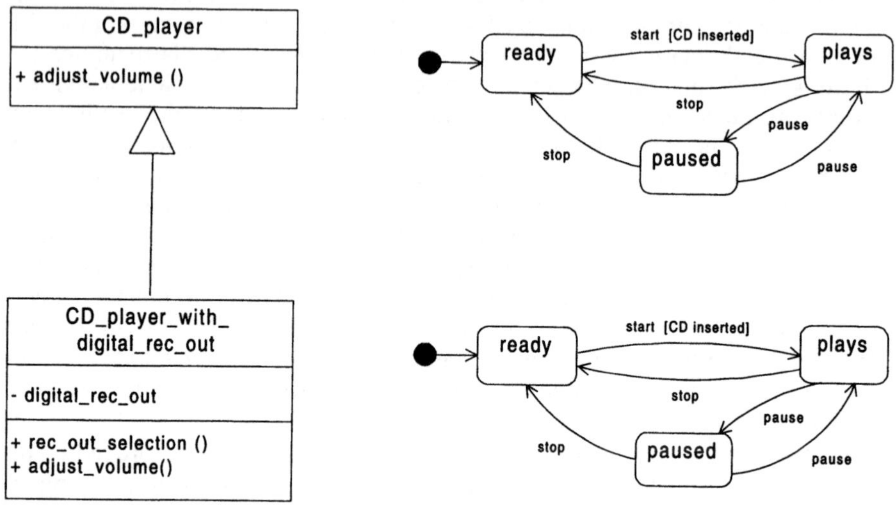

Figure 3: Unmodified state diagram

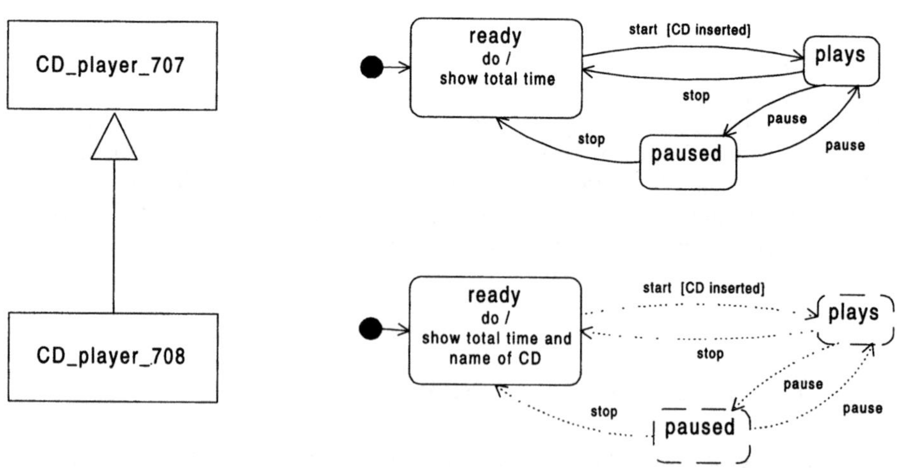

Figure 4: Redefinition of state activity

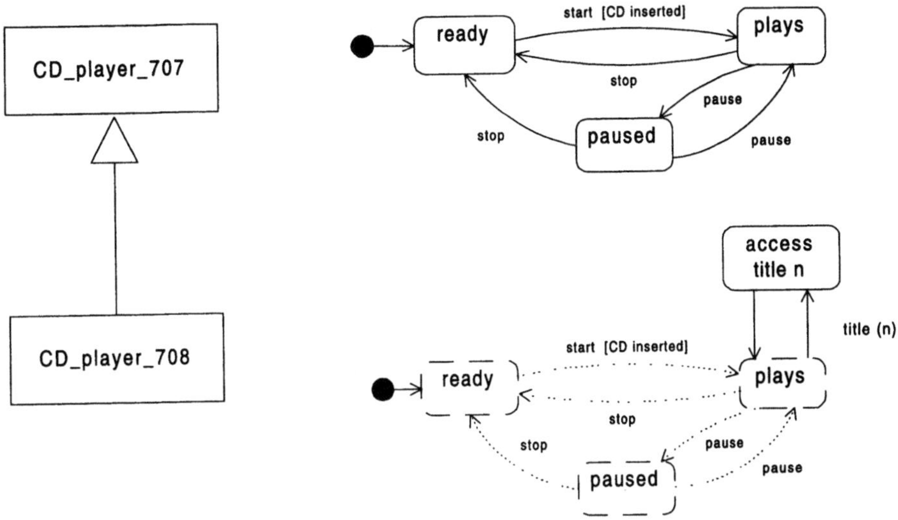

Figure 5: Additional states and transitions

3.2 Additional States and Transitions

We want to have direct access to the first 20 titles of the CD which can be selected by buttons. Therefore we need a new state defining the activity for accessing the chosen title. As shown in Fig. 5 the event of pushing the button fires a new transition which we draw from state 'plays' to the new state 'access title n'. The new state fires an unconditional automatic transition (a transition with no external event) leading back to the state 'plays'. When the selected title is not available, the CD player continues playing the title which was being played before the event 'title (n)' occurred.

3.3 Changing the Target State of a Transition

The next generation of the CD player is enhanced with a function 'program'. With this function we can determine which titles shall be skipped whenever a special CD is played. The information about what to skip can be saved in a program memory. After pushing the start button but before the CD is played, the CD player looks for a memory entry for the inserted CD. We define a new state 'program' and a new automatic transition to the state 'plays' (see Fig. 6). The target state of the transition initiated by the event 'start' must be changed to lead to the new state 'program'. The transitions fired by the event 'stop' are not concerned.

We are also allowed to change the target state of automatic transitions as automatic transitions are part of the internal behavior of an object (they are fired by completion of state activity) by which the object changes its state itself.

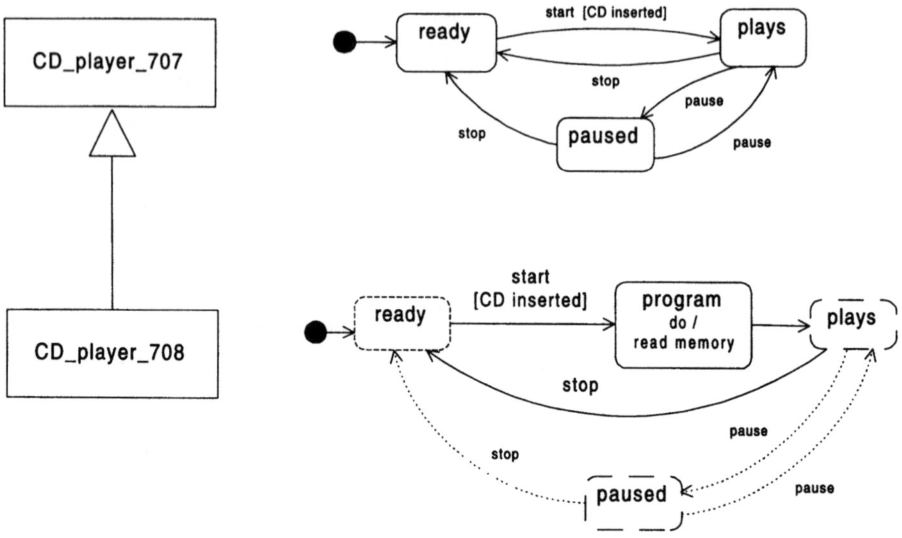

Figure 6: Changing the target state of a transition

3.4 Additional Transitions with External Events of the Superclass

We want the CD player to offer a function 'music scan' to play the first 10 seconds of each title, if we do not know the content of the CD. In order to initiate this function the button 'music scan' must be pushed. By pushing the start button the scan function is deactivated. The CD player will then switch to normal play mode and plays the last scanned title. We add a transition with the external event 'start' from the state 'music scanning' to the state 'plays' (see Fig. 7). Now there are two transitions fired by the same event. The event 'start' is accepted in two different states of the subclass.

3.5 Elimination of States

Now we ask an important question: Are be allowed to eliminate states of the superclass in the state diagram of the subclass or are the states of the superclass fully inherited? Thinking about deletion of states still produces an awkard feeling.

Answering this question consider the following example: The lifecycle of a biological cell consists of a state in which the cell gets to a definite size and then reproduces itself by division. In every division process the cell shortens its telomers (called telomerase). Telomers are base sequences at the end of the chromosomal DNA of the cell. When the telomers are used up, the cell cannot reproduce itselft any longer and will exist until it dies. A cell usually divides about 50 times, which is determined by the amount of its telomers. The state diagram in Fig. 8 shows a possible abstraction from the lifecycle of a cell.

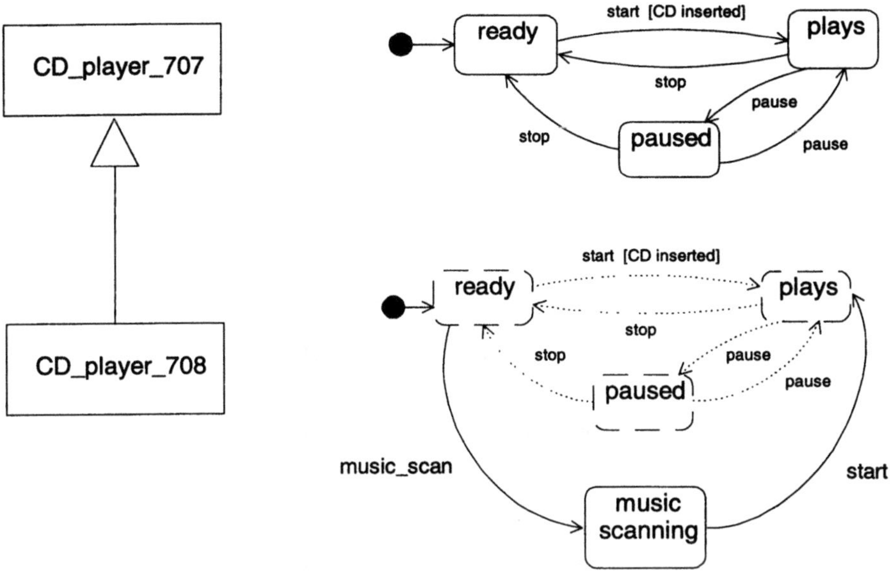

Figure 7: Additional transitions with external events of the superclass

Now we want to add a cancer cell to our system and model a state diagram for it. A cancer cell is a degenerated cell that never stops reproducing. The reason is that a cancer cell rebuilds the parts of the telomers that were cut off. Logically approached, the lifecycle of cancer cell shown in Fig. 9 of its own is a legitime abstraction. We could leave out the modeling of telomers because they are never used up.

After having introduced this new kind of cell we have to integrate it into our class hierarchy, which means establishing an inheritance relationship between the two classes 'cell' and 'cancer cell'. Obviously, the cancer cell is a special kind of a normal cell rather than the other way round. So we draw a generalization arrow from the cancer cell to the normal cell. This produces the hierarchy shown in Fig. 10.

The subclass 'cancer cell' now misses a state the superclass has, but leaving out a state on the subclass level is not so evident. Recalling the matching of state diagrams with class properties the class 'cell' would have a state method more than the class 'cancer cell' (state 'lives'). Regarding the inheritance on the class level the cancer cell does have the method for the state 'lives' because it inherits all attributes and methods of the class 'cell'. We realize an inconsistency: the cancer cell has a state method but there is no aquivalent state in its state diagram. This consistency problem between a model and source code occurs in all mentioned concepts for transformation of state diagrams (Shlaer and Mellor (1992), Harel (1997)) (see above).

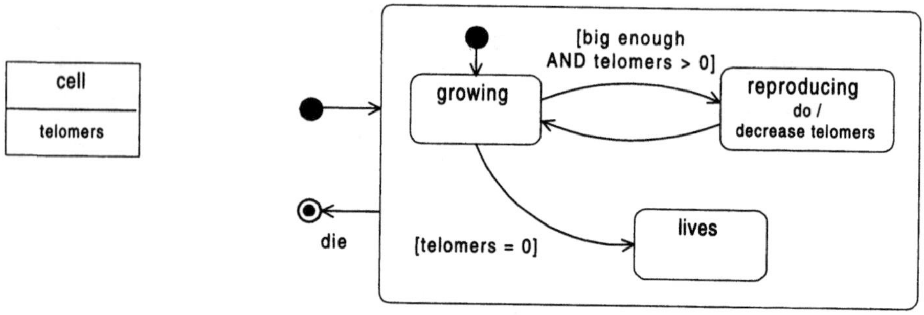

Figure 8: Life cycle of a cell

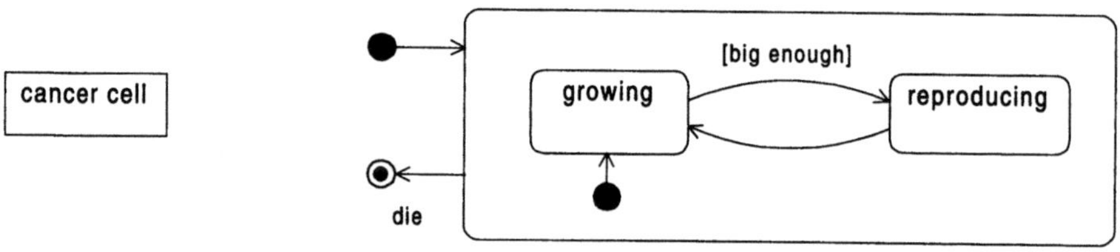

Figure 9: Life cycle of a cancer cell

We do not allow the elimination of states because of this inconsistency. This instruction is no problem since we can model the state diagram of the class 'cancer cell' in a different way. Either we redefine the activity of the state 'reproducing' so that the shortened telomers are reconstructed or we add an action with the same effect to the automatic transition between the states 'reproducing' and 'growing' (see Fig. 11).

Keeping the states and transitions of a superclass we could have left out in the state diagrams of a subclass makes sense in case that a subclass of the class 'cancer cell' may need this functionality again: We regard the development of a antidote for cancer what forces us to add a special cancer cell to our hierarchy as a subclass of the class 'cancer cell' that reacts to the antidote. We eliminate the action, wich we have added to the state diagram of the class 'cancer cell'. In this case we need the state 'lives' and the incoming automatic transition again. The new class then has the same state diagram as its super- superclass.

3.6 Elimination of Transitions

Contrary to elimination of states the deletion of transitions driven by external events causes no inconsistency concerning the matching with class properties, as long as at least one transition with a special event remains. The event method is modified so that the event is no longer valid for this state. If all transitions with a certain event are deleted, there are two problems. First, the interface conformity to the superclass is violated. This is because the subclass misses a public method

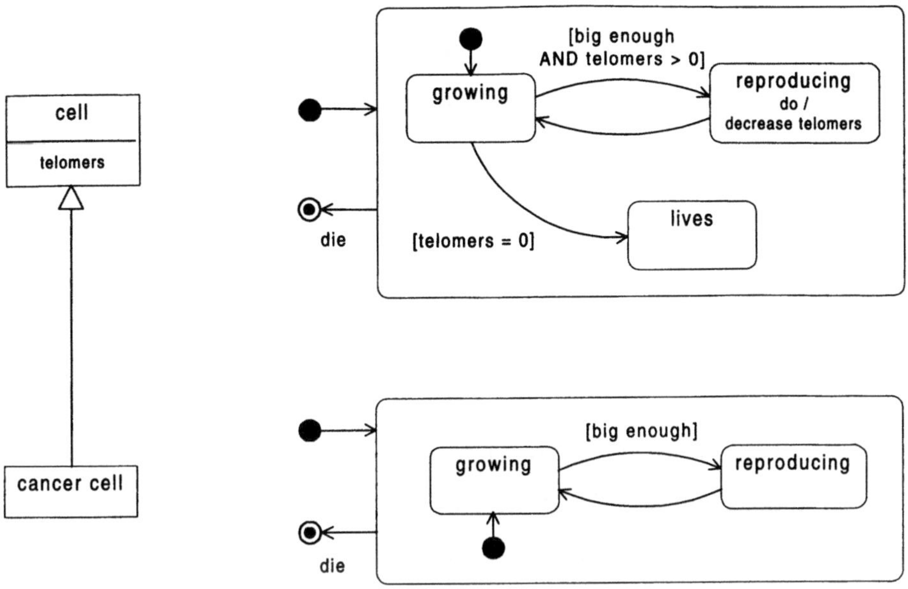

Figure 10: Elimination of states

its superclass has. Second, in the subclass no method for this event would be created during code generation. In fact, an object of the subclass would react to this event because the subclass inherits the event method on the class level.

In either case, the elimination of event driven transitions should not be recommended. We expect an object of a subclass to accept the same messages in the same states as an object of the superclass. We should be sure that an object responds in a particular state to the same events. The following activities or actions may differ, especially different state transitions sequences are allowed, but the reaction to events should conform to the dynamic of the superclass.

The elimination of automatic transitions can be allowed. The responsibility for triggering automatic transitions is up to the state activity. It will fire such a transition when having completed the activity. Thus we can interpret the triggering of automatic transitions as part of the internal behavior. Deletion of automatic transitions leaves the class interface unconcerned as they are not a reaction to external stimuli.

4 Summary of the Rules for Derivation of State Diagrams from a State Diagram of the Superclass

1. state diagram remains the same in the subclass
2. redefining state activities (polymorphic states)

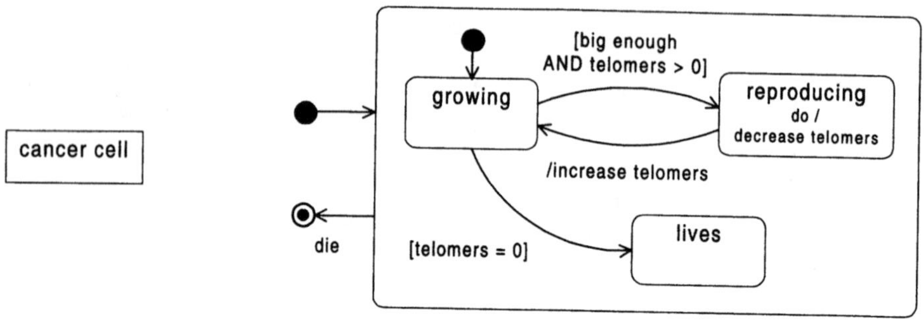

Figure 11: Elimination of states

3. additional states and additional transitions with new external events
4. additional transitions with given external events
5. additional transitions without external events (automatic transitions)
6. elimination of transitions without external events (automatic transitions)
7. additional conditions, actions and message-sending for transitions
8. elimination of conditions, actions and message-sending of transitions
9. changing the target state of a transition
10. isolate states (may happen by (8))

Inheritance of classes is based on redefining methods and adding methods, attributes and associations to the subclass. In reference to the concepts for matching state diagrams with classes we see, that the modeling rules for state diagrams support inheritance relationships between classes:
(2), (5), (6), (7), (8) complies with redefinition of state methods (4), (7), (8), (9) complies with redefinition of event methods (3) complies with additional methods Not allowed are the following actions:

11. elimination of transitions with external events
12. changing the source of a transition
13. elimination of states

As we have seen in the examples above, we cannot demand full behavioral conformity between two classes as this would not be observed in the real world. A class does not need to behave in the very same way in a certain state as its superclass and need not have identical state transitions. What we must ensure is that a class accepts the same events in a certain state as its superclass, but is free to define the following reaction. By avoiding the elimination of states and transitions and the changing of source states of a transition we can guarantee that a subclass reacts (not behaves) in the same way as the superclass. So to say we speak about "reaction conformity".

In (Harel (1997)) David Harel mentions that states and transitions can be added and that inherited states must not be deleted in the state diagram of the subclass (conforms to the points 1-5,7,8,9,13). Harel points out that the elimination of transitions is generally prohibited (conforms to point 11 but in contrast to point 6), but he suggests the implicit elimination of an automatic transition by making its guard false. Respecting point (12) Harel says that the source state of a transition must not be changed, but keeps a backdoor open: The change of a source state can be achieved by adding substates to this state and let the transition have one of these substates as its source. This proposal does not actually solve the problem: An event leading out of a superstate is global to all of its substates, so that the condition for the reaction of the superstate to this event is definately modified.

The aim of the presented modeling rules is to maintain structural, interface and reaction conformity with restrictions on what events are accepted in what order. Following these instructions we are able to build hierarchies of descriptions of dynamic behavior of classes that are clear and consistent and support reuse, maintainability and extensibility of source code as well as model elements. The intention of our approach is to serve as a piece of advice how to deal with problems of dynamic modeling in analysis and design and to suggest semantics for the inheritance of state diagrams.

5 Abstract State Diagrams

We have developed a set of consistent rules for modeling state diagrams and are able to match them with class properties. Thus we are now entitled to speak about "inheritance of state diagrams". As there is a many-to-many relationship between the type 'class' and the behavioral element 'state diagram' in the UML (Booch et al. (1997d), Booch et al. (1997b)), we can demand as a next step that also abstract classes can have state diagrams.

We introduce an abstract state diagram as a state diagram with at least one abstract state or one abstract transition. An abstract state is a stereotyped state with a defined name but undefined activities. In a concrete subclass the activities may be specified by another behavioral instance (Booch et al. (1997d), Booch et al. (1997b)) or a code sequence. An abstract transition can be defined as an automatic transition or a transition triggered by an external event. An abstract transition can have conditions, actions and message-sending. An abstract state diagram serves as an obligatory template for the behavior of a subclass. Fig. 12 shows a simple example for the specialization of an abstract class 'vehicle'.

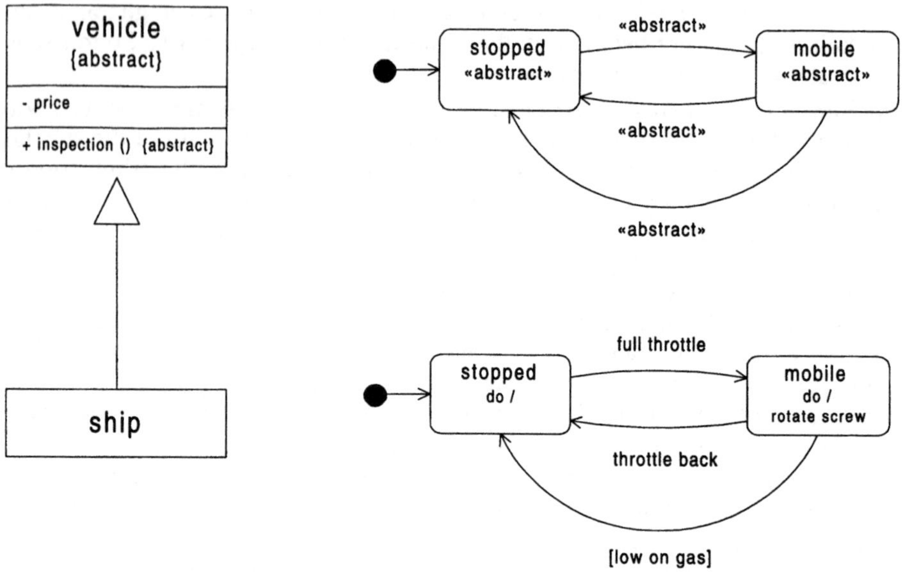

Figure 12: State diagrams of abstract classes

6 Result

The definition of modeling rules and semantics for the various possibilities of assignments of diagrams is a necessary and important step towards a useful application of the UML in object oriented software projects. This does not mean the definition of a method: The UML as a potential standard notation should give detailed instructions how to interpret each of these combinations, which is the basis for applying a method. This is essential for helping the software engineer reaching his goal to produce code from his models. The CASE-tool industry needs these definitions to develop consistency checkers, advanced code generators and documentation facilities for their products. The modeling of software by CASE-tools will then become more convenient, attractive and popular as it is today.

References

BOOCH, G. (1994): Object Oriented Analysis and Design with Applications, 2nd Edition, Benjamin/Cummings: Redwood City, California, 1994.

BOOCH, G. and RUMBAUGH, J. (1995): Unified Method for Object-Oriented Development, Documentation Set Version 0.8. Rational Software Corporation, 1995

BOOCH, G., RUMBAUGH, J., and JACOBSON, I. (1996): The Unified Modeling Language for Object-Oriented Development, Documentation Set Version 0.91 Addendum, Rational Software Corporation, Santa Clara, CA (USA), 1997, URL: http://www.rational.com

BOOCH, G., RUMBAUGH, J., and JACOBSON, I. (1997a): Unified Modeling Language, Notation Guide, Version 1.0, Rational Software Corporation, Santa Clara, CA (USA), 1997, URL: http://www.rational.com

BOOCH, G., RUMBAUGH, J., and JACOBSON, I. (1997b): Unified Modeling Language, UML Semantics, Version 1.0, Rational Software Corporation, Santa Clara, CA (USA), 1997, URL: http://www.rational.com

BOOCH, G., RUMBAUGH, J., and JACOBSON, I. (1997c): Unified Modeling Language, Notation Guide, Version 1.1, Rational Software Corporation, Santa Clara, CA (USA), 1997, URL: http://www.rational.com

BOOCH, G., RUMBAUGH, J., and JACOBSON, I. (1997d): Unified Modeling Language, UML Semantics, Version 1.1, Rational Software Corporation, Santa Clara, CA (USA), 1997, URL: http://www.rational.com

COAD, P. and YOURDON, E. (1990): Object Oriented Analysis. Yourdon Press Prentice Hall, 1990

COAD, P. and YOURDON, E. (1991): Object Oriented Design. Yourdon Press Prentice Hall, 1991

GAMMA, E., HELM, R., JOHNSON, R., and VLISSIDES, J. (1996): Design Patterns - Elements Of Reusable Object-Oriented Software. Addison Wesley 1996

HAREL, D. (1997): Executable Object Modeling With Statecharts. *Computer, 07/97*

JACOBSON, I., CHRISTERSON, M., JONSSON, P., and VERGAARD, G. (1992): Object-Oriented Software Engineering - A Use Case Driven Approach. Addison-Wesley Publishing Company, 1992

METZ, P. (1997): Code Generation Concepts And Methods For The Unified Modeling Language v1.0. diploma thesis, Fachhochschule Darmstadt, 1997

METZ, P. and WEBER, W.: Modeling Synchronous And Asynchronous Communication Between Objects. working group 'fundamentals of object-oriented modeling' (GROOM), German Association Of Computer Science

RUMBAUGH, J., BLAHA, M., EDDY, F., and LORENSEN, W. (1993): Objektorientiertes Modellieren und Entwerfen. Prentice Hall/Hanser, 1993

SHLAER, S. and MELLOR, S.J. (1992): Object Lifecycles - Modeling The World In States. Prentice Hall, 1992.

Part 3

Business Process Modeling and Applications

Application of UML Within the Scope of New Telecommunication Architectures

E. Holz

Humboldt-University Berlin

Department of Computer Science
A.-Springer-Str.54a
10117 Berlin, Germany
holz@informatik.hu-berlin.de

Abstract: The telecommunication market is one of the fastest growing markets in the last years. Deregulation in the provider market, new techniques and user demands lead to more flexibility but require also the coexistence of legacy telecommunication systems with new and more advanced technologies. Although being known conservative in the introduction of new technologies, the new requirements have forced the industry to increase the time-to-market for new services and to apply new reference architectures.

This paper investigates, how the new object oriented modeling language UML (Unified Modeling Language) can be applied in this domain.

1 Telecommunication Systems

Telecommunication systems can be roughly divided into three main areas: Communication protocols, telecommunication services and telecommunication management systems. A fourth group, which will not be considered here, comprises basic hard- and software (switches, routers) and customer premises equipment. Communication protocols include signaling protocols used to setup, control and tear down calls and connections and transport protocols used to transmit data between participants in a telecommunication system. Telecommunication services may be provided by the network operator (telecommunication company) or by 3rd parties. Typical current day examples include call-forwarding, voice-mail, video-conference etc. Management systems are used to control and administer telecommunication systems, Usual tasks here are authorization, authentication, subscription and unsubscription and billing.

The last years witness an increasing fading of the traditional boarders between telecommunications systems and information processing distributed computer networks. Common reference models as ODP lead to similar domain specific solutions and standards. Two major players are OMG's CORBA and the public network operators's TINA.

Due to the fact that telecommunication systems of different network providers have to cooperate worldwide, standardization of protocols, interfaces and services is necessary. Examples for such standards resp. families of standards are ISDN (Integrated Services Digital Networks), Broadband-ISDN, IN (Intelligent Network) or TMN (Telecommunication Management Network).

1.1 Reference Models and Description Techniques

Reference models serve as a framework for the development of telecommunication systems and standards. They provide an abstract architecture and a common terminology limiting thus the universe of discourse. The most recent result in the development of such reference models is the Reference Model of Open Distributed Processing (RM-ODP), which was a joint standardization activity of ITU-T and ISO. It clearly reflects the shift of the focus away from pure protocols and services towards open systems of distributed objects. The abstract infrastructure defined here enables objects to interact at there interfaces with other objects. To cope with the complexity of distributed systems the concept of viewpoints and transparencies has been introduced.

Two other standardization activities related to the RM-ODP are Common Object Request Broker Architecture (CORBA) by the OMG and Telecommunications Information Networking Architecture (TINA) by TINA-C. The purpose of these industry consortia is the employment of ODP to concrete application areas (distributed computer systems, telecommunication).

For the formalization of the standards as well as for the development of applications a series of different description and specification techniques is applied. Most notably are here SDL (ITU-T Specification and Description Language) and MSC (message Sequence Charts). Both are formal techniques developed by ITU-T and do find an increasing use. However, plain english text is still extensively used.

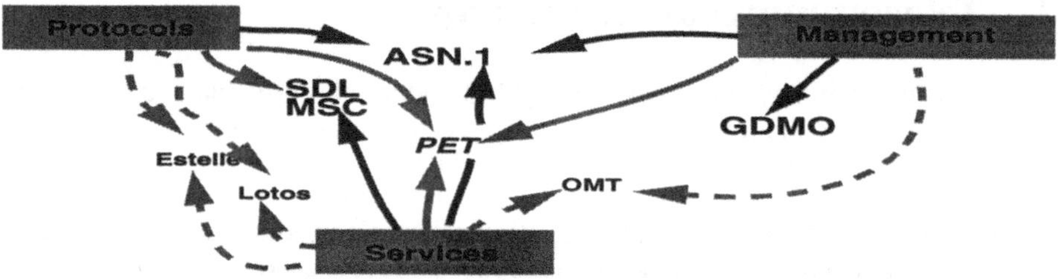

Figure 1: Description techniques for telecommunication systems.

2 Modeling Concepts of RM-ODP and TINA

The development of the Reference Model for Open Distributed Processing (RM-ODP) is an ongoing joint standardization activity of ITU-T and ISO. It aims at a framework to organize services within autonomous systems in order to facilitate interworking of software components distributed into larger and larger systems. The RM-ODP provides:

- a general modeling approach and a set of general concepts
- a method to divide a specification into five viewpoints in order to simplify the specification process

The RM-ODP standard is divided into four main parts:

1. Part 1 - Overview and Guide to Use
2. Part 2 - Foundations
3. Part 3 - Architecture
4. Part 4 - Architectural Semantics

A series of related standards defining languages and ODP components is currently under development, especially the ODP Trader and the Interface Definition Language (IDL). Although still in development the ODP standard has already influenced major developments in the area of distributed and telecommunication systems. The Telecommunication Information Network Architecture (TINA) is strongly applying the concepts of ODP. The following sections will give a short introduction into ODP/TINA and its concepts.

2.1 Concepts

Objects and actions are the most basic modeling concepts of ODP. An object as a model of an entity is characterized dually by its behavior and its state. A change in an objects state can only occur as a result of an internal action or an interaction with its environment (encapsulation). Such interactions with the objects environment occur at interaction points. Interfaces form partitions of the interactions of an object, they are abstractions of the behavior of objects consisting of a subset of the interactions together with a set of constraints on when they may occur. Informally, objects are said to perform functions and offer services. A service specification captures e.g. data representation, transport protocol, location etc.

To hide the aspects of a system that arise through its distribution an ODP infrastructure supports a set of distribution transparencies. Developers of applications can concentrate on the design of their application without addressing distribution aspects. Some important distribution transparencies are:

- Access Transparency
- Location Transparency
- Migration Transparency.

The management of the large amount of information usually involved in the complete specification of a complex distributed system is addressed by the concept of viewpoints. Viewpoints are separations of concern. They give a partial view of the complete system specification. Five different viewpoints are identified in the RM-ODP:

- Information viewpoint

- Enterprise viewpoint
- Computational viewpoint
- Engineering viewpoint
- Technology viewpoint.

Each viewpoint is associated with a viewpoint language expressing the rules which are relevant to the respective universe of discourse. To verify the conformance between real implementations and specifications and the compliance between two specifications the RM-ODP introduces the concept of reference points. Reference points are selected interaction points serving as potential conformance points. Four different classes of reference points have been introduced:

- Programmatic Reference Points
- Perceptual Reference Points
- Interworking Reference Point
- Interchange Reference Point

Additional information required when testing an implementation of an ODP specification is called Implementation eXtra Information for Testing (IXIT). Those information relate Implementation Conformance Statements (ICS)—i.e conformance points, required behavior etc.—to their realization in an implementation. In order to test the conformance of an implementation under test the tester has to provide sets of IXIT's and ICS relating the concepts and structures of the enterprise, information and computational specification of the system to its engineering specification and a set of IXIT's and ICS relating the concepts and structures of the engineering specification to the implementation choices made in the technology specification/implementation.

The RM-ODP defines concepts and common functions of distributed systems in a generic manner. Refinements and specializations of this model are explicitly encouraged and are currently under way (e.g. TINA-C). Standards for the realization of common functions, so called component standards, fill out the framework and are providing a base for the development of ODP applications. The Trader standard is one of the central component standards. It has reached the status of an International standard.

2.2 ODP Viewpoints

The viewpoint concept is essential for the whole RM-ODP. Each viewpoint is focusing on a subset of the properties of the system (cf. Table 1). The viewpoint concept can be applied at large at the whole system or at a different level of abstraction to individual components of the system.

Viewpoint	Focus on
Enterprise viewpoint	purpose scope policies
Information viewpoint	semantics of information information processing
Computational viewpoint	functional decomposition objects interacting at interfaces
Engineering viewpoint	mechanisms/functions required to support distributed interactions between objects
Technology viewpoint	choice of technology

Table 1: Viewpoints and their Focuses

The RM-ODP does not define a general mapping or correspondence between every pair of viewpoint languages, however, special relationships between the computational and information resp. the computational and engineering viewpoint are identified. The RM-ODP does also not prescribe any chronological order for the development of specifications for the different viewpoints, on the contrary—it favours a parallel development of the specifications. Nevertheless, a development process starting with the enterprise specification, followed by (possibly interleaved) specification of information, computational and engineering viewpoints and concluded by the technology specification seems to be an adequate way for the development of ODP systems.

Part 3 of the RM-ODP contains the abstract definition of the viewpoint languages. A concrete syntax for these languages is not given, the language definitions contain only the concepts and rules for the specification from the selected viewpoint. This allows to use existing or evolving languages/notation techniques as concrete viewpoint languages. The languages envisaged here range from natural languages over programming languages to formal description techniques (FDT). Mappings between the computational and information languages and the standardized FDTs SDL-92, LOTOS, Estelle, Z and ACT.ONE are given in Part-4 of RM-ODP.

2.2.1 Enterprise Viewpoint

An enterprise specification presents an ODP system and its environment as a community. The community is specified in terms of roles played by the objects of the community, the policies governing interaction, creation/deletion and configuration and the activities undertaken by the system. Fulfilling a role implies for an object that it becomes subject to permissions, obligations and prohibitions.

2.2.2 Information Viewpoint

The main concept for the description of the semantics of information and information-processing is the scheme. Three different kinds of schemes are defined for the information language:

- Invariant Schema
- Static Schema
- Dynamic Schema.

A template of an information object references to all three of these schemes. The invariant schema is a set of predicates constraining the possible states and state changes of an object. The static schema specifies a state of an information object and the dynamic schema the allowable state changes of that object. Schemes may apply to a single object or to a set of objects. Information object templates may be atomic (lowest level of abstraction) or are represented as a composition of other information object templates. An information specification needs not be apt for distribution.

2.2.3 Computational Viewpoint

The computational viewpoint specifies the functional decomposition of an ODP system. ODP applications and functions are defined in terms of computational objects interacting at interfaces. Computational interfaces are divided into stream interfaces (continuous information flows between producer and consumer) and operational interfaces (support of announcements and interrogations). A computational object may have multiple interfaces. In order for two computational object to interact, both objects have to provide the appropriate complementary interfaces and a binding between these interfaces must exist. Each attempt for interaction at an unbound interface fails. The computational language distinguishes between primitive binding and compound binding. Primitive binding enables the binding between two interfaces whereas compound binding connects a set of interfaces. In the latter case special binding objects support the binding. The computational language defines rules for the structure of a computational specification, for the interactions, the binding as well as failure and portability rules. Computational objects are potential candidates for distribution.

2.2.4 Engineering Viewpoint

In the engineering viewpoint an abstract infrastructure is defined to support the distribution of an ODP system. The specification is expressed in terms of engineering objects, activities within these objects and interactions between them.

The engineering languages imposes a structuring of the configuration of engineering objects into clusters, capsules and nodes. The atomic objects are the

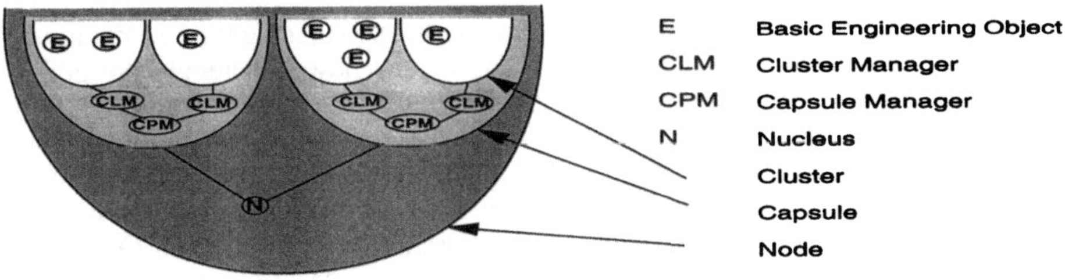

Figure 2: Structure of an engineering specification

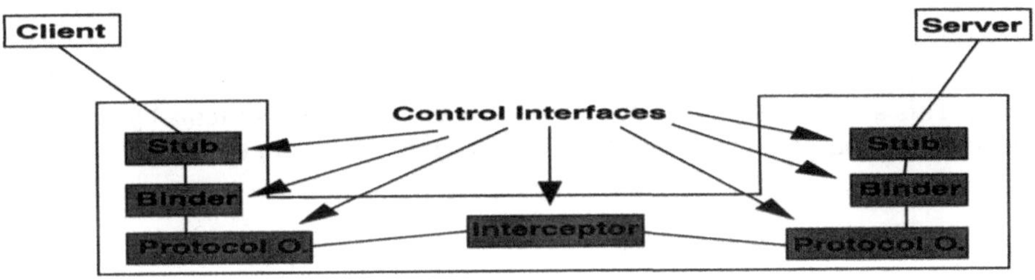

Figure 3: Engineering channel

basic engineering objects (i.e. objects that require the support of a distributed infrastructure).

Channels provide the means for the binding of interfaces of basic engineering objects. A channel is structured in stubs, binders protocol objects and interceptors.

2.2.5 Technology Viewpoint

A technology specification expresses how the specifications of an ODP system are implemented (e.g. programming language, infrastructure etc.) and defines the information required for testing from an implementors view (IXIT's).

3 Viewpoint Specification with UML

The specification and description of telecommunication systems can serve different purposes, which strongly influence the style of the specification. Standards and public specifications (i.e. specifications to be submitted to 3rd parties) have due to competition grounds a very descriptive nature. They do not prescribe any concrete implementation and hide technical solutions. Design specifications on the other side are prescriptive and will finally lead to an implementation. Within this paper mainly standard specifications will be considered.

Object oriented analysis and design techniques (OOAD) have been applied successfully for the development of large applications. Their advantage is that the object oriented paradigm is consistently applied through all stages of the design up to the implementation. The development of UML has now also adopted some key concepts for the development of distributed systems, e.g. interface and exception. This leads to the question whether UML is suited as a concrete viewpoint language for some or all viewpoints. First attempts to apply OOAD for the specification of viewpoints have been made by ODP and TINA-C, however this is restricted to the information viewpoint only. In both cases only the class diagrams of OMT, one predecessor of UML, have been used. The remaining part gives an outline, how the different models of UML can be applied within different viewpoints and how those viewpoint specifications can be related. The Trader is used as an example to explain the chosen approach. This example was selected due to the existence of a complete and standardized specification in the enterprise, information and computational viewpoint and its importance for distributed systems. The Trader allows server objects to advertise their services and client objects to find services they need. This supports the concept of openness in distributed systems by enabling the dynamic introduction, removal or modification of servers and clients.

3.1 Enterprise Viewpoint

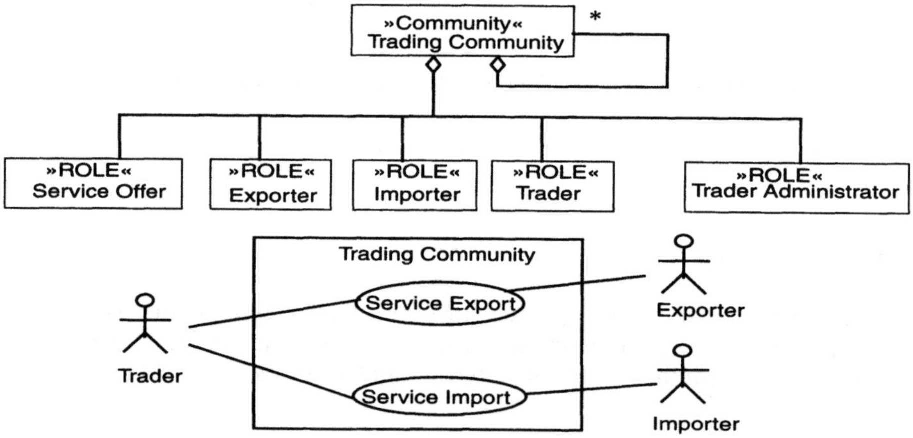

Figure 4: Engineering viewpoint.

In the engineering viewpoint a trading system is seen as a community which references 5 different roles which objects can play within the community. These roles are Exporter/Importer, Service Offer, Trader and Trader Administrator. Objects participating in a trader community may play more than one role, i.g. an exporter of some services may be importer for some other services, a trader itself may be an importer of another trading community. For administrative or technical reasons a trader community can be subdivided into other trader communities. The different activities of the trading community are reflected by use cases. The behavior of the single use cases may be specified by sequence charts as shown in Figure 5 or by collaboration diagrams.

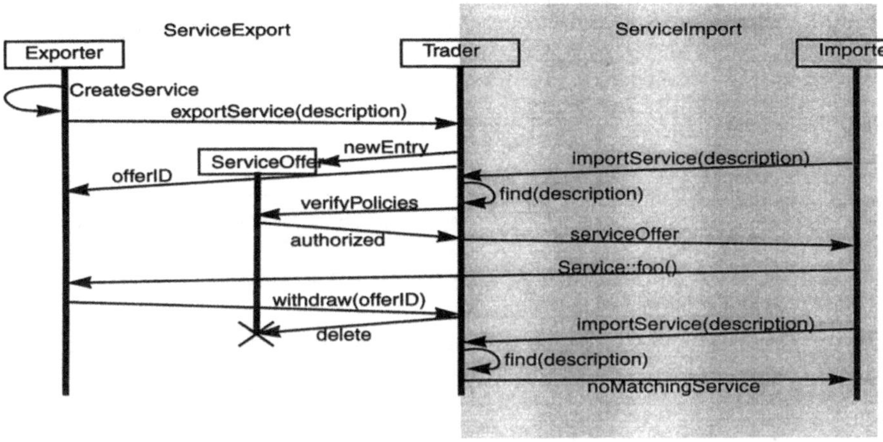

Figure 5: Engineering viewpoint - behavior.

3.2 Information Viewpoint

An information specification is given as a configuration of information objects. A template for an information objects references invariant, static and dynamic schemata. The static and invariant schemata are represented in UML by classes and objects, the dynamic schemata are additionally reflected by a set of state diagrams. A Trading systems consists of a configuration of interconnected nodes,

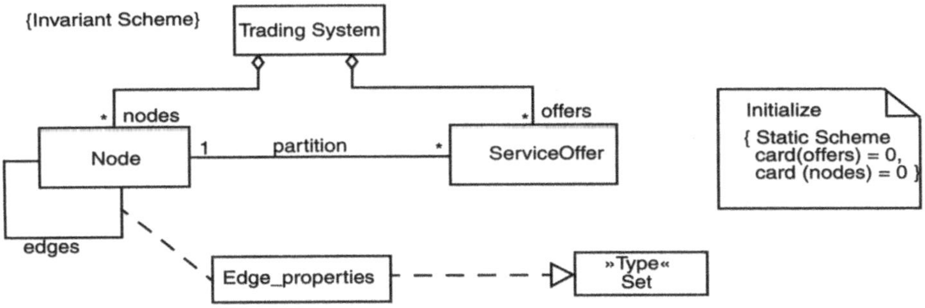

Figure 6: Information viewpoint.

which are used to partition the set of service offers. Each service offer belongs to exactly one node. Initially a trading system does not have nodes or service offers (static scheme initialize). In Figure 6 an example for a dynamic scheme is given in form of a collaboration diagram. It shows, how the state of the trading system is changed by the operation export. The OCL notation has been applied to formulate constraints and conditions. A Trader object template will reference a series of such collaboration diagrams (dynamic schemes), one for each trader operation. Alternatively activity diagrams or state diagrams may be used.

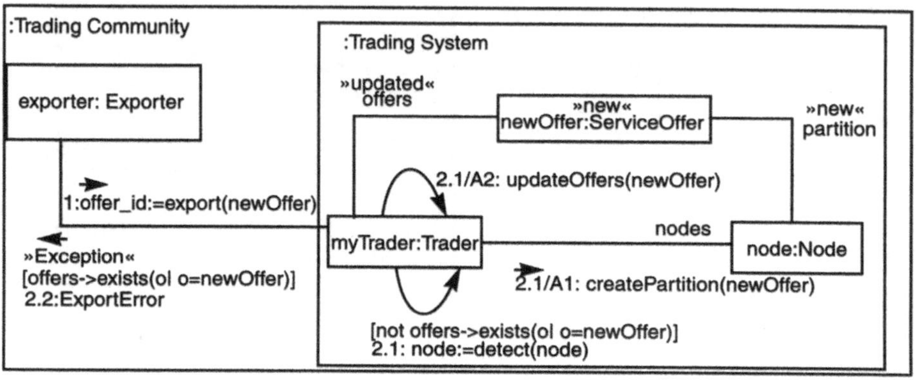

Figure 7: Information viewpoint - behavior.

3.3 Computational Viewpoint

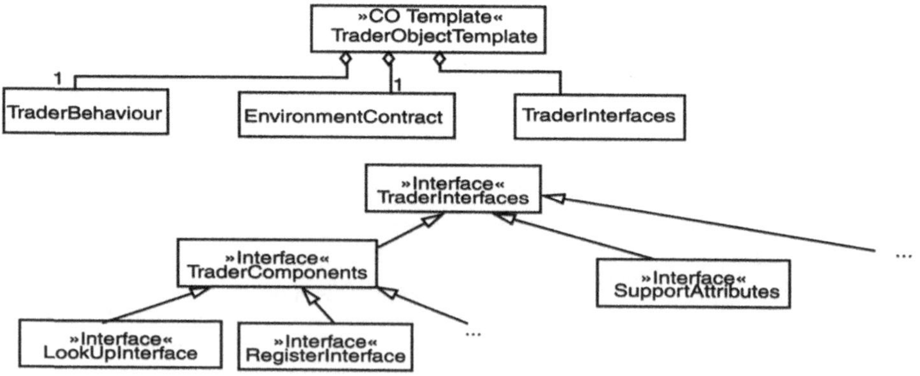

Figure 8: Computational viewpoint.

In the computational viewpoint the system is divided into objects which are potential candidates for distribution. These objects may interact at their interfaces. The object behavior and the interactions are governed by contracts. Consequently the computational object template for a Trader references the trader behavior, an environment contract and a set of templates for trader interfaces.

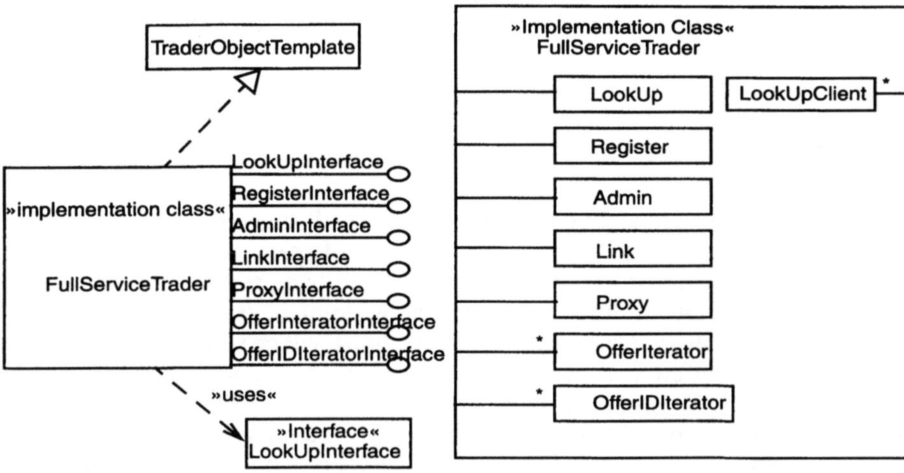

Figure 9: Computational viewpoint - concrete realization.

The different kinds of trader interfaces can be classified using a generalization/specialization hierarchy. In Figure 9 one concrete realization of the trader template, the FullServiceTrader, is shown. It provides all different Trader Interfaces, some of them may have multiple interface instances (e.g. OfferIterator). By attaching the stereotype »Implementation Class« it is indicated that FullServiceTrader is candidate for implementation as a single object within a distributed system.

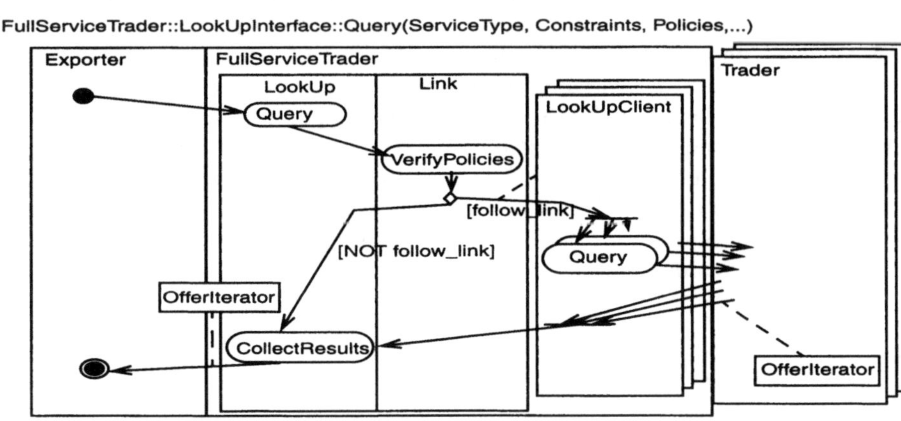

Figure 10: Computational viewpoint - behavior.

The behavior of the object can be specified by statecharts, its behavior in relation to other objects by collaboration diagrams or (as shown in Figure 10) by activity diagrams with swimlanes. It is clearly visible here, how the export operation is propagated to the FullServiceTrader and from there to other Traders of the community.

4 Conclusions

As an object oriented modeling language UML is well suited for the specification of object oriented systems. The direct reflection of many concepts, the variety of models supported and the semantics make it to one candidate for the specification of viewpoints in the telecommunication domain. By applying the same technique to different viewpoints, the specifications will be better understandable and the learning effort will be decreased. At the same time the transition between different viewpoints will be eased. The extension features of UML (e.g. stereotypes) make it possible to tailor the language to the application area, gaining more compact specifications. This could be supported by libraries/packages of predefined concepts. Tool support is a must for the specification and development of large systems. Currently a series of companies have started to develop tools for UML, supporting not only the specification development, but also code generation and reengineering. Especially the last two topics are of increasing importance. The pure generation of pure code skeletons is not sufficient, code generation for the behavior parts is required too (and supported by non-UML tools used in the telecommunications industry).

Nevertheless, the use of UML in the telecommunication domain is not without problems. Most of them stem from differences in the semantics of concepts. Whereas in UML interfaces are a pure typing concepts, ODP and TINA support interfaces as a more structural concept. They may be instantiated, deleted and addressed. Interactions between complementary interfaces (client/server) requires a dynamic binding of interfaces, what is also not supported by UML. This binding concept is an important feature for the specification of distributed and telecommunication systems. It abstractly models the different communication relations (calls, connections) and enables the dynamic reconfiguration and the evolution of such systems. Other important features missing in UML are models for continuous data communication (streams), which are needed for multimedia systems. This comprises not only different connectivity kinds (one-two-one, one-to-many or multipoint-to-multipoint) but also bundling of stream flows, synchronisation or splitting of streams.

5 Related Work

The application of oo techniques in the telecommunications industry is still in its introduction phases. Some important directions are the object oriented extensions to SDL (SDL-92, SDL-96), standardized by the ITU-T and combinations of SDL and OMT. These efforts do increase the importance of SDL in this application domain and make this language to a strong competitor to UML. However, it can be expected that UML will be used instead of OMT. Another development concerns object and interface definition languages. The language IDL, developed by OMG, is now a joint standard of ITU-T and ISO, the language ODL (Object Definition Language, developed by TINA-C is expected to become an ITU standard in near future (1998/1999).

References

ITU-T Rec. X.901 | ISO/IEC 10746-1 (1995): Open Distributed Processing - Reference Model Part 1: Overview, ITU-T

ITU-T Rec. X.902 | ISO/IEC 10746-2 (1995): Open Distributed Processing - Reference Model Part 2: Descriptive Model, ITU-T

ITU-T Rec. X.903 | ISO/IEC 10746-3 (1995): Open Distributed Processing - Reference Model Part 3: Prescriptive Model, ITU-T

ITU-T Rec. X.904 | ISO/IEC 10746-4 (1995): Open Distributed Processing - Reference Model Part 2: Architectural Semantics, ITU-T

ISO/IEC CD 14750 (1996): Open Distributed Processing - Interface Definition Language, ISO/ITU-T DIS

ITU-T Rec. X.950 | ISO/IEC 13235 (1995): Open Distributed Processing - Reference Model ODP Trading Function, ITU-T

ITU-T Rec. Z.100 (1992): ITU-T Specification and Description Language, ITU-T

RATIONAL (1997a): UML Semantics V1.1

RATIONAL (1997b): UML Notation Guide V1.1

TINA-C (1994): Overall Concepts and Principles of TINA, TINA-C

TINA-C (1996a): Object Definition Language - Manual Version 2.3, TINA-C

TINA-C (1996b): Computational Modeling Concepts, TINA-C

Using UML for Business Object Based Systems Modeling

A. Korthaus

Lehrstuhl für Wirtschaftsinformatik III,
Universität Mannheim, D-68131 Mannheim, Germany

Abstract: The development of business information systems based on business object components as defined by the OMG is going to complement and simplify the conventional approach to object-oriented software development. The intention is to enable end users and business experts to assemble "plug-and-play" business objects without the help of IT experts. In spite of the reduction of complexity to be expected, a model-based approach to systems development is still essential. Business objects are not only well suited as modeling concepts in software engineering, they may even be used in the context of business engineering. This paper describes different aspects of modeling business objects with the Unified Modeling Language and evaluates its aptitude for that purpose.

1 Introduction

Today, enterprises need to adapt themselves in a flexible way to a rapidly changing environment, in order to remain competitive. To keep up with the dynamic competition, a considerable number of measures has to be taken, for which buzzwords such as *Business (Re-)Engineering*, *Continuous Improvement* etc. have been coined (e.g. in Hammer and Champy (1994)). The basis for these measures is the modeling of the business and its business processes in order to cope with the complexities of the real world. Based on the business models, software systems have to be built, which are one of the most important enablers of modern successful business activities, not only since new WWW-based processes have become feasible (Davenport (1993)).

Recognizing the close connection between the business perspective and the software perspective, and trying to exploit the advantages of object technology (e.g. modularization, encapsulation, inheritance, polymorphism etc.), Taylor (1995) has propagated an integrated approach called *Convergent Engineering* (see Figure 1). This synergetic approach suggests the application of object-oriented concepts on every level of the system's lifecycle, from business engineering through analysis and design of information systems to the implementation. Thus, the use of information systems to support newly designed business processes is emphasized. The challenge is to ensure a quick implementation of changed or new business requirements, since timing aspects have become essential today (in addition to keeping the quality high and the costs low).

In the field of object-oriented software technology, mechanisms such as model-based specification, component technology, and solution assembly by end users, which are increasingly gaining attention, seem to be very promising in order to achieve these goals. The Object Management Group (OMG), the leading industry

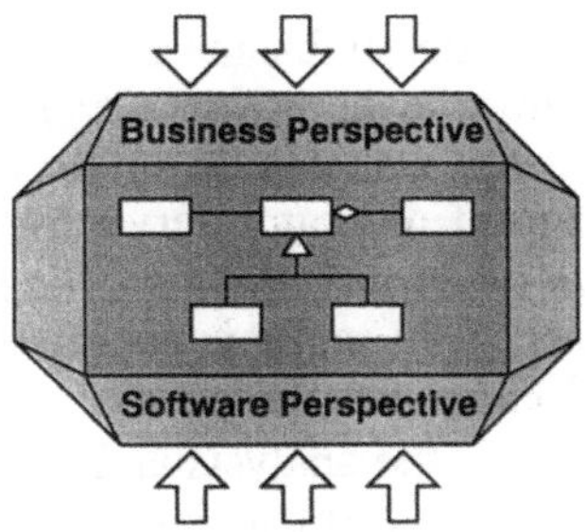

Figure 1: Convergent Engineering

consortium for object technology, is a key driver of these trends. It provides and seeks standards to facilitate the development of distributed information systems. In Nov. 1997, the *Unified Modeling Language* (Rational Software Corp. (1997a)–(1997d)) was adopted as the official standard for modeling languages, and revised proposals for so-called *Business Object* components and a *Business Object Facility* as an infrastructure for those components based on CORBA are currently being evaluated (OMG (1996)).

After clarifying the concepts of UML and OMG Business Objects, this paper will analyze exemplary requirements originating from business object based modeling and implementation of business and software systems.

2 Modeling with the UML

The UML version 1.1 is the new industry standard for object-oriented analysis and design modeling languages. It combines common concepts of earlier analysis and design methods, defines standard notational symbols for those concepts, and enhances the basic set with new modeling elements meeting the requirements of current modeling tasks. The UML is a general purpose language designed to be able to model a wide range of different types of systems, from purely technical (non-software) through software to business systems.

In this paper, the focus is on business and software systems. According to Eriksson and Penker (1998), business systems "describe the goals, the resources (humans, computers etc.), the rules (laws, business strategies, policies etc.), and the actual work in the business (business processes)". Information systems, on the other hand, "store, retrieve, transform, and present information to users. [They] Handle large amounts of data with complex relationships, which are stored in relational or object databases."

Modeling a system with UML means describing different views of the system under construction with the help of a number of diagrams, containing modeling elements. *Use Case Diagrams*, for example, express the externally visible behavior of the system and its interactions with actors, e.g. users or different systems. They are just right for modeling business processes or information system requirements on a very abstract level. *Class Diagrams* are the structural part of the system model, expressing elements or entities of the respective business or software system. A group of diagrams serves for describing behavioral aspects. Among them are *State Diagrams, Activity Diagrams, Sequence Diagrams* and *Collaboration Diagrams*. The implementation level may be described by *Component Diagrams* and *Deployment Diagrams*.

Compared with its predecessors, the analysis and design methods Booch, OMT and OOSE, UML adds some new elements: extensibility mechanisms (stereotypes, tagged values, constraints), modeling support for patterns and collaborations, Activity Diagrams, refinement, interfaces and components, and the Object Constraint Language (OCL). As will be shown in section 4, these are very valuable concepts in the context of business object based modeling.

3 OMG Business Objects

Using object-oriented modeling for business engineering is relatively new and not very wide-spread at present, although it is broadly acknowledged as an excellent approach of modeling and documenting businesses and business processes (Ferstl and Sinz (1995), Frank (1994), Jacobson et al. (1995), Taylor (1995)). Analyzing, improving, and implementing business processes is tightly bound up with designing and implementing the supporting information systems. Therefore, if the same object-oriented concepts and models are applied on each level of the system lifecycle, the result will be considerable synergistic effects.

The UML can be used for developing business models, which describe, among other things, resources (physical and informational), rules, goals, and actions (workflows), and for developing business software system models as well. Figure 2 shows an example of an incomplete inheritance hierarchy of typical business elements expressed with UML modeling constructs (classes, inheritance arrows, and constraints which indicate that there are possibly more subclasses that are missing in the hierarchy) as it might be used to build a taxonomy of business elements in an enterprise as a basis for communication. These concepts might be used further in object models describing organizational structures and processes of the same enterprise.

Recently, the OMG, whose focus used to be on technical aspects of distributed information systems solely, has been recognizing the fact that distributed object technologies can only become wide-spread if business users and application developers are addressed directly and can be shielded from technical IT details. In 1993, a Special Interest Group for Business Object Management (BOMSIG) was formed within the OMG, which was upgraded as Business Object Domain Task Force (BODTF) afterwards. BOMSIG issued a Request For Proposal for *Common Business Objects* and a *Business Object Facility*, which solicited proposals for the following two items, based on ideas of Sims (1994):

- "*Common Business Objects (CBOs):* Objects representing those business semantics that can be shown to be common across most businesses.

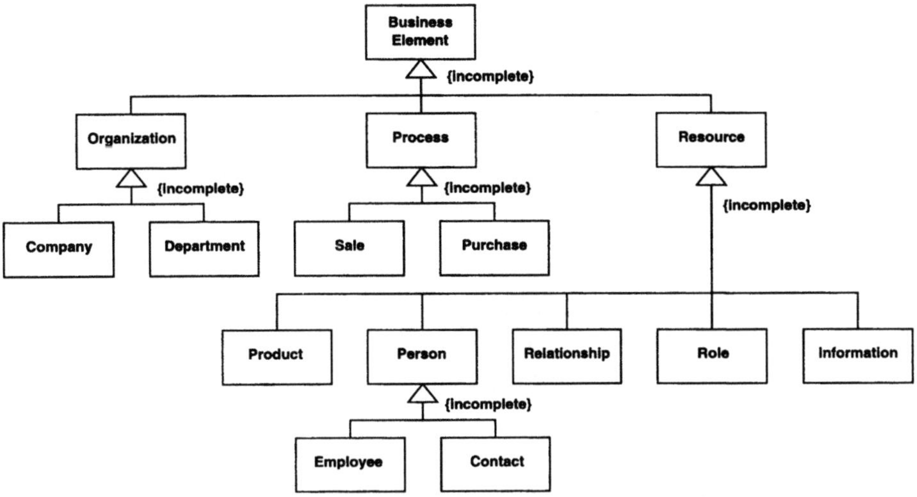

Figure 2: Part of a Specialization Hierarchy of Business Elements

- *Business Object Facility (BOF):* The infrastructure (application architecture, services, etc.) required to support business objects operating as cooperative application components in a distributed object environment." (OMG(1996))

The first part of the RFP asks for Common Business Objects, which represent concepts shared among different business domains (e.g. industry sectors such as finance, insurance, manufacturing etc.). Since it is very hard to reach an agreement on CBOs shared by different domains, the OMG is also trying to standardize domain variations as well as regional variations on CBOs and, of course, purely domain specific business objects not shared between different industry sectors.

After a long debate, the members of the CBO Working Group of the OMG BODTF are now arriving at a common understanding of the term business object. Business objects capture "information about a real world's (business) concept, operations on that concept, constraints on those operations, and relationships between that concept and other business concepts. [...] a business application can be specified in terms of interactions among a configuration of implemented business objects." (OMG (1997a))

Consequently, the term business object is used in two distinct ways, expressing the different areas of application, namely business engineering and software engineering:

1. The term *modeling business objects* designates the usage of business objects in business models to capture business concepts and express an abstract view of the business.

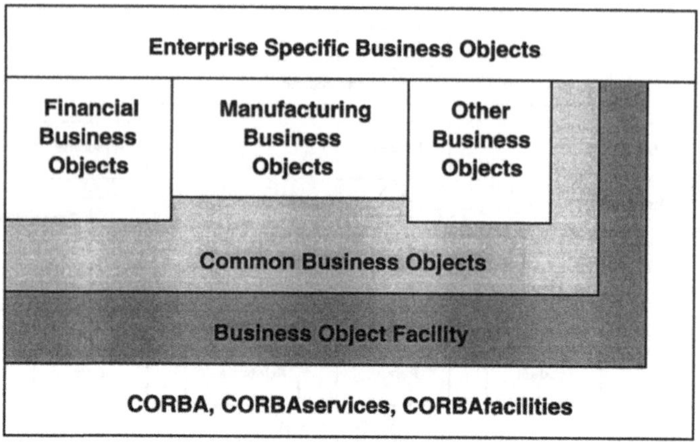

Figure 3: Architecture for Business Objects

2. The term *systems business objects* is used in the context of software system designs or program code. Systems business objects reflect the realization of business concepts (represented by modeling business objects) in software.

Business objects are organized into a taxonomy of *Entity Business Objects* (e.g. Involved Party, Location, Product, Agreement, Order, Financial Instrument), *Process Business Objects* (e.g. Order Fulfillment, Procurement, Making a Payment), and *Event Business Objects* (e.g. Account Overdrawn, End of Fiscal Year, Bond Mature).

Figure 3 (OMG (1996)) shows the proposed architecture for business objects. Integrated in OMG's Object Management Architecture (OMA), which includes a reference model for distributed object computing and defines OMG's objectives and terminology, the Business Object Facility (BOF), based on CORBA, provides the infrastructure for CBOs, domain specific BOs and enterprise specific BOs.

The major goals of the OMG Common Business Object (CBO) vision are:

- "Interoperability of OMG Business Objects as both design-time and run-time constructs including the possibility of ad-hoc integration.

- Simplicity, so that design and implementation, configuration and deployment is viable for the average developer." (OMG (1996))

These goals comprise the conceptual and the technical usage of business objects. On the technical level, ad-hoc integration means that run-time business object components (called application components in the RFP) must be able to plug-and-play, i.e. they can be put together in a run-time environment and will then work without any intervention by IT professionals. Furthermore, a newly plugged-in business object will be able to interact with other business objects in order to perform some business function. This interaction can take place even if it was not planned or foreseen by the developers of the business objects. Although originally addressed by the CBO/BOF RFP, efforts of enabling plug-and-play components have been shifted from the responsibility of the BODTF to the Corba Component Initiative (OMG (1997b)) in the meantime.

The CBO vision is aimed at a marketplace for standardized "off-the-shelf" modeling and systems business objects. Generalized descriptions of best business practices and templates for common constructs like Customer, Order, Product etc. will be sold in the form of business object models, supplemented by corresponding software components (systems business objects) which speed up development and are easily integrated with other business objects through the BOF.

4 Requirements for Modeling with Business Objects

Having clarified the context of business object based systems modeling and development, it has to be examined what is required from a modeling language used for this purpose. The requirements analyzed are typical of (but not inevitably restricted to) business object based systems. It is neither a systematic nor a complete evaluation of UML in the business object context, but a discussion of some examplary aspects worthwhile being considered.

4.1 Communication

Communication between domain experts, systems analysts, and software developers is essential for the success of reengineering a business and developing information systems. Divergent vocabulary and different background knowledge on the part of business and IT people often lead to severe problems of mutual understanding. A modeling language used for developing business and software models must be simple enough to allow for this understanding and at the same time detailed enough to specify the system elements unambiguously and sufficiently.

The business object approach emphasizes simplicity and a focus on business issues. Business and software models must be easy to discuss, to verify against the given requirements and easy to maintain. It is very important that concepts from the problem domain are used and expressed in the business terminology.

However, the UML is a general-purpose modeling language which is very complex and provides a considerable number of modeling elements whose semantics must be fully understood by the users of UML. While its complexity lays the foundation for its expressiveness, it also undermines communication with non-experts.

The solution to this problem might be to define different subsets of UML for different modeling purposes on different stages in systems development. For example, when dealing with domain experts, it is advisable to restrict the set of modeling elements to an expressive subset of basic elements useful for conceptual modeling in the business context (e.g. in Class Diagrams: renunciation of association classes, qualifiers, visibility markers etc.). The full variety of constructs is not needed until implementation oriented design tasks are carried out.

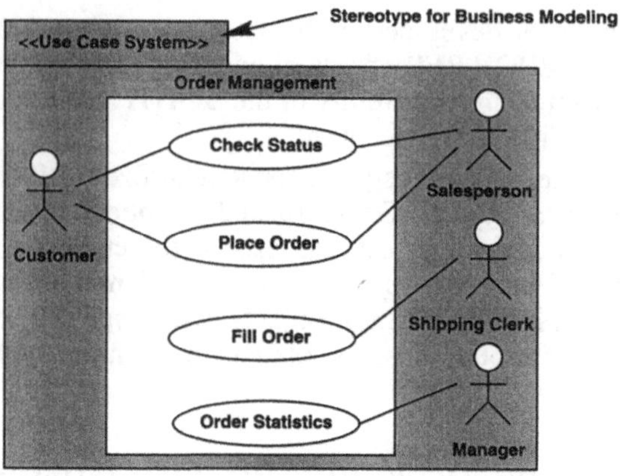

Figure 4: Modeling Business Processes and System Functionality with Use Cases

Another possibility to adjust the UML to the needs of business modeling or business information systems modeling is to use the UML extensibility mechanisms (i.e. stereotypes, tagged values, constraints). Particulary stereotypes applied to an existing metamodel element can help to add new semantics to the language. For example, the stereotype <<business object>> could indicate that a package or a class has certain semantics that are characteristic of business objects. Combining the stereotype with a new presentation icon for the new kind of modeling element may further increase understandability, if the look of the new icon is meaningful to the readers of the model. Rational has already defined an UML extension for business modeling that introduces a number of new stereotypes with corresponding icons and is primarily based on use cases as the central concept for modeling business processes (Jacobson et al. (1995), Rational Software Corp. (1997a)).

4.2 Modeling Goals, Business Processes and Workflows

All business activities are based on strategies, goals and policies which build the framework for the conduct of business and must be determined prior to any other steps during business planning or reengineering. The goals of the business motivate the workflows, where the resources are used in accordance with specified rules. Therefore, modeling activities have to start at the strategic level.

Although UML models can be used to establish a basic common set of concepts and express their relationships and semantics (see Figure 2), the UML is not powerful at this level. Textual commitments and figures will predominate in this context.

The modeling of business processes and workflow, though, can be done very well with the features provided by UML (although the diagrams used for this purpose, i.e. Use Case Diagrams and Activity Diagrams, are not really object-oriented in nature). Figure 4 shows, for example, a Use Case Diagram which represents a

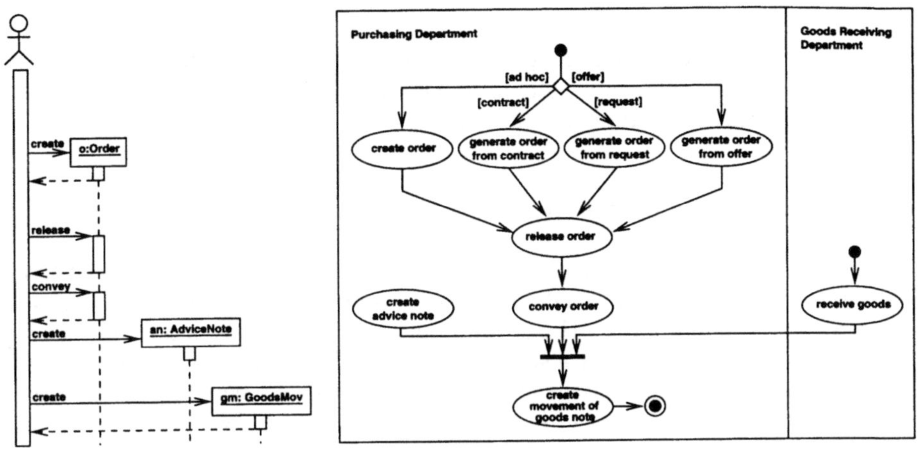

Figure 5: Mapping of Activity Diagrams to Sequence Diagrams

simplified model of the business process "Order Management". Like business objects, use cases can be applied to business modeling, which is portrayed in detail in Jacobson et al. (1995), and also to software systems modeling as described in Jacobson et al. (1992).

Activity Diagrams are a good mechanism for expressing workflow. Workflow designates the automation of a business process, in whole or part, during which documents, information or tasks are passed from one participant to another for action, according to a set of rules. In future application systems, workflow objects (special business objects) will interconnect other business objects (instead of applications). The OMG seeks proposals for a Workflow Management Facility (WMF) which will have to work together with the BOF at the infrastructure level (OMG (1997d)). Activity Diagrams are used to describe how the work is performed. In addition to showing workflow, they can be used for modeling dynamics of operations, classes, and use cases. The approach to modeling business processes with Activity Diagrams goes hand in hand with use cases or other techniques to capture the requirements of the business system.

A great advantage of Activity Diagrams is their explicit support of modeling concurrent activities, thus helping to reengineer business processes to increase their efficiency (Fowler and Scott (1997)). Activity Diagrams have the potential to replace the wide-spread approach of using Event-Driven Process Chain (EPCs) Diagrams for modeling business processes (for EPCs see Nüttgens et al. (1998)). Due to their flowchart heritage, a disadvantage of Activity Diagrams is the difficult mapping to object-oriented concepts, which is also very difficult for use cases. Figure 5 shows an idealized mapping of the action states in an Activity Diagram to the message flows in the corresponding software systems Sequence Diagram. This will not always be possible, e.g. if different levels of abstractions have been chosen or if parts of the Activity Diagram are performed manually. The mapping of information in Activity Diagrams to classes and objects can be achieved by organizing action states into swimlanes (vertical areas) which indicate the responsibilities of certain classes/objects.

4.3 Partitioning and Refinement

Business systems and their corresponding software systems are usually very complex in nature. Therefore, methods of partitioning and refinement are needed for modeling such systems. The partitioning of large models is not only useful for ergonomical reasons, but also allows for parallel activities of different developers/teams if the dependencies are not too numerous between the different parts of the model. In order to handle a large business object system, a hierarchical approach is needed to refine the basic requirements and incrementally add more detail. Because of the known problems, functional decomposition has to be avoided.

The UML provides a strong mechanism for structuring model parts: packages. Packages are shown as rectangles in a manila folder shape (see left side of Figure 10). By grouping model elements which logically belong together, packages serve for partioning and decomposing the models. Packages may contain other packages (the whole system is contained in a top-level package labeled with stereotype <<system>>), can reference other packages, and inheritance between packages may apply, which means conformity of interfaces and the support of polymorphism. Not only classes, but, in principle, all modeling elements of the UML can be organized in packages. To ensure a loose coupling, dependencies between packages should be minimized. A useful technique supporting this goal is the instantiation of the *Facade* pattern (Gamma et al. (1995)) to hide functional details of a package from other packages. Facades should be labeled with the predefined stereotype <<facade>>. Although the package concept of UML is very extensive, it should be noticed that its specification is not yet free of imprecisions or even contradictions (Schürr and Winter (1998)).

Another UML mechanism for complexity management are refinement relationships which are a special kind of dependency relationships. Like all dependencies, refinements are shown as dashed arrows between two model elements, labeled with the keyword <<refine>>. The refinement construct can be used to express a historical or derivation connection between two elements with a mapping between them.

4.4 Modeling Business Rules

In every organization there are rules which determine how several tasks have to be executed. These business rules define and lay down admissable proceedings, based on ethical, cultural, legal or internal business conditions. They often express policies and refer to administrative processes. Some of the rules are just implicitly part of the employees' know-how, others are explicitly written down

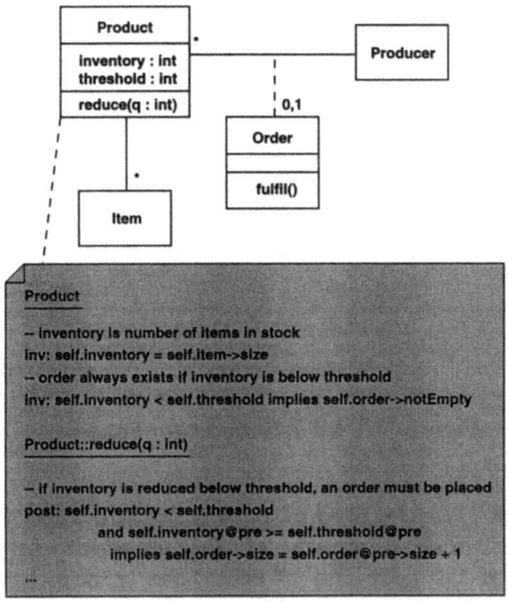

Figure 6: Expressing Business Rules in Object Constraint Language (OCL)

in organizational handbooks. If information systems have to be built to support the conduct of a business, these rules have to be represented in the applications (Knolmayer and Herbst (1993)).

Since business rules change frequently, they should not be scattered in code as they are in traditional applications, because this has led to poor maintainability. Most of the time, business rules will be implemented in the methods of the business objects affected by those rules. The CBOF proposal to the OMG RFP for CBOs/BOF (OMG (1996)) describes a business object architecture where rules may be expressed as components in their own right and can be plugged in and out as needed (CBOF (1997)). Another aspect to be considered is the fact that domain experts often are aware of business rules, which means that they are a good means of communication. As a result, modeling languages used for modeling business information systems must have an explicit support of business rule modeling.

UML version 1.1 includes a language for the specification of expressions during modeling, called Object Constraint Language (OCL). In the UML documentation, OCL is used to define well-formedness rules expressing the semantics of the UML modeling elements. The main advantage of OCL is its simplicity while at the same time it has got a certain degree of formalism. A considerable disadvantage of OCL might be its lack of rigor. There is no metamodel for OCL in the UML, and the specification of OCL is not always precise and free of ambiguities (see Gogolla and Richters (1998)).

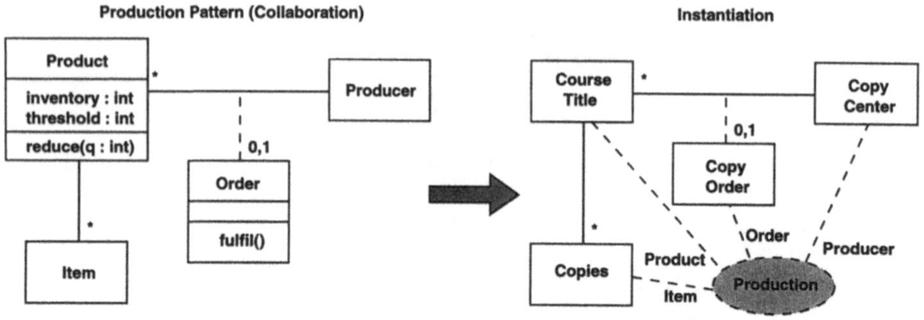

Figure 7: UML's Support for Patterns

To illustrate how OCL can be used to express business rules, Figure 6 provides an example. OCL expressions are very suitable for specifying pre- and postconditions of operations and invariants of operations or classes/types (see subsection 4.7). The example shows a simplified production pattern, which describes the production of different kinds of products by producers, based on orders. For each product type there is an inventory of items, the size of which is stored in the product object's attribute inventory. Furthermore, a threshold value is administrated which determines, when a new order has to be placed. The business rules behind this production pattern might well be defined as constraints in OCL, as can be partially seen in the figure.

4.5 Patterns and Reuse

One of the most important progresses in object-oriented analysis and design are the results of the ongoing research into analysis and design patterns (e.g. Fowler and Scott (1997), Gamma et al. (1995)). These patterns describe best-practice solutions to recurring analysis and design problems and facilitate high level reuse of model specifications. Having in mind the coarse granularity of useful business object components (implemented as collaborations of smaller business objects), patterns and collaborations can help very much in documenting and specifying the semantics of those components, thus laying the foundations for their efficient reuse. Thinking of ready-to-use, "off-the-shelf" systems business object components, patterns of corresponding modeling business objects could serve as documentation of their functionality and possible usage.

Collaboration Diagrams in UML are the means to document behavior implemented by sets of business objects that exchange messages within an overall interaction to accomplish a purpose. Patterns can be defined as parameterized collaborations in UML with types/classes, relationships, and operations as the instantiation parameters. Figure 7 repeats the production pattern of Figure 6 and shows an example of its instantiation into a problem specific UML Class Diagram.

The dashed ellipse symbol contains the pattern name and the dashed lines labeled with the pattern roles are attached to the participants of the pattern.

The use of this notational convenience in UML proves to be very useful, because it represents a design construction on a higher abstraction level than the basic elements, which can be repeatedly applied to different designs. Eriksson and Penker (1998) speak of UML patterns as "generators of design solutions", because they implicitly contain context and interactions, and thus, if not all parts of the design are shown, simplify the models.

Furthermore, building larger models by composing generic patterns is possible with this modeling construct. In this case, if two patterns are to be combined, there is at least one common class/type playing a different role in each pattern. Assuming that the semantics of business object components will be specified by collaborations, the composing of these specifications could be the modeling level preparation for plugging the corresponding systems business object components together. The construction of models and specifications by composition is described further in the Catalysis method (see Catalysis (1997)), D'Souza (1997)).

4.6 Roles and Actors

Separation of concerns is an important principle for design, specification and implementation of business object systems. Different departments and development teams will inevitably access and modify business objects in different models for different reasons. This variety of interest in single business objects was one of the factors which made monolithic enterprise objects impractical. The solution to this problem are roles. Roles represent aspects of objects connected with a certain view or a certain part of a model. A role expresses what an object represents in a special context, not what it is. Roles mirror types that can be adopted and released dynamically (see Reenskaug, Wold and Lehne (1996) for the OOram method, in which role modeling is the central concept).

An actor is a role a person or an external system takes over in regard to the system being modeled (see Figure 4: Customer, Salesperson...). For example, there might be many business partners who place orders, each of them playing the role of a customer. However, they are not restricted to that role, but might adopt other roles at the same time.

One way to express these semantics is the application of dynamic, multiple classification. Fowler and Scott (1997) describe how dynamic, multiple classification can be modeled in UML with the help of stereotypes (see Figure 8). If dynamic, multiple classification is allowed, objects can change their class over time and can belong to more than one class at a time. Thus, the requirements of role modeling are met. However, this concept is rarely used because it is usually not supported by programming languages.

An indirect way of modeling roles without the need for dynamic, multiple classification, is the application of role patterns. Figure 9 shows a delegation based design of the same problem domain as illustrated in Figure 8 on the basis of a role pattern instance.

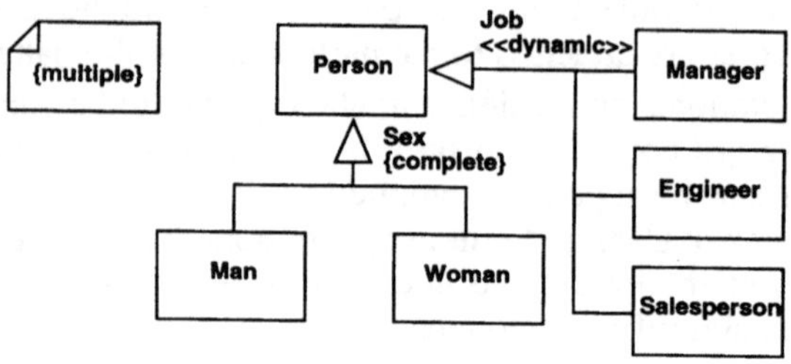

Figure 8: Dynamic, Multiple Classification

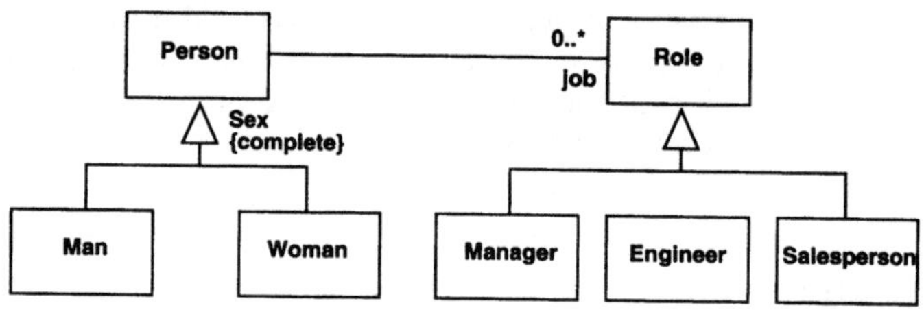

Figure 9: Role Pattern with Delegation

In UML, the concept of roles is supported directly in three more ways: In addition to roles in associations which have simpler semantics, roles are represented in UML by the actors in a use case and by the participants in a collaboration. An Actor element in a Use Case Diagram characterizes the role played by an outside object which may play several roles and therefore be modeled by several actors. In a collaboration, roles must be bound to actual classes when the collaboration is used. The roles may have their own names and possibly show only subsets of the attributes, operations and related objects known to actual classes playing the role. An actual class may play several roles in different collaborations (Rational Software Corp. (1997b)).

4.7 Component Technology

Another aspect which has to be considered is the fact that implemented OMG systems business objects will be runtime plug-and-play components. One goal of the business object approach is to enhance flexibility and extensibility of systems by enabling substitution of one business object component for another (e.g. a newer version of a component replaces an older one, or components from different vendors are interchanged).

To support the component character of business objects at the design stage, it is necessary to know the component model or rather the business object architecture that will finally be adopted. At the time of this writing, proposals for the CBO/BOF

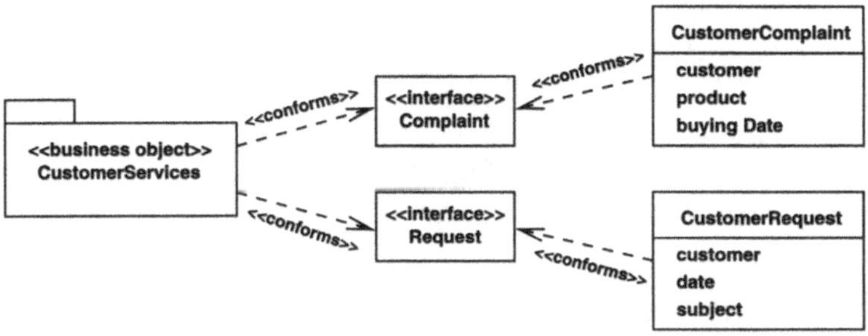

Figure 10: External and Internal View of Business Object Components

RFP (OMG (1997a)) and CORBA Component Model RFP (OMG (1997b)) are being evaluated. One promising BOF submission (CBOF (1997)) will be briefly addressed in section 5.

Bearing in mind current component models, it might be useful to concentrate on modeling with types and interfaces and to ensure separation of concerns and design by contract. Separation of interface from implementation is central in this context. Fortunately, the UML provides a number of techniques for this purpose.

First, the external and the internal view of business object components should be distinguished. Externally visible are the operations or services that are supported by the business object component. The internal realization of the component might be based on an encapsulation of highly interrelated classes, associations, operations, events and constraints. Figure 10 shows a coarse grained business object component CustomerServices modeled as a stereotyped package which exports two interfaces. The classes CustomerComplaint and CustomerRequest on the right belong to the internal realization of CustomerServices and provide those interfaces.

The distinction between an external and internal view is closely connected with the distinction between specification and implementation. Fowler (1997) describes three perspectives in modeling: conceptual, specification, and implementation. The conceptual perspective describes the concepts of the domain under study and is independent of implementation aspects. The specification perspective is concerned with interfaces and types, not implemention classes. Finally, in the implementation perspective, the actual implementation (with classes etc.) is laid bare.

When modeling business object based systems, all three perspectives are relevant. The conceptual perspective should be taken in early phases of systems development (especially business modeling). The specification perspective is very important. Specifying types and interfaces allows for designs that can be used for implementation or assembly of a BOF-based system independently of the source of the business object components that constitute the system. If a component is to be bought externally, its specification must be matched against the model, and its implementation is irrelevant. If the component is to be devel-

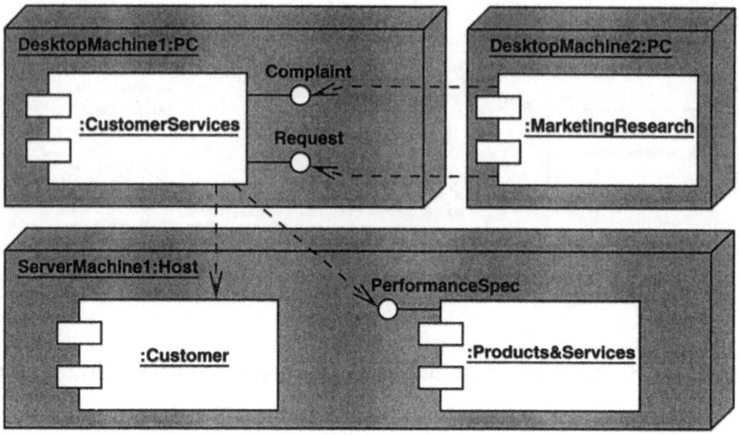

Figure 11: Component Architecture Shown in a Deployment Diagram

oped internally, the specification model has to be refined by a model from the implementation perspective. UML explicitly supports the concepts of types and interfaces. For example, there are two notational ways of presenting interfaces (see Figures 10 and 11), and types can be made explicit by using the predefined stereotype <<type>> in a class symbol. Modeling with types, interfaces and operations implies designing by contract, i.e. specifying boolean assertions which must always be true. There are three kinds of assertions to be distinguished, namely preconditions, invariants, and postconditions. Applied to an operation, a postcondition specifies what has to be the result of the operation without saying how to achieve this result, thus ensuring separation of interface and implementation. Preconditions describe the system state as expected by the operation before execution, thus defining the responsibilities of the caller. An invariant, applied to a class, holds always true at any moment an operation is called. In UML models, assertions should be expressed in OCL. Specifying functionality in this way is essential if implementational aspects are to be abstracted from in order to allow for business component substitution.

In the context of an implementation (and architectural) perspective, only one UML feature shall be mentioned here: Deployment Diagrams, which can be used to show business object components, their physical locations in a distributed environment, and the dependencies between them (see Figure 11). Although describing relevant aspects, Deployment Diagrams appear to be too complex for the benefit they bring.

As can be inferred from the above paragraphs, it is essential to define a suitable process of business object based systems development. The UML standard does not include or prescribe a development process. To allow for a specification based approach of business object component modeling, ideas might be taken from methods such as Catalysis (Catalysis (1997)) and COOL (Short (1997)). Catalysis, which builds on UML, puts collaboration patterns as specifications of components into the center of attention and describes a formalized process of building business models, requirements specs, designs, and code rapidly from reusable generic components and frameworks. Its main advantages (e.g. full model consistency, views and patterns synthesis) stem from its rigor and formality, which are, simultaneously, its main disadvantages, because it is hard to use for non-experts from the business domain.

5 Evaluation and Prospects

In this paper, exemplary aspects of a business object based systems modeling have been analyzed and related to the features and concepts of UML, the new industry standard for object modeling languages. It has been shown that UML is very powerful and provides numerous modeling elements needed for the special purpose under examination. On the other hand, it is necessary both to restrict and to extend certain parts of the UML to provide the semantics needed and to avoid undesired complexity. Furthermore, a systems development process for business object based systems which builds on UML is to be defined to use UML both efficiently and effectively.

With the adoption of a CBO/BOF proposal by the OMG, more information about how these problems have to be solved will become available. One of the most promising responses to the BODTF RFP (OMG (1997a)) is CBOF (1997) which defines a Business Object Architecture (BOA; a metamodel for the constructs and types that are used to build a business object system), a Component Definition Language (CDL; a language for the textual expression of business object specifications that use the metamodel), and an IDL mapping (to specify what interfaces are required to support BOA based models). The proposal is integrated in OMG's Object Management Architecture, i.e. builds on Corba and IDL, but adds the semantics of business components. The rationale for the introduction of CDL is, that it "provides a level of abstraction needed to express the semantics of business components and to combine (compose) medium-grain business components, a capability beyond the OMG's Interface Definition Language. CDL enhances IDL in that it can describe object semantics as well as interfaces. CDL (and semantic definition) is required to support the definition and standardization of common business objects, domain specific business objects and corporate standard business objects." (CBOF (1997))

The BOA model is described as an UML extension, i.e. shared concepts are kept and new concepts are introduced using the UML extension mechanisms. On the other hand, "the BOA and CDL represent a very specific and narrow subset of UML capabilities. Within its scope, however, CDL provides more rigor, more semantic depth for the targeted business object domains, and an unambiguous relationship with OMA." For example, the format of constraints and other expressions is Uninterpreted in UML (i.e. not standardized) whereas the BOA metamodel explicitly models expressions.

If the CBOF proposal should be adopted and a suitable mapping between UML and BOA/CDL metamodels can be defined, UML designs will be the starting point for business object modeling, and will be transformed into CDL specifications automatically. The CDL specification provides the relevant information needed by the business object infrastructure (Business Object Framework, Meta Object Facility (OMG (1997c))) so that business object components can be plugged in, generated by tools or implemented manually. UML models and CDL specifications will then serve as standardized documentation means of the structure and semantics of business object components. Future responses to business object RFPs will require specifications in this form.

References

CATALYSIS (1997): Catalyis—Next Generation Component-Based Development from Object Frameworks. URL: http://www.iconcomp.com/catalysis/.

CBOF (1997): Combined Business Object Facility—Business Object Architecture (BOA) Proposal. OMG Business Object Domain Task Force BODTF-RFP 1 Submission. Revision 1.0. Data Access Technologies et al. OMG Document bom/97-11-09.

COAD, P. and MAYFIELD, M. (1997): Java Design—Building Better Apps & Applets. Yourdon Press Computing Series, Prentice Hall, New Jersey.

DAVENPORT, T.H. (1993): Process Innovation—Reengineering Work through Information Technology. Harvard Business School Press, Boston, Massachusetts.

D'SOUZA, D. (1997): Framework: Java to UML/Catalysis. *Journal of Object-Oriented Programming, 10/5, 10–13.*

ERIKSSON, H.-E. and PENKER, M. (1998): UML-Toolkit. Wiley Computer Publishing, New York.

FERSTL, O.K. and SINZ, E. (1995): Der Ansatz des Semantischen Objektmodells (SOM) zur Modellierung von Geschäftsprozessen. *Wirtschaftsinformatik 37/3, 209–220.*

FOWLER, M. and SCOTT, K. (1997): UML Distilled—Applying the Standard Object Modeling Language. Addison-Wesley, Reading, Massachusetts.

FRANK, U. (1994): MEMO: A Tool Supported Methodology for Analyzing and (Re-) Designing Business Information Systems. In: R. Ege, M. Singh and B. Meyer (eds.): *Technology of Object-Oriented Languages and Systems.* Englewood Cliffs, 367–380.

GAMMA, E. , HELM, R., JOHNSON, R., and VLISSIDES, J. (1995): Design Patterns—Elements of Reusable Object-Oriented Software. Professional Computing Series. Addison-Wesley, Reading, Massachusetts.

GOGOLLA, and RICHTERS, M. (1998): On Constraints and Queries in UML. In: Schader, M. and Korthaus, A. (eds.): *The Unified Modeling Language—Technical Aspects and Applications.* Physica-Verlag, Heidelberg.

HAMMER, M. and CHAMPY, J. (1994): Reengineering the Corporation—A Manifesto for Business Revolution. Nicholas Brealey Publishing, London.

JACOBSON, I., CHRISTERSON, M., JONSSON, P., and ÖVERGAARD, G. (1992): Object-Oriented Software Engineering—A Use Case Driven Approach. Addison-Wesley, Wokingham, England.

JACOBSON, I., ERICSSON, M. and JACOBSON, A. (1995): The Object Advantage—Business Process Reengineering with Object Technology. Addison-Wesley, Wokingham, England.

KNOLMAYER, G. and HERBST, H. (1993): Business Rules. *Wirtschaftsinformatik 35/4, 386-390.*

NÜTTGENS, M., FELD, T., and ZIMMERMANN, V. (1998): Business Process Modeling with EPC and UML: Transformation or Integration? In: Schader, M. and Korthaus, A. (eds.): *The Unified Modeling Language—Technical Aspects and Applications.* Physica-Verlag, Heidelberg.

OMG (1996): Common Facilities RFP-4, Common Business Objects and Business Object Facility. Request for Proposal. OMG TC Document CF/96-01-04. Object Management Group.

OMG (1997a): Business Object DTF—Common Business Objects. OMG Document bom/97-11-11 Version 1.3. Object Management Group.

OMG (1997b): CORBA Component Model RFP. Request for Proposal. OMG Document orbos/96-06-12. Object Management Group.

OMG (1997c): Meta Object Facility (MOF) Specification. OMG Document ad/97-08-14. Object Management Group.

OMG (1997d): Workflow Management Facility RFP. Request for Proposal. OMG Document cf/97-05-06. Object Management Group.

RATIONAL SOFTWARE CORP. (1997a): UML Extension for Business Modeling. Version 1.1, 1 September 1997, Rational Software Corp. et al.

RATIONAL SOFTWARE CORP. (1997b): UML Notation Guide. Version 1.1, 1 September 1997, Rational Software Corp. et al.

RATIONAL SOFTWARE CORP. (1997c): UML Semantics. Version 1.1, 1 September 1997, Rational Software Corp. et al.

RATIONAL SOFTWARE CORP. (1997d): UML Summary. Version 1.1, 1 September 1997, Rational Software Corp. et al.

REENSKAUG, T., Wold, P. and Lehne, O.A. (1996): Working with Objects: The OOram Software Engineering Method. Greenwich, Manning.

SCHÜRR, A. and WINTER, A. (1998): Formal Definition of UML's Package Concept. In: Schader, M. and Korthaus, A. (eds.): *The Unified Modeling Language—Technical Aspects and Applications.* Physica-Verlag, Heidelberg.

SHORT, K. (1997): Component Based Development and Object Modeling. WhitePaper, Texas Instruments Software, Febr. 1997, Version 1.05. URL: http://cool.sterling.com.

SIMS, O. (1994): Business Objects—Delivering Cooperative Objects for Client-Server. IBM McGraw-Hill series. McGraw-Hill Book Company, london.

TAYLOR, D. (1995): Business Engineering with Object Technology. John Wiley & Sons, Inc., New York.

System Development with V-Model and UML

G. Müller-Ettrich

Industrieanlagen Betriebsgesellschaft mbH (IABG),
Abt. IS23,
D-85521 Ottobrunn, Germany

Abstract: The V-Model is an international recognized development standard for IT-systems which was developed by Industrieanlagen - Betriebsgesellschaft (IABG) on behalf of the German Ministery of Defense (BMVg) and was also taken over by the German Federal Ministery of the Interior. It is a generic process framework, that can be adapted to each type of system development project. The new version of the V-Model has integrated perfectly smooth the UML-Methods in the second level of the standard.

1 System Development with V-Model

1.1 What is the V-Model?

The V-model is an internationally recognized development standard for IT systems which uniformly and bindingly lays down what has to be done, how the tasks are to be performed and what is to be used to carry this out.
The V-model encompasses

- the Lifecycle Process Model,
- the Allocation of Methods, and
- the Functional Tool Requirements.

That is the clear outline of what steps are to be taken and which methods are to be applied for the development tasks and which functional characteristics the tools to be used must have.

1.2 Structure of the Lifecycle Process Model

The Lifecycle Process Model is structured into three parts:

1. Regulations

   This part contains binding regulations concerning worksteps to be performed (activities) and results (products).

2. Supplements with regard to Authorities

   This part exists once for the field of German Federal Armed Forces and once for the field of the civilian Federal Administration. It contains instructions to apply the Lifecycle Process Model in the respective field.

3. Collection of Manuals

   This part contains a set of manuals dealing with special topics, such as IT security or use of object-oriented languages.

1.3 How to Use the V-Model

The V-model was developed with several applications in mind. The focal application points are:

- **Basis for Contracts**

  In this instance, the scope of delivery of the software and the completeness of the software documentation are clearly defined.

- **Instruction**

  The V-model serves as guideline and concrete instruction for system development with its detailed descriptions of the activities and documents.

- **Communications Basis**

  By means of the description of the documents and the provision of a glossary, it serves as the basis for mutual understanding and reduces frictional losses between customer, user, contractor, and developer.

1.4 The V-Model in the Industrial Field

The provisions of the V-model are strictly organizationally impartial. They are restricted exclusively to the technical development process. Therefore, the V-model is not only suitable as the development standard in public administration but also in industry. It already has been taken over and is used as the corporate standard by a number of companies and is used both by software and system houses and also by users from many other different areas such as

- banks,
- insurance companies,
- car manufacturers,
- manufacturing industry,
- energy producers.

The use of the V-model in the industrial field is made considerably easier by the fact that its use is free of license fees. It is non-proprietary and not copy-protected, which means that the V-model can be copied as often as is wished for one's own use without infringing license regulations.

1.5 V-Model and Security

The V-model contains rules which are necessary for the generation of critical software. The currently valid security criteria (ITSEC) have been fulfilled with respect to their regulations governing the development process by the application of the V-model. A certification of the software so developed is hence considerably facilitated.

1.6 Participation of the Users in the Development and Maintenance of the V-Model

The influence of the users necessary for the maintenance and modification processes of the V-model is ensured by a change control board which meets roughly once a year with representatives from industry and authorities. The change control board is obliged, according to its orders of procedure, to process carefully all received change requests to the V-model.

1.7 Adaptation to the Projects and their Specific Requirements: "Tailoring"

An outstanding feature of the V-model is its *universal validity* and its *company and project independence*. To use it for a specific project, individual decisions have to be taken with respect to which activities and documents are necessary for the project for technical reasons. In each case, superfluous mountains of paper, senseless documentation, but also the lack of important documents are to be avoided. This project-specific adaptation is called **"Tailoring"**.

In the **"tailoring relevant for tendering" (Fig. 1)**, which is carried out before completion of the contract and start of the actual project, a selection of the necessary activities and products is to be undertaken. In addition, special deletion conditions are established under which certain activities which were held to be essential at the beginning can be deleted under particular circumstances in the course of the project. The resulting subset of the Lifecycle Process Model is laid down together with further agreements in the **Project Manual**. This Project Manual is an important part of the contract.

The tailoring relevant for tendering is also important even if a project is not externally awarded but is an in-house development.

During **"technical tailoring"**, the deletion conditions laid down in the Project Manual are evaluated and it is decided, which of the activities contained in the Project Manual are to be carried out. This occurs continuously during the course of the project.

1.8 V-Model as a Basis for Contracts

So that comparability of all offers with respect to the kind of project realization and documentation is comprehensively guaranteed, the project-specific adaptation of

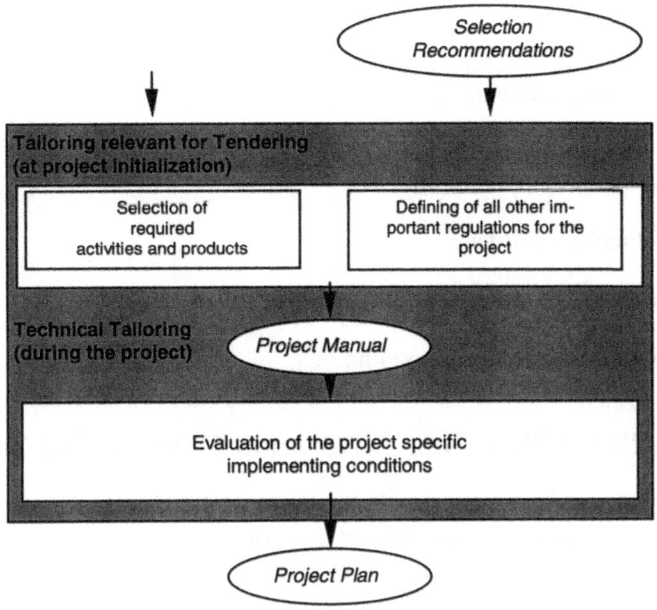

Figure 1: Tailoring Steps

the V-model for external contractual awards is undertaken *before* tendering begins. The Project Manual thus compiled defines the scope of the project to be realized by the contractor (and his subcontractors). The Project Manual therefore becomes the uniform action basis and guideline for all participants in the project.

1.9 The Updated V-Model

The V-model was originally developed by Industrieanlagen-Betriebsgesellschaft mbH (IABG) in Ottobrunn near Munich on behalf of the Federal Ministry of Defense (BMVg) and in cooperation with the Federal Office for Defense Technology and Procurement (BWB) in Koblenz. In the summer of 1992, it was taken over by the Federal Ministry of the Interior for the civilian Federal Administration domain and has been a binding obligatory regulation since June 1996 in this sector as well.
The V-model is a "living" standard, the further development of which is promoted and financed by the Federal Ministries of Defense and the Interior.
The most important specifications for the review and updating of the 1997 version were:

- Comprehensive approach, by means of the generation of an IT system development standard, with regulations governing the development of software and hardware as part of the system development.
- Changes to the requirements documentation into the User Requirements and the Technical Requirements.

- Reduction in the volume of the regulations part and division into a collection of explanatory manuals.
- Better support of new technologies, such as incremental system development and object-oriented methods.
- Use of standard software.
- Improvements to the project management submodel.
- Adoption to the ISO 8402 terminology.

1.10 The Three-Phase Standardization Concept (Fig. 2)

The necessity of standardization in IT development is today undisputed. Mainly seen as advantages of standardization are:

- Better planability of IT projects
- Curtailment of the development costs over the lifecycle
- Improvement in quality
- Improvement in the communication between customer and contractor.

The standard has the following three levels:

1. Procedure

   "*What* has to be done?"

   This level establishes what activities are to be performed in the course of system development, which results are to be produced in this process and what contents these results must have.

2. Methods

   "*How* is something to be done?"

   Here it is determined what methods are to be used to perform the activities established in the first level and what means of presentation are to be used in the results.

3. Tool Requirements

   "*What* is to be used to do something?"

   At this level, what is established is what functional characteristics must the tools have which are to be used during system development.

At all levels, the regulations are structured according to the areas of activity, the so called submodels

- project management (PM)
- system development (SD)
- quality management (QA), and
- configuration management (CM)

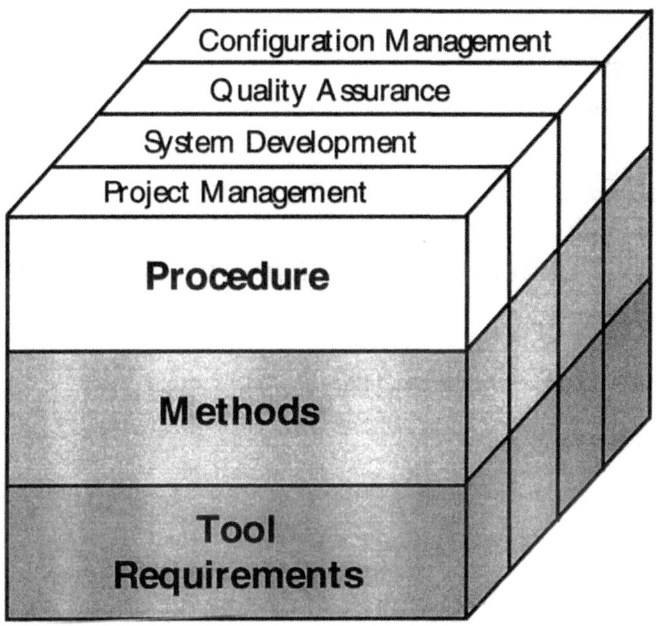

Figure 2: Tailoring Steps

1.11 The Submodels

The four submodels are closely linked to one another and influence each other concerning the exchange of products/results (Fig. 3, Fig. 4).

- **PM** plans, controls and informs the SD, QA and CM submodels.
- **SD** develops the system or the software.
- **QA** specifies quality requirements, test cases and criteria, and examines the products and the compliance with the standards.
- **CM** administrates the products generated.

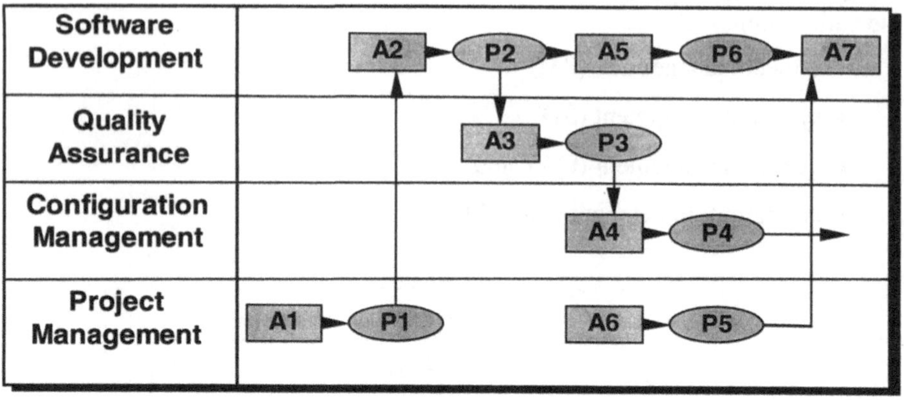

Figure 3: Example for the Activity and Product Flow within the Four Submodels

2 Object-Oriented Software Development with V-Model

Basically, the object-oriented procedure is identified by

- iterative development,
- incremental development,
- prototyping and
- use of object-oriented methods.

Iterative development allow the iterative assessment and improvement of preceding events. The incremental procedure allows the development of parts of the object-oriented architecture used, among others, to deliver first tangible results. In an object-oriented procedure, prototyping is primarily applied for the development of information systems in the sense of the explorative prototyping. This kind of prototyping is primarily applied to obtain information for the refinement, completion and clarification of User Requirements. In the development of technical systems, prototyping is predominantly used in the sense of the experimental prototyping.

By applying object-oriented methods, System Development (SD) activities are used to support the static and dynamic modeling of the object-oriented architecture. They are also used to collect the functional requirements and the description of the physical software design, the physical platform of the object-oriented architecture and the process structure required by the System.

The application of modular combinable modules (classes) makes changing architecture usually easy, i.e. with less effort as this is the case in classical (not

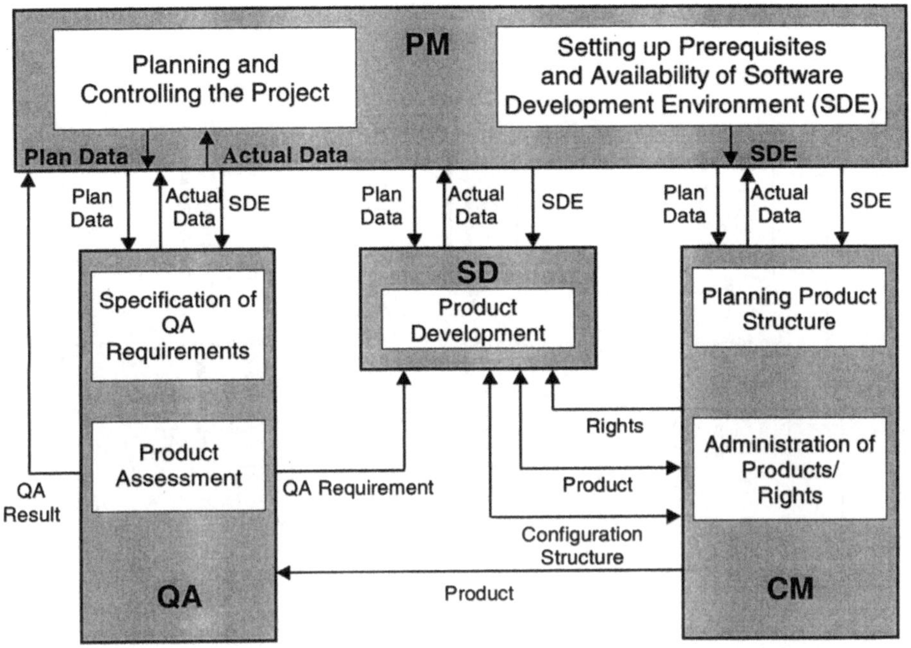

Figure 4: Cooperation of Submodels

object-oriented) procedures. Using class libraries and object-oriented methods, the application of ready parts in the sense of an off-the-shelf product-oriented development strategy is made easy. Development cycles are realized faster, since, as a rule, modular object-oriented architectures can be easily modified.

The regulations for project and configuration management and quality assurance are basically not influenced by the use of object-oriented methods, since the regulations of the V-model are defined independent of the methods.

Within the scope of an object-oriented procedure, User Requirements are the starting point for all other tasks/activities, they are binding for the entire system development, just as a work contract. The User Requirements in the object-oriented scenario refine the User Requirements for the overall System.

The sequence of the SD activities in an object-oriented procedure is illustrated in Figure 5.

2.1 Time T 0-Start

Initialization of the project and beginning of the tasks with regard to the content according to submodel SD.

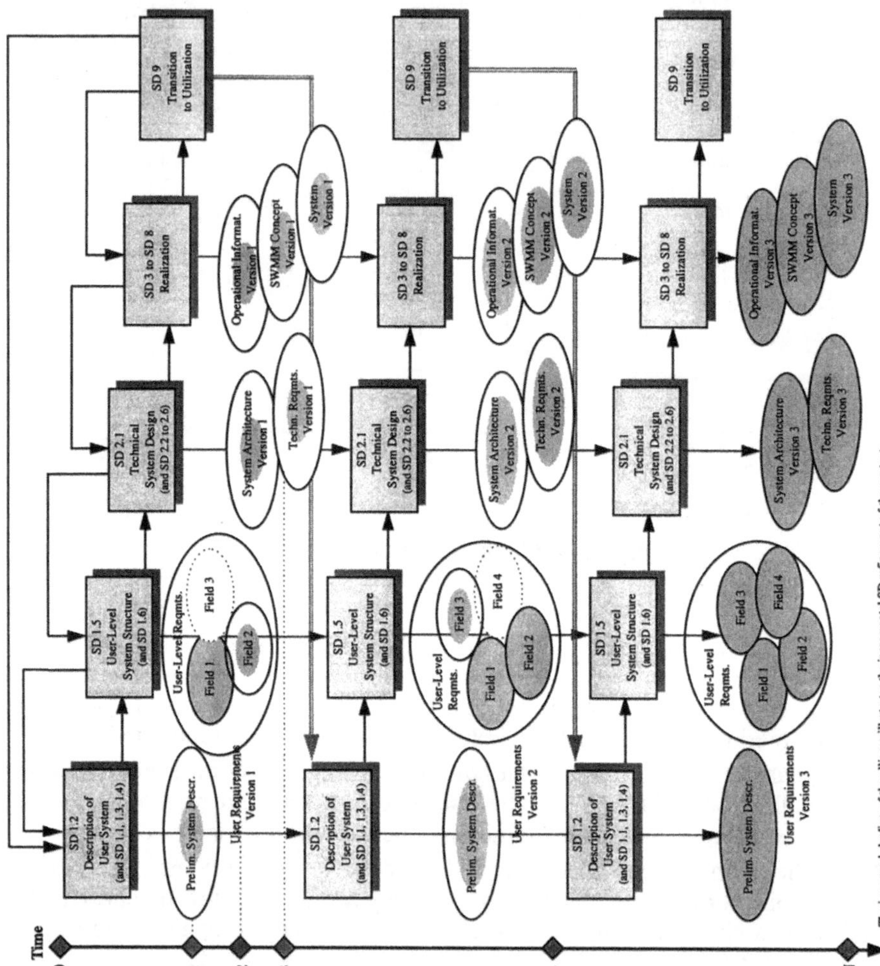

The increased shading of the ellipses illustrates the incremental SD refinement of the contents. Hatched ellipses refer to planned document portions.

Figure 5: Sequence of SD Activities in Object-Oriented Development

2.2 Time T 1-Preliminary System Description

A preliminary system description is available as a result of activity SD 1.2, it describes the core and the overall content for the system functionality. Here the System is first structured into fields whereby, from a user-level and conceptual point of view, each field represents a unit for the analysis. User requirements are described as use cases. With their functional requirements, the thus defined use cases represent a basis for finding classes and objects, for allocating functionality to classes, and for the interface design. They are also used to reach an understanding with the user himself about the User Requirements. In its overall size, the use cases specified for a System contain the application-oriented, functional requirements to the System. The object-oriented concepts of class and object modeling are used on this basis in order to be continually refined during the following processes, until they are ready for implementation. It is the essential tasks of the class and object modeling to collect the static aspects of object-oriented Systems. Dynamics and interaction within object-oriented Systems are collected, together with other object-oriented elementary methods.

For some fields identified in activity SD 1.5 (first increment level) parts of the user-level requirements are not complete (field 1), other parts have been incompletely generated (field 2).

The description of the functionality includes all use cases and the initial class structure based on these cases-predominantly describing the responsibilities of classes and their cooperation-as well as an initial representation of the dynamics and the interaction between the classes.

2.3 Time T 2-Integration of Predefined User-Level Modules

The presence and use of libraries with predefined classes is an important part in an advanced, object-oriented development.

Using predefined classes is to

- speed up the development activities by decreasing the development efforts,
- increase the quality by the integration of "matured" classes,
- base user-level and technically oriented design tasks on available modules in order to come up with more cost-effective solutions,
- promote future developments by evolutionary further development of class libraries as side effects of the system development's spin off.

The class library is not only to be used as a source for modules but also to support proven and possibly standardized user-level architectures. In case predefined field descriptions are already available for the application field in object-oriented form, they may be used.

Together, the results of activities SD 1.2 and SD 1.5 represent the User Requirements which are available in an initial version at time T 2.

2.4 Time T 3-Design of the Technical Solution

As a result of activity SD 2.1, the fields of the first increment are described with regard to their technical realization (both in the **System Architecture** and in the **Technical Requirements**).

The description of the System Architecture in the object-oriented field is done via class hierarchies, i.e. classes and objects defined on the basis of the User Requirements are completed by technical classes and objects and combined into an object-oriented architecture. In this connection, the user organization must be taken into consideration as an influential factor.

Technical classes and objects can be allocated to completing fields, e.g. fields for the data and system administration, fields with mechanisms and functions for the support of the user fields or fields with resources for the software implementation.

The technical structuring may be based on class libraries, just like user-level structuring.

By taking into consideration technical solutions within the scope of the SD 1 activities, a professionally sound and sufficiently defined specification is generated for the realization of the initial increment by the contractor. The System Architecture and the Technical Requirements are completed, and all further documents and development results related to the realization are generated.

The Technical Requirements and the System Architecture are object-oriented models that can be easily integrated as a specification for the implementation. During the implementation new-technical-objects might be created, for technical reasons, which are additionally integrated into the System Architecture and the Technical Requirements.

After completing the realization, the first increment is made available to be used.

2.5 Time T 4 to T N-1-Further Increments

At the time T 4, and as a result of the repeated realization of activity SD 1.2, a refined version of the preliminary system description is available. Usually, the refinements are within the scope of the overall system functions as defined at the time T 1. They represent a specification of the requirements. However, such refinements may also result in new fields.

The user-level requirements are defined for the integral parts of the second increment. In this connection, fields that were not taken into consideration before can be described, and those that were available before can be refined. *The user-level object-oriented models in particular will be updated and refined.* First reactions and feedback from the use of the first increment will be taken into consideration.

Thus, the **User Requirements** available in a second version represent the starting point for the refinement and completion of the **System Architecture** and the **Technical Requirements**.

The implementor, e.g. a contractor, expands the already productive system version 1 by the newly generated parts and integrates them within the scope of the integration steps. During the integration tasks, it may be necessary to make

changes for system version 1. After the realization has been completed, the second increment is made available for use.
These steps are repeated for each increment.

2.6 Time T N-Complete System Description

At the time of T N, User Requirements, System Architecture, and Technical Requirements are complete and have all been submitted. After realization and making the System available for use, the entire System is in use.

3 UML Integration within V-Model

It is an easy task to make it formally possible to develop systems with UML-Methods within the V-Model. You only have to add the UML-Methods to level two of the V-Model Standard. This was done in the new version of the V-Model. Now you can use the process model of the V-Model and develop object-oriented with the UML-Methods. In summary the following UML-Methods (with CRC) are integrated in level two of the V-Model:

- Use-Case Modeling (Use Cases)
- Class Object Modeling (Class Diagrams)
- Interaction Modeling (Sequence and Collaboration Diagrams)
- State Transition Modeling (State Diagrams)
- Process Modeling (Deployment Diagrams)
- Subsystem Modeling (Package Diagrams)
- Class-Responsibility-Collaboration

4 Summary

V-Model is a generic process framework. It can be adapted to each type of system development project. The new version of the V-Model has integrated perfectly smooth the UML-Methods in the second level of the standard.

References

The complete version of V-Model including further references can be found on our WEB-page: http://www.v-modell.iabg.de

Business Process Modeling with EPC and UML: Transformation or Integration?

M. Nüttgens, T. Feld, V. Zimmermann

Institut für Wirtschaftsinformatik (IWi) der Universität des Saarlandes,

D-66123 Saarbrücken, Germany

Abstract: *Process* and *object-orientation* are basic concepts of modeling, implementing and customizing information systems. In this paper we present two approaches of combining those concepts into a coherent way. In the first approach we discuss how to transform business process models *(Event-driven Process Chain (EPC) diagrams)* into object-oriented models *(Unified Modeling Language (UML) diagrams)*. The main focus is to support the co-existence of both modeling methods focusing on the modeling context. The second approach deals with the integration of both modeling methods extending the *EPC*-model by *business object classes*.

1 Business Modeling

Today, analysis and design of *business processes* are the major tasks of *business engineering* (Scheer (1994), Österle (1997), Hammer et al. (1993), Davenport (1993)). In research as well as in practice, the *Architecture of integrated Information Systems (ARIS)* (Scheer (1992)) is accepted as a standard framework for business process (re-)engineering. It supports the whole process management life cycle consisting of *process design, process management* , *process workflow* and *process application implementation* (Scheer (1996)).

The *Unified Modeling Language (UML)* (Rational Software (publisher) (1997)) is a common standard for object-oriented modeling. The *UML* is derived of a shared set of commonly accepted concepts which have successfully been proven in the modeling of large and complex systems, especially software systems. With the *UML extension for business modeling*, a first object-oriented *UML* terminology has been defined for the domain of *business modeling*.

ARIS as well as *UML* are based on integrated meta models supported by several modeling tools. The core business modeling concepts of both methodologies will firstly be introduced and compared afterwards.

1.1 Event-driven Process Chain (EPC)

The method of *Event-driven Process Chains (EPC)* (Keller et al. (1992), Nüttgens (1997)) has been developed within the framework of *ARIS* in order to model business processes. In the *EPC model*, a process consists of sequences of events triggering business functions, which are themselves the results of other functions apart from initial events triggering the whole process. By introducing boolean operators ("and", "or", "exclusive or"), the event-driven control structure can

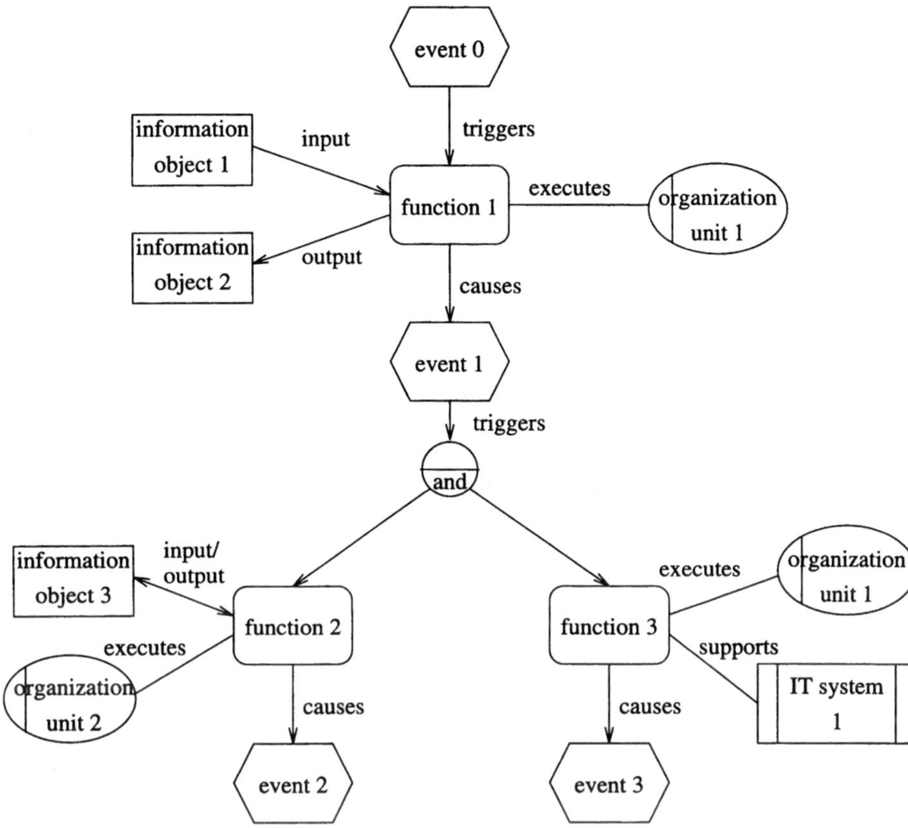

Figure 1: Event driven process chain (EPC)

be expanded to a variously complex *control flow* illustrating business relevant decisions.

This basic model of the *EPC* can be extended by further semantic components of description. The illustration of *data flows*, responsibility of *organizational units* and the use of *IT systems* are examples for such an extension (see figure 1).

Furthermore, on the basis of formal descriptions of the *EPC* method, tool-supported concepts for analysis and simulation are being developed. The approach of Langner/Schneider/Wehler (Langner et al. (1997)) aims at the translation of *EPC models* into *petri networks* and at the algorithmic verification of the resulting networks. In contrast to this, the approaches of Rump (Rump (1997)) and of Keller/Teufel (Keller and Teufel (1997)) are based on an own formal description of the *EPC*.

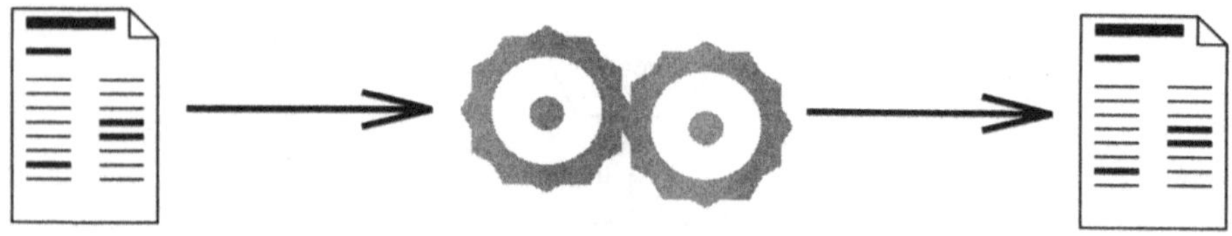

Figure 2: Example of special icons for entities and actions (Rational Software (publisher) (1997))

1.2 UML Extension for Business Modeling

The *UML extension for business modeling* (Rational Software (publisher) (1997)) consists of several *stereotypes* and introduces an object oriented terminology for *business modeling*. The extension does not currently introduce any explicit *tagged values* or *constraints* and is not meant to be a complete business modeling language at all.

On the top level, there is the *use case model* and the *object model* based on the *UML* meta class *model*. Models are partitioned into constructs, based on the *UML* meta classes *subsystem* and *package*.

The *use case model* describes the behavior and relationships between services and participants outside the focused information system, e.g. customers and suppliers. The *object model* focuses on the internal *business processes*. It consists of *object systems*, containing *organization units, work units, workers* and *entities*.

Figure 2 illustrates the entity *trade* in two states *[requested]* and *[processed*], where the *trade* is the dominant entity of a *trade document work unit. Client trading* is an action. The icons are designed to be meaningful in the particular problem domain. Nevertheless, the diagram is based on *use case diagrams*, using other symbols and another terminology.

The diagrams of the *UML Extension for Business Modeling* have the same structure as normal *UML class* and *behavior diagrams*. Hence, we do not go further in detail concerning the *UML extension for business modeling*, but compare the *EPC* directly with *class* and *behavior diagrams* of the *UML* in order to show contradictions and synergy.

2 Transformation Approach: From EPC to UML

As we have mentioned above, the *EPC method* and *UML* have different scopes of *business modeling*. Hence, it is not clear whether the results of the *EPC method* substitute the *UML* results or whether the methods are compatible at all. In this section, we describe an transformation approach which shows exemplary relationships between the *EPC* and the basic *UML* diagrams *use case, activity diagram, class diagram* and the *UML application architecture* at all. We give a short description of the UML *diagram*, followed by the comparison with the *EPC* and a rough transformation from *EPC* to *UML.*

2.1 UML Use Case Diagrams

Use case diagrams primarily define the behavior of a system or subsystem. Instances of the actors can use services of the system in any chronological order. The internal structure of the system, which makes the services available, can be regarded as a black box.

The relationship and interaction of *organization units* and *business functions* can also be illustrated using an *EPC diagram.* Moreover, the *control flow* is illustrated and scenarios can be linked to complex process models in *EPC.*

Use cases can be regarded as a representation of small and less structured business functions on a very detailed level, where is no need to define a control flow.

Furthermore, collecting all references from an *application system* to all *functions* and *organization units* concerned, a *use case diagram* for the *application system* can be made up. An example for the transformation is shown in figure 3.

2.2 UML Activity Diagram

An *activity diagram* is a combination of the *control flow* and *object flow* among its constituent *actions*, similar to the *control flow* and the *data flow* among the *functions* in the *EPC*. Thus, most of the *EPC diagram* constructs can be more or less easily transformed into *activity diagrams. EPC functions* provoke *activities, EPC events* cause *object flow states* and *EPC link operators* lead to *synchronized* or *splitted transitions.* Figure 4 illustrates those relationships. Because of the illustrative design of *control flow* and *data flow*, both models can also be applied in the context of *workflow modeling.*

2.3 UML Class Diagram

Although *class diagrams* describe the static structure of an information system, processes give a lot of information on objects, their structure and their relationships. Classes can be derived from *information objects* and *business functions* of *EPC diagrams* by detailing them. Within *ARIS*, the *Entity-Relationship Model (ERM)* or *function decomposition diagrams* can be used to discribe the static stucture. As shown in Figure 5, classes are not necessarily developed in a top down approach but can be derived in parallel to a business process model.

2.4 UML Application Architecture

A general grouping mechanism of the *UML application architecture* is provided by the *subsystem* and the *package* constructs. An *application system* can be modularized in *subsystems* and *packages.*

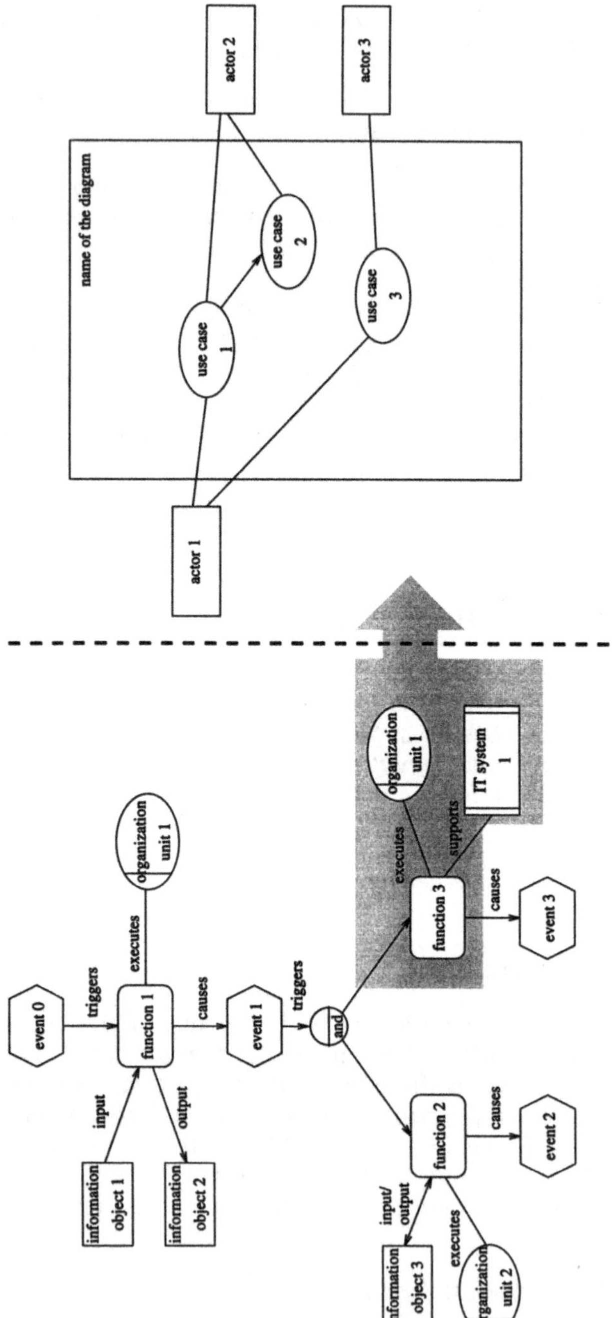

Figure 3: EPC - UML use case diagram transformation, see (Oestereich (1997))

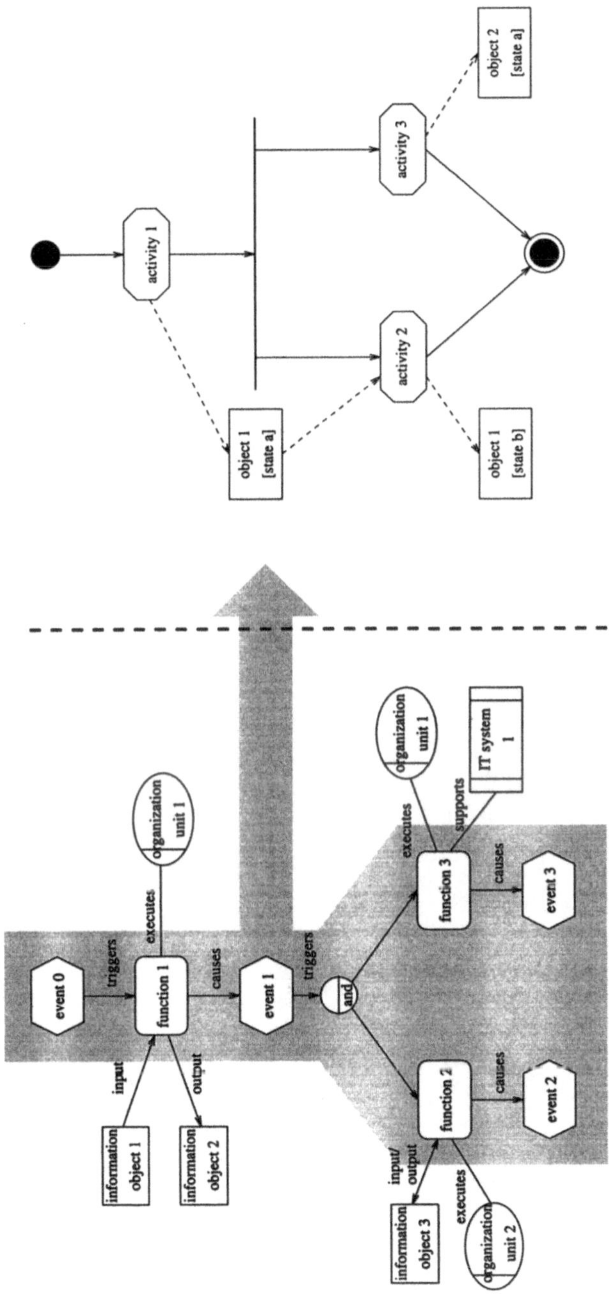

Figure 4: EPC - UML activity diagram transformation

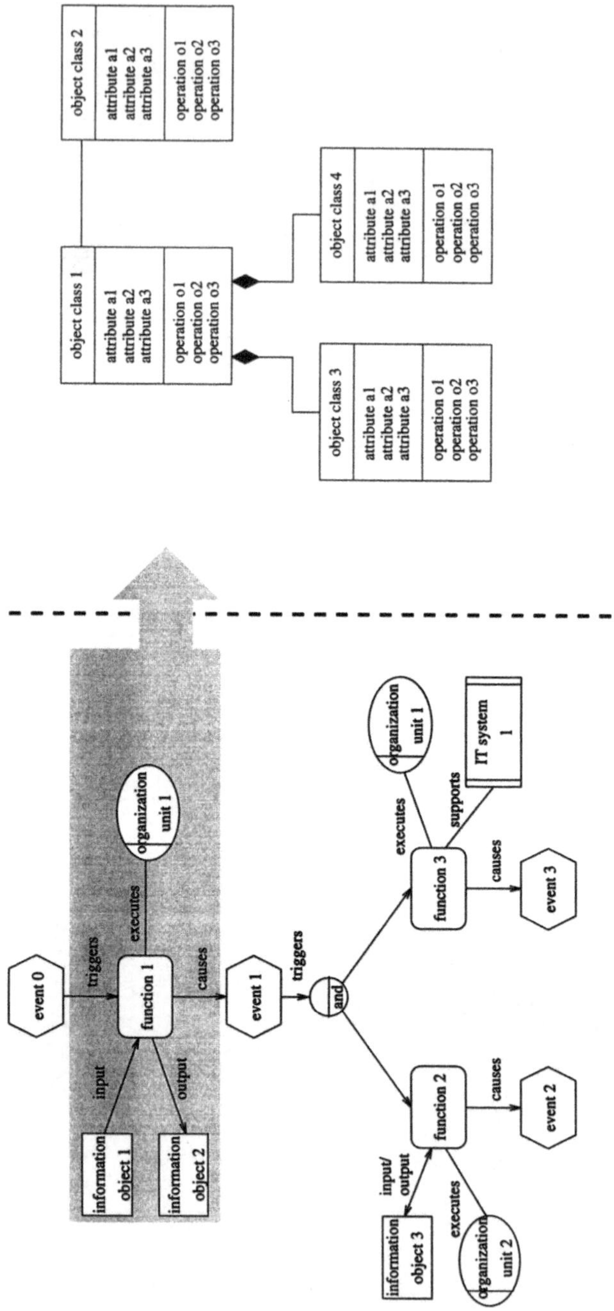

Figure 5: EPC - UML class diagram transformation

In an *EPC diagram*, the existing applications are described as an *IT-resource*, related to other kinds of resources like *organization units* and *information objects*. The relationship between *applications* and *business functions* and their support of complex business processes are also illustrated in the *EPC diagram. Application systems* defined in an EPC model are the basis for describing their interaction. Furthermore, in an *application architecture diagram*, application components can be represented by several *UML packages*. Each *package* can be specified in greater detail with the help of further *UML diagrams*, as it is indicated in figure 6.

3 Integration Approach: "Object-Oriented EPC"

The purpose of the following presented concept of the *object-oriented event-driven process chain (oEPC)* (Scheer et al. (1997)) is on the one hand to preserve the potential and the end users acceptance of the standard *EPC method* and on the other hand to integrate object-orientated methods.

In this context, a business process is defined as the event-driven processing and interacting of business objects. The oEPC differentiates between *business process business object*, the corresponding resources such as *organization units IT* and *production resources* and *rules/events*.

Within the object-oriented methodology, *business objects* are regarded as *generalized objects* which can usually be specialized. For instance, the business object *customer order* can be specialized into the objects *customer order header* and *customer order items*. Often, *business objects* are called *object clusters* or *complex objects*.

Events/rules describe the state transition of a *business object* at a certain time caused by the execution of one of its *operations*. They are defined as independent meta objects. Within the *oEPC* method *business objects* and *events/rules* are defined as *object classes* on type level. Hence, *business objects* can be described in greater detail by assigning *attributes* and *operations* to the classifying *business object class*.

Business process modeling focuses on finding and solving organizational problems and media incompatibilities in business processes. For this reason, *organization units* and *resources* can be assigned to *business objects* similar to the standard *EPC method*. The interaction between *business objects* is based on message exchange. *Messages* reflects the *control flow* i.e. the decision- and control mechanism of a business process. Messages can also describe a kind of *customer supplier relationship* of *business objects*. The message sender *(customer)* triggers the recipient *(supplier)* to produce a result, which the sender needs for the further execution of the process. But within business process modeling, *customer supplier relationships* do not come to the fore.

Furthermore, the *EPC method* disposes of a set of *boolean operators*, used to split a process or to combine different processes. Hence, the business decision interrelationship within the process execution can be illustrated. The combination of *boolean operators* and *events/rules* make up the link to common business roles in analogy to the standard *EPC*.

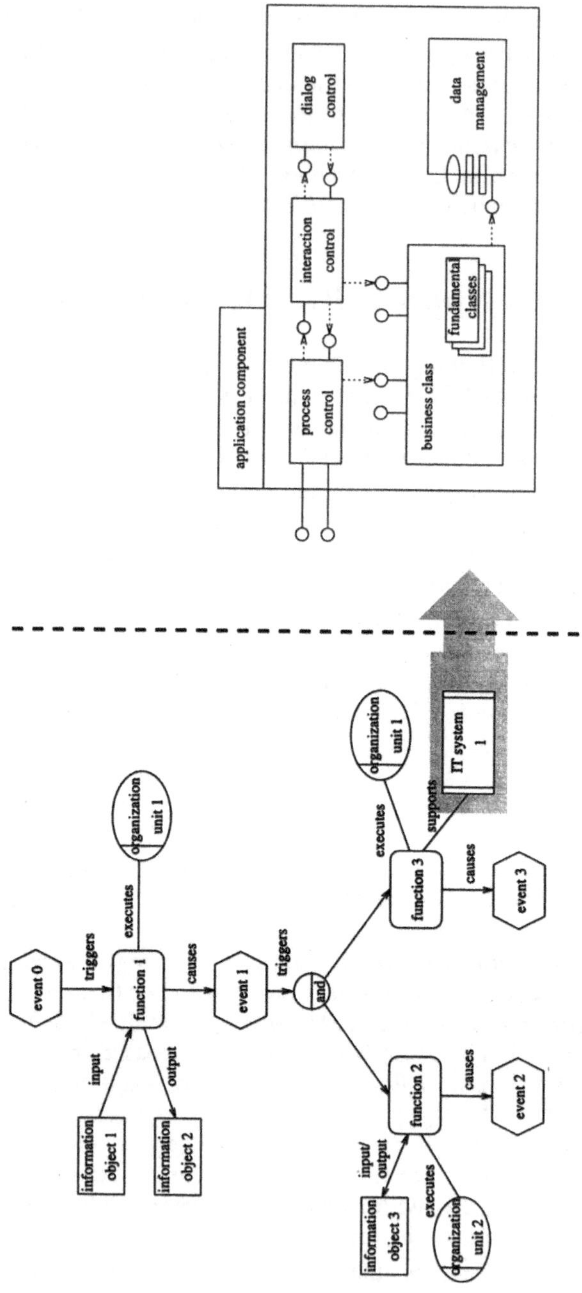

Figure 6: EPC - UML application architecture (Oestereich (1997)) transformation

In figure 7, the structure of a business process model is shown by means of *oEPC* symbols illustrating graphically the *control flow* defined by *event-driven messages*.

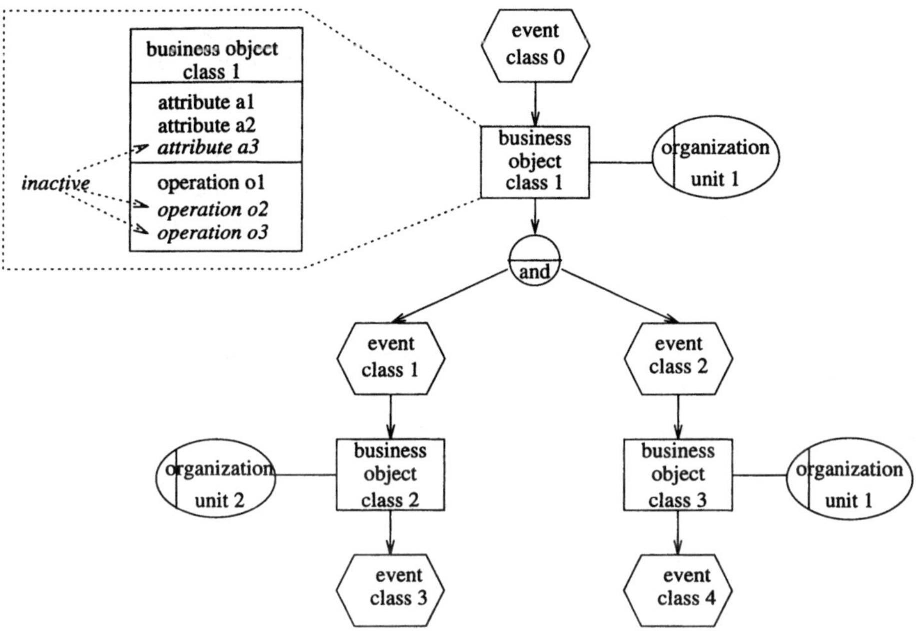

Figure 7: Example for the oEPC structure of a business process.

Because of the complementary usage of *object attributes* and *object operations*, the transformation of an *oEPC* model into a static *UML class model* is possible and can be the basis of a further coherent implementation specification.

4 Conclusion

Concepts for the modeling of the static structure of object classes, e.g. *UML class diagrams*, are methodically sophisticated approaches which are increasingly used in practice and which will probably replace other traditional approaches for static modeling like the *entity relationship modeling language*.

Even today, usefully adapted and simplified object oriented languages for static modeling can be used in the context of business modeling. In addition to this, trough refinement and consideration of IT relevant aspects, the business model can be transformed into an implementation specification.

The object oriented modeling of dynamic behavior, especially within business processes, and the relationships between *dynamic diagrams* and *static class diagrams* are just insufficiently analyzed and discussed. The main *UML* diagram framework still focuses on the implementation specification whereas the recent

UML extensions for business modeling just introduce other symbols for the existing diagram structures. Thus, the *UML extensions for business modeling* can hardly be used for business process modeling.

The presented *transformation approach* as well as *integration approach* are based on the idea of finding a synergetic combination of *process-* and *object-oriented* concepts in order to profit from the advantages of both methods. This idea, which is also increasingly used in literature, is changing the rather dogmatic discussion on methods into an discussion on integration of methods.

The further scientific work within the context of the presented *object-oriented event-driven process chains (oEPC)* will primarily deal with the development of a coherent proceeding model and the illustration with the help of modeling tools.

References

DAVENPORT, T.H. (1993): Process Innovation. Reengineering Work through Information Technology, Boston.

HAMMER, M.; CHAMPY, J. (1993): Reengineering the Corporation. A Manifesto for Business Revolution, New York.

KELLER, G.; NÜTTGENS, M.; SCHEER, A.-W. (1992): Semantische Prozeßmodellierung auf der Grundlage "Ereignisgesteuerter Prozeßketten (EPK)", *Veröffentlichungen des Instituts für Wirtschaftsinformatik, Heft 89*, Saarbrücken, URL: http://www.iwi.uni-sb.de/public/iwi-hefte/heft089.zip

KELLER, G. and TEUFEL, T. (1997): R/3 prozeßorientiert anwenden: Iteratives Prozeßprototyping zur Bildung von Wertschöpfungsketten, 2. edition, Bonn.

LANGNER, P., SCHNEIDER, C., and WEHLER (1997): Prozeßmodellierung mit ereignisgesteuerten Prozeßketten (EPKs) und Petri-Netzen, *Wirtschaftsinformatik 39*, 479-489.

NÜTTGENS, M. (1997): Event-driven Process Chain (EPK) - Some Links and Selected Publications, URL: http://www.iwi.uni-sb.de/nuettgens/EPK/epk.htm

OESTEREICH, B. (1997): Objektorientierte Softwareentwicklung mit der Unified Modeling Language, 3. edition, München 1997, 85ff.

ÖSTERLE, H. (1997): Business Engineering, Prozeß - Systementwicklung, Volume 1: Entwurfstechniken, Berlin.

RATIONAL SOFTWARE (publisher)(1997): UML Notation Guide 1.1, *Unified Modeling Language Version 1.1*, Santa Clara (USA), URL: http://www.rational.com/uml/documentation.html

RATIONAL SOFTWARE (publisher)(1997): UML Extension for Business Modeling version 1.1, *Unified Modeling Language version 1.1*, Santa Clara (USA), URL: http://www.rational.com/uml/documentation.html

RUMP, F. (1997): Erreichbarkeitsgraphbasierte Analyse ereignisgesteuerter Prozeßketten, *Technischer Bericht, Fachbereich Informatik, Universität Oldenburg*, URL: http://www-is.informatik.uni-oldenburg.de/~rump/paper/analyse/analyse.ps

SCHEER, A.-W. (1992): Architecture of Integrated Information Systems - Foundations of Enterprise-Modeling, Springer, Berlin.

SCHEER, A.-W. (1994): Business Process Engineering - Reference Models for Industrial Enterprises, 2nd edition, Springer, Berlin.

SCHEER, A.-W. (1996): ARIS-House of Business Engineering, *Veröffentlichungen des Instituts für Wirtschaftsinformatik, Heft 133,* Saarbrücken, URL: http://www.iwi.uni-sb.de/public/iwi-hefte/heft133.zip

SCHEER, A. W., NÜTTGENS, M., and ZIMMERMANN, V. (1997): Objektorientierte Ereignisgesteuerte Prozeßkette (oEPK) - Methode und Anwendung, *Veröffentlichungen des Instituts für Wirtschaftsinformatik, Heft 141*, Saarbrücken, URL: http://www.iwi.uni-sb.de/public/iwi-hefte/heft141.ps

Conventions for the Practical Use of UML

A. Schroff, A. Teichrieb

Fraunhofer-Institut Informations- und Datenverarbeitung (IITB),
D-76131 Karlsruhe, Germany

Abstract: We describe our experiences with the use of the Unified Modeling Language (UML) in a job floor control system project. Firstly, we analyze what is new for the daily project work when using UML. The powerfulness and the extensibility of the UML, its changing character at the moment, and insufficiencies of the available tools make conventions a very important aspect of UML use in the practice. We give some examples of naming and structuring conventions and show how workarounds influence modeling.

1 Project

The Fraunhofer Institut Informations- und Datenverarbeitung Karlsruhe is developing in co-operation with Heinz+Baretzky Consulting, Markdorf/Bod. a job floor control system for the textile industry. Five firms are involved as suppliers of requirements and pilot users of the system. We start by describing the project in which we achieved our UML experience because from our point of view several circumstances of the specific project have to be considered when investigating the practical applicability of UML.

The character of the project as a business information system with, for example, strong emphasis on data modeling allows covering a large number of the problems by means of object-oriented modeling . The complexity of the system makes tool support an important prerequisite for the success of the project.

The co-operation with consultants who are experts in the textile industry but with less knowledge of object-oriented modeling leads to the requirement of easy-to-understand models, at least at a certain level. Particulary, this point proves to be essential in our project, or even in software development like Fowler (1997) emphasises.

The existence of several customers results in further aspects, e.g. a strong demand for model reusability and a high probability of changing requirements even in later project phases.

While some project members had experience of projects with OMT and Shaelor-Mellor, several others had less background in object-oriented modeling at the start of the project. Naturally, this also has consequences for the way of applying UML.

Finally, the technology used in addition to UML modeling has some impact on modeling aspects. The business process models are developed with the ARIS toolset and therefore the UML models are not stand-alone but with interdependency models based on other modeling languages. The use of Java causes the reverse engineering of large numbers of classes. The use of object-oriented databases brings special requirements for describing persistence in the models.

2 New Aspects Through UML

We consider the question of how the appearance of the UML influences practical daily work. Regarding our project, several aspects become obvious:

- Powerfulness: The UML contains many more modeling elements, diagrams etc. than its predecessors like OMT or Booch.
- Extensibility: Extension mechanisms are parts of the language itself.
- Changing character: The development of UML has brought several versions with quite strong modifications within two years.
- Discrepancy to the tool: The UML described in the specification differs strongly from what the available tools support.
- Insufficiency of tools: Because of the changing character and the short time since the appearance of the UML, the time for which the UML tools on the market are in practical use is rather short, which naturally leads to some problems with bugs.

We emphasise the role of tool support in this list because the success of UML use strongly depends on the existence of appropriate tools.

All these points make - in a way - conventions necessary. The broad range of modeling capabilities causes the need to select certain kinds of diagrams. An uncontrolled use of the extension mechanisms in a project may lead to inconsistency and confusion in the project. Particularly, the practical work with tools is not possible without conventions, formulated in order to use the existing functionality optimally and to work around the bugs.

3 Naming

In general, naming conventions improve the readability and support the exchange of artefacts and team development. The existing UML documentation uses conventions. The *Naming Conventions and Typography* paragraph in *UML Semantics* (Rational (1997a)) explains what conventions are used for defining the UML itself. Furthermore, the *UML Notation Guide* (Rational (1997b)) contains a proposal for naming.

But the rules in the UML documentation do not cover the whole range of the UML. Here, we can identify the first point that makes naming in UML models special: We have many more model elements and kinds of diagrams in UML than in other modeling approaches. Thus, the naming conventions may become complex if there is no strong intent to simple rules.

A second aspect of UML naming is the existence of the tagged value mechanism. We can use it for example to provide additional names for model elements. In some cases it can help if implementation names are used in addition to the normal name in the UML. Then a tagged value can be used to attach it to the model entity. Further, we applied the tagged value mechanism to add an "Abbreviation" to most of the model elements:

{ImplementationName = "Operation", "Abbrevation = "Op"}

These abbreviations are especially used for qualifying. Due to a significant insufficiency in our modeling tool, qualifying is a central aspect in our daily modeling work. While UML introduces packages as name spaces, the implementation of our tool ignores this demand. Because we are then not allowed to have for example two classes called "Operation" anywhere in different packages, we always have to qualify until the names are unique. This is a particular disadvantage in our project, because with Java we use a programming language which supports packages as namespaces so that we would not even have to force unique class names in the implementation.

We distinguish between class and package names because we hope that in a later version of our modeling tool, name spaces will be supported. The names of the classes appear in the bodies of the methods which are not generated by automatic code generation. The code lines which include the names of the packages like, for example, the import statements are fully generated. So we have the opportunity to exchange the package names in a later project phase just by a new execution of the code generation procedure if our tool will support name spaces. Thus, we qualify the package names and the class names in different ways. The developer has to find a name for a class which makes sense to him in that form because the names are thought to survive until the end. For the package names we use a simple rule. We add the name of the hierarchically superior package in front of the package name to make it unique. We may apply this rule several times hierarchically. This leads to names like the example of Figure 1.

A last impact of missing name space support concerns working with reverse engineered class libraries. Oestereich (1997) emphasises the important aspect that the team members have to become familiar with the libraries. In order to support this, we always generate UML models of the libraries. Because the names of the classes are already given, we can not include them simultaneously if they have some class names in common. In that case, the developer has to switch between different libraries in the model.

The last example of conventions is the naming of reverse engineered packages. For modeling the work with the object-oriented data base, we had to generate models of packages of the data base vendor (Odi (1997)). Figure 2 shows an example.

Fortunately, we do not have problems with the package names for the libraries. It is true that names like "util" appear quite often as package names in libraries, but we can force unique names for library packages simply by dropping some levels of the hierarchy. The names resulting this conventions can be seen in Figure 3.

Here, we have a combination of naming conventions and conventions concerning the package structure. These conventions we investigate in the next paragraph.

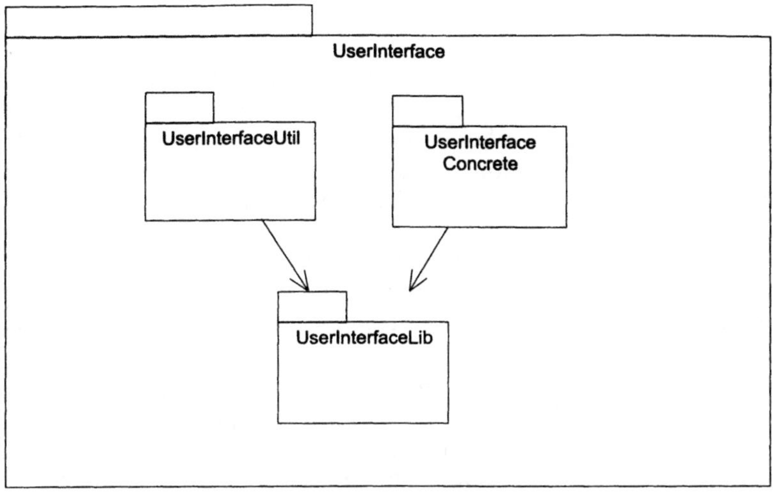

Figure 1: Packages

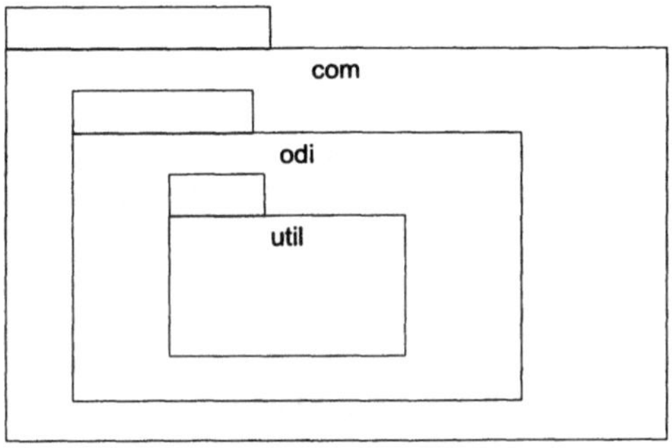

Figure 2: Library packages

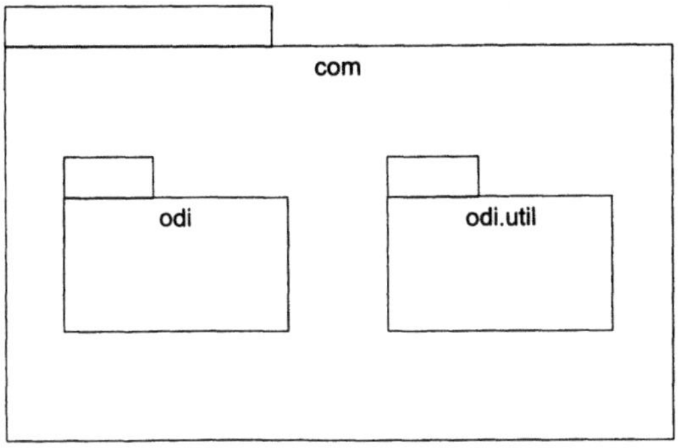

Figure 3: Library package names

4 Structuring

UML includes with the package a general mechanism for grouping model elements. If there were no conventions for the structure of the models, it would become impossible to look at other developers' packages, navigate through them or understand them. One developer would use a deep hierarchy of packages and group the elements in a certain manner, the next would do it in totally different way, the third would pack everything in one package, and so on. This danger of confusing structures is particularly valid for UML modeling because there are many more kinds of modeling elements than other approaches offered previously. Developers with less experience need guidance for structuring and diagram selection.

One approach would be to restrict the use of diagrams and modeling elements. One could restrict the UML capabilities to be used in a project. But to us it seems more appropriate to formulate some diagrams each package must include and leave the further expression capabilities to the creativity of the developer.

As an example, we describe our conventions for the models of the logical view (Rational (1996)). We have a diagram for each package named in the same way and including all entities defined in it. In order to achieve easy-to-handle packages this overview diagram still should not be too complex. Such a diagram helps enormously to navigate through the package hierarchy and to get an overview at a glance.

Another issue of common interest are the interdependencies to other packages of our models. So we have a "Dependency"-diagram which describes which associations, dependencies, specialisations and generalisations the classes in a package have.

For the design of a Java implementation the use of the language packages is an important aspect. Quite often a review of the Java use in the package is necessary, for instance when an update of the Java classes happens. Therefore, we have a "Dependency java" diagram in each package which contains all associations, dependencies, specialisation of java classes.

Finally, we have "Dependency roguewave" (see Roguewave (1997)) and "Dependency djgl" (see Objectspace (1997)) diagrams which contain the interdependencies to these libraries in the same manner.

All other diagrams, such as sequence or collaboration diagrams, are in the "Details" package. In summary, these conventions lead to packages as depicted in Figure 4.

5 Workarounds

When looking at the rapid development of the UML, it becomes obvious that providing appropriate tool support is a difficult problem. This is true even for vendors directly involved in the UML definition process. The tools we looked at do support certain parts of the UML as specified in *UML Semantics* (Rational (1997a)) and *UML Notation Guide* (Rational (1997b)). Other things are not

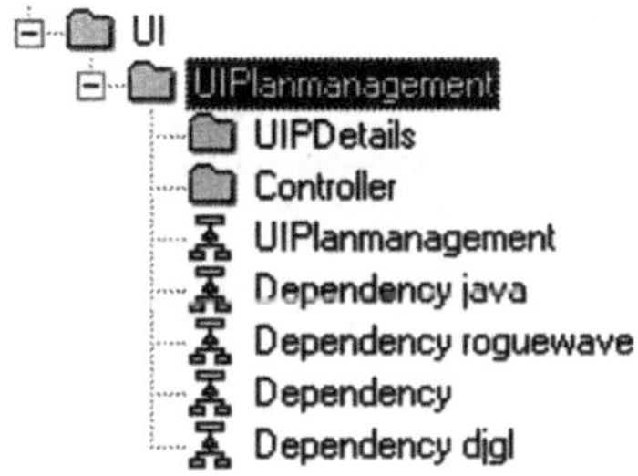

Figure 4: Package structure

supported. Finally, some things are supported, but not in the right way. We do not want to over-emphasise the role of tools and their insufficiency in this paper, but it is a fact that a tool has a great impact on the modeling work in a project. It is interesting to see what diagrams UML provides, but for the daily work the UML dialect of the tool is decisive.

In this paragraph we show how workarounds influence UML models. The first example is a workaround for a UML model element which is not supported by our tool: The *UML Notation Guide* describes an n-ary association as an association among 3 or more classes, with the diamond notation as depicted in Figure 5 (Rational (1997b)).

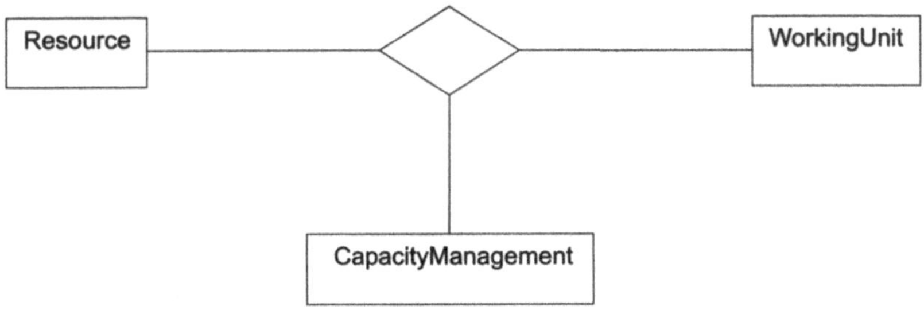

Figure 5: N-ary association

Because we cannot model n-ary associations in our tool in that way, we model them as classes. In order to make the original sense clear, and to help later correction processes when the tool capabilities are extended, we introduce a stereotype "N-ary association" (see Figure 6).

The second example concerns code generation. When we have a reflexive association as shown in Figure 7, the code generation procedure of our tool always ignores one side.

This means that "Resource" has only code for the "super" role. Therefore, we model a reflexive association twice. Figure 8 shows the result.

We mark the two associations with (A) and (B) to preserve the original sense, and to mark the workaround.

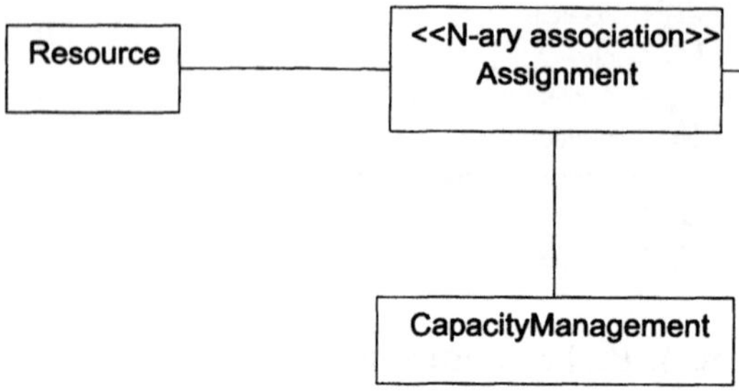

Figure 6: N-ary association workaround

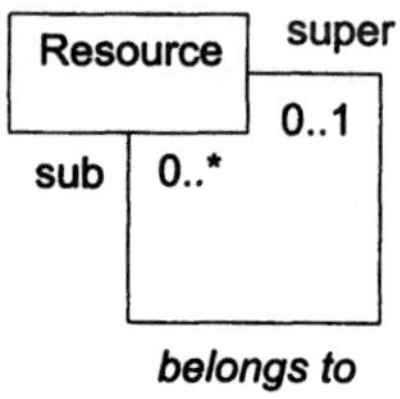

Figure 7: Reflexive association

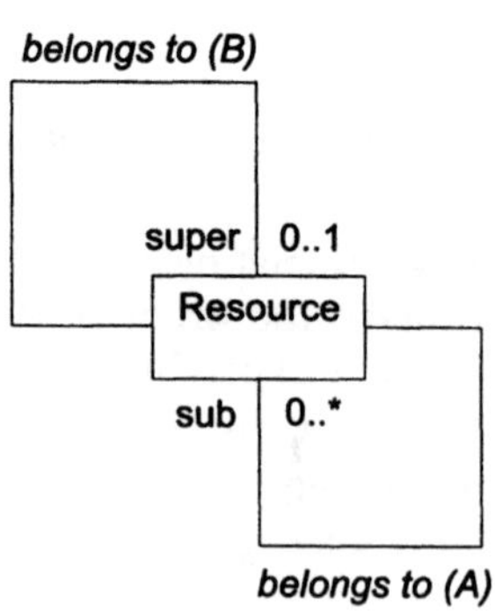

Figure 8: Reflexive association workaround

Marking a workaround is an essential aspect, as the following example shows. In the first version of our tool, a bug causes errors when a class has more than 17 non-abstract methods. We worked with the following convention: In each case of a class with more than 17 methods, an abstract class was introduced, called <class> + "help", which contains some of the methods. Then a generalisation of stereotype "help" was added, so that the original class inherited these methods. Because we did a proper marking of these workarounds, we were able to correct our models by a simple script, after the bug was fixed in a new version.

Further workarounds are already described in the naming paragraph.

6 Describing Conventions

While we show why conventions are necessary in our UML project in the above, we now want to consider the question of how to express conventions.

Naming conventions do not make sense as hard restrictions. Therefore, we still leave such questions to the creativity of the developer. But other restrictions have to be followed very carefully.

We give an example. Each package of our UML model may be saved in a different file due to efficient version control and team development. But packages are a general grouping mechanism. So somebody can have associations in one package, while the connected classes are assigned to another package. Naturally, this will cause problems when independent versions of these packages are generated. We cannot avoid such problems totally, but we claim that an association has to be in the same package as at least one of the classes. This is an example of a convention, or rather a restriction, we would like to express in a formal way and to check it by the system. Therefore, we currently investigate the capabilities of the Object Constraint Language (OCL) in the *Object Constraint Language Specification* (Rational (1997c)).

7 Summary

The goals of the UML described in the *UML Summary* are oriented on the requirements of the daily project work (Rational (1997d)). But at the moment not all the advantages are achievable for the user. UML modeling cannot be done without tool support. So for the users it is relevant what language the tools support. UML is a relatively new approach with numerous recent changes in the specification. Thus, the tools do not support the UML as described in the UML specification (Rational (1997a)). Together with other properties of the UML this has resulted in the strong use of conventions to achieve efficient use of UML for object-oriented modeling.

References

FOWLER, M. and SCOTT, K. (1997): UML Distilled – Applying the Standard Object Modeling Language. Addison-Wesley, Reading, Massachusetts.

OBJECTSPACE (1997): ObjectSpace JGL à The Generic Collection Library for Java, URL: http://www.objectspace.com/jgl/

ODI (1997): Making Java Objects Persistent, URL: http://www.odi.com/papers.html

OESTERREICH, B. (1997): Objektorientierte Softwareentwicklung: Analyse und Design mit der Unified Method Language, Oldenbourg, Mnchen

RATIONAL (1996): A Rational Approach to Software Development Using Rational Rose, Rational Software Corporation, 2800 San Tomas Expressway, Santa Clara, CA 95051-0951

RATIONAL (1997a): UML Semantics, Version 1.1, URL: http://www.rational.com/uml/1.1/ad970804_UML11_Sematics2.zip

RATIONAL (1997b): UML Notation Guide, Version 1.1, URL: http://www.rational.com/uml/1.1/ad970805_UML11_Notation2.zip

RATIONAL (1997c): Object Constraint Language Specification, URL: http://www.rational.com/uml/1.1/ad970804_UML11_OCL.zip

RATIONAL (1997d): UML Summary, Version 1.1, URL: http://www.rational. com/uml/1.1/ad970804_UML11_Summary.zip

ROGUEWAVE (1997): Freshly brewed Java Solutions, URL: http://www.roguewave .com/products/java.html

Software Engineering Process with the UML

M. Wolf[1], R. Burkhardt[2], I. Philippow[1]

[1] Technical University of Ilmenau, Faculty of Informatics and Automation
Institute of Theoretical and Technical Informatics,
P.O. Box 100 565, D - 98684 Ilmenau

[2] OWiS Software GmbH - Society for object-oriented and knowledge-based systems
Ltd., Ilmenau,
Lindenstrasse 28, D - 98693 Ilmenau

Abstract: In this contribution at first the Unified Modeling Language (UML) on the basis of the different diagrams (Class-Structure-, Use-Case-, Sequence-, Collaboration-, Component-, Distribution-, State- and Activity diagram) is briefly introduced as the result of the efforts to standardize modeling languages. Furthermore, the framework of an activity flow model for the software development in professional projects is introduced. Basing on this framework a possible activity flow model for the software development on the basis of UML is introduced, which has been adapted to a professional project of a leading german organisation in the banking sector.

1 Introduction

The modeling of a system is performed in order to obtain an abstract, understandable description of the architecture and structure in a formal or semi-formal notation (modeling language) and an involved activity flow model which gives a guideline or instruction for modeling and development respectively. The object oriented modeling exploits the concepts of object technology and uses them as a means of description for the representation of object oriented systems.

In the field of object oriented modeling the Unified Modeling Language (UML) (Booch, Rumbaugh and Jacobson (1997a), Booch, Rumbaugh and Jacobson (1997b), Burkhardt (1997)) is the de-facto standard which was submitted first for standardisation to the Object Management Group (OMG) in early 1997 by Booch, Jacobson and Rumbaugh as a suggestion for harmonising the different modeling strategies. The UML though does not include an activity flow model for the description of the sequence of the various modeling activities. A book on the description of the modeling process is by the "Amigos" (Booch, Jacobson, Rumbaugh) is announced for May or August of 1998. Other approaches about the modeling process are for example described in Fowler and Scott (1997) and Jacobson et al. (1997).

In cooperation with the corp. OWiS/Ilmenau a framework for the object oriented software development process (called SEPP/OT) has been developed, which will be introduced in the following along with possible concrete activities. The basis for modeling will be the UML. This activity description has been adapted to a professional project of a leading german organisation in the banking sector and is there applied to the software development process.

2 Object Oriented Modeling with the UML

Different views on an information domain let completely different aspects of a single field of application be the uppermost. A model always represents only a certain part of a real system. Such a restricted point of view is helpful in order to concentrate on the important aspects which are to be investigated. A basic distinction from the modeling standpoint is made in terms of dynamic, static and architectural aspects.

The UML defines on the one hand a notation and on the other hand a meta model of the object technology. The notation supports the fundamental concepts of object technology and provides a homogenous object oriented modeling environment by making consequent use of a well defined set of models and descriptive elements. The meta model given in UML notation is useful on the one hand as a description of the basic elements of object technology (classes, objects, instantiations, etc.) and on the other hand for the description of the construction of the defined models.

2.1 Models of the UML

The UML contains partly redundant views on the information domain which support a respective proprietary diagram notation. These are:

- Use-Case Model -UCM (Use-Case Diagram - UCD)
- Interaction Model - IM (Sequence Diagram - SD, Collaboration Diagram)
- Class Structure Model - CSM (Class Structure Diagram - CSD)
- Component Model -CM (Component Diagram - CD)
- Distribution Model -DM (Distribution Diagram - DD)
- State Model - SM (Statechart Diagram -SD, Activity Diagram - AD)

For the last model we apply the Object Process Model (OPM / Object Process Diagram), developed at the TU Ilmenau (Burkhardt (1994), Wolf (1995)), which allows for a complete object oriented modeling of the attribute related object states and a simulation on Petri Net level and which definitely harmonises very well with the UML(Burkhardt (1997)).

2.2 Modeling Process

In the following the term modeling process, or activity flow model, is used to denote the representation of sequences in a project, whereas the methodology specific modeling process and the project related activity flow model have to be distinguished.

The methodology related modeling process describes the exact activities which are required for the software development from the point of view of the project team. At this time the applied method and the used tool come to the fore. The project related activity flow model are oriented towards the business management requirements of an enterprise and the means by which the flow of the project should be controlled while taking into account the available resources.

3 Demands on the Object Oriented Development Process

Object oriented development processes are always motivated by one or more basic ideas which are giving the impulses during the flow of the project. In Jacobson (1997) a Use-Case driven, architecture centred, iterative and incremental activity flow has been demanded.

The essential driving forces that are proven in practical application and which have to be taken into account in every modern software development process are introduced next.

- Iterative approach
  Typical for the iterative approach is the repetition of individual activities of an otherwise concretely given activity sequence. The iterative approach can be found for instance in Booch (1994) as a micro process.

- Incremental approach
  With the incremental approach the disadvantage of the iterative approach, that the effect of an iteration is not necessarily recognisable and thus, can hardly be verified, adressed. The idea is to require a certain increment per run which eventually has to be specified further. All increments summarised result - pictorially spoken - in the building which is constructed during the project: the software product. The most widely known approach for the additional consideration of the grow of the result with every iteration is the Spiral Model according to Boehm (1986). Another approach is the activity sequence shown in Burkhardt (1994).

- Evolutionary approach
  A variation of the incremental development strategy is the evolutionary prototyping, which especially focuses on obtaining first visible results as early as possible which either almost completely realise a narrow segment or realise the nearly complete domain of application in the way of an overview. The step-by-step extension of the prototype leads it to the target system after a not exactly predictable number of cycles trough the activity flow model.

- Event-oriented approach
  The software development process can not run according to a fixed, predefined scheme but has to be able to respond to events.

- Architecture-centred approach
  The architecture-centred approach bases on the reuse of known architectures as: logical architecture (classes, roles, ...), component architecture (closed software packages) and physical architectures (hardware elements).

- Use-Case-driven approach
  When defining cases of application taking into account the requirements

given by the experts or the customer one achieves the opportunity to restrict the part of the entire domain of information which needs to be considered (Jacobson et al.(1992)).

These aforementioned features have to be sufficiently combined during within the flow of activities. The activity flow model should though give a concrete action directive, however, it needs to provide sufficient freedom for adaptions as well.

4 Framework for an Activity Flow Model for the Software Development

In the following the framework for a software development process with UML called SEPP/OT (Software Engineering Process for Professional projects based on the Object Technology) for the methodology specific software development is introduced which meets the aforementioned criteria.

4.1 Overview

The SEPP/OT is divided into four "Use Cases" which stay active throughout the entire duration of the project and describe the main columns of the actions. The activity flow model describes five views on these Use Cases, i.e. the perspective of a group of persons motivated in a certain way or of members of the project staff that play a particular role. Components of this Use Cases are activities which are the real flow entities in the SEPP/OT. Each activity belong to exactly one Use Case. These activities run connected by pre- and postconditions. As long as these preconditions are not fulfilled they must not start. As long as the postconditions are not fulfilled they must not terminate. The basic model is illustrated in Figure 1.

4.2 Views

The activity flow model knows the aforementioned five points of view (illustrated in Figure 1) the software development in the project is seen from. Different priorities of an observer of the project result in different views on the course of the activity flow model. The views are in detail:

- Project management view (PM-View)
- Method view (M-View)
- Security view (S-View)
- Quality management view (QM-View)
- Reuse view(R-View)

The different standpoints are adopted by team members that are responsible for a corresponding function (e.g. project management view: project manager or

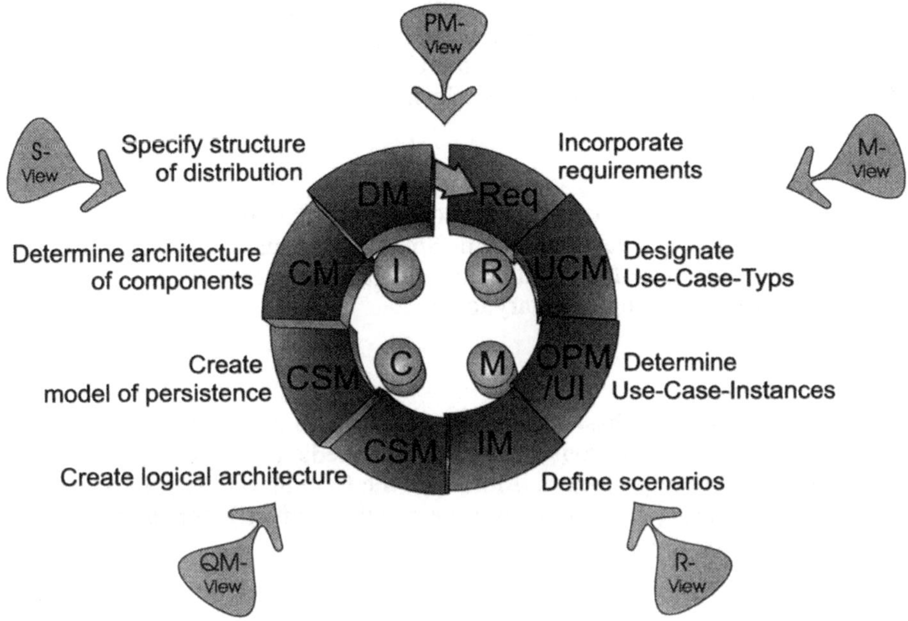

Figure 1: Framework of the Software Engineering Process with the UML

safety view: safety revisor in the project). However, there is nothing said at the moment about which of the tasks can be fulfilled by a single person. In every instance of the activity flow model or any other activity flow model roles have to be established. The concrete project organisation however, is sensibly fixed individually and with respect to the actual project.

4.3 Use Case

Separate actions that run parallel within the activity flow model result in Use Cases consisting of single activities. These Use Cases run usually in parallel; they start with the beginning of the project and finish with its end. The Use Cases are requirements capture, modeling, conversion and introduction.

- Requirements capture
  The main issue during the requirements capture is the registration of the requirements of the specialist departments and the technical description of the business process. But also the further guidance up to formalised requirements or to the Use Case is assigned to this part.

- Modeling
  The modeling consists of the analysis (what has to be done) and the development (how has it to be done in principle). The activities in this part are essentially accompanied by the UML notation and are supported by a modeling tool like OTW (Object Technology Workbench (1997)).

- Conversion
  The implementation contains the coding in a programming language environment (e.g. Visual Age C++ or Smalltalk, Visual Cafi or C++-Builder) as well as the test of the application and its components in this environment or by means of supplementary tools.

- Introduction
  The introduction phase consists of the installation and implementation of the respective final products or of an intermediate outcome in the form of an evolutionary prototype. Moreover, the training on the product and the coaching during the introductory phase of the product in its real environment are allocated to this process.

In the scope of each Use Case a set of activities is defined describing the actions possible within the respective Use Case during the different stages of development and depending on the originating point of the development.

4.4 Activities

Activities represent the entities in the activity flow model containing the actual instructions for actions during the real project period. The activities can be basically passed through in different order. Condition for an instance of actions adequate to the specification of the activity flow model is that it allows the compliance with the pre- and postconditions included in the activities. The different activities on the top level refer to the individual UML diagrams

Each shown activity on the top level (Figure 1) is refined by further activities of lower levels. Therefore, the activity flow model is a collection which already defines some structures and correlations but has to be concretely refined further in particular cases.

The several activities refer on the one hand to the various UML diagrams which in total represent the overall model or the object model respectively, on the other hand they refer as well to fundamental description elements existing independently of diagrams (object, class, inheritance). For the different elements and documents involved state attributes are defined by means of which the pre- and postconditions are formulated.

Activity	Considered models
Incorporate requirements	no formal model, requirement forms with a pattern pre-set
Designate Use-Case-Typs	Use-Case Model (UCM)
Determine Use-Case-Instances	Object Process Model (OPM)
Define scenarios	Interaction Model (IM) (Object Process Model - OPM)
Create logical structure	Class Structure Model (CSM)
Create model of persistence	Persistence feature of fundamental description elements (class, object), e.g. in the Class Structure Model (CSM)
Determine architecture of components	Component Model (CM)
Specify structure of distribution	Distribution Model (DM)

Table 1: Activities with their associated models

5 Concrete Activity Flow Model for the Software Development

As explained, SEPP/OT is not a concrete instance of an activity flow model but rather a framework on the basis of which the instantiation of the entire activity flow model can be performed. This framework can be completed specific to a project and an enterprise or according to other requirements. In order to obtain a concrete course of actions for one or more projects this framework has to be instantiated. The instantiation describes the transformation of the Use Cases into executable processes. For this purpose the activities relevant to the concrete actions are considered as instances of an Use Case. These instances of Use Cases are processes which describe the operations required for the fulfilment of the Use Case.

The result is an instance of the SEPP/OT framework belonging to an actual company specific activity flow model. In Figure 2 such an instance is shown as a path connecting the various activities of different Use Cases with each other. All instances of activity flows basically suffice the principle illustrated in Figure 2. From the project management point of view the project supervision follows the start of the project immediately, thus, running parallel to the actual project work. The work on the project is performed on the basis of the formal specifics of the modeling method and with help of the activities of the SEPP/OT. During the cyclic process activities can be differentiated depending on the current cycle. The concrete activities to be performed in the first run may be different from those of further passes. On the occasion of respective activities at first the prototype-like and later the shipping software product will be made available. Throughout the entire development phase the project team is permanently working towards finishing resp. improving the product.

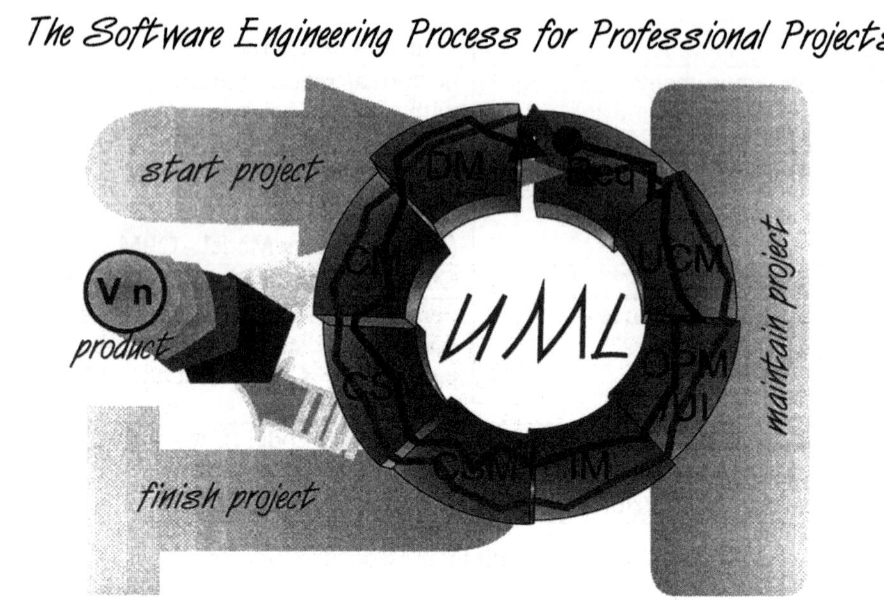

Figure 2: Instance of a Software Engineering Process with the UML

5.1 Business Process Driven Development

In the following the business process driven development will be briefly introduced as an example for a concrete instance of the SEPP/OT. The business process driven development is a pattern that has been described in Burkhardt (1997) for a certain type of project.

This concrete procedure is to be understood as a complete path through the activity flow model involving more than 100 activities. This software development process is Use Case driven, iterative, incremental, architecture centred and event oriented. Moreover, it takes safety-, quality- and reuse aspects into account.

The starting point for the business process driven development is the activity "designate Use Case types"; basing on the Use Case types the corresponding Use case instances are described which are depicted by scenarios. Subsequently, the logical structure defining the persistence model is determined by a series of activities, the component model is generated, the component architecture is stated and the distribution model is created. The iteration over these activities with a respective gain of information assures the steady model extension and application development.

The particular focus on the business process driven development is given by the choice and combination of relevant activities for this type of software development.

6 Summary

In the presented paper a framework of an activity flow model for the object oriented software development basing on the UML has been introduced. Within this framework (SEPP/OT) constraints have been mentioned that have to be met for all special software developments.

In order to carry through a concrete software development process the framework has to be instantiated by choosing the necessary activities and sorting them in a respective order.

A possible instance of this kind has been adapted to a professional project of a major german organisation in the banking sector (SIZAE-OO (1997)). Other modeling processes deal with instances of modeling activities on a more abstract level Fowler and Scott (1997). In Jacobson et al. (1997) the modeling of business processes by means of the UML was described. There, pictograms in conjunction with stereotypes are intensely used and thus, modeling is opened to other professionals than computer science specialists too. In the described approach (SEPP/OT) activities are described very detailed and associated to types. The experience made in the carried through project was that the quantity of activities used was probably too high. Therefore, a reduction of the numbers of processes will be done in the near term.

At the Technical University Ilmenau the UML based software development process is further investigated and improved in Cupertino with OWiS, whereas attention is focussed mainly on the formal representation of the design process as an object process model and on the conception of tools for simulation and workflow control respectively.

The firm OWiS is offering the SEPP/OT framework as consulting service.

References

BOEHM, B. W. (1986): A Spiral Model of Software Development and Enhancement, *Software Engineering Notes, vol. 11(4), p. 22, 8/1986.*

BOOCH, G. (1994): Object Oriented Analysis and Design with Applications, 2nd Edition, Benjamin/Cummings: Redwood City, California, 1994.

BOOCH, G., RUMBAUGH, J., and JACOBSON, I. (1997b): Unified Modeling Language Notation, Version 1.1, Rational Software Corporation, Santa Clara, CA (USA), 1997, URL: http://www.rational.com

BOOCH, G., RUMBAUGH, J., and JACOBSON, I. (1997a): Unified Modeling Language Notation, Version 1.1, Rational Software Corporation, Santa Clara, CA (USA), 1997, URL: http://www.rational.com

BURKHARDT, R. (1994): Modellierung dynamischer Aspekte mit dem Objekt-Prozess-Modell, Technische Universität Ilmenau, Dissertation, 1994 (in German).

BURKHARDT, R. (1997): Die Unified Modeling Language, Objektorientierte Modellierung für die Praxis, Addison-Wesley, 1997 (in German).

FOWLER, M. and SCOTT, K.: UML-Distilled, Applying the Standard Object Modeling Language, Addison-Wesley, 1997.

JACOBSON, I. (1997): Im Gespräch: Ivar Jacobson beantwortet Fragen anläßlich seines Vortrags zur "Unified Modeling Language" auf der OOP '97 in München, *OBJEKTspektrum (1997) 3: S.20-22* (in German).

JACOBSON, I., CHRISTERSON, M., JONSSON, P., and OEVERGAARD, G. (1992), Object-Oriented Software Engineering: A Use Case Driven Approach, Addison-Wesley, 1992.

JACOBSON, I., GRISS, M., and JONSSON, P.(1997): Software Reuse: Architecture, Process and Organisation for Business Success, Addison Wesley: New York, 1997.

OBJECT TECHNOLOGY WORKBENCH (1997): Object Technology Workbench OTW(2, Manual, OWiS Software GmbH Martinroda/Ilmenau, 1997, URL: http://www.otw.de

SIZAE-OO (1997): Sparkasseninformatik-Zentrum Handbuch der objektorientierten Software-Entwicklung, Bonn, 1997 (in German).

WOLF, M. (1995): Validierung und Optimierung dynamischer Modelle auf der Basis des Objekt-Prozess-Modells, Technische Universität Ilmenau, Diploma Thesis, 1995 (in German).

Author and Subject Index

The numbers given in this index refer to the first page of the respective papers.

GPSR Compliance

The European Union's (EU) General Product Safety Regulation (GPSR) is a set of rules that requires consumer products to be safe and our obligations to ensure this.

If you have any concerns about our products, you can contact us on ProductSafety@springernature.com

In case Publisher is established outside the EU, the EU authorized representative is:

Springer Nature Customer Service Center GmbH
Europaplatz 3
69115 Heidelberg, Germany

Batch number: 10577878

Printed by Printforce, the Netherlands